Stress, Trauma, and Wellbeing in the Legal System

American Psychology-Law Society Series

Books in the Series

Trial Consulting
Amy J. Posey and Lawrence S. Wrightsman

Death by Design
Craig Haney

Psychological Injuries
William J. Koch, Kevin S. Douglas, Tonia L. Nicholls, and Melanie L. O'Neill

Emergency Department Treatment of the Psychiatric Patient
Susan Stefan

The Psychology of the Supreme Court
Lawrence S. Wrightsman

Proving the Unprovable
Christopher Slobogin

Adolescents, Media, and the Law
Roger J. R. Levesque

Oral Arguments Before the Supreme Court
Lawrence S. Wrightsman

God in the Courtroom
Brian H. Bornstein and Monica K. Miller

Expert Testimony on the Psychology of Eyewitness Identification
Edited by Brian L. Cutler

The Psychology of Judicial Decision-Making
Edited by David Klein and Gregory Mitchell

The Miranda Ruling: Its Past, Present, and Future
Lawrence S. Wrightsman and Mary L. Pitman

Juveniles at Risk: A Plea for Preventive Justice
Christopher Slobogin and Mark R. Fondacaro

The Ethics of Total Confinement
Bruce A. Arrigo, Heather Y. Bersot, and Brian G. Sellers

International Human Rights and Mental Disability Law
Michael L. Perlin

Using Social Science to Reduce Violent Offending
Joel Dvoskin, Jennifer L. Skeem, Raymond W. Novaco, and Kevin S. Douglas

Children Who Resist Postseparation Parental Contact
Barbara Jo Fidler, Nicholas Bala, and Michael A. Saini

Stress, Trauma, and Wellbeing in the Legal System
Monica K. Miller and Brian H. Bornstein

Stress, Trauma, and Wellbeing in the Legal System

Edited by

Monica K. Miller

Brian H. Bornstein

OXFORD
UNIVERSITY PRESS

OXFORD
UNIVERSITY PRESS

Oxford University Press is a department of the University of Oxford.
It furthers the University's objective of excellence in research, scholarship, and education by publishing worldwide.

Oxford New York
Auckland Cape Town Dar es Salaam Hong Kong Karachi
Kuala Lumpur Madrid Melbourne Mexico City Nairobi
New Delhi Shanghai Taipei Toronto

With offices in
Argentina Austria Brazil Chile Czech Republic France Greece
Guatemala Hungary Italy Japan Poland Portugal Singapore
South Korea Switzerland Thailand Turkey Ukraine Vietnam

Published in the United States of America by
Oxford University Press
198 Madison Avenue, New York, NY 10016

Library of Congress Cataloging-in-Publication Data
Stress, trauma, and wellbeing in the legal system / edited by
Monica K. Miller, Brian H. Bornstein.—1st ed.
p. cm.—(American psychology-law society series)
Includes bibliographical references and index.
ISBN 978-0-19-982999-6
1. Justice, Administration of—United States—Psychological aspects
2. Stress (Psychology)—United States. 3. Therapeutic Jurisprudence—United States.
I. Miller, Monica K. II. Bornstein, Brian H.
KF8700.S77 2013
347.73001'9—dc23
2012024740

Printed in the United States of America
on acid-free paper

To Dad and Mom, who taught me the value of working hard. And to Bart, Zoe, and Maggie, who have taught me the value of not working *too* hard.

—Monica

To Christie, Lillian, and Melissa—the bastions of my wellbeing.

—Brian

Contents

Series Foreword

This book series is sponsored by the American Psychology-Law Society (APLS). APLS is an interdisciplinary organization devoted to scholarship, practice, and public service in psychology and law. Its goals include advancing the contributions of psychology to the understanding of law and legal institutions through basic and applied research; promoting the education of psychologists in matters of law and the education of legal personnel in matters of psychology; and informing the psychological and legal communities and the general public of current research, educational, and service activities in the field of psychology and law. Members of APLS include psychologists from the academic, research, and clinical practice communities, as well as members of the legal community. Research and practice is represented in both the civil and criminal legal arenas. APLS has chosen Oxford University Press as a strategic partner because of its commitment to scholarship, quality, and the international dissemination of ideas. These strengths will help APLS reach its goal of educating the psychology and legal professions and the general public about important developments in psychology and law. The focus of the book series reflects the diversity of the field of psychology and law, as we will publish books on a broad range of topics.

In the latest book in the series, *Stress, Trauma, and Wellbeing in the Legal System*, Monica Miller and Brian Bornstein have compiled a series of chapters, each dealing with the ways in which the legal system positively or negatively affects the wellbeing of individuals who have contact with various legal entities. The chapters cover numerous aspects of the legal system, as well as various types of individuals involved, including victims, witnesses, and other lay participants; legal professionals; and legal decision makers (judges and jurors). Each chapter reviews the relevant literature and points out where research is lacking for each specific population involved in the legal system. Both positive and negative aspects of wellbeing are included to provide a broad perspective on wellbeing in the legal system. The result of this approach is a broad perspective with unique insights into how the legal system can be changed to promote wellbeing on both an individual and a societal level.

Miller and Bornstein begin by providing an introduction to stress and wellbeing within the legal system and how the law can be used to enhance wellbeing. In part II, the literature for various types of lay participants is reviewed, including victims of domestic violence; children, families, and the professionals who work with them; child witnesses; civil plaintiffs; and older adults. Each of these chapters provides unique insights into issues of stress, trauma, and wellbeing for each type of lay participant. Part III deals with the experiences of legal professionals, including law enforcement, probation officers, and attorneys. Part IV deals with legal decision makers—judges and jurors—and both includes important suggestions for change and highlights the areas in which our knowledge is lacking. Finally, a series of conclusions and directions for the future are provided.

Stress, Trauma, and Wellbeing in the Legal System presents a comprehensive and detailed analysis of issues most relevant to improving the experiences of individuals who participate in the legal system at various levels and in various roles. Scholars, researchers, policymakers, and practitioners will undoubtedly find that this book has the potential to help to shape the future of interactions within the legal system.

Patricia A. Zapf
Series Editor

Preface

Got stress? Only if you are human. Or, only if you are working in a system charged with delivering justice in an efficient and fair manner. Even the justice system itself operates under stress. Those of us who have spent our careers in the legal system know that stress is a major component of our lives, both in and out of the courthouse. Over the past 40 years, I have worked in police stations, jails, and pretrial release programs; I've worked as a prosecutor, a defense attorney, a civil litigator, and a judge. I have seen firsthand that many law enforcement officers, advocates, and judges thrive on stress. Law enforcement officers may well be adrenalin junkies—their job has been described as consisting of hours of boredom, followed by moments of sheer terror. Many litigators and judges also like living on the brink, managing cases by the "miracle of the courthouse steps"—cases settling at the last minute—and the requirement of thinking on their feet and dealing with ambiguity. Some of us live for the moments when it comes down to us—we make the difference in others' lives.

This stress and trauma often comes at a cost for both humans and the delivery of justice. While some individuals thrive on this stress, many experience inconvenience, anxiety, depression, heart disease, substance abuse, or other stress-related ailments. Their families may also suffer the side effects of this stress, whether it is dealing with health concerns, safety concerns, or relationship difficulties. Sometimes this stress can be beneficial—after all, we do not want legal decisions made lightly—but it is possible that stress could result in hasty or disproportionate decisions or arrests, further violence, or the inability to fully meet the needs of those involved in the system. This book investigates whether, and how, the justice system might be changed to improve the quality of justice and the quality of life of those who come into contact with the justice system by choice or by happenstance. All of the authors also identify areas for further research and suggest how policymakers might consider restructuring the civil and criminal justice system—areas of interest for legislators, citizens, and those in charge of applying limited financial resources to resolve legal disputes.

You may be reading this because you are most interested in the impact stress and trauma have on the delivery of justice by the individuals directly involved in the system—judges, lawyers, police officers, caseworkers, or parole officers—as well as those who have the justice system thrust upon them—victims of crimes, partners or children in violent relationships, jurors, parties to lawsuits, witnesses, or citizens trying to understand the results of a case. You may be primarily interested in how the justice system itself can (or whether it should) be changed to improve wellbeing—exploring different approaches to problem solving such as therapeutic jurisprudence, specialized treatment-based courts (such as for substance abuse cases, domestic abuse cases, sex workers, or women with children), peer courts for teens or young adults, and courts that focus on specific age groups (e.g., elders) or that take a more holistic view of family dynamics. All of these perspectives are examined and thoughtfully presented in this book.

The authors challenge readers to think about the stressors in many aspects of the U.S. justice system. The views presented are research and evidence based, not mere opinions. The variety of perspectives in this book will spark discussions across various disciplines from psychology to biology to jurisprudence; it offers a refreshing mix of social and physical science with legal theory. As decision makers try to shape the justice system for efficiency, cost savings, and effectiveness, or as the system and its players try to cope with the individual effects of stress (including heart disease, substance abuse, burnout, or change of career), they can turn to these data to reach informed decisions, or continue the research, in order to improve the system for all participants.

The good news is that some of the authors' recommendations may be immediately and easily implemented at no or low cost. This includes alterations such as accommodating police officers who are just completing an overnight shift and want to report to court to testify immediately rather than reporting hours later; providing clear information to witnesses, jurors, and others who are trying to find their way around courthouses; allowing jurors to ask questions (during trial) in order to reduce their confusion about evidence and increase their feeling of control in the decision-making process; and evaluating whether arbitrarily imposed case management timelines or prosecution policies may actually adversely impact victims or children.

Readers of this book can apply the policy suggestions, continue research, shape policy, or step up to a leadership role by promoting change in the legal system to make it more human, and more humane. We do not have to accept trauma and stress as conditions of employment in the delivery of justice, or as side effects of involvement in the system. Thoughtful, research-based decisions will result from continuing the dialogue started by these authors.

Celeste F. Bremer, J.D., Ed.D.
U.S. Magistrate Judge
Des Moines, Iowa

Acknowledgments

This book is the culmination of nearly a decade of research, discussion, daydreaming, planning, writing, and editing. Our interest in stress in the legal system began in 2001, when one of us (Brian) was awarded a grant from the University of Nebraska Tobacco Settlement Biomedical Research Enhancement Fund. This award funded a project investigating jurors' perceptions of stress and tested the effects of a "jury debriefing" intended to reduce stress brought on by jury duty. As the research assistant, Monica got to spend all summer in Lincoln, Nebraska courtrooms, trying to wrangle jurors into participating. We observed that the jurors who did not want to participate were exactly the ones we most wanted to study—those who participated in more stressful trials such as homicides. The publications that resulted from this project, and other similar papers published before and after ours, are described in chapter 11. Our interest in this area is still growing today, especially when we hear of trials containing graphic evidence or highly complicated evidence, and especially when we hear of jurisdictions implementing protective measures for jurors in stressful trials.

Years later, our interest in juror stress expanded to include judge stress. Thanks to collaborations with the National Judicial College, the National Council of Juvenile and Family Court Judges, and the Grant Sawyer Center for Justice Studies at the University of Nevada, Reno, we were able to study the stressors judges face. Our publications, and those of others interested in the topic, are discussed in chapter 12. Still today, our interest is piqued when we hear of judges who experience stress—for instance, the Wisconsin Supreme

Court justices who literally fought amongst themselves in a 2011 incident that suggested that the stresses of the job had become unmanageable.[1]

In 2009, the idea of putting together a book on stress in the legal system was born. Once we began to look at the issue from a broader perspective, we realized that there was no component of the legal system, and no actors within the system, that were exempt from stress. It is fair to say that it is ubiquitous. The challenge then became how to limit the topic to a single volume. We were fortunate to recruit many well-respected authors from various disciplines, and we have managed to put together a book that details the stressors, innovations to reduce stress, and policy suggestions for a variety of groups involved in the legal system. We hope it educates and inspires both researchers and those working within the system to address the problems associated with stress in the legal system.

In addition to the pleasant intellectual experience of writing the book, we experienced the joy of expanding a friendship and professional partnership that began as a student–mentor relationship over a decade ago. The opportunities to keep in touch, swap research ideas, and collaborate on our chapters were some of the best parts of working on this project.

As with any project, especially one of this magnitude, there are many individuals who provided helpful guidance and assistance along the way. Both before and during the production of this book, there were many who graciously dedicated time to giving us feedback along the way, whether it was at a conference, after a guest speaking engagement, or through an e-mail. We especially appreciate the input of Tim Robicheaux and Mike Havercamp. The reviewers of the book prospectus were very helpful in providing thoughtful and encouraging feedback even before we began the book itself. We also thank all the chapter authors who provided their insights, were unusually responsive to feedback, and put up with all the "reminder" e-mails for almost 2 years. A special thanks goes to Patty Zapf, editor of the American Psychology-Law Society book series. Without her patience and valuable input, this book would not have been possible. And, of course, Sarah Harrington, Andrea Zekus, and everyone else at Oxford University Press deserve a great big "thank you" for making the "nuts and bolts" side of publishing a book relatively painless.

And finally, we give our warmest appreciation to the significant others, friends, colleagues, and family who supported us in this effort—and all our efforts. Our supporters kindly listened to us as we described the ups and downs

[1] See Hughes, T. (2011, August 26). *Report detailing confrontation between two Wisconsin Supreme Court justices released.* OrlandoSentinel.com. Retrieved from http://www.orlandosentinel.com/topic/witi-20110826-prosser-report,0,5239547.story?track=rss-topicgallery; Richmond, T. (2011, August 25). David Prosser, Wisconsin Supreme Court justice, won't be charged in alleged Ann Bradley choking case. *Huffington Post.* Retrieved from http://www.huffingtonpost.com/2011/08/25/david-prosser-wisconsin-supreme-court-choking_n_936366.html

of editing a book and rambled about how great the project was going to be, and they tolerated our absences as the work piled up. These folks and many other friends and family members—you know who you are!—contributed to our efforts more than they know. The celebration of the completion of this book would mean little if we did not have them to join in on our celebration. In the spirit of the book's theme, we thank you for all that you do to enhance our wellbeing.

About the Editors

Monica K. Miller, J.D., Ph.D., is an Associate Professor with a split appointment between the Criminal Justice Department and the Interdisciplinary Ph.D. Program in Social Psychology at the University of Nevada, Reno. She is also an adjunct faculty member at the Grant Sawyer Center for Justice Studies and a Faculty Associate for the Women's Studies Program. Her interests involve the application of psychological theories and justice principles to laws and policies. Specifically, she is interested in the role of religion in the legal system; how the law regulates sexual behavior, pregnancy, and family issues; jury decision making; and community sentiment and public policy. She has authored or edited four books and over 100 journal articles and book chapters. She has received grant funding from the National Science Foundation and other sources. Dr. Miller teaches courses in law and social sciences at both the graduate and undergraduate levels.

Brian H. Bornstein, Ph.D., M.L.S., is Professor of Psychology and Courtesy Professor of Law at the University of Nebraska-Lincoln, where he serves as the associate director of the Law and Psychology Program. Dr. Bornstein is coeditor of the journal *Psychology, Crime & Law*, and he writes a blog on juries for *Psychology Today.* His research interests include jury decision making, especially in civil cases; the reliability of eyewitness memory; and the application of decision-making principles to everyday judgment tasks, as in medical decision making and distributive justice. He has authored or edited eight books and over 100 journal articles and book chapters. He has received grant funding for his research from several agencies, including the National Science Foundation and the National Institute of Justice. Professor Bornstein teaches courses on human memory, psychology and law, decision making, and the history of psychology at the graduate and undergraduate levels.

Contributors

Sarah J. Beal, Ph.D.
Cincinnati Children's Hospital & Medical Center

Brian H. Bornstein, Ph.D.
University of Nebraska-Lincoln

Hon. Celeste F. Bremer, J.D., Ed.D.
U.S. District Court, Southern Iowa

Jared Chamberlain, Ph.D.
Argosy University

Deborah Epstein, J.D.
Georgetown University

Warren D. Franke, Ph.D.
Iowa State University

Sheri C. Gibson, M.A.
University of Colorado-Colorado Springs

Lisa A. Goodman, Ph.D.
Boston College

Edie Greene, Ph.D.
University of Colorado-Colorado Springs

Gwen Hullman, Ph.D.
University of Nevada, Reno

W. Wesley Johnson, Ph.D.
University of Southern Mississippi

Bradley D. McAuliff, J.D., Ph.D.
California State University Northridge

Monica K. Miller, J.D., Ph.D.
University of Nevada, Reno

Jodi A. Quas, Ph.D.
University of California, Irvine

Sandra L. Ramey, Ph.D., RN
University of Iowa

Krystia Reed
University of Nebraska-Lincoln

James T. Richardson, J.D., Ph.D.
University of Nevada, Reno

Elizabeth Rush
University of California, Irvine

Lorie L. Sicafuse
University of Nevada, Reno

Risdon N. Slate, Ph.D.
Florida Southern College

Mary White Stewart, Ph.D.
University of Nevada, Reno

Victoria Weisz, Ph.D.
Center on Children, Families, and the Law
University of Nebraska-Lincoln

Twila Wingrove, J.D., Ph.D.
Appalachian State University

Steven M. Wood, M.S.
University of Nevada, Reno

Part I

INTRODUCTION TO STRESS AND WELLBEING IN THE LEGAL SYSTEM

1

Stress, Trauma, and Wellbeing in the Legal System: An Overview

Monica K. Miller and Brian H. Bornstein

Participants in the justice system are charged with many functions that are integral to society. Police investigate and arrest alleged criminals. Judges and jurors decide matters of law and fact in order to settle legal issues. Lawyers represent the state, the defendant, and civil litigants who have been accused of or are accusing other people of causing harm. Witnesses and victims provide information and testimony. Probation and parole officers keep tabs on those who have been convicted of crimes but have been released into the community under supervision. While the participation of each of these groups is necessary to promote justice, this participation may lead to negative consequences for participants. Judges have been threatened, jurors have witnessed extremely graphic evidence of crimes, children have had to identify their abusers in open court, and domestic violence victims have had to face their abusers in court.

Some of these individuals are legal professionals (e.g., judges, attorneys, police officers) who choose to put themselves in this position. Even so, some of these individuals experience negative outcomes such as occupational burnout, secondary traumatic stress, and stress-related health problems. Other individuals are laypersons (e.g., victims, litigants) who do not choose to be involved in the legal system. Many stressors are minor but nonetheless cause disruption to one's life. On occasion, the impact on legal participants can be profound; some experience anxiety, depression, alcoholism, and heart disease. Trauma and stress have the potential to affect the behavior and performance of victims, litigants, witnesses, judges, jurors, police, and attorneys; this in turn can influence the functioning of the legal system as a whole. Trauma and stress can also affect individuals on a more personal level, affecting their relationships, job satisfaction, and overall health.

Scholars have long recognized that the legal system can have therapeutic or nontherapeutic effects. David Wexler and Bruce Winick coined the term *therapeutic jurisprudence* to refer to a set of principles that legal actors can follow to ensure that their actions avoid putting undue stress on individuals in the legal system (e.g., Winick & Wexler, 2003). For instance, judges can try to avoid rescheduling or postponing a trial that would delay a child's testimony and force her to mentally prepare again at a later date. On a larger scale, "problem-solving courts" have been developed to address underlying problems (e.g., mental health or drug abuse) that are related to certain crimes. Such steps help attenuate stress and promote wellbeing among legal participants.

While the legal system can cause stress in some respects, participation in the legal system can also produce positive outcomes. For instance, participation in the legal system can promote wellbeing for many individuals, such as victims who feel that justice was served and jurors and judges who feel they have helped preserve the integrity of the legal system. The justice system takes criminals off the streets, removes children from dangerous homes, compensates victims of others' negligence, and protects people with diminished capacity (e.g., some elders) from making bad decisions. Such actions certainly promote wellbeing for many individuals.

On a societal level, participation in the legal system can have benefits in terms of greater trust in public institutions and greater civic engagement. As discussed in the chapter on juries, many individuals have more positive perceptions of the legal system *after* participating as compared to before. Thus, serving as a juror can diminish negative perceptions of jury duty and encourage jurors to speak positively of jury duty in the future, leading friends and family to participate in the future. Similarly, a child who feels that the legal system paid attention to her wishes as to whom to live with after her parents' divorce may feel that the legal system helped her cope with a difficult situation. A victim might feel relieved and safe after her abuser is imprisoned, and an elderly prisoner may reap physical and emotional benefits from having accommodations that better suit her physical abilities. In such instances, the legal system has promoted wellbeing. Such actions can encourage individuals to trust the legal system again in the future; for example, they may be more likely to report future crimes and encourage others to do so. Positive attitudes can also encourage individuals to be more actively involved in the legal system or community in general, perhaps by voting or volunteering.

It is important to note that some degree of stress in many legal situations is actually appropriate. It would certainly be undesirable for judges and juries to make cavalier decisions without feeling a certain weight of responsibility. Similarly, an awareness of what is at stake will prevent civil litigants from entering the legal arena without a great deal of thought, thereby discouraging frivolous lawsuits. Finally, a certain amount of stress will lead all individuals involved in a trial (e.g., prosecutors, civil and criminal defendants) to expend due diligence in developing the case.

The purpose of this book is to illustrate how the legal system positively or negatively affects the wellbeing of individuals who have contact with various legal entities. The book will review the literature and summarize the existing research (or point out where research is lacking) concerning how involvement in the legal system affects a variety of populations. It focuses on both negative and positive aspects of wellbeing in order to provide a broad perspective on wellbeing in the legal system. This approach offers insights into how the legal system can be changed to promote wellbeing on both an individual basis and a societal level.

What Are Stress, Trauma, and Wellbeing?

Even though they are frequently used in our everyday lives, terms such as *stress*, *trauma*, and *wellbeing* are difficult to define. All three terms are interwoven and possibly best defined by keeping the other terms in mind. For instance, wellbeing could mean anything from positive emotional or physical health to the absence of stress or trauma. In this book, *wellbeing* is often used when discussing innovations designed to prevent or reduce stress.

Courts have adopted measures to address jurors' mundane stressors (e.g., not knowing where to park) and clinically significant stressors (e.g., viewing graphic and violent photographs of crime scenes). Courts have also allowed children to testify behind screens or through closed-circuit television in order to avoid retraumatizing them or causing them further stress (e.g., by having to talk about being abused in front of strangers and the accused abuser). Legislatures have passed laws to address judges' safety concerns and to require individuals to report child or elder abuse. Police departments have adopted wellness programs to promote the physical health of officers. Such measures are certainly addressing the wellbeing of these individuals. These measures aside, being involved in the legal system can promote or hinder one's wellbeing. Attorneys sometimes become substance abusers, in part due to the pressures of the job; and police officers suffer higher rates of cardiovascular disease and obesity than the general public. Victims sometimes refuse to cooperate with police because they anticipate a reduction in their wellbeing if they do so. Thus, while wellbeing is somewhat of an inclusive yet elusive term, it generally refers to one's positive mental or physical health.

Trauma and stress are related but separate constructs, as is noted in the psychological term *posttraumatic stress disorder* (PTSD), which is discussed in many chapters as a measure of how one's wellbeing has been negatively affected by some situation or event. Trauma is most commonly discussed in terms of victims' experiences, but it can also be used to refer to the experiences of others; for instance, the term *secondary traumatic stress* is experienced by those who help victims or are exposed to details of the victim's trauma. While the chapters on judges and jurors note studies specifically on secondary or vicarious stress, it certainly could apply to individuals such as attorneys, police officers, foster parents, and the people who work with families involved in dependency courts. Trauma is typically associated with a specific event or series of events, such as being victimized or experiencing the divorce of one's parents. Alternatively, the term *trauma* is used as a descriptor of the type of stress one experiences, as in the term *traumatic stress*, as opposed to less serious types of stressors.

The terms *stress* and *trauma* are often used together in clinical diagnoses. The two types of clinical disorders most related to stress are PTSD and acute stress disorder; while these have been recognized by clinicians only in recent decades, some form of stress disorder has been recognized by mental health professionals since they formally began to document disorders. The first version of the *Diagnostic and Statistical Manual of Mental Disorders* (DSM) used the term *gross stress reaction* to describe the reactions to extreme stress such as a catastrophic event (see Follette & Ruzek, 2006, for review). While the first DSM (also referred to as DSM-I) did not list any criteria for diagnosing this disorder, it noted that the syndrome could apply to anyone who had experienced stress that was so significant that it could not be tolerated. In the revised 1968 version of the DSM (DSM-II), the term *transient situational disturbance* was used instead and was a broader disorder that emphasized "overwhelming" stressors. In the 1970s, clinicians started recognizing such disorders as rape trauma syndrome and battered women syndrome. Partially in response to such developments, in 1980 the DSM-III first used the term *posttraumatic stress disorder* and described the traumatic stressor as being an abnormal event likely to cause distress. The 1994 DSM-IV and the 2000 "text revised" DSM-IV-TR no longer require that the traumatic stressor be abnormal, recognizing that a broad range of stressors that are quite common can produce PTSD (Monson & Friedman, 2006).

The DSM-IV-TR is the current manual used by mental health clinicians; it defines stress in the context of the two stress disorders mentioned earlier (see generally Fink, 2000). Acute stress disorder is similar to PTSD in that both are reactions to a traumatic stressor and are marked by "reliving" the event multiple times, avoiding events or things that cause the person to relive the event, and experiencing anxiety and/or negative arousal. However, the disorders are differentiated in three ways: (1) acute stress disorder lasts up to 4 weeks, while PTSD lasts over 4 weeks; (2) acute stress disorder includes a criterion that the person is suffering from dissociative symptoms, while PTSD does not; and (3) acute stress disorder specifies that the symptoms are not due to substance use, medical, or psychiatric conditions, whereas PTSD does not have such a specification.

Both acute stress disorder and PTSD are *disorders*, indicating that they are not normal responses to stress. This abnormality is what makes this type of stress deserving of a diagnosis in the DSM. While such extreme and abnormal reactions are certainly deserving of being researched, less traumatic stressors—and accompanying stress reactions that do not reach clinically diagnosable levels—are also worthy of study. While the exact frequency of clinical and subclinical stress is not known, it seems likely that subclinical—and therefore less severe—stress would be much more common. In fact, it may be quite common in some groups; for instance, nearly all jurors report experiencing some level of stress—mostly subclinical stress—as a result of jury duty. Because of its frequency, it is important to address these somewhat less serious stressors.

Traumatic stress aside, the term *stress* can also connote a more general sense of lacking wellbeing, whether it is from experiencing a specific trauma (or the trauma of others) or from experiencing a long-term situation such as being overworked and publicly criticized for one's job performance. Because the general term *stress* is more commonly used than *trauma* or *wellbeing* in the fields of study in this book, we will focus a bit more on this term in the next section.

First, though, it is important to note that stress, trauma, and wellbeing are not uniform constructs. In this book, we take a broad approach, allowing chapter authors to approach their topics using the definitions and measures most commonly studied in their field. For instance, juror stress is often measured by depression, anxiety, or boredom. In contrast, police stress has been measured by stress-related health markers, and stress in children witnesses has been measured through physical reactions such as crying. As such, the terms are not used strictly in the clinical sense, but are used more broadly. Other terms, such as anxiety or distress, might be differentiated from—or related to—stress, trauma, and wellbeing, but we do not distinguish them here. This wide variety of terms and measures reflects the reality that stress can manifest itself in many ways, which include physical reactions, emotional responses, and disease. With these definitions and caveats in mind, it is easier to understand the causes of stress and the ways in which it has been measured.

Causes of Stress

There are a great number of stressors among participants in the legal system. Some can be quite general; for instance, trial delays can be stressful for judges, jurors, attorneys, law enforcement officers, and witnesses. Other stressors are very role dependent; for instance, the stressors faced by a domestic violence victim, such as the fear and shame involved in accusing her husband of abusing her, are quite unique to that situation.

As discussed in multiple chapters, stress can be categorized as resulting from several types of sources. One typology includes external, operational, and organizational stressors, while another typology includes mundane versus clinically significant stressors. A third typology categorizes stressors as personal, external to one's agency, internal to one's agency, or task related.

Although applied primarily to law enforcement, the external/operational/organizational typology could apply to many other groups as well, especially judges, attorneys, and probation officers. External stress refers to stressors that arise because of difficulties balancing one's family and job or because of criticism from the public or other external sources. Any of the professionals discussed in this book could face these challenges. In contrast, operational stress is a result of one's actual duties in the legal profession. Probation officers, judges, and other such professionals also may deal with potentially dangerous individuals, make difficult decisions, and face dangerous situations. Finally, organizational stress is a result of dealing with bureaucracy associated with the job; most legal professionals likely deal with such issues on a regular basis.

Causes of stress for other groups also vary and can range from mild inconveniences (e.g., jurors not being able to check their e-mail) to extreme emotional distress (e.g., a victim experiencing PTSD years after being victimized). For laypersons, stress can result from being in an unusual situation and not knowing what to expect. Parents who have had their legal rights revoked, children who have to testify against their accused abuser, plaintiffs who have to discuss personal issues in open court, and older adults who have their decision-making competency questioned might all experience stress simply because of their contact with the legal system. Stressors can also result from *not* being involved in the legal system as much as one wants to be involved. As discussed in several chapters herein, plaintiffs in civil cases and children in criminal, divorce, and dependency cases often want to be "heard" but are not allowed to tell their stories, at least to the extent that they wish to do so. Probation officers (and other employees) may not have as much input into their job duties or performance evaluations as they would like. In sum, the causes of stress are quite varied.

Measures of Stress

As just discussed, the terms *stress*, *trauma*, and *wellbeing* are somewhat difficult to define. As might be expected, there are a wide variety of assessments used to measure stress. While some have been used specifically on one population, they might also be used (possibly with small adaptations) for other groups in future research.

Some measures focus on physical effects related to stress. For instance, much of the research concerning police officers measures instances of cardiovascular disease and obesity; this could also be used on other groups that experience high levels of stress in their occupations, such as attorneys, judges, and probation officers. While there are clear differences (e.g., police officers are the only members of this group who regularly put themselves in potentially violent situations), it is possible these measures could be used on a variety of populations.

Other measures of stress focus on psychological aspects of stress, such as anxiety and depression. Common measures include the Beck Depression Inventory, the Center for Epidemiological Studies Depression Scale, and the State-Trait Anxiety Inventory. Other related psychological measures are for detecting secondary traumatic stress or vicarious trauma. While these measures are largely used in research on judges and jurors, they are general enough to be used for a wide variety of participants in the legal system.

Psychologists have also begun to define and assess forensic stress disorder (FSD), litigation response syndrome (LRS), and litigation-induced trauma syndrome (LITS). Symptoms of such disorders or syndromes are similar to those of PTSD, but instead of being caused by a traumatic stressor, they are caused by participation in the legal system itself. Much like a clinical diagnosis, there are criteria for diagnosing these symptoms. For instance, FSD's symptoms include sleeplessness, obsessive thoughts, reliving the forensic experience (e.g., testifying), and avoidance of things associated with that forensic experience (Cohen & Vesper, 2001). All three of these syndromes/disorders focus on civil litigants, especially victims of accidents or malpractice; however, they could be useful in studying the stress experienced by other types of victims, defendants, and perhaps even families involved in divorce or dependency cases.

Some measures of stress involve evaluating one's performance. For instance, assessments of the quality of children's memories and the accuracy of their testimony can be used as a proxy for how much stress children are experiencing. Some measures of stress target specific job-related performance measures such as occupational burnout. Performance measures could be used to assess all legal professionals and even some types of witnesses.

Some measures focus on stress related to safety. These measures are used primarily with judges, but they are certainly relevant to all individuals in legal professions in which there is concern that one's wellbeing could be compromised by violence. Jurors, attorneys, and witnesses could also have safety issues that are measurable in this way.

Finally, some measures are designed to assess a person's *risk* for experiencing stress, rather than measuring stress itself. For instance, there are formulas for measuring risk in police officers. Similar formulas might be used in other groups that have prolonged exposure to legal stress, such as law enforcement officers, attorneys, or judges. Other formulas could be developed to assess jurors' risk of stress, which might help develop stress interventions that are tailored to the amount of stress experienced by each individual juror.

As an aside, some measures recognize that stress has a temporal element. While many symptoms of stress are apparent immediately, others might not appear until months or years later. Further, stress can be either acute or chronic. For instance, divorce is detrimental to the wellbeing of both parents and children, leading to both short-term and long-term effects. Most stressors that jurors experience are relatively short in duration and lessen over time; however, some jurors may experience a delayed reaction to stress long after the trial is over. Police officers' stress-related health symptoms can last a lifetime, as can the effects of being a domestic violence victim or experiencing injury due to another's negligence. Thus, while much stress is alleviated quickly, other stress reactions are longer lasting; researchers have often recognized this and have measured it accordingly.

As this brief review demonstrates, there is a broad variety of measures of stress (or related constructs) used in legal settings. Some are clinical-type diagnoses (e.g., LITS), some are Likert-type scales (e.g., State-Trait Anxiety Inventory), and some are observational measures (e.g., observations of whether a child seems upset). While some measures are relatively well known (e.g., Beck Depression Inventory), others are less widely used, such as the measures used to assess stress in civil litigants. As might be expected, measures vary in whether they have been tested for reliability and validity. Future research can help better develop such stress measures and the relationships among them.

Should the Legal System Address Problems Related to Stress?

While the legal system is designed to promote justice, it sometimes threatens the wellbeing of those who are involved. And although being involved in the legal system certainly can affect one's wellbeing, it is important to recognize that the system is not necessarily designed to promote wellbeing. However, it often does take steps to reduce harm from the trauma and stress of being involved in the legal system; the chapters in this book detail many of these efforts. But the question remains: *Should* the legal system be obligated, or at least encouraged, to address the stress that it has caused?

While that is a normative question to which the answer could vary based on who is answering, there are reasons that someone might say no. For instance, one might argue that it is not the legal system's place to address the psychological needs of participants. The effective functioning of the legal system is of utmost importance, and it should not be disrupted or altered for other purposes. Employers in general are not required to take extensive steps to protect the wellbeing of their employees or people who interact with the business. Thus, the legal system should not necessarily be required to address stress any more than other businesses.

On the other hand, there are many reasons that the answer to the question "Should the legal system help address the stress it has caused?" should be yes. First, the legal system should help promote wellbeing and prevent undue stress simply because the functioning of the legal system depends on it. If individuals have negative impressions of the legal system, they may fail to participate. Witnesses will not testify, jurors will not show up, and victims will not pursue justice by reporting crimes or assisting prosecutors in bringing charges against the perpetrators. Further, only a small subsection of the population will seek careers in the legal field if they fear experiencing a great deal of untreated stress or being stigmatized if they seek help. Also of concern is the possibility that workers' performance might suffer due to stress. Judges, attorneys, probation officers, and other legal professionals under stress may be prone to making biased decisions, and overly stressed police officers may use undue force in dealing with suspects or fail to follow up on important leads.

Second, stress experienced by those who come in contact with the legal system can also have personal and societal consequences. Individuals who suffer a great deal of stress could experience personal difficulties in their relationships, which could lead to divorce, violence, or other maladies. Further, stress may come at the cost of increased health care expenses, missed days of work, alcoholism, and suicide—all of which are costly for the individual and his or her employer. These outcomes are also costly for society as a whole—as are reductions in civic participation (e.g., voting), as discussed earlier.

For all these reasons, it is important for the legal system to recognize stress and promote wellbeing. If legal actors do decide to take action to address stress, there is a variety of steps they can take, discussed next.

What Can the Legal System do to Promote Wellbeing and Reduce Stress?

In the United States and abroad, legal systems have taken steps to address stress and wellbeing. For instance, many countries are taking steps to protect child witnesses, such as hiring intermediaries who can reword questions in developmentally appropriate ways; similarly, courts around the world are taking measures such as hiring counselors to address jurors' stress. In some arenas, the legal system has gone to great lengths to protect these individuals. Some of these measures have good empirical data on their effectiveness, but many are still untested.

In recent years, researchers and other entities (e.g., the National Center for State Courts) have increased their attention to studying and addressing the stressors experienced by a range of individuals in the legal system. There have been a variety of actions taken, such as mentoring programs for judges, laws requiring individuals to report suspected elder abuse, and allowing police officers to retire early if they are disabled by their work-related health issues such as cardiovascular disease. There are even specialized courts that are tailored to meet the unique needs of specific populations (e.g., mentally ill, prostitutes, drug abusers). Each of the chapters of this book evaluates existing innovations and makes suggestions for what additional steps can be taken to promote wellbeing.

Overview of the Book

This book contains 5 parts with 13 chapters. This introductory chapter is followed by a chapter discussing the concept of therapeutic jurisprudence, which runs through much of the remainder of the book, and an overview of how the principles of therapeutic jurisprudence have been used to address stress in the legal system in general. Part II contains five chapters discussing how the legal system promotes wellbeing and can lead to stress in victims, families, child witnesses, civil litigants, and older adults. Each of these groups contains individuals who are lay participants in the legal system. Although some have chosen to be involved in the system (e.g., plaintiffs in civil cases, divorcing parents), most are unwilling participants (e.g., child victims, domestic violence victims). Whether willing or not, most of these individuals have little experience in the legal system and frequently encounter unfamiliar situations, procedures, and people. In contrast, the groups in Part III have chosen to be involved in the legal system by their selection of profession. These three chapters discuss the stressors experienced by law enforcement, state and federal probation officers, and attorneys. While these individuals have chosen to be part of the legal system, this does not mean that they are immune to stress. In fact, they may be particularly susceptible to stressors related to their jobs, especially in environments in which expressing distress is not acceptable (e.g., police officers might not let others know that they are experiencing distress because they think it is a sign of weakness). Part IV contains two chapters discussing the stressors experienced by jurors and judges—two groups responsible for making ultimate outcome decisions in the court system. These two groups both share some stressors and experience stressors that are unique.

The chapters in Parts II, III, and IV share a number of similarities; each chapter (1) addresses the research that exists concerning the effects of involvement in the legal system for this particular population, (2) identifies gaps in the existing research, (3) discusses future research that can fill these gaps, (4) analyzes any current interventions designed to promote the wellbeing of this population, and (5) provides policy recommendations for promoting the wellbeing of this population. In addition, the chapters present other information that is unique to their particular topic.

The concluding chapter, which makes up Part V, identifies some of the overarching themes discussed in multiple chapters throughout the book. It also briefly examines two groups that might experience stress but have not yet been thoroughly studied in this regard: eyewitnesses and individuals involved in alternative dispute resolution. The chapter concludes with some recommendations for future research and policy.

Conclusion

All individuals face stress in their daily lives; this may be particularly true for those who enforce the law, administer justice, or are forced into the legal system. Such involvement can result in negative behaviors, burnout, reduced efficiency, risk taking, mental illness, or physical symptoms ranging from colds to suicide. When such phenomena occur, it is time to reassess old habits and devise approaches to inoculate those in the justice system from stress. This book presents theory, research, and scholarship from a variety of disciplines and offers suggestions for those interested in exploring and improving the wellbeing of those who are voluntarily (e.g., police, probation officers, civil plaintiffs, lawyers, judges, court staff) or involuntarily (e.g., jurors, criminal and civil defendants, witnesses, children) drawn into the legal system. The first step in promoting wellbeing among these groups is the dissemination of knowledge; that is what this book is designed to do.

References

Cohen, L. J., & Vesper, J. H. (2001). Forensic stress disorder. *Stress: The International Journal on the Biology of Stress, 25*(1), 1–21.

Fink, G. (2000). *Encyclopedia of stress*. San Diego, CA: Academic Press.

Follette, V. M., & Ruzek, J. I. (2006). *Cognitive behavioral therapies for trauma* (2nd ed.). New York, NY: Guilford Press.

Monson, C. M., & Friedman, M. J. (2006). Back to the future of understanding trauma: Implications for cognitive-behavioral therapies for trauma. In V. M. Follette & J. I. Ruzek (Eds.), *Cognitive-behavioral therapies for trauma* (2nd ed., pp. 1–16). New York, NY: Guilford Press.

Winick, B. J., & Wexler, D. B. (2003). Introduction. In B. J. Wexler & D. B. Winick (Eds.), *Judging in a therapeutic key: Therapeutic jurisprudence and the courts* (pp. 3–7). Durham, NC: Carolina Academic Press.

2

Using the Law to Enhance Wellbeing: Applying Therapeutic Jurisprudence in the Courtroom

Lorie L. Sicafuse and Brian H. Bornstein

Traditionally, the law has largely functioned to maintain social order, preserve individual rights, and protect the public from harm (Senna & Siegel, 1999). These goals are primarily accomplished through the threat or administration of punishment for legal transgressors. Purportedly, punishing wrongdoers helps to prevent future transgressions, reinforces social values, and restores a sense of justice or equity among victims and community members (Tyler & Smith, 1998).

Within the past two decades, many legal scholars and professionals have argued that the scope of the law should be expanded to promote individual wellbeing (e.g., Rottman, 2000; Wexler, 1995; Winick, 1997). Specifically, they propose that legal decision making should be guided by *therapeutic jurisprudence*, defined as "the study of the role of the law as a therapeutic agent" (Wexler, 1995, p. 220). In practicing therapeutic jurisprudence, legal actors aim to maximize positive physical, psychological, and social outcomes for offenders, victims, and community members while minimizing the law's anti-therapeutic consequences (Casey & Rottman, 2000).

Therapeutic jurisprudence is not necessarily inconsistent with the more conventional purposes of the law and the U.S. legal system, but it does require a more careful consideration of the measures taken to achieve justice. For instance, proponents of therapeutic jurisprudence acknowledge that legal sanctioning is often appropriate and necessary (Winick & Wexler, 2003); yet they also recognize that punishment alone does little to promote wellbeing among those affected by the law and can often lead to unintended antitherapeutic outcomes (Winick & Wexler, 2003).

Although therapeutic jurisprudence provides a guiding framework for legal analysis and practice, this chapter focuses specifically on the application of therapeutic jurisprudence in the courtroom. In particular, it illustrates how legal professionals can utilize therapeutic principles to promote individuals' wellbeing. First, the emergence of therapeutic jurisprudence from mental health law and the main tenets of this approach will be discussed, as will its suitability to particular offenses and defendants. Second, this chapter presents an overview of prior applications of therapeutic jurisprudence and its short-term impact on defendants' wellbeing, focusing on cases involving drug offenses, domestic violence, and juvenile delinquency. Third, it describes the most recent efforts to address other crimes characterized by high rates of recidivism, such as gambling and prostitution, through therapeutic principles. Fourth, it highlights other common cases in which the courts could consider applying therapeutic jurisprudence to target the underlying causes of offending while promoting the wellbeing of defendants, victims, and the community. Fifth, it summarizes potential advantages and negative consequences of approaching law breaking from the perspective of therapeutic jurisprudence. Applications of therapeutic jurisprudence have yielded promising short-term outcomes, but additional research is needed to determine if increased court efforts to maximize therapeutic outcomes for those involved in and affected by crime lead to long-term wellbeing and decreased recidivism.

Therapeutic Jurisprudence: Foundations in Mental Health Law

Considering its emphasis on the promotion of wellbeing, it seems appropriate that the concept of therapeutic jurisprudence emerged from an analysis of mental health law and policy (Wexler & Winick, 1991). At its inception in the 1970s, mental health law was initially guided by a concern for patients' rights (Wexler & Winick, 1991). In particular, scholars and former mental health patients advocated for the right to refuse treatment; some even argued that the practice of involuntary civil commitment be entirely abandoned (see Mechanic, 1987. Less extreme proposals aimed at protecting patients' rights mandated that the mentally ill be afforded the same rights as criminal defendants, such as the right to appointed counsel in civil commitment hearings (Ennis, 1971). However, this patient-centered approach remained unpopular among policymakers and the courts and essentially became obsolete over the next two decades as courts focused on civil commitment as a means of promoting "community security" (Mechanic, 1987; Reisner & Slobogin, 1990; Wexler, 1992). Moreover, there was little consideration of the effects of mental health policy on the wellbeing of patients, families, or practitioners (Wexler, 1992). Based on these observations, Wexler and Winick introduced therapeutic jurisprudence as a framework for evaluating and improving mental health policy and practices.

Early applications of therapeutic jurisprudence in mental health law primarily focused on two broad areas affecting both law-abiding citizens and criminal defendants: civil commitment/coercion and competency judgments. Drawing on research from counseling, clinical, and social psychological disciplines, legal scholars and researchers elucidated the antitherapeutic consequences of civil commitment (i.e., involuntary psychiatric hospitalization) and coerced treatment (e.g., Tyler, 1996; Wexler & Winick, 1991; Winick, 1992, 1997). Specifically, they argued that the loss of autonomy patients experience when institutionalized and/or treated against their will likely minimizes the intended therapeutic effects of these interventions. Coerced patients are likely less motivated to participate in their treatment plan and work toward recovery (or improvement) than those afforded some degree of choice in their treatment decisions; they also may be less inclined to seek treatment voluntarily in the future for fear of being institutionalized (Winick, 2008). In general, coerced treatment and civil commitment could result in a variety of negative psychological consequences: depression, hopelessness, and a loss of self-efficacy (see Wexler & Winick, 1991; Winick, 2008, for a review of the potential antitherapeutic effects of coercion).

The antitherapeutic effects of civil commitment and coercion can extend beyond the patient. Therapists might experience a sense of inefficacy or inadequacy upon treating such reluctant patients (Winick, 2008); family members dissatisfied with the process or outcomes of civil commitment hearings might be less inclined to seek treatment on their loved one's behalf and develop negative attitudes toward the courts and the legal system in general (Kennedy, 2003; Tyler, 1996). Accordingly, these authors made several recommendations aimed at promoting the wellbeing of mental health patients, practitioners, and participants (e.g., family members, attorneys) in the civil commitment process. Specifically, they suggested that coercion and/or involuntary hospitalization be reserved for extreme cases in which patients pose significant danger to themselves or others (Winick, 2008); that the patients' perspective be carefully considered in civil commitment hearings; and that they be afforded choice to the extent possible in determining their treatment plan (Tyler, 1996; Winick, 2003, 2008). Based on justice theory, Kennedy and Tyler further asserted that the courts and legal professionals should strive to treat such individuals and their families with the utmost respect and consideration throughout these legal processes.

Much of the early therapeutic jurisprudence literature also explored issues related to legal determinations of competency. These analyses encompassed the potential outcomes of incompetency labeling for both criminal defendants (i.e., adjudicating a defendant incompetent to stand trial) and mentally ill individuals in general (e.g., competency in making decisions regarding treatment, finances, or marriage). Across these different cases, advocates of therapeutic jurisprudence have again utilized social science research to illustrate how incompetency labeling can negatively affect individuals' wellbeing. Primarily,

Winick (1996a, 1996b) highlighted the aversive psychological consequences of the objectification and loss of control that typically results from incompetency labeling: helplessness, hopelessness, depression, and low self-esteem. As with civil commitment and/or coerced treatment, patients adjudicated as incompetent might be unmotivated and unwilling to participate in their own treatment plans, thereby undermining any well-intended therapeutic objectives of such assessments (Wexler & Winick, 1991; Winick, 2008). Some antitherapeutic effects of incompetency labeling are unique to cases involving criminal defendants. For example, bail is not an option for individuals adjudicated as incompetent; thus, they are often isolated from their family and friends, which can negatively affect the recovery process (Winick, 1996b). Further, incompetent defendants accused of misdemeanors might be institutionalized for a significantly longer period of time than they would have spent in a correctional facility had they simply pled guilty (Winick, 1996b).

Proposals to help address these issues include narrowing competency standards so that only those with extremely impaired decision-making abilities are rendered incompetent, modifying terminology so that individuals unable to make decisions on their own behalf because of mental illness are labeled "temporarily impaired" (Winick, 1996a), and replacing the formal competency process with a series of trial continuances for defendants who might be incompetent (Wexler & Winick, 1991). Such changes should help to minimize the stigmatizing effects of an official incompetency label on individuals' psychological and social wellbeing. In addition, Winick further suggested allowing individuals who would otherwise be labeled as incompetent to make their own decisions to the extent that such choices are supported by professionals or patients' advocates (e.g., allowing defendants to plead guilty if attorneys agree that this decision is in their client's best interest).

These examples illustrate how therapeutic jurisprudence can be used to analyze policies and procedures, as well as to promote changes in legal practice that can enhance individuals' wellbeing. As many of the aforementioned proposals have proven controversial among lawmakers and constituents (Winick, 1996b, 2008), few changes in substantive mental health law have emerged from policy evaluations guided by therapeutic jurisprudence. However, legal professionals can and do use therapeutic jurisprudence to guide *applications* of the law both within and outside of the mental health realm. The next section further describes the main tenets of therapeutic jurisprudence as they developed from analyses of mental health law, with the remainder of the chapter focusing on selected applications of therapeutic jurisprudence within the criminal justice system.

Principles of Therapeutic Jurisprudence

Wexler and Winick (1991), along with other legal scholars and professionals, soon broadened the scope of therapeutic jurisprudence to encompass multiple areas within substantive and applied law (see Wexler, 1995; Winick, 1997).

At present, therapeutic jurisprudence can best be conceptualized as a framework guiding legal decision making across disciplines. Legal rules, procedures, and applications of the law should be viewed in terms of their propensity to produce therapeutic or antitherapeutic outcomes (Wexler & Winick, 1996a). Since its development in mental health law, therapeutic jurisprudence has been widely practiced in the fields of correctional law, criminal law, juvenile and family law, personal injury law, and several other areas regarding laws, legal practice, and legal evidence (Wexler, 1996).

As practiced in the courts, therapeutic jurisprudence primarily entails careful consideration of the law's applications, rather than the purposes and effects of substantive law. Judges, attorneys, and other legal actors can all work to promote the wellbeing of offenders, victims, families, and the community as a whole (Casey & Rottman, 2000). This typically involves developing and implementing interventions to address the underlying issues that brought defendants into the courtroom (Casey & Rottman, 2000; Rottman, 2000). However, therapeutic jurisprudence can be practiced during multiple phases of a case involving law breaking, and legal actors can make therapeutic decisions that are not directly related to sentencing or trial outcomes. For instance, an attorney could consider whether allowing a victim to testify would yield therapeutic or antitherapeutic consequences, or a judge might promote wellbeing among jurors by holding a posttrial debriefing session (Miller & Bornstein, 2004; also see chapter 11, this volume; Shuman, Hamilton, & Daley, 1996). In all contexts, legal actors applying therapeutic jurisprudence must adhere to several important principles inherent within this perspective.

First, therapeutic jurisprudence is an interdisciplinary, research-oriented approach to the law. Although judges and other legal actors may use their own knowledge and experiences as a basis for their decisions, they should also incorporate expert opinions and draw on theory and research from a broad range of social science and health disciplines (Wexler & Winick, 1991). For instance, legal professionals could utilize research conducted by clinical psychologists and physicians in order to determine whether a drug offender should be sentenced to prison or referred to treatment (Hora, Schma, & Rosenthal, 1999), or they could consult social workers and family therapists to develop the most appropriate interventions in a child abuse case (Brooks, 1999). It follows that legal actors must take a collaborative approach to maximizing the therapeutic outcomes of the law. Judges and attorneys for both parties must work together rather than against one another, and they must establish close working relationships with law enforcement, legal advocates, treatment facilities, and community organizations to address the needs of offenders and victims (Stolle, Wexler, Winick, & Dauer, 1997).

Second, legal actors viewing cases through the lens of therapeutic jurisprudence must refrain from applying a "blanket solution" to legal transgressions. Rather, they must carefully consider the unique aspects of each case and the needs of all parties involved. Therapeutic approaches to maladaptive behaviors may only be appropriate for certain offenders. Interventions involving psychological counseling and education are best suited to defendants amenable to treatment, and judges should not waive prison sentences upon successful completion of a treatment program for extremely dangerous offenders. Legal actors also must consider whether the complex issues underlying a defendant's behavior can be sufficiently addressed through therapeutic interventions. If a robbery was motivated by drug addiction or poverty, a judge might consider referring the defendant to a drug treatment program and ordering attendance at job training and GED classes. Conversely, these measures may be inappropriate if this robbery was committed by an extremely violent offender who had previously been noncompliant with court-ordered treatment.

In addition, identical legal interventions or impositions might have therapeutic consequences for some offenders and antitherapeutic consequences for others (Wexler, 1995). For instance, mandated inpatient treatment likely benefits many drug offenders, but it could be undesirable for pregnant drug abusers or single mothers. Some legal decisions might promote positive psychological or social outcomes among defendants, yet undermine the wellbeing of victims or community members. Although sex offenders might benefit socially and psychologically from being reintegrated into the community, this practice can threaten local residents' sense of security. Thus, although applications of therapeutic jurisprudence tend to focus on minimizing antitherapeutic consequences for offenders, legal professionals must also anticipate the impact of their actions on victims and the more distal outcomes of these actions (e.g., effects on the community or the legal system as a whole; Winick, 2000).

Third, therapeutic considerations should not trump justice principles or important social values. Although legal actors should contemplate the therapeutic consequences of their decisions, they must also consider a multitude of other factors such as individual rights and autonomy, public safety, and financial considerations (Wexler & Winick, 1996a). For instance, an offender who poses a significant threat to his wife and children's safety might need to be incarcerated, even if incarceration has some antitherapeutic consequences for the offender and his family. Legal judgments incorporating therapeutic jurisprudence must adhere to current legal standards and regulations, and it is essential that offenders be held accountable for their actions (Winick, 2000). Therapeutic jurisprudence and punishment are not mutually exclusive; legal actors viewing cases from this perspective simply must consider the *purpose* and *potential outcomes* of legal sanctioning. To the extent possible, judges also should refrain from "forcing" defendants into treatment or other diversion programs, but rather frame therapeutic options as a choice (Wexler & Winick, 1996b). Not only must legal actors respect the rights of the victim and community members, but they also must acknowledge the rights and autonomy of defendants.

In sum, although therapeutic jurisprudence originated in mental health law, it has since branched out into numerous legal disciplines and can be viewed as an innovative approach to the law and legal procedures in general.

Legal actors who view law breaking through the lens of therapeutic jurisprudence aim to maximize the wellbeing of all parties affected by a crime and target the social and psychological underpinnings of crime. Incorporating therapeutic considerations into legal decisions requires considerable effort and collaboration among legal actors, as well as a sufficient knowledge of social science research and community resources. Applications of therapeutic jurisprudence must cohere with existing law and justice principles and may be of limited utility for certain types of crimes and offenders. Overall, therapeutic approaches may be most beneficial in cases involving first-time, relatively minor offenses or in cases involving defendants with treatable conditions (e.g., substance abuse, poor social or anger management skills) underlying their offending. Despite these limitations, thousands of U.S. courts have used therapeutic jurisprudence to address a broad range of legal transgressions (Winick & Wexler, 2003).

Therapeutic Jurisprudence: From Theory to Practice

As with any well-developed justice principle, therapeutic jurisprudence is ultimately rooted in theory and scholarship. Specifically, it involves "the use of social science to study the extent to which a legal rule or practice promotes the psychological or physical wellbeing of the people it affects" (Slobogin, 1996, p. 775). Although therapeutic jurisprudence has a solid theoretical foundation, it has become increasingly more applied in nature. Therapeutic jurisprudence has surged in popularity over the last decade and is widely practiced in general and specialized courts (i.e., courts designed to address specific crimes; Rottman, 2000). However, legal actors often continue to disregard therapeutic considerations in favor of a more punitive approach to law breaking (Winick, 2000).

This section describes ways in which therapeutic jurisprudence can be applied in the courts to enhance individuals' wellbeing. First, it reviews more well-established and routine applications of therapeutic jurisprudence that commonly occur within specialty courts. Next, it discusses more recent efforts to address the underlying causes of prostitution and gambling crimes through therapeutic jurisprudence. Finally, it identifies cases in which victims, offenders, and their families would likely benefit from therapeutic interventions.

Prior and Prevalent Applications

Therapeutic jurisprudence has been applied frequently to cases involving drug-related offenses, domestic violence, and juvenile offenders. Such cases are often adjudicated in specialty courts (e.g., drug treatment court, domestic violence and family court, and various specialty courts for juveniles; Winick & Wexler, 2003). Although these courts share a common goal, they take different approaches to maximizing therapeutic outcomes among those affected by crime, given differences in the kinds of offenses and offenders they deal with (see, generally, Wiener & Brank, in press).

Drug treatment courts. The early establishment and apparent success of drug treatment courts catalyzed the development of many other specialty "problem-solving courts" throughout the past two decades. The first drug treatment court (DTC) was founded in Miami in 1989 and provided a forum for expanding therapeutic jurisprudence beyond mental health law (Hayes, 2003). Therapeutic approaches to drug-related crimes were rapidly adopted; as of 2007, over 1,600 DTCs were operating in the United States (BJA Drug Court Clearinghouse Project, 2007).

Drug treatment courts increased in popularity as legal actors (namely, judges and attorneys) began to recognize the ineffectiveness of traditional approaches to drug-related crimes (Hayes, 2003; Hora et al., 1999). Drug offenders were largely unresponsive to supervised parole or incarceration, as these punitive measures failed to target the addiction underlying delinquency in this population (Hora et al., 1999). This led to the characterization of the legal system as a "revolving door" for drug offenders; judges were repeatedly faced with the same defendants committing the same types of crimes. As a result, drug-related cases were putting a significant strain on already limited court resources (Winick & Wexler, 2003).

Different DTCs adopt varying approaches, but their primary focus is to address the drug addiction that brought defendants into the legal system. Drug offenses may be processed initially by DTCs or transferred from traditional courts. Prosecutors, defense attorneys, and judges must work together to assess a defendant's suitability for DTC and corresponding therapeutic interventions (Senjo & Leip, 2001a). Consistent with the main tenets of therapeutic jurisprudence, defendants are only referred to DTC if they are willing to admit guilt and accept responsibility for their transgressions. In contrast to many traditional courts, DTCs aim to process drug-related cases in a timely, efficient manner, and many defendants are placed in a treatment program within 3 days of their arrest or release from jail (Senjo & Leip, 2001b). Such early intervention is an essential component of the DTC model, as addicts are often most amenable to treatment during periods of crisis (Hora et al., 1999).

DTC treatment programs are intensive and typically involve three to four phases including detoxification, stabilization, aftercare, and counseling. During the aftercare phase, defendants receive academic and occupational training intended to prevent them from returning to their "old lifestyle" (Hora et al., 1999). Throughout this process, defendants are closely monitored by the courts; they must submit to frequent drug testing and make regular court appearances to inform the judge of their progress (Senjo & Leip, 2001b). Because DTCs accept the "medical model" of drug addiction, they generally recognize that relapse is often a part of treatment and strive to be as nonpunitive as possible (Hora et al., 1999). However, sanctions are imposed for defendants who repeatedly fail urinalysis tests, and those who do not adhere to program requirements (e.g., regular attendance at therapy sessions or job training) are referred back to the traditional court system and typically face incarceration (Hayes, 2003). Conversely, prosecutors often dismiss the charges against defendants who successfully complete the program (Hora et al., 1999).

Drug treatment courts have received strong legal and community support (Wilson, Mitchell, & Mackenzie, 2006), and therapeutic approaches to drug offenses are significantly more cost-effective than more traditional punitive approaches such as incarceration (Hayes, 2003). Unlike many other specialty courts adopting a therapeutic perspective, drug treatment courts have been subject to frequent evaluations. Although Hora et al. (1999) report promising findings from treatment courts located in Florida, Michigan, Maryland, and California, most evaluations reveal mixed and inconsistent results. The methodology employed in such research is often questionable, as evaluators may lack appropriate comparison groups and often simply report program graduation rates rather than attending to other outcomes indicative of DTC performance (e.g., relapse, recidivism, successful transition back into the community; Wilson et al., 2006). Reviewing 37 published and unpublished evaluations of DTCs, Belenko (2003) found that fewer than half (47%) of those sentenced to DTC programs graduate, though drug use and criminal activity are substantially reduced during participation in the program. Wilson et al.'s meta-analysis of 55 DTC evaluations revealed that such courts lead to a modest reduction in recidivism, but that some drug courts are more effective than others. Specifically, DTCs that establish clear incentives for program completion such as dismissal or reduction of charges tend to yield higher program graduation rates and lower recidivism rates among participants than those that do not (Wilson et al., 2006). Researchers agree that the long-term impacts of DTCs are unknown (Belenko, 2003; Senjo & Leip, 2001a, 2001b; Wilson et al., 2006), and it is unclear if the temporary therapeutic outcomes of DTCs have more distal effects on the wellbeing of offenders, offenders' family members and friends, or the community as a whole.

Domestic violence courts. Domestic violence courts (DVCs) are relatively new outgrowths of the problem-solving court movement. Separate courts processing domestic violence cases first appeared in the mid-1990s. There are approximately 300 specialty DVCs throughout the United States, with plans to establish many more in the coming years (Shelton, 2007).

As a recent phenomenon, DVCs vary considerably in scope and nature. Some have extremely limited functions and are designed primarily to facilitate the processing of civil protection orders. Some DVCs handle only misdemeanor charges, while others deal with felony charges and other serious criminal cases linked to domestic violence (Shelton, 2007). Integrated DVCs are typically best equipped to promote wellbeing, as they handle both civil protection orders and criminal charges and have strong ties to community organizations and resources that can help address the needs of victims and offenders (Winick, 2000). Although DVCs aim to address domestic violence offenses therapeutically, there is no well-developed model guiding their operations as with DTCs (Levey, Steketee, & Keilitz, 2000). Thus, more so than other specialty courts, DVCs often differ in their approaches to domestic violence.

Despite a lack of consensus regarding the most therapeutic means of addressing domestic violence, most DVCs strive to ensure offender accountability and the wellbeing of battered spouses and their children (Hartley, 2003). Here, DVCs diverge from DTC models and problem-solving courts in two respects. First, legal actors involved in domestic violence cases recognize that strong sanctions are often appropriate and necessary (Levey et al., 2000), whereas DTC judges try to avoid punishing offenders (Hora et al., 1999). Second, although problem-solving courts in general aim to maximize therapeutic consequences for all those affected by a crime, DVCs place an explicit focus on the wellbeing of victims and their families. The offender's rehabilitation, though desirable, is often a secondary concern (Shelton, 2007).

First and foremost, DVCs address victims' wellbeing by prioritizing safety. Cases are often adjudicated within days of the offense, and most DVCs ensure streamlined processing of protection orders at no cost to the victim (Levey et al., 2000). Victims' advocates are assigned in each case and provide referrals to battered women's shelters and other community services for victims and their families (Levey et al., 2000). Social workers might provide immediate counseling for battered women and children while facilitating access to more intensive psychological treatment (Hartley, 2003). Domestic violence courts also can assist victims in obtaining medical care, child support, or job training, depending on their individual needs (Winick, 2000). Judges also aim to incorporate the victim's desires into their sentencing decisions (Gover, MacDonald, & Alpert, 2003).

Although primacy is always placed on the victims' needs, DVCs differ in the extent to which they also aim to address the underlying causes of the defendant's behavior. As in other types of problem-solving courts, defense attorneys often assume a nontraditional role by encouraging their client to admit guilt and accept responsibility for their actions (Winick, 2000). In some instances, offenders might simply be sentenced to jail or prison and receive any type of treatment that those facilities provide (Shelton, 2007). In many other cases, however, offenders are ordered to complete an intensive treatment program consisting of substance abuse treatment, cognitive and behavioral therapy, and/or anger management classes (Gover et al., 2003; Hartley, 2003). Noncompliant offenders are swiftly sanctioned through increased court appearances, fines, or incarceration, whereas judges may often minimize the sentences imposed for adherent defendants (e.g., via reduced or suspended fees and jail time; Gover et al., 2003). Winick (2000) emphasizes that offenders' suitability for such diversion programs should be based on actuarial risk assessment models and social science research rather than on legal actors' intuitions or clinical predictions.

Despite an increased focus on the problem of domestic violence and the most appropriate types of treatment for offenders (Wallace, 2005), very few researchers have examined the outcomes of DVCs. Evaluations of DVCs in Salt Lake City and in rural South Carolina suggest that these courts increase convictions in domestic violence cases and significantly reduce the likelihood of recidivism (Gover et al., 2003; Rivera, 2003). Evaluators of the DVC in Lexington County, South Carolina, controlled for factors such as prior arrests and specific type of offense, revealing that this court was also successful in decreasing recidivism among multiple and repeat offenders (Gover et al., 2003). However, both studies utilized a comparison group (offenders charged prior to the implementation of the DVCs) rather than a pure control group. Further, no published studies to date have examined the impact of DVCs on the wellbeing of victims and their families or systematically compared the outcomes of DVCs with differing therapeutic orientations. With the rapid expansion of DVCs throughout the United States, more research is urgently needed to assess their capacity for promoting therapeutic outcomes among those affected by domestic violence.

Juvenile specialty courts. Juvenile delinquency is commonly attributed to a combination of developmental and social factors (Tolan & Titus, 2009). Essentially, many instances of juvenile delinquency are believed to be the product of unfortunate circumstances (e.g., parental abuse and neglect) and the poor decision-making capabilities of adolescents (e.g., susceptibility to peer pressure, lack of foresight and understanding of long-term consequences) rather than to a more permanent "criminal personality" (Siegel & Welsh, 2005). Consequently, juvenile offenders are typically viewed as more amenable to treatment than adult offenders, and most do indeed develop into law-abiding adults (Siegel & Welsh, 2005). Based on these observations, U.S. courts have historically taken a therapeutic approach to juvenile delinquency. Since 1899, many cases involving juveniles have been adjudicated in separate courts designed to promote rehabilitation and wellbeing among troubled youth (Winick & Wexler, 2003). Although lawmakers and community members have advocated for a more punitive, "get tough" approach to juvenile delinquency in recent years, specialty juvenile courts have continued to proliferate. Throughout the United States, there are several juvenile specialty courts designed to address truancy, domestic violence, substance abuse, sex-related crimes, and cases involving juveniles with mental illnesses (Tolan & Titus, 2009). Because a comprehensive description of each type of juvenile court is beyond the scope of this chapter, this section provides a brief overview of two of the most popular juvenile specialty courts: juvenile drug treatment court (JDTC) and teen court.

Juvenile drug treatment courts. Juvenile drug treatment courts are an outgrowth of adult DTCs, and both were established for similar purposes: to provide a more efficient means of processing drug-related cases and to address the addiction underlying delinquent behavior (Hora et al., 1999). In addition, JDTCs aim to *prevent* addiction, as many juveniles charged with substance-related crimes have not yet developed a chemical dependency (Cooper, 2002). Such courts handle a wide range of offenses, from truancy and DUIs to drug possession and theft.

Juvenile drug treatment courts and adult DTCs follow the same basic model, and their judges typically order similar therapeutic interventions:

mandatory inpatient or outpatient drug treatment, frequent drug testing, psychological counseling, and regular court appearances (Tolan & Titus, 2009). However, judges and other legal actors within JDTCs must have a thorough understanding of youth development and the unique needs of juvenile drug offenders. Adolescents often respond to a crisis differently from adults; they also are more inclined to engage in risk-taking behaviors, experience difficulty in severing destructive peer relationships, and generally have less control over their family and social situations (Cooper, 2002). Some common practices in adult DTCs might be ineffective or antitherapeutic for juvenile offenders, and different factors may underlie substance use in juveniles and adults. For instance, the threat of jail time might motivate an adult offender to comply with a drug treatment program but be ineffective for youth who consider referral to detention to be a "badge of honor" (Cooper, 2002, p. 220) or who view detention as an opportunity to escape a harmful family or school environment. In addition, substance use among juveniles is often a product of a malfunctioning family system; parents might not provide adequate supervision, or they might be addicts themselves (Henggeler et al., 2006). In such cases, JDTC judges must assess the stability of the offender's living situation and family structure and make appropriate referrals to family services, therapy, or parenting classes (Cooper, 2002).

Although approximately 300 JDTCs are currently operating in the United States, they have not been subject to the same routine evaluations as adult DTCs (Henggeler et al., 2006). Some individual programs have reported significant reductions in recidivism and substance use based on small samples (e.g., Thompson, 2001), and Henggeler et al. found that youth offenders randomly assigned to juvenile drug courts had better outcomes than those assigned to traditional family courts. The long-term outcomes of individual JDTCs on recidivism and the wellbeing of juvenile offenders in general are unknown (Belenko, 2003; Cooper, 2002).

Teen courts. Teen courts are less formal diversion programs intended for first-time juvenile offenders charged with very minor crimes (e.g., Class C misdemeanors such as theft under $50, traffic tickets, and alcohol possession; Elliot, 2003). Hearings are typically held in an actual courtroom presided over by a judge, attorney, or other community official, while the offenders' peers serve as jury members and counsel (Tolan & Titus, 2009). "Trials" in teen court are scaled-down versions of those occurring in formal court, involving opening and closing statements, questioning of the offender, and jury deliberations (Stickle, Connell, Wilson, & Gottfredson, 2008). Defendants are typically sentenced to community service and must serve as jurors in future trials; they also may be ordered to write apology letters, complete educational projects, or undergo substance abuse evaluations and counseling (Elliot, 2003; Tolan & Titus, 2009). Teen courts have become increasingly popular, with more than 1,000 such programs established in communities throughout the United States (Pearson & Jurich, 2005).

Several aspects of teen court should lead to therapeutic outcomes for juvenile offenders, victims, and youth within the community. Like other restorative approaches to justice, teen courts urge juvenile offenders to accept responsibility for their actions and to consider the ways in which their behaviors harmed the victim and the community (Tolan & Titus, 2009). Offenders are judged by a jury of their peers, which can enhance their perceptions of procedural fairness, increase the likelihood of adherence to court orders, and facilitate reintegration back into the community (Stickle et al., 2008). If offenders successfully complete their sanctions, they can have their record expunged, avoiding the stigma of labeling and other antitherapeutic consequences associated with a formal juvenile record (Stickle et al., 2008). Further, teen courts provide local youth with a sense of empowerment and responsibility, as well as an opportunity to learn about the legal system (Elliot, 2003).

Like many other problem-solving courts, teen courts enjoy strong public and professional support but have received little empirical attention. Evidence of their effectiveness is primarily anecdotal, and most evaluations of teen courts simply report recidivism rates with no reference to comparison groups (e.g., Harrison, Maupin, & Mays, 2000; Minor, Wells, Soderstrom, Bingham, & Williamson, 1999). The only evaluation of teen court outcomes involving random assignment yielded discouraging findings, as juveniles processed in teen court were actually *more* likely to self-report engagement in delinquent behaviors than juveniles processed through standard juvenile courts. Moreover, those referred to teen court had significantly lower scores on a scale of belief in conventional rules, and recidivism rates were similar among both groups (Stickle et al., 2008). Stickle and colleagues offered numerous explanations for these unexpected findings, ranging from methodological issues (i.e., attrition) to potential unintended consequences of the key principles of teen courts. Primarily, these researchers argued that restorative approaches might be less effective for cases involving minor offenses typically adjudicated in teen court than for cases involving more serious transgressions. In addition, they proposed that teen courts might be more successful in shaming than reintegrating the offender. That is, the embarrassment offenders experience when adjudicated by their peers may lead to social withdrawal, further isolating them from the community.

As this section demonstrates, therapeutic jurisprudence is widely practiced in specialty courts handling a broad range of offenses. Although courts can tailor their approaches to the particular aspects of the case, they all aim to promote positive physical, social, and psychological outcomes among those affected by the law. As many specialty courts are still in their infancy, methodologically sound evaluations of their propensity to promote wellbeing and reduce recidivism are often lacking. Some studies suggest that specialty courts founded on therapeutic principles are minimally effective in reducing delinquent behaviors (e.g., Stickle et al., 2008), but others provide preliminary support for these approaches to law breaking (e.g., Gover et al., 2003; Wilson et al., 2006). Because therapeutic jurisprudence provides a means of addressing the issues underlying delinquency, however, it is likely that specialty courts and applications of therapeutic principles in general will persevere.

New and Potential Applications

Therapeutic jurisprudence is continually expanding into new legal arenas. Lawmakers, legal professionals, and social scientists have begun to recognize the potential value of therapeutic approaches to other types of criminal offenses characterized by high rates of recidivism. For example, efforts to address complex social problems therapeutically have materialized in newly established specialty gambling and prostitution courts. However, therapeutic jurisprudence remains underutilized in traditional courtrooms. Applications of therapeutic jurisprudence could be particularly beneficial in cases involving drug use during pregnancy and other forms of parental delinquency, which are often addressed through more punitive measures (Brosh & Miller, 2008; Coleman & Miller, 2006; Miller & Sicafuse, 2009).

Gambling courts. Judge Mark Farrell established the first gambling court in 2001 in Amherst, New York. Although social scientists have recently advocated for the implementation of specialty gambling courts in other states, Judge Farrell's court remains, to our knowledge, the only one of its kind. Based on the DTC model, the gambling treatment court aims to address the social and psychological underpinnings of gambling addiction that are responsible for defendants' crimes (e.g., theft or embezzlement; Hinshaw, 2005). Recognizing that problem gambling is an illness rather than a vice, the court orders defendants (who must admit guilt prior to referral to the court) to complete a multifaceted treatment program, including group and individual therapy and debt counseling (American Gaming Association, 2006). In doing so, the court aims to promote the wellbeing not only of defendants but also of their family members, who are deeply affected both economically and psychologically by their loved one's addiction (see http://www.gamblingcourt.org/).

Accountability is key in Judge Farrell's court, as defendants undergo regular credit checks and meet with Judge Farrell a minimum of twice a month (Belson, 2007). Sanctions for defendants who fail to comply with the program (e.g., missing therapy sessions or Gamblers Anonymous meetings, relapsing) can range from increased supervision and more frequent courtroom visits to jail time. Alternatively, adherence to the program can be rewarded with formal court recognition and reduced supervision and courtroom visits. Upon successful completion of the program, defendants typically receive reduced or suspended jail time and fees (American Gaming Association, 2006).

Judge Farrell's gambling court handles a small number of cases involving misdemeanors of $1,000 or less (e.g., forgery, theft, check fraud). As of 2007, more than half of the 100 defendants referred to the court successfully completed treatment, and only one had been rearrested for an offense (and this offense was not directly connected to gambling; Belson, 2007). Although these statistics are promising, more data are clearly needed to establish the efficacy of gambling courts. Moreover, gambling-related crimes are difficult to identify (Hinshaw, 2005), and the small number of such cases may not justify the establishment of specialty gambling courts in many jurisdictions. However, they could be worthwhile in jurisdictions where gambling is an especially prominent feature of the local landscape, such as Clark and Washoe counties in Nevada.

Prostitution courts. Although some large community problem-solving courts have been handing prostitution cases throughout the past decade (e.g., New York City's Midtown Community Court; Quinn, 2006), courts have traditionally addressed prostitution through punitive measures. There is very little literature documenting the existence, operation, and outcomes of therapeutic approaches to prostitution in the courtroom. Recognizing the need for a more widespread and comprehensive means of addressing prostitution, Sanchez and Miller (2009) proposed a framework for the development of a specialty prostitution treatment court. In line with therapeutic principles, Sanchez and Miller emphasized the need for specialty courts to address the issues underlying prostitution (e.g., homelessness, lack of education and job skills, drug abuse; see also Farley, 2004) in lieu of imposing jail sentences or other punitive sanctions. They also argued that such courts should ensure that defendants receive psychological counseling and health care. Like other specialty courts, prostitution courts must address this complex social problem through collaborative efforts among legal actors, law enforcement, treatment centers, and other community organizations; it is also critical to ensure accountability for the defendants' crimes and adherence to the program (Sanchez & Miller, 2009).

Specialty prostitution courts have recently been established in Dallas, Texas; Washington, DC; Allegheny County, Pennsylvania; and Reno, Nevada. These courts aim to enhance the wellbeing of defendants by ordering interventions such as psychological treatment, job training, addiction counseling, and mandatory drug testing (Banks, 2006; Ellis, 2009; Russell, 2010). Consistent with Sanchez and Miller's (2009) recommendations, these courts rely on team efforts in taking a therapeutic approach to prostitution and promote defendant responsibility. Development of a specialized prostitution treatment court is currently under way in Baltimore, Maryland (Justice Policy Institute, 2010), and community courts are increasingly viewing prostitution cases through the lens of therapeutic jurisprudence.

Despite the growing enthusiasm over problem-solving approaches to prostitution, some have suggested that they may be ineffective (see Quinn, 2006; Thompson, 2002). Although the Midtown Community Court's (MCC) "crackdown" on prostitution dramatically decreased prostitution arrests and the incidence of "streetwalking," there is evidence that New York City prostitutes have simply learned to operate more covertly or have migrated to other jurisdictions (see Wolf, 2001). Quinn also argued that the seemingly therapeutic approaches employed by the MCC and problem-solving courts in general are coercive and dehumanizing. Specifically, she observed that defendants have little choice but to participate in their rehabilitation, and that extensive community involvement in such courts (e.g., collaboration with outside services, promoting problem-solving courts by encouraging the public to attend hearings) unnecessarily subjects them to shame and humiliation. More generally, critics have charged that the "therapeutic" interventions that are commonly imposed (e.g., community service, group counseling sessions) are too broad in scope to address the needs of prostitutes (Quinn, 2006; Thompson, 2002). It should be noted that the majority of these criticisms are based on the practices of community courts and the MCC in particular, rather than those of specialty courts that deal only with prostitution. The newly developed prostitution courts could potentially offer a more individualized approach to those charged with prostitution and could establish stronger relationships with outside experts and community organizations that are better suited to meet the needs of prostitutes. Ultimately, the efficacy of both prior and more recent therapeutic approaches to prostitution has yet to be determined.

New directions for therapeutic jurisprudence. Within the U.S. court system, therapeutic jurisprudence is most frequently practiced in problem-solving specialty courts (Wiener & Brank, in press). Specialty court judges and staff have extensive knowledge of defendants' and victims' issues, and these courts are well equipped to coordinate interventions tailored to the unique aspects of a case (Rottman, 2000). Nonetheless, applications of therapeutic jurisprudence need not be confined within courts dealing with highly specific offenses, nor even within the criminal justice system—therapeutic jurisprudence has relevance to civil litigation as well (Greene, 2008). Several types of crimes involving defendants, victims, and families who may benefit from a more therapeutic approach continue to be addressed through punitive measures in traditional or generalized family courts. Many of these cases involve controversial charges stemming from child endangerment, abuse, or neglect.

As previously discussed, many cases involving drug-related offenses are addressed therapeutically through DTCs. Within this realm, judges, attorneys, and social service professionals work together to target the underlying cause of drug crimes and promote wellbeing among defendants and community members (Hora et al., 1999). However, such therapeutic considerations are often lacking in cases involving prenatal drug use. Guided by existing state laws, many judges respond to prenatal drug users through punitive measures. Although rulings may vary from state to state (see Hoffman & Miller, 2009, for a review), women who use drugs during pregnancy often face jail time or prison sentences, and they may be charged with homicide if their drug use leads to stillbirth (see *State v. McKnight*, 2003). South Carolina mandates arrest for women who test positive for drugs prior to or immediately after giving birth, and prenatal drug users can lose custody of their infant and other children (Bornstein, 2001; Paltrow, 1999).

Such responses to prenatal drug use can lead to antitherapeutic consequences for women, children, and society (Bornstein, 2003; Coleman &

Miller, 2006). For instance, the threat of arrest and loss of parental rights could discourage many drug-abusing women from seeking prenatal care or substance abuse treatment. Incarcerated pregnant women might not receive adequate medical care and nutrition, and they are unable to care for their existing children. Moreover, minority women may be disproportionately affected by punitive approaches to drug use during pregnancy (Brosh & Miller, 2008). Although White and African American women are similarly inclined to engage in prenatal drug use (Roberts, 1991), African American women are significantly more likely to be reported to authorities and to undergo mandatory drug testing during pregnancy (Chasnoff, Landress, & Barrett, 1990; Schmall, 1993). Most significantly, these sanctions are likely ineffective in minimizing substance abuse among pregnant women, due to their failure to treat addiction and the widespread availability of illegal drugs in many prisons (Okie, 2007). Thus, Coleman and Miller suggest that the courts and legal professionals should address the wellbeing of prenatal drug users by ordering substance abuse treatment and other therapeutic interventions (e.g., counseling, parenting classes). As with any therapeutic approach, judges, attorneys, and social service professionals involved in such cases should closely monitor the defendant's progress and ensure accountability. In targeting the precise issues that brought prenatal drug users into the legal system, legal actors can promote the wellbeing of mothers and children, and they can also help reduce the strain that such cases place on taxpayers and the foster care system.

Although prison sentences and loss of parental rights might be common responses to neglectful or abusive parents, some judges have imposed even more extreme sanctions on defendants charged with such crimes. Specifically, judges have administered procreation restrictions to both male and female defendants in response to a variety of transgressions, ranging from failure to pay child support (*State v. Oakley*, 2001, to child abuse and neglect (*Trammell v. State*, 2001), to check forgery (Associated Press, 2006). Like responses to prenatal drug users, procreation restrictions do not address the complex social and psychological issues underlying parental delinquency, and they could have a negative impact on parents' and children's wellbeing. Procreation restrictions can have disproportionate effects on women, who might feel compelled to obtain an abortion or starve themselves in order to hide their pregnancy (Miller & Sicafuse, 2009). Mothers who become pregnant under procreation restrictions face incarceration and loss of existing parental rights, which again places the burden of childrearing on the community and increases the likelihood that these children will experience serious psychological problems (Brooks, 1999). Furthermore, procreation restrictions infringe upon individuals' rights to privacy, bodily autonomy, and reproduction (Miller & Sicafuse, 2009).

Judges and other legal professionals considering therapeutic alternatives to procreation restrictions must have a thorough understanding of the underlying causes of parental delinquency and the most appropriate means of addressing them. Poverty, drug abuse, mental illness, and lack of parenting skills can all perpetuate child maltreatment (Asawa, Hansen, & Flood, 2008). Thus, judges could order delinquent parents to attend parenting or anger management classes, job training, or GED classes; they should also ensure that these parents and their children receive psychological counseling and any other appropriate forms of treatment (e.g., substance abuse treatment, nutritional counseling, medical care). Some have suggested that removal of children from their parent's care should be used as a last resort and considered only after all therapeutic means of addressing parental delinquency have failed (Miller & Sicafuse, 2009).

Cases involving prenatal drug use and procreation restrictions are among a much larger sample of cases that could be effectively addressed through therapeutic jurisprudence. For instance, researchers have suggested applying therapeutic principles to cases involving childhood obesity (Hayes & Sicafuse, 2010), statutory rape (Jehle, 2009), and other sex-related crimes (Birgden, 2004; Edwards & Hensley, 2001). Such applications need not be limited to specialty courts and could occur in larger family courts, which typically adjudicate a variety of cases in which a therapeutic perspective is warranted. However, judges and other legal actors practicing in both broader and more tailored courts must consider the potential costs and benefits of therapeutic approaches.

Assessing the Value of Therapeutic Approaches: Benefits and Criticisms

Since its emergence nearly two decades ago, the therapeutic approach to justice has become increasingly popular among lawmakers, legal professionals, and community members (Hoffman, 2002). The movement has received strong support in both academic and clinical arenas, and applications of therapeutic jurisprudence have captured the attention of mainstream media (e.g., see Belson, 2007; Ellis, 2009). However, as therapeutic jurisprudence continues to develop and expand, it is also important to consider its potential shortcomings.

The potential benefits of addressing law breaking therapeutically have been highlighted throughout this chapter. Not only do therapeutic approaches promote wellbeing among offenders, but they also maximize therapeutic outcomes for victims and families. Such attention to the physical and psychological health of those directly and indirectly affected by crime is rare in traditional responses to offending. In this sense, therapeutic jurisprudence is related to the idea of restorative justice (Strang & Sherman, 2003). Restorative justice focuses mainly on the needs of victims and the community in resolving criminal matters, as addressed by features like apologizing and taking responsibility for the harm one has caused, and making reparations (Umbreit, Vos, Coates, & Lightfoot, 2005; Zehr, 2002). To the extent that specialty courts involve victims and attend to their interests, needs, and preferences in dealing with offenders—as many of them do—they can serve these restorative goals.

Admitting guilt and assuming responsibility for one's transgressions can also be therapeutic for the offender. Not only is this admission a prerequisite for successful rehabilitation, but it also restores dignity to the offender and reconnects the wrongdoer to the community (Greene, 2008). Restorative justice policies are becoming widespread, both in the American criminal and juvenile justice systems (Umbreit et al., 2005) and globally (Sullivan & Tifft, 2006). Their proliferation offers yet another opportunity to integrate principles of therapeutic jurisprudence into the dispute resolution process and management of criminal offending.

Therapeutic approaches to law breaking also can yield many practical advantages. Most notably, they are cost-effective and reduce prison overcrowding. Although therapeutic interventions often require significant amounts of funding and other resources, they are typically much less expensive than more punitive responses to law breaking. To illustrate, it costs $25,000 to $50,000 per year to incarcerate a drug offender, whereas the most comprehensive DTC systems spend approximately $3,000 on each defendant per year (Hayes, 2003). In addition, because therapeutic approaches aim to address defendants' needs in a respectful manner, they can enhance offenders' perceptions of procedural justice and government legitimacy. Both of these outcomes can increase the likelihood of adherence to therapeutic interventions and compliance with the law in general (Tyler, 2006). Most significantly, therapeutic approaches target the complex social and psychological issues underlying criminal behavior. To the extent that these issues are addressed effectively, applications of therapeutic jurisprudence in the courts help to promote the wellbeing of society as a whole.

Despite these benefits, there are staunch opponents of the therapeutic jurisprudence movement. Numerous scholars (e.g., Hoffman, 2002; Petrila, 1996; Quinn, 2007) equate therapeutic jurisprudence to paternalism. From this perspective, therapeutic jurisprudence presents defendants with the illusion, but not the reality, of choice. To avoid incarceration and other sanctions (e.g., large fines, loss of parental rights), many defendants might essentially feel compelled to submit to medical and psychological treatment (Quinn, 2007). Quinn further argues that the availability of treatment alternatives and pressure from well-intended judges and attorneys to accept responsibility might elicit guilty pleas from innocent defendants. Such criticisms are problematic on two grounds. First, the main tenets of therapeutic jurisprudence specify that courts and legal actors must respect defendants' rights and autonomy (Wexler & Winick, 1996b). Wexler (2004) notes that judges and attorneys should not discount presumptions of innocence, and that litigants' perspectives regarding their treatment needs (or lack thereof) should be carefully considered and incorporated into legal decisions. Second, therapeutic approaches require that judges, attorneys, and other legal actors work to ensure that defendants understand their options (e.g., adjudication in a traditional vs. specialty court, plea bargaining) and their potential consequences (e.g., acquittal, jail time, drug treatment; Wexler, 2004; Winick, 2003). Thus, to the extent that therapeutic jurisprudence is practiced in accordance with its underlying principles, this common criticism is largely unfounded.

Legal scholars also object to the shift in judges' and attorneys' roles to therapeutic agents. Because the therapeutic framework is loosely defined, judges, attorneys, and mental health professionals decide what constitutes therapeutic and antitherapeutic outcomes (Petrila, 1996). This lack of clear decision rules is the basis for arguments that applications of therapeutic jurisprudence in the courts impinge on the legislative function. According to Hoffman (2002, p. 2096), "It is for legislators, and not self-described therapeutic judges, to decide not only whether a certain behavior is a crime or a disease, but also in many circumstances to set a range of punishment." Similarly, Hoffman and others (Arrigo, 2004; Petrila, 1996; Quinn, 2007) emphasize the dangers in allowing judges and attorneys to assume the role of "experienced therapists" and defendants' "activists." Quinn fears that legal professionals' lack of mental health expertise could lead to unintended antitherapeutic outcomes, and Hoffman claims that these purported expansions of the judicial role undermine judges' autonomy and truth seeking. Once again, the concerns appear to stem from a misunderstanding of how therapeutic jurisprudence is and should be practiced. Applications of therapeutic jurisprudence must be discretionary in order to address the motivations for law breaking and the needs of the defendant, victim, and community effectively. Nonetheless, therapeutic interventions must remain within the purview of substantive law, and they should not trump justice concerns (Winick, 1997). From a therapeutic perspective, illness and addiction sometimes underlie crime but are distinct from the criminal act itself. Therapeutic approaches do not emancipate defendants from guilt or accountability, nor do they preclude punishment. Moreover, judges should not be activists for the defendant, but should rather strive to promote wellbeing among all those affected by a crime (Winick & Wexler, 2003).

Critics have further charged that applications of therapeutic jurisprudence overwhelm the courts and divert community resources away from law-abiding citizens in need (Hoffman, 2002). It is true that the establishment of specialty courts is often followed by a dramatic increase in criminal charges within the purview of these particular courts (see Belenko, 2003; Gover et al., 2003). However, one could argue that it is more advantageous to address these crimes in this manner than to ignore them for the sake of efficiency. To the extent that therapeutic approaches reduce recidivism, both traditional and specialty courts are likely to see a decrease in cases involving repeat offenders in the long run (see Hora et al., 1999; Rivera, 2003). In addition, community resources linked to these courts not only are expended on defendants but also are used to help promote wellbeing among victims and offenders' families, who are typically law-abiding citizens in need of assistance.

Accusations that therapeutic approaches to justice lack empirical support (Arrigo, 2004; Hoffman, 2002) are more well founded than these other concerns. The efficacy of therapeutic interventions is usually assessed by program compliance rates or by changes in offenders' attitudes and self-reported behaviors (e.g., see Hora et al., 1999; Minor et al., 1999; Wilson et al., 2006). Evaluations of specialty courts often lack comparison or control groups and are plagued by methodological issues. Although some studies suggest that therapeutic approaches to minor offenses may be misguided (see Stickle et al., 2008; Quinn, 2006), well-designed evaluations of DTCs and DVCs have yielded positive results (Gover et al., 2003; Wilson et al., 2006). Taken together, the existing research does not demonstrate that therapeutic approaches to justice are ineffective. As many specialty courts are still in their infancy (Cooper, 2002), it is highly likely that future research will provide a more comprehensive portrayal of the utility of therapeutic jurisprudence in the courtroom.

Conclusions

Proponents of therapeutic jurisprudence have expanded upon more traditional conceptualizations of the purposes of law, arguing that the law should function as a therapeutic agent and be applied in a manner that promotes wellbeing among both victims and offenders (Wexler & Winick, 1996a). Although therapeutic jurisprudence was initially used as a basis for evaluating mental health policy, it has subsequently flourished into an overarching perspective guiding legal actors' decisions both inside and outside of specialty courts (Rottman, 2000).

Many specialty courts provide a forum for viewing a broad range of transgressions through the lens of therapeutic jurisprudence (Wiener & Brank, in press). Such courts aim to promote wellbeing among those affected by drug-related crimes, domestic violence, and juvenile delinquency. As the value of therapeutic approaches is increasingly recognized, specialty courts will likely continue to proliferate and diversify. Most recently, specialty courts have been established to target prostitution and gambling-related crimes. The growth of specialty courts notwithstanding, therapeutic jurisprudence should also be practiced by judges, attorneys, and other legal actors in more traditional courts. Controversial crimes such as prenatal drug use, certain types of sex offenses, and others might be best addressed through therapeutic rather than punitive measures.

Therapeutic approaches to justice are favored by many legal professionals and community members, but others question the use of the law to promote wellbeing (Arrigo, 2004). Many criticisms aimed at therapeutic jurisprudence are unfounded or based on an insufficient understanding of therapeutic principles. However, there is little empirical evidence supporting the effectiveness of therapeutic approaches to law breaking. Some research has shown that therapeutic approaches reduce recidivism and promote offenders' physical and psychological wellbeing by minimizing substance abuse (Gover et al., 2003; Hora et al., 1999). Despite these promising findings, few (if any) researchers have examined the effects of therapeutic approaches on the wellbeing of victims, families, and community members and the relationship between therapeutic jurisprudence and restorative justice.

Therapeutic jurisprudence is a unique and innovative approach in one other important respect: It aims to address the complex social and psychological issues that underlie offending. Many other justice approaches (e.g., retributive justice, procedural justice, restorative justice) can yield positive physical or psychological outcomes among certain individuals (i.e., victims) affected by law breaking, and they can also minimize recidivism through deterrence or incapacitation (Tyler & Smith, 1998). However, as evidenced by relatively stable victimization rates and swelling prison populations (Bureau of Justice Statistics, 2010), these approaches alone are insufficient means of reducing crime. Although more research is needed to assess the long-term outcomes of therapeutic jurisprudence in the courts, its potential value in promoting individual and social wellbeing seems clear.

References

American Gaming Association. (2006). *Alternative sentencing: How a NY gambling treatment court is shaking up the system in 2006.* Retrieved fromhttp://www.americangaming.org/newsroom/newsletters/responsible-gaming-quarterly/alternative-sentencing-how-ny-gambling-treatment

Arrigo, B. A. (2004). The ethics of therapeutic jurisprudence: A critical and theoretical inquiry of law, psychology, and crime. *Psychiatry, Psychology, and Law, 1*, 23–43.

Asawa, L. E., Hansen, D. J., & Flood, M. F. (2008). Early childhood intervention programs: Opportunities and challenges for preventing child maltreatment. *Education and Treatment of Children, 31*, 73–110.

Associated Press. (2006, October 18). *MO judge tells woman: No more pregnancies.* Retrieved from http://www.informationliberation.com/?id=17117

Banks, G. (2006, May 30). Prostitution court: A struggle for a new life. *Pittsburgh Post-Gazette.* Retrieved from http://www.post-gazette.com/pg/06150/694217–85.stm

Belenko, S. (2003). Research on drug courts: A critical review, 2001 update. In B. J. Wexler & D. B. Winick (Eds.), *Judging in a therapeutic key: Therapeutic jurisprudence and the courts* (pp. 25–27). Durham, NC: Carolina Academic Press.

Belson, K. (2007, May 1). New York gambling treatment court stresses help. *New York Times.* Retrieved from http://www.nytimes.com/2007/05/01/nyregion/01gamble.html?pagewanted=1

Birgden, A. (2004). Therapeutic jurisprudence and sex offenders: A psycho-legal approach to protection. *Sex Abuse: A Journal of Research and Treatment, 16*, 351–362.

BJA Drug Court Clearinghouse Project. (2007). *Drug court activity update.* Retrieved from http://www1.spa.american.edu/justice/documents/1956.pdf

Bornstein, B. H. (2001). Seize this urine test: The implications of *Ferguson v. City of Charleston* for drug testing during pregnancy. *Journal of Medicine and Law, 6*, 65–79.

Bornstein, B. H. (2003). Pregnancy, drug testing, and the Fourth Amendment: Legal and behavioral implications. *Journal of Family Psychology, 17*, 220–228.

Brooks, S. L. (1999). Therapeutic jurisprudence and preventative law in child welfare proceedings: A family systems approach. *Psychology, Public Policy, and Law, 5*, 951–965.
Brosh, J. E., & Miller, M. K. (2008). Regulating pregnancy behaviors: How the Constitutional rights of minority women are disproportionately compromised. *Journal of Gender, Social Policy and the Law, 16*, 437–457.
Bureau of Justice Statistics. (2010). *Key facts.* Retrieved from http://bjs.ojp.usdoj.gov/index.cfm?ty=kfa
Casey, P., & Rottman, D. B. (2000). Therapeutic jurisprudence in the courts. *Behavioral Sciences and the Law, 18*, 445–457.
Chasnoff, I. J., Landress, H. J., & Barrett, M. E. (1990). The prevalence of illicit-drug or alcohol use during pregnancy and discrepancies in mandatory reporting in Pinellas County, Florida. *New England Journal of Medicine, 322*, 1202–1206.
Coleman, E. E., & Miller, M. K. (2006). Assessing legal responses to prenatal drug use: Can therapeutic responses produce more positive outcomes than punitive responses? *Journal of Law and Health, 20*, 35–67.
Cooper, C. S. (2002). Juvenile drug user treatment courts in the U.S.: Initial lessons learned and issues being addressed. In L. Harrison, F. Scarpitti, M. Amir, & S. Einstein (Eds.), *Drug courts: Current issues and future perspectives* (pp. 213–240). Huntsville, TX: Office of International Criminal Justice.
Edwards, W., & Hensley, C. (2001). Restructuring sex offender sentencing: A therapeutic jurisprudence approach to the criminal justice process. *International Journal of Offender Therapy and Comparative Criminology, 45*, 646–662.
Elliot, J. (2003). Youths face a jury of their peers: Teen court offers a chance to clear records of minor offenses. In B. J. Wexler & D. B. Winick (Eds.), *Judging in a therapeutic key: Therapeutic jurisprudence and the courts* (pp. 49–54). Durham, NC: Carolina Academic Press.
Ellis, T. M. (2009, August 15). *Court program aims to put prostitution in the past.* Retrieved from http://www.wfaa.com/news/local/64593482.html
Ennis, B. J. (1971). Civil liberties and mental illness. *Criminal Law Bulletin, 7*, 101–127.
Farley, M. (2004). "Bad for the body, bad for the heart": Prostitution harms women even if legalized or decriminalized. *Violence Against Women, 10*, 1087–1125.
Gover, A. R., MacDonald, J. M., & Alpert, G. P. (2003). Combating domestic violence: Findings from an evaluation of a local domestic violence court. *Criminology and Public Policy, 3*, 109–131.
Greene, E. (2008). "Can we talk?" Therapeutic jurisprudence, restorative justice, and tort litigation. In B. H. Bornstein & R. L. Wiener (Eds.), *Civil juries and civil justice: Psychological and legal perspectives* (pp. 233–256). New York, NY: Springer.
Harrison, P., Maupin, J. R., & Mays, G. (2000). Are teen courts an answer to our juvenile delinquency problems? *Juvenile and Family Court Journal, 51*, 27–34.
Hartley, C. C. (2003). A therapeutic jurisprudence approach to the trial process in domestic violence felony trials. *Violence Against Women, 9*, 410–437.
Hayes, G. (2003). Breaking the cycle of addiction: Officials seek to spread the word on drug treatment courts. In B. J. Wexler & D. B. Winick (Eds.),

Judging in a therapeutic key: Therapeutic jurisprudence and the courts (pp. 21–24). Durham, NC: Carolina Academic Press.

Hayes, J. A., & Sicafuse, L. L. (2010). Is childhood obesity a form of child abuse? Factors to consider in judicial rulings. *Judicature, 94*, 20–27.

Henggeler, S. W., Halliday-Boykins, C. A., Cunningham, P. B., Randall, J., Shapiro, S. B., & Chapman, J. E. (2006). Juvenile drug court: Enhancing outcomes by integrating evidence-based treatments. *Journal of Consulting and Clinical Psychology, 74*, 42–54.

Hinshaw, C. D. (2005). Taking a gamble: Applying therapeutic jurisprudence to compulsive gambling and establishing gambling treatment courts. *Gaming Law Review, 9*, 333–342.

Hoffman, L., & Miller, M. K. (2009). Inconsistent state court rulings concerning pregnancy-related behaviors. *Journal of Law and Health, 22*, 279–293.

Hoffman, M. B. (2002). Therapeutic jurisprudence, neo-rehabilitationism, and judicial collectivism: The least dangerous branch becomes most dangerous. *Fordham Urban Law Journal, 29*, 2063–2098.

Hora, P. F., Schma, W. G., & Rosenthal, J. (1999). Therapeutic jurisprudence and the drug treatment court movement: Revolutionizing the criminal justice system's response to drug abuse and crime in America. *Notre Dame Law Review, 74*, 439–538.

Jehle, A. (2009). Therapeutic jurisprudence for teen sex-related issues. In M. K. Miller (Ed.), *Contemporary perspectives on legal regulation of sexual behavior: Psycholegal research and analysis* (pp. 145–149). New York, NY: Nova.

Justice Policy Institute. (2010). *Baltimore behind bars: How to reduce the jail population, save money and improve public safety.* Retrieved from http://www.justicepolicy.org/images/upload/10-06_REP_BaltBehindBars_MD-PS-AC-RD.pdf

Kennedy, C. J. (2003). Judicial behavior and the civil commitment practitioner. In B. J. Wexler & D. B. Winick (Eds.), *Judging in a therapeutic key: Therapeutic jurisprudence and the courts* (pp. 158–164). Durham, NC: Carolina Academic Press.

Levey, L. S., Steketee, M. W., & Keilitz, S. L. (2000). *Lessons learned in implementing an integrated domestic violence court: The District of Columbia experience.* Retrieved from http://contentdm.ncsconline.org/cgi-bin/showfile.exe?CISOROOT=/famct&CISOPTR=173

Mechanic, D. (1987). Correcting misconceptions in mental health policy: Strategies for improved care of the seriously mentally ill. *Melbank Quarterly, 65*, 203–230.

Miller, M. K., & Bornstein, B. H. (2004). Juror stress: Causes and interventions. *Thurgood Marshall Law Review, 30*, 237–269.

Miller, M. K., & Sicafuse, L. L. (2009). Legal restrictions on procreation: Therapeutic jurisprudence suggests alternatives that avoid unintended legal, health, and gender-based consequences. In M. K. Miller (Ed.), *Contemporary perspectives on legal regulation of sexual behavior: Psycholegal research and analysis* (pp. 77–90). New York, NY: Nova.

Minor, K. I., Wells, J. B., Soderstrom, I. R., Bingham, R., & Williamson, D. (1999). Sentence completion and recidivism among juveniles referred to teen courts. *Crime and Delinquency, 45*, 467–480.

Okie, S. (2007). Sex, drugs, prison, and HIV. *New England Journal of Medicine, 356*, 105–108.
Paltrow, L. M. (1999). *Punishment and prejudice: Judging drug-using pregnant women.* Retrieved from http://advocatesforpregnantwomen.org/articles/ruddick.htm
Pearson, S. S., & Jurich, S. (2005). *Youth court: A community solution for embracing at-risk youth.* Washington, DC: American Youth Policy Forum. Retrieved from http://www.aypf.org/publications/Youth%20Court%20-%20A%20Community%20Solution.pdf
Petrila, J. (1996). Paternalism and the unrealized promise of *Essays in Therapeutic Jurisprudence.* In D. B. Wexler & B. J. Winick (Eds.), *Law in a therapeutic key: Developments in therapeutic jurisprudence* (pp. 685–705). Durham, NC: Carolina Academic Press.
Quinn, M. C. (2006). Revisiting Anna Moscowitz Kross's critique of New York City's Women's Court: The continued problem of solving the "problem" of prostitution with specialized criminal courts. *Fordham Urban Law Journal, 33*, 665–726.
Quinn, M. C. (2007). An RSVP to Professor Wexler's warm therapeutic jurisprudence invitation to the criminal defense bar: Unable to join you, already (somewhat similarly) engaged. *Boston College Law Review, 48*, 539–595.
Reisner, C., & Slobogin, C. (1990). *Law and the mental health system: Civil and criminal aspects.* St. Paul, MN: West Group.
Rivera, R. (2003). Court cracks down on domestic violence. In B. J. Wexler & D. B. Winick (Eds.), *Judging in a therapeutic key: Therapeutic jurisprudence and the courts* (pp. 55–57). Durham, NC: Carolina Academic Press.
Roberts, D. E. (1991). Punishing drug addicts who have babies: Women of color, equality, and the right to privacy. *Harvard Law Review, 104*, 1420–1482.
Rottman, D. B. (2000). Does effective therapeutic jurisprudence require specialized courts? *Court Review, 37*, 22–27.
Russell, T. (2010). *Court created for local prostitutes.* Retrieved from http://www.kolotv.com/news/headlines/80666932.html
Sanchez, M. H., & Miller, M. K. (2009). Using therapeutic jurisprudence to design a special treatment court to address illegal prostitution. In M. K. Miller (Ed.), *Contemporary perspectives on legal regulation of sexual behavior: Psycholegal research and analysis* (pp. 63–76). New York, NY: Nova.
Schmall, L. (1993). Addicted pregnancy as a sex crime. *Northern Illinois University Law Review, 13*, 263–333.
Senjo, S. R., & Leip, L. A. (2001a). Testing and developing theory in drug court: A four-part logit model to predict program completion. *Criminal Justice Policy Review, 12*, 66–87.
Senjo, S., & Leip, L. A. (2001b). Testing therapeutic jurisprudence theory: An empirical assessment of the drug court process. *Western Criminology Review, 3* [Online]. Retrieved from http://wcr.sonoma.edu/v3n1/senjo.html?ref=Sex%C5%9Ehop.com
Senna, J. P., & Siegel, L. G. (1999). *Introduction to criminal justice.* Belmont, CA: Wadsworth.
Shelton, D. E. (2007). *The current state of domestic violence courts in the United States, 2007.* Retrieved from http://contentdm.ncsconline.org/cgi-bin/showfile.exe?CISOROOT=/famct&CISOPTR=173

Shuman, D. W., Hamilton, J. A., & Daley, C. E. (1996). The health effects of jury service. In D. B. Wexler & B. J. Winick (Eds.), *Law in a therapeutic key: Developments in therapeutic jurisprudence* (pp. 949–978). Durham, NC: Carolina Academic Press.

Siegel, L. J., & Welsh, B. C. (2005). *Juvenile delinquency: The core.* Belmont, CA: Thomson Wadsworth.

Slobogin, C. (1996). Therapeutic jurisprudence: Five dilemmas to ponder. In D. B. Wexler & B. J. Winick (Eds.), *Law in a therapeutic key: Developments in therapeutic jurisprudence* (pp. 673–694). Durham, NC: Carolina Academic Press.

State v. McKnight, 576 S.E. 2d 168 (S.C. 2003).

State v. Oakley, 629 N.W. 2d 200 (Wis. 2001).

Stickle, W. P., Connell, N. M., Wilson, D. M., & Gottfredson, D. (2008). An experimental evaluation of teen courts. *Journal of Experimental Criminology, 4*, 137–163.

Stolle, D. P., Wexler, D. B., Winick, B. J., & Dauer, E. A. (1997). Integrating preventative law and therapeutic jurisprudence: A law and psychology based approach to lawyering. *California Western Law Review, 34*, 15–51.

Strang, H., & Sherman, L. W. (2003). Repairing the harm: Victims and restorative justice. *Utah Law Review, 1*, 15–42.

Sullivan, D., & Tifft, L. (2006). *Handbook of restorative justice: A global perspective.* London: Routledge.

Thompson, A. C. (2002). Courting disorder: Some thoughts on community courts. *Washington University Journal of Law and Policy, 10*, 63–99.

Thompson, K. M. (2001). *A preliminary outcome evaluation of North Dakota's juvenile drug court-recidivism analyses.* Retrieved from http://www.ndcourts.com/_court/news/ndcourts2006.pdf

Tolan, P. H., & Titus, J. A. (2009). Therapeutic jurisprudence in juvenile justice. In B. L. Bottoms, C. J. Najdowski, & G. S. Goodman (Eds.), *Children as victims, witnesses, and offenders: Psychological science in law* (pp. 255–274). New York, NY: Guilford Press.

Trammell v. State, 751 N.E. 2d 283 (Ind Ct. app. 2001).

Tyler, T. R. (1996). The psychological consequences of judicial procedures: Implications for civil commitment hearings. In D. B. Wexler & B. J. Winick (Eds.), *Law in a therapeutic key: Developments in therapeutic jurisprudence* (pp. 3–16). Durham, NC: Carolina Academic Press.

Tyler, T. R. (2006). Psychological perspectives on legitimacy and legitimation. *Annual Review of Psychology, 57*, 375–400.

Tyler, T. R., & Smith, H. J. (1998). Social justice and social movements. In D. T. Gilbert, S. T. Fiske, & G. Lindzey (Eds.), *The handbook of social psychology* (4th ed., Vol. 2, pp. 595–532). New York, NY: Oxford University Press.

Umbreit, M., Vos, G., Coates, R., & Lightfoot, E. (2005). Restorative justice in the 21st century: A social movement full of opportunities and pitfalls. *Marquette Law Review, 89*, 251–304.

Wallace, H. (2005). *Family violence: Legal, medical, and social perspectives.* Boston, MA: Allyn & Bacon.

Wexler, D. B. (1992). Putting mental health into mental health law: Therapeutic jurisprudence. *Law and Human Behavior, 16*, 27–38.

Wexler, D. B. (1995). Reflections on the scope of therapeutic jurisprudence. *Psychology, Public Policy, and Law, 1*, 220–236.
Wexler, D. B. (1996). Applying the law therapeutically. In D. B. Wexler & B. J. Winick (Eds.), *Law in a therapeutic key: Developments in therapeutic jurisprudence* (pp. 831–844). Durham, NC: Carolina Academic Press.
Wexler, D. B. (2004). Therapeutic jurisprudence and the rehabilitative role of the criminal defense lawyer. *St. Thomas Law Review, 17*, 743–774.
Wexler, D. B., & Winick, B. J. (1991). Therapeutic jurisprudence as a new approach to mental health law policy analysis and research. *University of Miami Law Review, 45*, 979–1004.
Wexler, D. B., & Winick, B. J. (1996a). Introduction. In D. B. Wexler & B. J. Winick (Eds.), *Law in a therapeutic key: Developments in therapeutic jurisprudence* (pp. xvii–xx). Durham, NC: Carolina Academic Press.
Wexler, D. B., & Winick, B. J. (1996b). Patients, professionals, and the path of therapeutic jurisprudence: A response to Petrila. In D. B. Wexler & B. J. Winick (Eds.), *Law in a therapeutic key: Developments in therapeutic jurisprudence* (pp. 707–712). Durham, NC: Carolina Academic Press.
Wiener, R. L., & Brank, E. M. (in press). *Special problem solving courts: Social science and legal perspectives.* New York, NY: Springer.
Wilson, D. B., Mitchell, O., & Mackenzie, D. L. (2006). A systematic review of drug court effects on recidivism. *Journal of Experimental Criminology, 2*, 459–487.
Winick, B. J. (1992). On autonomy: Legal and psychological perspectives. *Villanova Law Review, 37*, 1705–1777.
Winick, B. J. (1996a). The side effects of incompetency labeling and the implications for mental health law. In D. B. Wexler & B. J. Winick (Eds.), *Law in a therapeutic key: Developments in therapeutic jurisprudence* (pp. 17–58). Durham, NC: Carolina Academic Press.
Winick, B. J. (1996b). Incompetency to proceed in the criminal process: Past, present, and future. In D. B. Wexler & B. J. Winick (Eds.), *Law in a therapeutic key: Developments in therapeutic jurisprudence* (pp. 77–112). Durham, NC: Carolina Academic Press.
Winick, B. J. (1997). The jurisprudence of therapeutic jurisprudence. *Psychology, Public Policy, and Law, 3*, 184–206.
Winick, B. J. (2000). Applying the law therapeutically in domestic violence cases. *University of Missouri-Kansas Law Review, 69*, 33–90.
Winick, B. J. (2003). The judge's role in encouraging motivation for change. In B. J. Wexler & D. B. Winick (Eds.), *Judging in a therapeutic key: Therapeutic jurisprudence and the courts* (pp. 181–188). Durham, NC: Carolina Academic Press.
Winick, B. J. (2008). A therapeutic jurisprudence approach to dealing with coercion in the mental health system. *Psychiatry, Public Policy, and Law, 15*, 25–39.
Winick, B. J., & Wexler, D. B. (2003). Introduction. In B. J. Wexler & D. B. Winick (Eds.), *Judging in a therapeutic key: Therapeutic jurisprudence and the courts* (pp. 3–7). Durham, NC: Carolina Academic Press.
Wolf, R. V. (2001). New strategies for an old profession: A court and a community combat a streetwalking epidemic. *Justice System Journal, 22*, 347–359.
Zehr, H. (2002). *The little book of restorative justice.* Intercourse, PA: Good Books.

Part II

VICTIMS, WITNESSES, AND OTHER LAY PARTICIPANTS

3

Domestic Violence Victims' Experiences in the Legal System

Deborah Epstein and Lisa A. Goodman

Since the early 1970s, activists in the domestic violence movement have fought to shift the public's perception of and response to intimate partner violence (IPV).[1] They strove to demonstrate that the problem was not a private, family matter but a serious public one, requiring state-sponsored solutions (Goodman & Epstein, 2008). Activists focused much of their efforts on the justice system, urging the state to protect survivors and treat IPV as seriously as they would any other crime (Epstein, 1999).

This effort was highly successful. The criminal justice system changed substantially through the adoption of mandatory arrest laws, which require police to arrest in cases of intimate partner violence, and no-drop prosecution policies, which promote the pursuit of criminal charges against accused perpetrators regardless of whether the victim chooses to cooperate (Miccio, 2005). In the civil system, every state enacted a protection order law, authorizing judges to award a wide variety of protections that are tailored to meet survivors' individual needs (Epstein, 1999). These reforms have resulted in a dramatic increase in battered women's access to justice. According to one national study of 8,000 women in the United States, 27% of women assaulted by an intimate partner reported that police were involved in the most recent

[1] This chapter focuses on intimate partner violence, which represents only one form of the larger universe of domestic abuse. In general, domestic abuse may include not only physical violence but also psychological and emotional abuse. Domestic abuse also covers not just relationships between couples, but virtually any form of family relationship.

incident of abuse (Tjaden & Thoennes, 2000).[2] Another study found that among those IPV survivors who sought help from public agencies, 77% called the police and 61% filed a complaint against their abusive partner (Anderson et al., 2003).

Despite these improvements, numerous obstacles to victim safety remain. The reforms that have been implemented across the country tend to be based on a one-size-fits-all approach that fails to respond to the particular situations and perspectives of many individual women (Goodman & Epstein, 2008). As a result, the justice system still frequently fails to effectively support battered women; in some cases, it may even have a detrimental impact on their emotional and physical wellbeing.

This chapter analyzes the historical development, level of effectiveness, and limitations of recent criminal and civil justice system reforms in terms of survivors' safety and wellbeing, and then suggests policy reforms for the future.

The Criminal Justice System

History and Current Status

Historically, police officers have failed to recognize intimate partner abuse as a crime, ignoring domestic violence calls to 911 or purposefully delaying their response to such calls. When officers did respond, they were trained to mediate and to "avoid arrest if possible" (Eisenberg & Micklow, 1974). As a result, arrests were rare; studies estimate that they occurred in only 3% to 14% of all intimate partner violence cases to which officers actually responded (Buzawa & Buzawa, 1992). Battered women were left with little access to the criminal justice system.

This situation changed dramatically after the publication of the Minneapolis Domestic Violence Experiment. This well-publicized research effort concluded that arrest dramatically reduced the risk of reassault against the same victim during a 6-month period; it had a substantial influence on public policy (Sherman & Berk, 1984). The same year the study's results were published, the U.S. Attorney General's Task Force on Family Violence recommended arrest as the standard response to all cases of misdemeanor domestic assault. In response to this pressure, states began to enact statutes *requiring* arrest in IPV cases. Oregon passed the first mandatory arrest law in 1977, and other states soon did the same. By 2005, 26 states and the District of Columbia either required arrest or had adopted a pro-arrest policy (Miccio, 2005). These policies dramatically increased arrest rates for intimate partner violence and had a profound impact on survivors, at least in terms of police responsiveness.

---

[2] Although men can be victims of intimate partner violence, this chapter focuses on women's experience, both because they are the focus of the research reviewed and because they are the predominant users of the relevant sectors of the justice system.

The police were not the only sector of the criminal justice community that historically failed to take violence between intimate partners seriously. Prosecutors did the same, often discouraging victims from pursuing cases (Epstein, 1999). Even when mandatory arrest laws increased the number of incidents brought to their attention, prosecutors rarely pressed charges, and when they did, they rarely followed through and took the case to trial (e.g., Epstein, 1999). District attorneys nationwide explained that "because victims simply do not follow through in domestic violence cases, there is no need to waste precious prosecutorial resources on them" (Cahn, 1992, p. 163).

This "always drop" policy ceded to perpetrators an enormous degree of control over the criminal justice process. All a batterer had to do was coerce his victim—through threats, violence, guilt, or apologies—into asking the prosecutor to drop the charges; once she did so, he no longer risked jail time and therefore had far less incentive to refrain from abuse. Although some prosecutors recognized that batterers might be pressuring victims into asking that charges be dropped, they found themselves unable to distinguish between a battered woman who was communicating her true feelings and one who had a literal or figurative gun to her head. Accordingly, the government adopted a uniform approach and dropped charges in every case in which a woman requested it (Epstein, 1999).

During the 1980s and 1990s, the efforts of advocates against IPV resulted in substantial reform of these policies. In a growing number of states, prosecutors adopted "no-drop" policies (Epstein, 1999). Pursuant to such a policy, once charges are brought, a case proceeds regardless of the victim's wishes, as long as sufficient evidence exists to prove criminal conduct beyond a reasonable doubt. Such evidence can include recorded calls to 911, photographs and hospital records documenting injuries, and testimony from eyewitnesses or police officers who responded to the crime scene (Epstein, 1999). Even in cases in which the victim refuses to cooperate with the government or recants her original story and testifies for the defense, prosecuting attorneys often persevere, relying on these alternative sources of evidence (Epstein, 2002; Mills, 1999). Thus, IPV prosecutions are now in a position of rough parity with those of stranger violence. As with mandatory arrest, no-drop prosecution strategies proved quite useful in improving the ability of victims to access justice.

Effectiveness

In many ways, mandatory arrest laws and no-drop prosecution policies represent enormous progress for victims of domestic violence within the criminal justice system. First, these policies represent an important symbolic shift: The state has made a clear declaration that it no longer condones IPV (Ford & Regoli, 1993). Second, the experiences of victims have changed substantially. Battered women seeking to avoid abuse now have a far broader range of tools available to them. Indeed, some scholars and activists argue that mandatory arrest and no-drop prosecution are the most effective ways to prevent a perpetrator from escaping punishment through his ability to threaten victims into dropping charges (e.g., Hanna, 1996). Finally, some victims report that participation in the criminal justice system itself has psychological benefits. For example, 75% of victims surveyed by Ford and Regoli (1993) reported feeling more in control of their situation as a result of prosecution, independent of case outcome. Similarly, Dobash and colleagues found that victims reported having significantly more self-respect and less fear after their partner was convicted, regardless of the specific sanctions he received (Dobash, Dobash, Cavanaugh, & Lewis, 2000).

But the situation is more complex than these results suggest. No clear picture exists regarding the actual impact of mandatory arrest and no-drop prosecution on overall rates of offender reabuse (and, accordingly, on victim safety); however, what we do know gives rise to some real concerns. Since the original Minneapolis Domestic Violence Experiment, numerous additional studies have analyzed the impact of arrest on recidivism rates. A relatively recent reanalysis of the pooled data from these studies showed that mandatory arrest has, at best, a mixed impact on reabuse. The rate of effectiveness varies based in part on the perpetrator's employment status (Maxwell, Garner, & Fagan, 1999). In the aftermath of a mandatory arrest, perpetrators who are employed are less likely to commit a future assault resulting in rearrest than are unemployed perpetrators. The difference could stem from a lower "stake in conformity" on the part of unemployed batterers, or from a lower likelihood that survivors will call the police in cases in which the batterer or his family believe they have more to lose (Wooldredge & Thistlethwaite, 2002). The bottom line for many battered women, however, is that they remain vulnerable to reassault.

No-drop prosecution appears to be similarly problematic in terms of its effectiveness in reducing recidivism rates. The only experimental study to look directly at no-drop prosecution and reabuse rates found that victims who followed through with prosecution were less likely to experience violence within the subsequent 6 months *only if* they made a personal choice to participate. Those whom the government coerced into participation experienced no similar reduction in violence (Ford & Regoli, 1992). More research is needed here, but again, battered women are far from fully protected.

Further, mandatory policies *themselves* can create risks for battered women. Many victims fear that prosecution will provoke a batterer into retaliatory abuse against them and their children. In one study (Erez & Belknap, 1998), approximately 500 victims of IPV rated fear of the batterer as the most important reason they were unwilling to cooperate with the prosecution. It is important to note that such fears are realistic. Data show that separation from the batterer—an integral component of a prosecution—is the time of greatest risk of serious violence and homicide for battered women (see, e.g., Fleury, Sullivan, & Bybee, 2000). Several studies indicate that 20% to 30% of arrested offenders reassault their partners either before the court process has concluded or shortly afterward, often in retaliation for the victim's role in the process (e.g., Finn, 2003; Goodman, Bennett, & Dutton, 1999). A National Institute of Justice study found that increased prosecution rates for IPV were associated with increased levels of homicide among White married couples, as well as Black and White unmarried couples, even when controlling for other relevant variables (Dugan, Nagin, & Rosenfeld, 2001).

Despite this fact, prosecutors regularly subpoena reluctant victims and force them to testify (Epstein, Bell, & Goodman, 2003). This can lead to yet another safety risk: As survivors learn that their individual needs will not be taken into account, some of them will choose to avoid police and prosecutors altogether, reducing the gains society has made in access to justice and leaving them more vulnerable than ever to their partners' abuse.

Together, these findings have resulted in growing concern about the degree to which mandatory arrest and no-drop prosecution policies actually are effective in keeping women safe (see, e.g., Mills, 1998; Weisz, 2002). Many advocates for battered women are now rethinking their early enthusiasm for criminal justice mandates.

Limitations of Criminal Justice System Reforms

One of the principal reasons that mandatory criminal justice system interventions have not been more effective in protecting women's safety is that, given the enormous complexity of intimate partner violence, no single response can meet the needs of every woman, and many responses that are well suited to one situation can worsen another. But mandatory arrest laws and no-drop prosecution policies are designed to operate on a one-size-fits-all basis. They lack sufficient flexibility to permit effective responses to particularized situations and leave little room for a contextualized understanding of an individual battered woman's life circumstances. Pursuant to these mandates, once a woman, or her neighbor or friend, makes an initial call to the police, she is swept into a process over which she has little control. Her personal wishes and needs become largely irrelevant. This can have a substantial negative impact, both on a woman's physical safety and on her psychological wellbeing.

Such harm may be particularly acute for battered women who are financially dependent on their abusive partners. A victim may seek to have charges dropped so that her partner can continue to work, provide her with financial support, and prevent her family from ending up homeless. For these and other reasons, insufficient economic resources create a real obstacle to survivors' willingness to cooperate with prosecutors (Hare, 2006). Even so, prosecutors typically refuse to drop charges in situations in which abuse victims are financially reliant on their abusive partners, reasoning that dropping the case would not serve the interests of the state in deterring future batterers from harming women. From their perspective, it sends a mixed message if charges can be dropped for batterers whose families are dependent on their income. Such reasoning may be sound in theory, but in practice it may sacrifice individual survivors' safety and wellbeing in favor of general deterrence of intimate partner violence.

Criminal justice mandates applied in a one-size-fits-all manner also can damage a survivor's connections to her community. As one example, federal law provides that an immigrant convicted of a domestic violence offense becomes deportable, even if he has previously obtained lawful permanent resident status (Omnibus Consolidated Appropriations Act of 1997, 1996). Many women are realistically concerned that if their actions trigger the deportation of their partners, they will be ostracized from their cultural communities. This concern is particularly strong if the perpetrator might be subjected to political persecution if forced to return to his home country. A robust body of research demonstrates the devastating impact of isolation from family and friends on survivors' emotional wellbeing and physical safety (Adkins & Kamp Dush, 2010; Bybee & Sullivan, 2005; Goodman & Smyth, 2011). Faced with inflexible, one-size-fits-all policies, women often choose to remain silent about abuse or refuse to cooperate with criminal justice actors (Loke, 1997).

In fact, those survivors who perceived the justice system as unresponsive to their preferences were significantly less likely to report a new incident of abuse that occurred at some point over the next year (Buzawa, Hotaling, & Byrne, 2006). Similarly, those reporting less empowering experiences also described weaker intentions to use the system in the future if the need arose (Bennett Cattaneo & Goodman, 2010).

Finally, mandatory criminal justice interventions can undermine a survivor's relationship with her children. Research shows that children are at high risk of physical harm when separation occurs (Fleury et al., 2000). Not surprisingly, victims rank concern for their children's safety high on the list of factors that lead them to decline to cooperate with a prosecution (Erez & Belknap, 1998). As a result, many victims choose to remain in an abusive relationship in order to better protect their children. Despite the logic of such a decision, justice system officials often assume that a "good" mother would always leave an abusive relationship. Many prosecutors threaten to refer "uncooperative" victims to child protective services, so action may be taken to remove their children (Epstein, 1999). Such practices create an antipathy between government officials and battered women that leaves some women deeply reluctant to use the justice system as a resource.

The Civil Justice System

History and Current Status

In the late 1960s and early 1970s, activists grew frustrated with the slow pace of criminal justice reform and turned their attention to the civil justice system. Their efforts resulted in the widespread adoption of protection order statutes, which authorize judges to create flexible, individually responsive solutions for survivors of intimate partner violence. Today, every state has a protection order statute, though both eligibility criteria and the scope of available protections and other remedies vary (DeJong & Burgess-Proctor, 2006). The most basic protection orders typically direct a batterer to refrain from assaulting or threatening a victim and, often, to avoid all contact with her. Frequently, these orders also address a wide range of additional issues, including custody, visitation arrangements, child support, access to housing, and reimbursement for medical expenses or property damage (Logan, Shannon, & Walker, 2005). The inclusion of a broad range of remedies is crucial to battered women's wellbeing. For example, one of the primary reasons that victims return to their abusive partners is the pressure created by a loss of financial support (Goodman, Smyth, Borges, & Singer, 2009). For a woman with children, a support award may be the key to freedom. Similarly, because the potential for renewed violence is particularly acute during visitation exchanges, carefully structured pick-up and drop-off provisions that are designed to eliminate victim–perpetrator contact also can significantly reduce the risk of future violence (Finn & Colson, 1990).

In contrast to the criminal justice one-size-fits-all approach, protection order statutes were developed expressly to provide individually tailored legal remedies for battered women. For example, a perpetrator might be ordered to attend parenting counseling, provide spousal support, reimburse the victim for injury-related medical bills, or refrain from contacting the victim's employer. In most states, protection orders remain in effect for 1 to 3 years and may be extended upon demonstration of continued need. In addition, every state has adopted criminal enforcement mechanisms for protection orders (Epstein, 2002). These statutes make violation of a protection order a criminal offense, punishable by fine or incarceration.

Effectiveness

In light of this dramatic expansion in legal protection, it is perhaps not surprising that several studies suggest that a majority of women who obtain protection orders report feeling both safer and better about themselves after doing so (Fischer & Rose, 1995; Keilitz, Hannaford, & Efkerman, 1997). Research comparing reabuse outcomes for women with and without protection orders indicates that orders provide some real physical protection for IPV survivors. Although the data are mixed, several of the largest and most rigorous studies indicate that those women who obtained a protection order reported considerably less reabuse over time compared to those who reported an incident to the police but did not file for a protection order (Holt, Kernic, Wolf, & Rivara, 2003; Logan, Shannon, Walker, & Faragher, 2006).

Still, a small group of studies exploring the effectiveness of civil protection orders in terms of victim safety sound a cautionary note (e.g., Holt et al., 2003; Keilitz et al., 1997; Klein, 1996; Logan & Walker, 2009; McFarlane et al., 2004). These studies use a variety of data sources, including victim follow-up, police reports, and new restraining order applications. Follow-up periods range from 4 months to 2 years. Overall, they indicate that between 23% and 70% of batterers recidivate in violation of protection orders. The methodology is crucial here; victim report–based studies revealed far higher violation rates than did studies based on official records. Averaging across 32 studies, Spitzberg (2002) reported that batterers violate approximately 40% of protection orders. Several studies further suggest that a substantial portion of violations occur rapidly—within the first 3 months after issuance of the order (Harrell & Smith, 1996; Keilitz, 1997; Klein, 1996). These findings suggest that women who feel empowered by the protection order process may have a false sense of security; this, in turn, could result in a premature lowering of their guard (Goodman & Epstein, 2008).

Limitations of Civil Justice System Reforms

A variety of factors contribute to the fact that civil protection orders are an imperfect tool for promoting survivors' wellbeing. One substantial problem stems from a judicial failure to fully implement the civil laws. This failure arises in large part from an insufficient judicial understanding of the social and psychological dynamics of domestic violence. For example, many judges become frustrated with petitioners whom they perceive as simply "refusing" to leave the abusive relationship (Epstein, 1999). When a woman files a civil protection order suit after dropping previous cases, judges have made comments such as, "Oh, it's you again"; "How long are you going to stay away this time?"; and "You want to go back and get beat up again?" (Maryland Gender Bias Task Force, 1989).

Judges also may misinterpret victim behavior that is symptomatic of the psychological trauma induced by extended abuse. Survivors of prolonged or severe domestic violence often exhibit some symptoms or meet the full diagnostic criteria for posttraumatic stress disorder (PTSD; Golding, 1999). This diagnosis produces three major categories of symptoms: "hyperarousal" (being in a constant state of alertness for and expectation of danger), "intrusion" (reliving the violent experience as if it were continually recurring in the present, through flashbacks and nightmares), and "dissociation" (a numbing response that includes repressing memories of violent incidents; Herman, 1992). These symptoms can profoundly affect the way a battered woman appears in court and, in turn, how she is perceived by a judge. For example, dissociation may cause a survivor to testify about emotionally charged incidents with an entirely flat affect or to be unable to remember details of violent incidents. Hyperarousal can cause a victim to seem highly paranoid or subject to unexpected outbursts of rage in response to relatively minor incidents. But these explanations of battered women's behavior are not intuitively obvious, and because they are substantially different from the behavior and demeanor that a judge encounters in his normal experience, they may be misinterpreted as indications of a lack of credibility (Epstein, 1999).

These misunderstandings can, in turn, lead judges to identify with the batterer, distance themselves from the victim (Hanna, 1996), and apply artificially heightened standards of proof (Kinports & Fischer, 1993). A judge may refuse to issue civil protection orders when documentary or other physical evidence is absent; when unbiased eyewitnesses are not available; when the only witnesses are the parties and, therefore, a credibility determination is required; or when the victim has failed to follow through with a protection order case on a prior occasion (Epstein, 1999). These kinds of standards have no basis in law and are not applied in other family law cases (Epstein, 1999). They also are antithetical to the wellbeing of survivors, both in terms of the failure to provide physical protection and the psychological harm of being disbelieved.

Another significant obstacle to victim wellbeing in the protection order system stems from failures of enforcement (Kane, 2000). Police still frequently refuse to arrest batterers who have violated protection orders. This practice can substantially undermine a woman's faith in the justice system, making her far less likely to rely on it in the future. She is likely to be deeply reluctant to risk her abusive partner's wrath when an order turns out to be "nothing but a piece of paper," just as he told her it was.

In addition, like the criminal justice system, the civil protection order system has given rise to unanticipated negative consequences for survivors. Here, too, these challenges stem from officials' tendency to adopt a uniform view of battered women. The most significant problem is that in practice, the protection order system rests on the assumption that all survivors wish—or should wish—to exit their abusive relationships (Goodman & Epstein, 2008). But in fact, women may have numerous reasons for choosing to stay in such a relationship. As noted earlier, survivors may stay to avoid retaliatory violence against themselves and their children, or because they rely on their abusive partners (for financial support, childcare, or housing) and may not be able to survive without continued contact. Accordingly, they may want the violence to stop but not yet be ready to end the relationship. These women need support in their efforts to become more economically self-reliant, but such assistance is not offered by the justice system or by most community programs (Logan et al., 2006). Immigrant women may be particularly unlikely to choose separation from their partners for reasons having to do with religion, tradition, economic dependence, or a desire to remain part of a community that would not condone such an action (Latta & Goodman, 2005).

By assuming that all battered women should end their relationships, judges in civil cases often substitute their own judgment for that of a victim seeking assistance in their courtrooms. Some judges fine or even imprison battered women for initiating contact with an abusive partner during the effective period of a protection order (e.g., Goodmark, 2003). These actions demonstrate how little tolerance judges in civil protection order cases have for women who do not conform to government expectations, as well as how willing judges are to use criminal sanctions to enforce officially "appropriate" behavior. They harm the women who bring these cases, as well as others in the community who hear these stories and are deterred from using the system's protective resources.

This pressure toward separation is particularly problematic when juxtaposed with evidence that many judges presiding over contested custody proceedings fail to credit or refuse to consider allegations of intimate partner violence. Instead, these judges emphasize the importance of dual parent involvement and award joint custody—thus forcing survivors to maintain unwanted close contact with abusive partners (Meier, 2003). As a result, survivors find themselves on the receiving end of inconsistent judicial messages—you must separate from your abusive partner, regardless of your preference, except if you have children, in which case you must remain in regular contact with him even if you wish to leave. As is clear from both of these situations, civil judges, like their criminal justice counterparts, often use their substantial power to control the lives of victims.

Where Do We Go From Here?

The rapid pace and broad scope of changes in the criminal and civil justice systems have been truly breathtaking. But these responses still fail to reach many battered women, and recent reforms have themselves created new, unanticipated risks and challenges for numerous survivors, in terms of both physical safety and emotional wellbeing. So where do we go from here? How can we alleviate the harms that the justice system can inflict on survivors?

Perhaps most important, the criminal and civil justice systems need to become more individualized so as to meet the diverse needs and priorities of a variety of women (Bell, 2007). Although mandatory arrest laws and no-drop prosecution policies were adopted in large part to promote battered women's safety, they tend to be rigidly applied, even when doing so may expose women to more violence and feelings of disempowerment. Similarly, civil protection orders can be enormously helpful to survivors' safety and sense of empowerment, but the court process may pressure women to separate from their partners when they do not wish to do so. As an initial step forward, three changes would enhance the justice system's responsiveness to survivors' individualized needs as they themselves define them: greater communication between survivors and court actors, better developed and more responsive advocacy for survivors in court, and new civil remedies that consider survivors' own wishes rather than imposing separation.

Communication

Within the context of the criminal justice system, increased flexibility is dependent on increased communication with individual victims. For prosecutors to choose a course that will best meet the needs of survivors, they must have all pertinent information at their disposal at the initial, charging stage. Yet they typically have limited time to devote to an individual case, especially at the outset, and therefore tend to focus on the most recent incident of violence, without access to information regarding the larger context and historical patterns within the relationship. If it is possible to create opportunities for advocates, attorneys, and survivors to better communicate about the history and context of the most recent incident, prosecutors might be able to add charges that otherwise never would have been brought. These additional charges may increase the length of a jail sentence for the perpetrator, giving the victim additional time and space to create a new, safer life. Or, when appropriate, such discussions could result in a prosecutor agreeing to *decline* pursuit of certain charges, where doing so would increase the victim's sense of support and general willingness to cooperate (see Epstein et al., 2003, for an example of one such collaboration).

Similarly, increased communication might enable police and prosecutors to decide, in collaboration with a victim, whether her particular circumstances dictate a decision to decline arrest and prosecution altogether. Prosecutors could take one step in this direction by considering the postponement of prosecution in some, limited situations. They could accumulate the evidence necessary to go forward but delay filing charges while the victim receives the advocacy services she needs to assess her situation with greater clarity and then take action to move beyond the batterer's psychological and physical control. The potential effectiveness of such strategies is supported by a study that found that women who were given a choice about whether to drop charges reported an increased sense of the court's fairness, while those who felt they were subjected to coercive treatment by prosecutors reported diminished perceptions of the court's fairness (Finn, 2003). More generally, greater control over the court process is associated with more positive feelings toward the justice system and a greater sense of empowerment (Hotaling & Buzawa, 2003; Lewis, Dobash, Dobash, & Cavanagh, 2000; Ptacek, 1999; Zweig, Burt, & Van Ness, 2003).

Broader efforts at increased communication, such as unified domestic violence courts, also can have positive results. Around the country, such courts are structured in a variety of ways, but they typically include (1) a limited number of judicial officers who are assigned to hear only domestic violence cases, (2) partnerships between the court and community agencies to improve service provision, and (3) efforts to increase the consistency of court orders that affect a single family.[3] Some unified domestic violence courts have brought together civil and criminal cases into a single unit; others have brought together protection order and family law cases (Epstein, 1999). In many ways, these courts appear to have a positive impact on victims' experiences. One large-scale study found that the more battered women perceived different agencies as communicating effectively and working together, the more highly they rated them in terms of helpfulness and effectiveness and the more satisfied they were both

[3] See Sicafuse and Bornstein, chapter 2, this volume, for a longer discussion of domestic violence courts.

with the legal system in general and with their own individual case outcomes in particular (Zweig & Burt, 2006).

By increasing communication within the criminal justice system and throughout the courts, it is possible to move closer toward an individually responsive approach to battered women's lived experiences.

Advocacy

Although a variety of advocacy services already exist in courthouses, prosecutors' offices, and the occasional police department, more intensive programs are needed. An increase in advocacy services is particularly important given the widespread concern that while a victim is under the physical threat or psychological thrall of an abusive partner, she is likely to be severely hampered in her ability to make well-considered, self-protective decisions. This reality makes it far more challenging for police or prosecutors to move to a more survivor-centered system; the government must retain control over the decision-making process on a woman's behalf. The solution lies in expanded advocacy services. Intensive advocacy can help survivors to obtain the emotional space and empowerment necessary to make the important decisions that police and prosecutors now make for them. Intensive advocacy also can increase a victim's perception of social support, improve her mental health, and increase her physical and psychological safety.

In an evaluation of law school domestic violence clinics, for example, Bell and Goodman (2001) found that women who worked intensively with legal advocates in seeking civil protection orders reported significantly less physical and psychological abuse and marginally better emotional support 6 weeks after the initial interview than did women not receiving this intensive advocacy. Similarly, intensive, nonlegal advocacy services can have a real, positive impact on battered women. After 10 weeks of support from college students involved in an advocacy program, women leaving a shelter reported improvements in physical safety, social support, and effectiveness in obtaining necessary resources, as well as less depression, fear, and anxiety, as compared to those who did not receive advocacy services (Sullivan & Bybee, 1999). Impressively, some of these improvements lasted for up to 3 years after the intervention had ended (Bybee & Sullivan, 2005). By offering substantially expanded advocacy services within the criminal and civil justice systems, it might be possible to move toward a far more individualized system that would better promote survivors' physical and emotional wellbeing.

Removing Bias in Favor of Separation

Finally, the civil justice system could increase its flexibility and responsiveness to victims' individual needs through the eradication of the current reflexive judicial bias in favor of partner separation. Judicial training might begin to alleviate this problem, but many judges are not particularly receptive to advocacy-based training programs (Epstein, 1999). Solid research comparing the psychological and physical security of battered women who choose to stay and those who are forced to leave against their will could be extraordinarily useful in any project designed to expand judicial perspectives.

Conclusion

Over the last several decades, the justice system has made substantial strides toward taking intimate partner violence seriously and responding more forcefully to the needs of victims. But there is still a long road ahead before the justice system is able to respond directly to the particular obstacles, needs, and goals of diverse battered women; minimize the potential harmful impact of IPV; and truly promote the wellbeing of survivors. Increased communication between prosecutors and advocates, private attorneys, and survivors themselves could amplify survivors' sense of empowerment and positive feelings about the justice system. Similarly, an expansion of intensive advocacy services could increase battered women's perceptions of available practical support, as well as tangible physical and psychological safety. Finally, eradicating the existing judicial bias in favor of partner separation could make the current justice system far more responsive to the particular needs of individual survivors. These reforms, at a minimum, are crucial to continued efforts to ensure that the justice system promotes victim wellbeing.

References

Adkins, K. S., & Kamp Dush, C. M. (2010). The mental health of mothers in and after violent and controlling unions. *Social Science Research.*

Anderson, M., Gillig, P., Sitaker, M., McCloskey, K., Malloy, K., & Grigsby, N. (2003). "Why doesn't she just leave?": A descriptive study of victim reported impediments to her safety. *Journal of Family Violence, 18*, 151–155.

Bell, M. E. (2007). Empowerment and disempowerment for victims of intimate partner violence: An overview of the effects of criminal justice system practices. In K. A. Kendall-Tackett & S. Giacomoni (Eds.), *Intimate partner violence* (pp. 21.1–21.15). Kingston, NJ: Civic Research Institute.

Bell, M. E., & Goodman, L. A. (2001). Supporting battered women involved with the court system: An evaluation of a law school-based advocacy intervention. *Violence Against Women, 7,* 1377–1404.

Bennett Cattaneo, L., & Goodman, L. A. (2010). Through the lens of therapeutic jurisprudence: The relationship between empowerment in the court system and wellbeing for intimate partner violence victims. *Journal of Interpersonal Violence, 25,* 481–502.

Buzawa, E. S., & Buzawa, C. G. (1992). The scientific evidence is not conclusive: Arrest is no panacea. In R. J. Gelles & D. R. Loseke (Eds.), *Current controversies in family violence* (pp. 337–341). Thousand Oaks, CA: Sage.

Buzawa, E., Hotaling, G. T., & Byrne, J. (2006). Understanding the impact of prior abuse and prior victimization on the decision to forego criminal justice assistance in domestic violence incidents: A life-course perspective. *Brief Treat Crisis Intervention.* doi:10.1093/brief-treatment/mhl020

Bybee, D., & Sullivan, C. M. (2005). Predicting re-victimization of battered women 3 years after exiting a shelter program. *American Journal of Community Psychology, 36,* 85–96.

Cahn, D. D. (1992). *Conflict in intimate relationships.* New York, NY: Guilford Press.

DeJong, C., & Burgess-Proctor, A. (2006). A summary of personal protection order statutes in the United States. *Violence Against Women, 12,* 68–88.

Dobash, R. E., Dobash, R. P., Cavanagh, K., & Lewis, R. (2000). *Changing violent men.* Thousand Oaks, CA: Sage.

Dugan, L., Nagin, D., & Rosenfeld, R. (2001). *Exposure reduction or backlash? The effects of domestic violence resources on intimate partner homicide: Final report.* Washington, DC: U.S. Department of Justice.

Eisenberg, S., & Micklow, P. (1974). *The assaulted wife: "Catch 22" revisited.* Unpublished manuscript.

Epstein, D. (1999). Effective intervention in domestic violence cases: Rethinking the role of prosecutors, judges, and the court system. *Yale Journal of Law and Feminism, 11,* 3–50.

Epstein, D. (2002). Procedural justice: Tempering the state's response to domestic violence. *William and Mary Law Review, 43,* 1843–1905.

Epstein, D., Bell, M. E., & Goodman, L. A. (2003). Transforming aggressive prosecution policies: Prioritizing victims' long-term safety in the prosecution of domestic violence cases. *Journal of Gender, Social Policy and the Law, 11,* 465–498.

Erez, E., & Belknap, J. (1998). In their own words: Battered women's assessment of the criminal processing system's responses. *Violence and Victims, 13,* 251–268.

Finn, M. A. (2003). *Effects of victims' experiences with prosecutors on victim empowerment and re-occurrence of intimate partner violence, final report.* Washington, DC: National Institute of Justice.

Finn, P., & Colson, S. (1990). *Civil protection orders: Legislation, current court practice, and enforcement.* Washington, DC: National Institute of Justice.

Fischer, K., & Rose, M. (1995). When "enough is enough": Battered women's decision making around court orders of protection. *Crime and Delinquency, 41,* 414–429.

Fleury, R. E., Sullivan, C. M., & Bybee, D. I. (2000). When ending the relationship doesn't end the violence: Women's experiences of violence by former partners. *Violence Against Women, 6,* 1363–1383.

Ford, D. A., & Regoli, M. J. (1992). The preventive impacts of policies for prosecuting wife batterers. In E. S. Buzawa & C. G. Buzawa (Eds.), *Domestic violence: The changing criminal justice response* (pp. 181–207). Westport, CT: Auburn House.

Ford, D. A., & Regoli, M. J. (1993). The criminal prosecution of wife assaulters: Process, problems, and effects. In N. Z. Hilton (Ed.), *Legal responses to wife*

assault: Current trends and evaluation (pp. 127–164). Newbury Park, CA: Sage Publications.
Golding, J. M. (1999). Intimate partner violence as a risk factor for mental disorders: A meta-analysis. *Journal of Family Violence, 14*, 99–132.
Goodman, L. A., Bennett, L., & Dutton, M. A. (1999). Obstacles to domestic violence victims' cooperation with the criminal prosecution of their abusers: The role of social support. *Violence and Victims, 14*, 427–444.
Goodman, L. A., & Epstein, D. (2008). *Listening to battered women: A survivor-centered approach to advocacy, mental health, and justice.* Washington, DC: American Psychological Association.
Goodman, L. A., & Smyth, K. F. (2011). A call for a social network-oriented approach to services for survivors of intimate partner violence. *Psychology of Violence, 1*(2), 79–92.
Goodman, L. A., Smyth, K. F., Borges, A. M., & Singer, R. (2009). When crises collide: How intimate partner violence and poverty intersect to shape women's mental health and coping. *Trauma, Violence and Abuse, 10*, 306–329.
Goodmark, L. (2003). Law is the answer? Do we know that for sure? *St. Louis University Public Law Review, 23*, 7–48.
Hanna, C. (1996). No right to choose: Mandated victim participation in domestic violence prosecution. *Harvard Law Review, 109*, 1850–1910.
Hare, S. C. (2006). What do battered women want? Victims' opinions on prosecution. *Violence and Victims, 21*, 611–628.
Harrell, A., & Smith, B. A. (1996). Effects of restraining orders on domestic violence victims. In E. S. Buzawa & C. G. Buzawa (Eds.), *Do arrests and restraining orders work?* (pp. 214–242). Thousand Oaks, CA: Sage.
Herman, J. L. (1992). *Trauma and recovery.* New York, NY: Basic Books.
Holt, V., Kernic, M., Wolf, M., & Rivara, F. (2003). Do protection orders affect the likelihood of future partner violence and injury? *American Journal of Preventive Medicine, 24*, 16–21.
Hotaling, G. T., & Buzawa, E. S. (2003). *Victim satisfaction with criminal justice case processing in a model court setting.* Washington, DC: National Institute of Justice.
Kane, R. J. (2000). Police responses to restraining orders in domestic violence incidents: Identifying the custody-threshold thesis. *Criminal Justice and Behavior, 27*(5), 561–580.
Keilitz, S. L. (1997). *National Center for State Courts: Civil protection orders: The benefits and limitations for victims of domestic violence.* Williamsburg, VA: National Center for State Courts.
Keilitz, S. L., Hannaford, & Efkerman (1997). *Civil protection orders: The benefits and limitations for victims of domestic violence.* Williamsburg, VA: National Center for State Courts.
Kinports, K., & Fischer, K. (1993). Orders of protection in domestic violence cases: An empirical assessment of the impact of the reform statutes. *Texas Journal of Women and Law, 20*, 173.
Klein, A. R. (1996). Re-abuse in a population of court-restrained male batterers: Why restraining orders don't work. In E. S. Buzawa & C. G. Buzawa (Eds.), *Do arrests and restraining orders work?* (pp. 192–213). Thousand Oaks, CA: Sage Publications.

Latta, R. E., & Goodman, L. A. (2005). Considering the interplay of cultural context and service provision in intimate partner violence. *Violence Against Women, 11*, 1441–1464.
Lewis, R., Dobash, R. P., Dobash, R. E., & Cavanagh, K. (2000). Protection, prevention, rehabilitation or justice? Women's use of the law to challenge domestic violence. *International Review of Victimology, 7*, 179–205.
Logan, T., Shannon, L., & Walker, R. (2005). Protective orders in rural and urban areas: A multiple perspective study. *Violence Against Women, 11*, 876–911.
Logan, T. K., Shannon, L., Walker, R., & Faragher, T. M. (2006). Protective orders: Questions and conundrums. *Trauma, 7*, 175–205.
Logan, T. K., & Walker, R. (2009). Civil protection order outcomes: Violations and perceptions of effectiveness. *Journal of Interpersonal Violence, 24*, 675–692.
Loke, T. (1997). Trapped in domestic violence: The impact of United States immigration laws on battered immigrant women. *Boston University Public Interest Law Journal, 6*, 589–628.
Maryland Gender Bias Task Force. (1989). *Report of the Maryland Special Joint Committee on Gender Bias in the Courts.* Annapolis, MD: Maryland Court of Appeals.
Maxwell, C. D., Garner, J. H., & Fagan, J. A. (1999, June). *The impact of arrest on domestic violence: Results from five policy experiments.* Paper presented at the Research in Progress Seminar, Washington, DC.
McFarlane, J., Malecha, A., Gist, J., Watson, K., Batten, E., Hall, I., et al. (2004). Protection orders and intimate partner violence: An 18-month study of 150 black, Hispanic, and white women. *American Journal of Public Health, 94*, 613–618.
Meier, J. (2003). Domestic violence, child custody, and child protection: Understanding judicial resistance and imagining the solutions. *Journal of Gender, Social Policy and the Law, 11*, 657–725.
Miccio, G. K. (2005). A house divided: Mandatory arrest, domestic violence, and the conservatization of the battered women's movement. *Houston Law Review, 42*, 237–323.
Mills, L. G. (1998). Mandatory arrest and prosecution policies for domestic violence: A critical literature review and the case for more research to test victim empowerment approaches. *Criminal Justice and Behavior, 25*, 306–318.
Mills, L. G. (1999). Killing her softly: Intimate abuse and the violence of state interventions. *Harvard Law Review, 113*, 550–613.
Omnibus Consolidated Appropriations Act of 1997, 104 Pub. L. 208, § 350 (1996), codified at 8 U.S.C. § 1227(a)(2)(E)(2006).
Ptacek, J. (1999). *Battered women in the courtroom: The power of judicial responses.* Boston, MA: Northeastern University Press.
Sherman, L. W., & Berk, R. A. (1984). The specific deterrent effects of arrest for domestic assault. *American Sociological Review, 49*, 261–272.
Spitzberg, B. H. (2002). The tactical topography of stalking victimization and management. *Trauma, 3*, 261–288.
Sullivan, C. M., & Bybee, D. I. (1999). Reducing violence using community-based advocacy for women with abusive partners. *Journal of Consulting and Clinical Psychology, 67*, 43–53.

Tjaden, P., & Thoennes, N. (2000). *Full report of the prevalence, incidence, and consequences of violence against women: Findings from the National Violence Against Women Survey.* Washington, DC: U.S. Department of Justice. Retrieved from https://www.ncjrs.gov/pdffi les1/nij/183781.pdf

Weisz, A. N. (2002). Prosecution of batterers: Views of African American battered women. *Violence and Victims, 17,* 19–34.

Wooldredge, J., & Thistlethwaite, A. (2002). Reconsidering domestic violence recidivism: Conditioned effects of legal controls by individual and aggregate levels of stake in conformity. *Journal of Quantitative Criminology, 18,* 45–70.

Zweig, J. M., & Burt, M. R. (2006). Predicting case outcomes and women's perceptions of the legal system's response to domestic violence and sexual assault: Does interaction between community agencies matter. *Criminal Justice Policy Review, 17,* 202–233.

Zweig, J. M., Burt, M. R., & Van Ness, A. (2003). *The effects on victims of victim service programs funded by the STOP formula grants program.* Washington, DC: Urban Institute.

4

The Legal System Experiences of Children, Families, and Professionals Who Work with Them

Victoria Weisz, Sarah J. Beal, and Twila Wingrove

This book has set out to review factors related to the legal system that promote or are detrimental to the wellbeing of those involved in a variety of contexts. This chapter is specifically designed to address the experiences of children and their families as they interact with the legal system in two specific court contexts: divorce and dependency court, where dependency court refers to situations in which the court system has intervened based on concerns about child abuse or neglect.

Families typically enter the legal system because adults' dysfunctional relationships or behaviors have made them unable to solve problems, make decisions, or carry out basic parental functions. The legal system then imposes its often highly structured framework for problem resolution onto the families. Consequently, highly stressed families are often relying on an inflexible, rule-driven legal system to solve the highly significant, deeply personal, and richly detailed problems of family dissolution, family violence, or parental neglect.

It is likely that subjecting one's personal family life to an adversarial process and court scrutiny would be stressful on families. Those families who come under court jurisdiction come with preexisting vulnerabilities, undoubtedly making the experiences particularly difficult for many. This fact also contributes to a fundamental research challenge in teasing apart the stress contribution of the legal process from the stress that family members have already experienced and may be continuing to experience. For example, in situations with divorce, children may experience stress via attending court or being asked to speak to a judge regarding their preferences for living or custody arrangements, but they are often also experiencing the stress of changes in residence or observing parental conflict and tension. While these factors are not a result of legal involvement and are therefore beyond the scope of this chapter, they do provide an important context in which to understand the role of the legal process in either increasing or ameliorating stress. This chapter will review the small existing literature that has attempted to identify the experiences of children and families in the legal system that are separate or distinct from the stressors these families are experiencing more broadly, acknowledging the limitations and challenges of this approach. We have organized the chapter into three broad sections: the first section addresses experiences of children and families in the divorce context; the second addresses experiences of children, families, childcare providers (i.e., relative and foster caregivers), and legal actors in the dependency court setting; and the third section discusses areas for future research and provides some policy recommendations.

Divorce Court

A divorce is a court decree that ends a marriage. In addition to dissolving the marriage, the court divides property, awards spousal support, and, if there are minor children, awards custody and orders child support. States vary in the laws that govern divorce, although all states have moved generally toward a "no fault" approach. Further, only about 5% of divorces require a contested trial. In most cases, the parties negotiate and settle issues regarding property, support, and custody, often with the assistance of attorneys (American Bar Association, 2011). Trained mediators are sometimes used to assist divorcing couples in their negotiations, and in some states there are requirements for some form of mediation or collaborative process, especially when there are children involved. The collaborative law movement has been growing in some parts of the country over the past decade. It is a method of collaborative practice in which clients and attorneys sign a contract promising not to litigate and only work toward a noncourt settlement (Pruett, Insabella, & Gustafson, 2005). The development of these nonadversarial approaches has been motivated by assumptions that the adversarial process itself causes or exacerbates stress in parents and children. The following sections will review the sparse empirical literature on this topic.

The Nature of Children's Involvement in Divorce Cases: Current Research

There is no doubt that their parents' divorce can be a stressful, sometimes even traumatic, event for children, especially in the short term. Over the past 30 years or more, an abundance of research has been published detailing the immediate and long-term sequelae of divorce (for reviews, see Ahrons & Marquardt, 2010; Amato, 2007, 2010; Barczak et al., 2010). Researchers have studied how divorce directly impacts parenting quality (e.g., DeGarmo & Forgatch, 1999; Hetherington & Stanley-Hagan, 2002), socioeconomic status (e.g., Fischer, 2007), and child wellbeing (e.g., Amato, 2006; Cherlin, Chase-Lansdale, & McRae, 1998; Pruett & Barker, 2009). However, very few researchers have narrowly studied what impact the legal system itself might have on children's wellbeing, either positively or negatively. That narrower focus is the purpose of this chapter.

While it is impossible to get exact figures, it is safe to say that in the majority of divorce cases, children have limited contact with the legal system. Most divorces are not contested (Jackson & Donovan, 1990), meaning that there is no hearing or set of hearings in front of a judge where the judge must make final decisions regarding the dissolution of the marriage or child custody. Even when cases are contested, the children often have no need to be present in the courtroom and most parents choose to protect their children from witnessing their parents' clash during this adversarial process.

Those cases in which children are required to be present in the courtroom often involve either allegations of child maltreatment or child custody disputes. In such cases, children may be asked to testify during the proceedings. For a thorough discussion of the impact of testifying in court on children, see chapter 5 of this book. While that chapter is not devoted specifically to testifying in divorce cases, the research described about children's stress and wellbeing surrounding being asked to testify in the courtroom, as well as interventions designed to reduce children's stress, applies equally in divorce cases. Therefore, this chapter will not review that literature. Instead, we turn our attention to other experiences of children and families that contribute to stress or promote wellbeing, including the structure and process of the legal setting, interactions between families and legal actors, and policy changes, for example.

In contested custody cases in which children are not asked to testify, they may still be somewhat "involved" in the legal process. Children may be required to undergo custody evaluations, usually conducted by clinical psychologists (Emery, Otto, & O'Donohue, 2005). Custody evaluations are among the most common type of assessment conducted by psychologists. As such, there is a wide range of resources available to guide psychologists in making recommendations (e.g., American Psychological Association, 2010; Martindale et al., 2007; Powell & Lancaster, 2003). While there appears to be no research exploring the impact that the evaluations themselves have on promoting or hindering children's wellbeing, a central tenet of all recommendations is that they are child centered and conducted in a way that minimizes children's stress. Whether *any* stress related to custody evaluations is acceptable is somewhat of an open question, given that the reliability of conclusions based on custody evaluations is uncertain (Emery, Otto, et al., 2005). These researchers contend that the custody evaluations are often the central focus of custody disputes and that, in fact, these evaluations contribute to exacerbating the conflict between divorcing parents. That increased parental conflict, they conclude, has a negative impact on the children's wellbeing.

Rather than finalizing the divorce in a courtroom, most parents finalize their divorce outside of the courtroom, mostly through mediation programs or, more informally, on their own with the aid of attorneys. During mediation, there is certainly the potential for children to be involved (Garwood, 1989–1990; Saposnek, 2004; Schoffer, 2005), but again, there is little evidence that parents or mediators regularly involve children.

It is this *lack* of formal involvement in the legal system that has caused concern for some scholars, both legal and psychological (Saposnek, 2004). They have argued that allowing children to be active participants in the legal system, especially with reference to the custody decision, may serve to provide children with a sense of agency and control during a time when they have very little of it (James & James, 1999; Kaltenborn, 2005; Kurki-Suonio, 2000; Szaj, 2002). In other words, the argument is that an opportunity to be more actively involved in making the custody decision may actually promote wellbeing, or at least buffer against the negative consequences of the divorce itself. This argument has been countered by those who are concerned that requiring, or even encouraging, children's participation in the custody decision might actually increase stress, by forcing children to choose one parent over another (Starnes, 2003).

This debate has not yet been settled empirically. However, as guided by the Uniform Marriage and Divorce Act (1979), which includes as part of the best interests determination "the wishes of the children regarding their custodian," many state laws require formal consideration of children's wishes in contested custody cases. State statutes vary widely in how much guidance they give judges in how they solicit children's wishes and how much weight they should give them. Through judicial surveys, researchers have demonstrated that age plays a primary role: Judges are more likely to seek children's preferences and defer to them when they are older (Crosby-Currie, 1996; Scott, Reppucci, & Aber, 1988; Wallace & Koerner, 2003).

These studies also demonstrate that judges are concerned about protecting children from the risk of increased stress associated with being asked to state a preference, and many judges seek alternative methods for obtaining that preference rather than through traditional in-court testimony. For example, Crosby-Currie (1996) found that many judges relied on custody evaluators to obtain that information during the course of their evaluation. In special circumstances, judges may also speak to children in chambers, with the presumption being that children will feel less stress speaking to the judge informally than sitting on the witness stand and being questioned by the attorneys.

When considering the relationship between children's participation in the custody process and their wellbeing or stress in divorce cases, it is important to keep in mind that "participation" does not necessarily mean "control" or even "influence," nor does it mean requiring a child to provide an opinion. The concerns of those who oppose children's involvement are most relevant when a family or the court is considering placing them in a position of high influence over the custody decision. If involving children means merely giving them the opportunity to have their opinions heard should they so desire, then the number of people in opposition would likely dwindle.

The second answer to the debate over children's participation is an empirical one. The question is whether participation in the custody decision, however it is defined, is harmful or beneficial to children. The answer is that we do not yet know. Qualitative researchers have begun to tackle the question (e.g., Wallerstein, Lewis, & Blakeslee, 2000). Kaltenborn (2001a, 2001b) interviewed children who participated in custody decisions and found that a greater proportion of children whose wishes were not granted ended up effecting changes in their custody arrangements after the divorce. The idea that children can have a great effect on postdivorce changes in living arrangements was also found by Cashmore and Parkinson (2008).

In another study, Smith and Gollop (2001) interviewed children whose parents had divorced several years earlier. The strongest themes that emerged were the children's desire to be kept informed by their parents, to be listened to and respected, and for their views to be considered during the decision-making process. While this research does not speak directly to whether participation in the decision-making process benefits or harms children, it does suggest that many children themselves desire some amount of input. Taken together, the majority of studies provide support for the notion that children want to be involved in the decision but do little to explore the psychological impact, positive or negative, of involvement, either short term or long term.

The Experiences of Parents in the Divorce Legal System

There is a fair amount of evidence that divorce impacts the short-term adjustment of most individuals and the long-term adjustment of some (Clarke-Stewart & Brentano, 2006; Hetherington & Kelly, 2002; Johnson & Wu, 2002; Lorenz et al., 1997). Little research has been conducted on the impact of the legal system itself on parents' stress levels or psychological adjustment; most of the studies involve small samples of self-report data. The following brief section will summarize that research.

Parental perception of the divorce legal system is generally unfavorable, although there are differences among various demographic groups. In one study, the majority of parents entered the system with the hope of a fair experience, but only 12% ended the process with a positive attitude about the system (Pruett & Jackson, 2001). Leite and Clark (2007) also found relatively low overall satisfaction with the system, but they found that higher educated and higher income parents were more satisfied than their lower educated and lower income counterparts. Further, the parents in this study tended to be more satisfied with the way they were treated by judges than by their attorneys and most satisfied with court-based social services that were offered to them. Pruett et al. (2005) argue that the adversarial legal process creates situations where less confident people are especially vulnerable. They cite particular parental concerns about being under the scrutiny of the legal system and being exploited by one's spouse through manipulation of the legal system. Attorneys tend to agree that there is a negative impact on parents by legal actors. A survey of family law lawyers found a high level of belief in the notion that what lawyers did in divorce cases raised the emotional level of disputes (Braver, Cookston, & Cohen, 2002).

Other research that explores the impact of the legal system on parents' stress is the limited research that compares parents in the adversarial court system to parents in the alternative dispute resolution system. A more complete review of the stress related to alternative dispute resolution approaches can be found in chapter 13 of this volume. The development of alternative approaches to the adversarial divorce process, such as mediation, came about because of beliefs that litigation increased acrimony between parents and created psychological distress for them (Beck & Sales, 2001). Despite these beliefs, early research did not find that mediation resulted in improved psychological adjustment of divorcing spouses (Emery & Wyer, 1987). Mothers and fathers appeared to have different perceptions of litigation (Emery, Matthews, & Wyer, 1991). Mothers reported that they felt their rights were protected about the same in litigation and mediation; fathers reported that their rights were significantly more protected in mediation as compared to litigation. Further, mothers were more likely to report that they "won what they wanted" in litigation as compared to mediation; fathers reported the reverse. The authors speculate that the mother preference bias in judicial custody decisions that was very dominant 20 years ago may have contributed to fathers feeling they were more likely to achieve desired outcomes outside of the courtroom.

More recent research has found that parents are generally less satisfied with the adversarial process as compared to mediation and that mediation is related to improved relationships between parents and their children and each other (Emery, Sbarra, & Grover, 2005). These studies have not directly examined stress with the legal process.

Parents in the midst of a divorce are dealing with a multitude of stresses including, but not limited to, grief over the end of a relationship, dislocation, financial worries, and concerns about children. Despite popular agreement that the adversarial system exacerbates the stresses, there is not sufficient empirical research to determine whether the legal system significantly adds to the stress. Nonetheless, parents want the system to treat them fairly and they often feel that it does not (Pruett & Jackson, 2001). Alternatives to litigation may provide parents with a more positive experience, but much more research is needed to determine if that is so.

Dependency Court

State officials have the authority to intervene in families, an otherwise private realm protected from state intervention, when there are alleged or proven concerns about children's safety or basic wellbeing. Dependency courts have the purpose of providing oversight to the child welfare agency's interventions and ensuring that children are protected from harm, that parents are provided reasonable needed rehabilitative services, and that children return to their families or another permanent family as soon as possible. There is considerable state variability regarding the specificity of the court's authority (e.g., states vary as to whether courts can order specific services and placements), the nature and extent of legal representation or other advocacy of children and parents (e.g., some states require attorneys for all children and for all parents of limited income; some states require nonattorney advocates for children and do not provide attorneys for parents), and the degree of adherence to a formal adversary approach. Nonetheless, a growing federal regulatory framework combined with targeted federal resources toward improving dependency courts through adoption of best practices (Court Improvement Project, 1993) has resulted in a fair amount of consistency regarding the general progress of cases through dependency courts. One distinguishing feature of dependency court, as compared to other courts, is that the adjudication by a court that a child meets the state definition of an abused or neglected child (states vary on terms and definitions) does not end court involvement. In fact, in many cases, the adjudication is near the beginning of the court's involvement and will be followed by a dispositional hearing, dispositional review hearings, and permanency hearings, as well as potential hearings establishing guardianships, terminating parental rights, and finalizing adoptions. Thus, while the stress related to court involvement in most other legal cases may focus on one primary judicial decision, in dependency courts there are decisions at each hearing that significantly impact children and families, including decisions about where children live, how often they see their parents and siblings, and required parental services and treatment.

Current Research Involving Children

While it is true that it is difficult to separate the stress of being maltreated or neglected from the stress caused by the child welfare system itself, there is no doubt that the latter does cause significant stress independent of the former. Stress is likely to be most pronounced for children during periods of transition—for example, after their initial removal from the home, during placement changes, and, perhaps, as they are placed in what is expected to be their permanent home. While there is more empirical research on parental and foster caregiver stress, there are a small number of studies that focus on stress levels in children related to being in foster care. As expected, these studies support the expectation that children in foster care would experience, on average, more stress than those who have never entered foster care. For example, Glover and Glenwick (2009) compared the mental health records of foster care and non–foster care children in treatment and found that children in foster care had twice as many life stressors, many of which involved instability of relationships.

While the research on children's stress levels in foster care is limited, a greater number of research studies have investigated foster children's mental health. The conclusions to be drawn depend on the comparison sample being used. Compared to non–foster care children, children in foster care have significantly more mental health problems (e.g., Jee et al., 2010; Pears, Fisher, Bruce, Kim, & Yoerger, 2010). Many of these problems can be attributed to having been raised in families with significant problems and having experienced maltreatment, but the legal system quite possibly plays a contributing role. This section will review research examining children's general involvement in the child protection system, then review the research on children's involvement in the court process, more specifically.

Clearer evidence that the legal system likely also impacts children's mental health and stress levels can be found in research that focuses on various decision points in the system. Specifically, a large number of researchers focus on the differential impact of various placement and case closure options. These studies are rarely framed as an examination of the legal system, but placement and closure are *legal* decisions, so children's adjustment is necessarily a reaction to the legal system, at least in part. For example, some researchers have compared children currently in foster care to children who have been reunified with their biological families. In general, these studies show that children who remain in foster care actually have better developmental outcomes, on average, than children who are reunified with their families (Kernan & Lansford, 2004). Taussig, Clyman, and Landsverk (2001) conducted a large-scale longitudinal study of foster children and found that those children who were reunified with their biological families had more behavioral problems, both internalizing and externalizing; lower school grades; and higher dropout rates than those children who remained in foster care.

As the studies described in the previous paragraph imply, the legal decision to reunify children with their biological parents might be detrimental to children's mental health largely because the parents have not fully addressed the problems and behaviors that led to the initial removal. As further support for this contention, a number of studies have found significant re-entry rates for children in the child protection system (e.g., Fluke, Shusterman, Hollinshead, & Yuan, 2008; Frame, Berrick, & Brodowski, 2000; Shaw, 2006). For example, Barth, Weigensberg, Fisher, Fetrow, and Green (2008) found that roughly 16% of the 273 children in their sample re-entered foster care within 36 months of reunification. Other studies have reported even higher rates. In their review of the literature, Kernan and Lansford (2004) concluded that most studies have reported re-entry rates between 20% and 30%. When reunification decisions are made prematurely, children are subjected not only to recurrent maltreatment but also to the stress of repeated changes in living situations brought on by court reintervention.

Importantly, many of these studies were conducted prior to full implementation of the Adoption and Safe Families Act (ASFA) in 1997. The passage of ASFA was intended to facilitate two major goals. The first goal was to move children more quickly through the system. ASFA imposed timelines requiring courts to begin making decisions about where a child should permanently live within 12 months after a child entered foster care and move toward termination of parental rights if the child has been in care for 15 of the previous 22 months. The second goal was to protect the wellbeing of children, which was codified by requiring that children's health and safety be paramount in child maltreatment decision making. If ASFA has been effective in its goals, then re-entry rates should have decreased.

Whether ASFA has brought positive changes for children's wellbeing is an empirical question. A number of studies have investigated the impact of ASFA on case progression and case decision making (Green, Rockhill, & Furrer, 2006; McWey, Henderson, & Tice, 2006; Noonan & Burke, 2005). Yet, surprisingly, no research has been published directly studying the impact of ASFA on child wellbeing. Researchers who have conducted their studies of the child welfare system after the passage of ASFA can make some inferences about what impact the federal legislation has had on children's outcomes, but such inferences are difficult to rely on given the likelihood that myriad other system-level changes have also happened since then.

Thus far, this section has discussed the impact of children's general involvement in the child protection system. Another important consideration is the potential impact of a narrower kind of involvement—involvement in the court process. In the last 10 years or so, many researchers have studied children's perceptions of their involvement in foster care (e.g., Johnson, Yoken, & Voss, 1995; Lee & Whiting, 2007; Leeson, 2007; Mitchell & Kuczynski, 2010). A smaller group of researchers have narrowed in on children's perceptions of their participation in the legal system, including its effects on their stress and wellbeing (Block, Oran, Oran, Baumrind, & Goodman, 2010; Quas, Wallin, Horwitz, Davis, & Lyon, 2009; Weisz, Wingrove, Beal, & Faith-Slaker, 2011; Weisz, Wingrove, & Faith-Slaker, 2007–2008). According to the American Bar Association Center on Children and the Law (2007), there has been an increase in children's participation, with many jurisdictions now either requiring or encouraging children's attendance at dependency hearings. Despite the increasing acceptance of children's participation in their hearings, there have been few studies that have examined the impact of participation.

On the whole, research tends to suggest that participation leads to more benefit than harm. For example, the authors of this chapter interviewed children who attended and did not attend their dependency review hearings to explore their perceptions of the process (Weisz et al., 2011). The authors found that children who attended their hearings had more positive attitudes about the process. For example, they indicated greater trust in the judge, greater perceptions of procedural fairness, and more comfort with their guardians ad litem and caseworkers. Consistent with these findings, Block et al. (2010) interviewed children immediately after they attended their child protection hearings and found that children reported, on average, neutral to positive attitudes about their court experience. However, importantly, children in this sample reported dissatisfaction with their level of participation. For example, in answers to qualitative questions, children reported feeling that they had not been heard.

Weisz et al. (2011) also measured self-reported emotions immediately before and after hearings. They found no evidence of high distress surrounding court attendance. This is consistent with Quas and colleagues (2009), who found that children's prehearing and posthearing ratings were generally positive. Specifically, on a 5-point scale from very negative (1) to very positive (5), all pre- and posthearing ratings averaged above 3. Block et al. (2010) measured children's posthearing anxiety and found that children's state anxiety was slightly elevated following their hearings.

Aside from the few studies described in the previous paragraphs, the majority of research exploring children's views on their involvement in the dependency process have been qualitative in nature (e.g., Johnson et al., 1995; Lee & Whiting, 2007; Leeson, 2007; McLeod, 2007; Mitchell & Kuczynski, 2010). In 2002, Cashmore reviewed the literature that existed at that time and concluded that children generally prefer to have some involvement in the legal process and feel that they do not have as much opportunity to do so as they would like. Research published since then is generally consistent with this summary (Davies & Wright, 2008). For example, Munro (2001) interviewed "looked after" children in the United Kingdom and found that one theme was children's perception that they did not have a voice at reviews. Similarly, Winter (2010) interviewed children between 4 and 7 years old about their experiences in care and identified "not being listened to" as a consistent theme.

The majority of this research exploring children's experiences in the child protection system has been conducted abroad; however, thus far, those few published studies using North American samples have found similar results. For example, Mitchell, Kuczynski, Tubbs, and Ross (2010) asked children to give advice to other children in the system, foster caregivers, and social workers. When asked to give advice to social workers, one consistent theme was that children wanted to be active participants in the process. Similarly, children expressed a strong desire to be kept informed about the details of their case, especially where placement changes were concerned.

In sum, the sparse existing literature suggests that children in the foster care system experience more stress than children not in the system, but that direct participation in the court system is not a particularly stressful experience. Moreover, children express desire to participate and to have a voice in decisions; they are disappointed when they do not feel listened to.

Parents' Perceptions of Their Involvement in a Dependency Context

It is not surprising that interactions with the legal system should also result in stress for parents. The very nature of parent involvement in dependency court is that a legal finding has been or is being made in which parents are evaluated and, in many cases, determined to have failed to adequately meet their responsibilities for childcare and protection as established by social expectation and subsequent law in a particular community (Garbarino & Kostelny, 1995). As parents' behaviors and abilities to provide for their children are being examined and questioned, parents begin forming perceptions and attitudes toward the legal system and those professionals involved in it.

Parents often report feeling judged by those in the legal system and viewed as "bad parents" (Hardy & Darlington, 2008), yet parents may not see themselves as bad parents. In a qualitative study of parental perceptions, Dale (2004) found that parents rejected labels commonly used in the legal arena (e.g., physical abuse, neglect) and instead expressed that there was *concern* for children's physical or emotional wellbeing. Parents perceived the terms *abuse* and *neglect* as inferring causality—that parents had willingly or intentionally brought harm or unsafe situations upon their children. This causal attribution was inconsistent with parents' self-perceptions of being equally helpless in the abuse or neglect situation, unable to prevent the events that led to court involvement because of their own vulnerabilities.

Dale (2004) asked parents how helpful they thought legal intervention involving the child protection service was. Approximately 28% of parents reported that services did not help or made things worse. However, half of parents reported that intervention was helpful to some extent or very helpful, suggesting that many parents hold some positive perceptions of the child protection system as a whole. Based on results from a study conducted by Hardy and Darlington (2008), several factors appear to relate to positive perceptions of the child protection system. First, parents appreciated working with professionals (attorneys, caseworkers, etc.) who were available and would follow through with what they said they would do. Second, parents wanted to be involved in the process and the decisions being made about their families and desired acknowledgment for their role as parents in the case. Hardy and Darlington also found that partnership relationship styles between professionals and parents were perceived more positively by parents than the adversarial relationship experienced in some instances. It is possible that these more positive experiences, in which parents are involved and feel like they are listened to, results in achievement of positive outcomes and goals (Hardy & Darlington, 2008).

In another small qualitative study of parental perceptions, Dumbrill (2006) asked parents about their relationships with legal actors (caseworkers, attorneys, etc.). Parents reported feeling that legal professionals either had "power over" them or "power with" them. Parents who perceived legal actors as having power over them tended to view the court system as a means by which the parent could challenge those individuals, when the opportunity presented itself. However, in cases where parents felt they were working "with" legal actors, they tended to describe a team effort in fighting against the court or against the bureaucracy of the legal system. In that same study, Dumbrill categorized parent responses to the legal system using three classifications: parents who fought the system, challenging caseworkers and attorneys in court and refusing compliance; parents who played the game, pretending to cooperate in order to meet the minimum requirements to get their children back; and parents who were genuinely cooperative. Few parents in Dumbrill's study were classified as fighting the system—the vast majority of parents discussed either "playing along" or "working with" the system.

Parental Stress in a Dependency Court Context

It is likely the case that parental stress during involvement with the dependency legal system is unavoidable, as parents face the real possibility of temporarily or permanently losing the custody of their children. Parents are evaluated and required to do things they otherwise would not do as a result of their involvement in the legal system (Hardy & Darlington, 2008), which likely results in anxiety for parents. It is difficult to separate what stress results from the legal system itself versus other factors that led to parental involvement, and little research has been conducted that separates stressors in these distinct but related domains (Waterhouse & McGhee, 2009). In this section, we will review some research that provides preliminary insight about the legal system as a stressor for parents.

In part, parental stress stems from parents' awareness that the court system is evaluating them and will be making decisions about their competence as parents and, ultimately, the future of their families. For many parents, the outcome of their case is uncertain, which contributes to the stress and anxiety parents are experiencing (Waterhouse & McGhee, 2009). Many parents report feeling disenfranchised from the courts and perceive themselves as being punished by the court rather than being a partner in the process (Bass, Shields, & Behrman, 2004).

Early interactions with the court (i.e., first appearance hearings, prehearing conferences) are also a source of increased stress for parents. Parents report that they remember these events more vividly than any other experience they had while involved in the system (Dale, 2004). Parents mentioned feeling defensive, confused about the process and the language being used, and that no one took the time to explain things to them. Parents also reported feelings of shame and embarrassment and did not understand why there were so many "strangers" involved in their case. Even the formal architecture of courthouses and juvenile courtrooms may be intimidating and anxiety producing for some parents (Goltsman, 1992).

The experience of mothers in the legal system may be especially stressful. A small qualitative study suggests that stereotypes about mothering—in which mothers are expected to be all-knowing, sacrificing, and nurturing toward their children (Epstein, 1999)—can result in mothers being held to a higher standard in parenting than fathers; it also can result in mothers perceiving that they are being harshly judged. A small study of battered mothers' perceptions indicate that many mothers feel as though the court places more requirements on them than on the fathers (Johnson & Sullivan, 2008).

Research on the Experiences of Foster, Adoptive, and Other Caregivers

Involvement in the legal context also results in stress for child caregivers, whether that be foster and relative caregivers or adoptive parents. Like the experiences of biological parents, it is somewhat difficult to separate the stress stemming from the legal system and stress resulting from the other factors associated with being a primary caregiver. Further, while there are some similarities in the experiences of these caregivers, not all findings generalize across foster, relative, and adoptive caregiver scenarios. For example, nonrelative foster caregivers may benefit from positive stereotypes about their altruism.

With regard to foster caregivers, there is evidence to suggest that the legal system is an independent source of stress. These individuals often report experiencing a lack of support from the legal system (Bass et al., 2004; Chipungu & Bent-Goodley, 2004). In interviews with foster caregivers, Chipungu and Bent-Goodley reported that caregivers experienced a lack of validation, both in the context of positive feedback and understanding of negative experiences, and minimal involvement in the decisions made for children in their care, especially in the legal setting. In another study of foster caregiver perceptions and stress, participants reported feeling devalued by professionals, which added to the stress they were already experiencing related to issues of care provision, finances, and retention in care (Bass et al., 2004). Thus, it appears that for foster caregivers, a lack of involvement with and acknowledgment by the legal process is a source of stress. This stress likely impacts more than just the primary caregivers; foster caregivers report that they perceive formal support from and involvement in the legal system as a key element in successful placements (Brown, 2008).

In the past several years, new federal law (Orderly and Timely Interstate Placement of Foster Children Act of 2004) as well as new laws in many states have required that courts give foster caregivers notice of hearings and an opportunity to "be heard" in court. Nebraska, for example, now requires that courts provide notice of hearings and make an information form available to foster caregivers that can be completed and returned to the court. The form provides foster caregivers an opportunity to provide detailed information about the children in their care, including information about the child's health, mental health, education, relationships, activities, service needs, and so forth (Nebraska Revised Statutes, 2007). The rationale for these federal and state laws has been to provide foster caregivers a more active role in the legal case in response to the advocacy of foster caregiver organizations for such an increased role. Whether these statutory changes have reduced the negative experiences that foster caregivers reported in earlier research has not been evaluated yet, but would be an important area of further research.

Recent federal law and policies have encouraged and/or required state child welfare agencies to increase the use of relatives as care providers to children who must be removed from their parents' care (Fostering Connections to Success and Increasing Adoptions Act, 2008). Importantly, relative or kinship care does not require a biological relationship in all states; for example, in Ohio, a kinship placement is placement with anyone in a significant relationship with the child, including teachers or neighbors (Ohio Department of Job and Family Services, 2011). Placement with relatives, as compared to foster care with previously unknown caregivers, appears to be related to more positive outcomes for children, although there are some mixed findings (Farmer, 2009; Metzger, 2008; Ryan, Hong, Herz, & Hernandez, 2010; Winokur, Crawford, Longobardi, & Valentine 2008). Relative caregivers tend to be older, be more economically disadvantaged, be lone caregivers, have more health problems, and live in more overcrowded conditions than nonrelatives (Bass et al., 2004; Farmer, 2009). These caregivers also tend to persist in providing care to more difficult children and for longer (Farmer & Moyers, 2008). Despite the relatively higher needs of relatives, they generally receive less assistance and fewer services than nonrelatives (Bass et al., 2004). When compared to nonrelative caregivers, relatives also tend to have an already established relationship with the child, which enables them to provide more information to professionals about the child or situation and can result in increased involvement in the legal process (Bass et al., 2004). Relatives typically have more legal rights than nonrelatives, especially when they have a biological connection to the child. So while relative caregivers may have more social support and perceive their involvement in the system more positively than nonrelative caregivers, it is likely that they may be experiencing significant stress. They may also be reluctant to ask for what they need because they may feel that they should be able to provide care for their grandchild, niece, or nephew without outside assistance.

A third group of caregivers that experience stress stemming from the legal system is that of adoptive parents. During the adoption process, adoptive parents experience increased levels of stress and anxiety more generally (Brodzinsky, Lang, & Smith, 1995; McKay, Ross, & Goldberg, 2010). While sources of stress are not all directly tied to the legal context, the system itself may add to stress experienced by adoptive parents. Uncertainty surrounding the legal process and timelines to adoption appears to be related to increased stress and anxiety of adoptive parents and also depletes the parents' ability to prepare and plan for an event (i.e., the start of a family) when it is not clear when that event will occur (Brodzinsky et al., 1995). Two other legal requirements for adoption have also been identified as sources of stress by adoptive parents. The "home study," which is often required as part of the adoption process, is meant to evaluate, train, and empower adoptive parents. However, parents themselves often report feeling anxious, that the process was overly invasive and taxing, and a lack of overall satisfaction with the experience. In contrast to research with adoptive parents, the foster caregiver literature does not mention stress related to the home study process. It is possible that the different stakes of the home study for foster caregivers and adoptive parents contribute to a different experience with the process—even if the process is similar and not inherently stressful. Potential foster caregivers may fear disappointment that they will not be able to foster unknown children. In contrast, potential adoptive parents may fear losing a child they love and have cared for and whom they already view as their child. The significance of concerns about the decision for the home study is supported by findings that adoptive parents often report the probationary period between them receiving their child and the finalization of the adoption as the most stressful experience in the legal process of adoption. During this time, parents are bonding with their child, adapting to being parents of a child they are unfamiliar with, and simultaneously fearful that they may lose the child if the adoption is not finalized (McKay et al., 2010). While some of these legal stressors may be unavoidable, support services and interventions may help to minimize stress and enhance wellbeing. Identifying sources of stress and factors that promote adjustment and coping in adoptive parents is a much-needed area of future research.

Perceptions of Caseworkers and Legal Personnel in the Dependency System

While caseworkers, attorneys, and judges are often seen as sources of stress by parents and others involved in dependency court, there are aspects of the legal process that result in stressful experiences for legal personnel as well. In many ways, it is easier in this context to distinguish stress as a result of the legal process from other stressors than it was for other populations. As a result, more research has been conducted with caseworkers and attorneys, and to a lesser extent judges, than with other adult populations involved in the dependency court context.

One source of stress for legal actors is that of policy or federal regulations. While these laws and guidelines are meant to clarify processes and expectations and promote the best interests of children, they can also lead to confusion and anxiety for professionals in the system. The Human Rights Act (UK Parliament, 1998) and ASFA (1997) offer two examples of changes in policy that have been examined by researchers. The Human Rights Act incorporated the rights enumerated in the European Convention on Human Rights into British law, including core rights in child welfare contexts. The ASFA clarified earlier child welfare federal law and established various requirements regarding timeliness of different events and specific requirements in legal findings.

The Human Rights Act stipulates rights to private and family life and mutually enjoyable parent–child relationships as fundamental to family life (Munro & Ward, 2008). These stipulations have resulted in additional scrutiny in cases where children were removed from biological parents, and requirements for evidence to demonstrate that the wellbeing of a family member can only be protected through separation from one or more family members. Further, the act stipulates that delay in legal processing is prejudicial to child welfare.

Munro and Ward (2008) found that since the Human Rights Act, there has been an increase in the number of proceedings without a corresponding increase in the number of judges on the bench or judges' working hours. As legal requirements and best practice recommendations encourage more frequent hearings that may also last longer, judges report struggling to have docket time available to meet the demands (Beckett, McKeigue, & Taylor, 2007), and many courts have not increased the number of judges on the bench to match new recommendations and requirements. These stressors impact judges directly but likely have indirect effects on other legal actors, and on parents and children, as judges cope with the increasing demands and time constraints of new policy requirements. (See chapter 12 in this volume for more information about judge stress).

The Human Rights Act has also resulted in judges being concerned about whether there is enough evidence to suggest that reunification is not a possibility (Munro & Ward, 2008). This has resulted in increased reliance on evaluations and orders for multiple evaluations and assessments within a case, which places increased demand on expert witnesses and professionals and contributes to delays in the case. As cases are staying in the system longer, children are also experiencing less stability in their foster placements, and there has been a reduction in the pool of adoptive parents, especially with minority ethnic and multiple-sibling adoptions.

In their evaluation of ASFA, Humphrey, Turnbull, and Turnbull (2006) interviewed caseworkers, judges, attorneys, and families as part of a qualitative study. Participants from multiple groups reported that ASFA shortened the amount of time families had to address problems with children outside the home, that termination of parental rights was more frequent, and that reasonable efforts had become a more central part of proceedings and decision-making processes. Participants had mixed feelings about the impact of shortened timeframes, with some perceiving it as positive (i.e., families were reunified faster, fewer out-of-home placements) and others viewing it negatively (i.e., not giving parents enough time to correct issues, judges feeling forced into making decisions earlier than they would like). Judges also reported that they felt ASFA pushed them toward termination of parental rights, with mixed feelings about whether that had a positive or negative impact on child outcomes. Finally, there were mixed feelings about the impact of ASFA on reasonable efforts and family services, with some participants perceiving the act as preventing unnecessary removals and providing in-home services, others feeling ASFA decreases services to families, and a third group stating that ASFA had no meaningful impact on family services. These studies suggest that policy changes have an impact on legal actors and their perceptions of the process and the role they play in it.

Caseworkers and attorneys approach dependency cases from very different perspectives, which also contributes to tension and stress in this context. Caseworkers perceive the legal process as requiring an unnecessarily high level of evidence to demonstrate danger for children, resulting in children being harmed rather than being protected by earlier interventions (Beckett et al., 2007). In one study of caseworkers' perceptions of the court system, participants reported that the need for a specific event to catapult families into the legal context may result in a delay of legal intervention for chronic abuse cases (Beckett et al., 2007). Similarly, attorneys have reported experiencing stress and frustration as a result of caseworkers making claims without strong evidence to support them (Dickens, 2007).

Requirements for legal evidence are also a source of stress for caseworkers, especially within the context of a proceeding, where there are often competing goals of minimal length of time in care and resolution of the problems that led to court involvement, which can take some time (Beckett et al., 2007). Beckett and colleagues reported that caseworkers expressed concerns about the number of evaluations being conducted, suggesting that they may result in unnecessary delays to case proceedings and simultaneously not be informative. These individuals also felt that their own evaluations and experiences with families were devalued by the court system, and that judges and attorneys would prefer to rely on "artificial" observations made by professional counselors and expert witnesses. This left caseworkers feeling disrespected and, in many ways, unfairly treated by other legal professionals (Dickens, 2007); simultaneously, caseworkers report low confidence in their knowledge and ability to apply legal rules to their decisions about the cases they work with (Braye, Preston-Shoot, & Wigley, 2011). Interestingly, attorneys in another study expressed concern that change in family circumstances or behavior may influence the decision judges made, and therefore they valued the evidence provided by experts and multiple evaluations throughout the life of the case (Dickens, 2007). Attorneys in that study also reported frustration with caseworkers about their lack of preparedness in the courtroom, feeling that the lack of understanding of the legal process led to confusion and poor evidence and testimony.

Surprisingly, caseworkers do not seem to worry about whether removing children from the home was a mistake (Beckett et al., 2007), despite the stressors associated with removal and foster care experiences for children (see previous section for that discussion). However, caseworkers (Taylor, Beckett, & McKeigue, 2008) and attorneys (Dickens, 2007) did report stress related to a lack of or failed social or legal intervention, expressing concern that something may happen to children they may have failed to protect and that they may be held responsible for those incidents (Taylor et al., 2008). Families were also a source of stress for attorneys, who expressed frustration when parents were cooperating enough to be making progress but not as quickly as attorneys thought they could, leading to additional delays in the case (Dickens, 2007).

Dickens (2006) summarizes perspectives that suggest some of the conflict between attorneys and caseworkers derives from differences in their views of the purpose of legal intervention in the abuse and neglect context. This summary suggests that attorneys, who focus primarily on the law and individual rights, see themselves as a mechanism by which civil liberties are protected and aim to ensure rights are respected and intervention is warranted. Social workers, on the other hand, seek to meet the needs of the whole: protecting children while gaining consensus, unity, and growth for the family involved. In his study of caseworker and attorney differences, Dickens (2006) asked caseworkers and attorneys to provide their perspectives on each other. Caseworkers reported that they respect attorneys' value of the legal process and can appreciate their use of logic rather than emotion in legal proceedings. They also reported that they appreciated it when attorneys were supportive of them and communicated value, and that attorney feedback on their testimony and court reports could be very valuable. Caseworkers reported that they respected attorneys who were strong advocates in court and sensitive to the needs of children and parents. Attorneys reported that they appreciated it when caseworkers kept them informed of events and that they respected caseworkers' competing demands and sensitivity to family needs.

In sum, judges, attorneys, and social workers in the dependency system work in extremely difficult family circumstances, with high-stakes outcomes (child safety, family integrity), demanding legal requirements, and potential conflicts between their respective professional roles. All these factors contribute to stress.

Conclusions and Future Research

When it comes to understanding the impact of the legal system on children in divorce and dependency cases, the large questions remain poorly answered. First, what is the nature of children's involvement to begin with? We know that many children will experience their parents' divorce during their childhood and that there is a smaller but still significantly sized group of children who will come into the child welfare system each year. While the fates of these children are always under the jurisdiction of the legal system, we do not know how many of these children have direct contact with the legal process itself and what the nature of the contact is. How many testify in contested cases, participate in mediation programs, or are informally brought into the process through family conversations? There is preliminary evidence that participation in the legal process is not harmful to children and may provide some benefits, that children appear to experience less stress when they are armed with more knowledge about the process, and that children desire to have their perspective heard by decision makers (Quas et al., 2009, Weisz et al., 2011).

Similarly, the research on parent perspectives on their involvement in the legal system suggests more questions than answers but also indicates that, like children, parents (including other types of caregivers) desire to have their voice heard by the court and experience negative feelings when they perceive that is not happening (Bass et al., 2004).

There is a need for considerably more research that can be more specific about child, parent, and legal process characteristics that are optimal for the wellbeing of the involved individuals. As much of the research on child and parent involvement has been qualitative in nature, the field would benefit from increased methodological rigor, including adoption of standardized research instruments. Further, a more firm grounding in psychological theory, such as procedural justice theories (e.g., Tyler & Blader, 2003) and moral reasoning theories (e.g., Cohn, Bucolo, Rebellon, & Gundy, 2010), would advance our understanding of parents' and children's reactions to participation in the legal system.

This chapter and this book focus on stress associated with legal involvement, and there may be an inherent assumption that stress should be reduced. Parents and children involved in the divorce or dependency court system are in extremely difficult situations, and their greatest concern may not be to have a low-stress legal experience, but rather the best legal outcome for their situation. In a recent study by the authors of this chapter that examined the impact on foster children of their direct participation in their court hearings, a young adolescent girl cried during and after the hearing upon hearing of her mother's failures in drug treatment (Weisz et al., 2011). She reported that she experienced considerable anxiety during the hearing. Nonetheless, in the follow-up interview 10 days later, she reported that she was very glad that she better understood the reality of her situation and that she very much wanted to know what was going on in the hearings, even if it was upsetting at the time to hear disappointing information. This girl experienced a "high stress" court experience, but it was her preference to be there even if it was stressful.

Perhaps the goals of interventions for participants in divorce and dependency cases should be to reduce court processes that unnecessarily increase the stress of people who come before them, to prepare participants for the legal process with information and resources, and to increase the sensitivity of legal actors to the stress that participants are unavoidably experiencing. Most important, legal systems can provide all participants an opportunity to provide their perspectives to the decision maker so that they feel that the stress they might experience is for a reason.

References

Adoption and Safe Families Act, P.L. 105–189 (1997).

Ahrons, C., & Marquardt, E. (2010). Does divorce have positive long-term effects for the children involved? In B. Slife (Ed.), *Clashing views on psychological issues* (16th ed., pp. 134–154). New York, NY: McGraw-Hill.

Amato, P. R. (2006). Marital discord, divorce, and children's well-being: Results from a 20-year longitudinal study of two generations. In A. Clarke-Stewart & J. Dunn (Eds.), *Families count: Effects on child and adolescent development* (pp. 179–202). New York, NY: Cambridge University Press.

Amato, P. R. (2007). Life-span adjustment of children to their parents' divorce. In S. J. Ferguson (Ed.), *Shifting the center: Understanding contemporary families* (3rd ed., pp. 567–588). New York, NY: McGraw-Hill.

Amato, P. R. (2010). Research on divorce: Continuing trends and new developments. *Journal of Marriage and Family, 72*(3), 650–666. doi:10.1111/j.1741-3737.2010.00723.x

American Bar Association. (2011). *ABA family legal guide: Family law: Divorce.* Retrieved from http://public.findlaw.com/abaflg/flg-3–4c-2.html

American Bar Association Center on Children and the Law. (2009). *State-by-State summary of youth involvement in court.* Washington, DC: Author. Retrieved from https://docs.google.com/viewer?a=v&q=cache:AqJKP4po7_8J:www.americanbar.org/content/dam/aba/migrated/child/PublicDocuments/youth_in_court_state_chart_6_26_09.authcheckdam.doc+&hl=en&gl=us&pid=bl&srcid=ADGEEShz91qXlsV-fCslkZGCa2AJl12SAjR_nEzOBxCIR-99qIwAt8iSNqG5_6XkfR_FfmPXxTN--5ZaSumy5qM8-gRt1tip2Pn7z8EY1QXKCNQh7LyE65BUthpfznfZ0jjm4Xxo_Vfc&sig=AHIEtbQHU4xzOnLTaMATgMHZYuInwXp5FQ

American Psychological Association. (2010). Guidelines for child custody evaluations in family law proceedings. *American Psychologist, 65*(9), 863–867. doi:10.1037/a0021250

Barczak, B., Miller, T. W., Veltkamp, L. J., Barczak, S., Hall, C., & Kraus, R. (2010). Transitioning the impact of divorce on children throughout the life cycle. In T. W. Miller (Ed.), *Handbook of stressful transitions across the lifespan* (pp. 185–215). New York, NY: Springer Science + Business Media. doi:10.1007/978-1-4419-0748-6_10

Barth, R. P., Weigensberg, E. C., Fisher, P. A., Fetrow, B., & Green, R. L. (2008). Reentry of elementary aged children following reunification from foster care. *Children and Youth Services Review, 30*(4), 353–364. doi:10.1016/j.childyouth.2007.10.002

Bass, S., Shields, M., & Behrman, R. (2004). Children, families, and foster care: Analysis and recommendations. *Future of Children, 14*(1), 5–29. doi:10.2307/1602752.

Beck, C. J. A., & Sales, B. D. (2001). *Family mediation: Facts, myths, and future prospects.* Washington, DC: American Psychological Association.

Beckett, C., McKeigue, B., & Taylor, H. (2007). Coming to conclusions: Social workers' perceptions of the decision-making process in care proceedings. *Child and Family Social Work, 12*(1), 54–63. doi:10.1111/j.1365-2206.2006.00437.x

Block, S. D., Oran, H., Oran, D., Baumrind, N., & Goodman, G. S. (2010). Abused and neglected children in court: Knowledge and attitudes. *Child Abuse and Neglect, 34*(9), 659–670. doi:10.1016/j.chiabu.2010.02.003

Braver, S. L., Cookston, J. T., & Cohen, B. R. (2002). Experiences of family law attorneys with current issues in divorce practice. *Family Relations, 51*(4), 325–334. doi:10.1111/j/1741-3729.2002.00325.x

Braye, S., Preston-Shoot, M., & Wigley, V. (2012). Deciding to use the law in social work practice. *Journal of Social Work.* doi:10.1177/1468017311431476

Brodzinsky, D. M., Lang, R., & Smith, D. W. (1995). Parenting adopted children. In M. H. Bornstein (Ed.), *Handbook of parenting, Vol. 3: Status and social conditions of parenting* (pp. 209–232). Hillsdale, NJ: Lawrence Erlbaum Associates.

Brown, J. D. (2008). Foster parents' perceptions of factors needed for successful foster placements. *Journal of Child and Family Studies, 17,* 538–554.

Cashmore, J. (2002). Promoting the participation of children and young people in care. *Child Abuse and Neglect, 26*(8), 837–847. doi:10.1016/S0145-2134(02)00353-8

Cashmore, J., & Parkinson, P. (2008). Children's and parents' perceptions on children's participation in decision making after parental separation and divorce. *Family Court Review, 46*(1), 91–104.

Cherlin, A. J., Chase-Lansdale, P., & McRae, C. (1998). Effects of parental divorce on mental health throughout the life course. *American Sociological Review, 63*(2), 239–249. doi:10.2307/2657325

Chipungu, S., & Bent-Goodley, T. (2004). Meeting the challenges of contemporary foster care. *Future of Children, 14*(1), 75–93. doi:10.2307/1602755

Clarke-Stewart, A., & Brentano, C. (2006). *Divorce: Causes and consequences.* New Haven, CT: Yale University Press.

Cohn, E. S., Bucolo, D., Rebellon, C. J., & Gundy, K. (2010). An integrated model of legal and moral reasoning and rule-violating behavior: The role of legal attitudes. *Law and Human Behavior, 34*(4), 295–309. doi:10.1007/s10979-009-9185-9

Court Improvement Project. Omnibus Budget Reconciliation Act of 1993 (P.L. 103–66).

Crosby-Currie, C. A. (1996). Children's involvement in contested custody cases: Practices and experiences of legal and mental health professionals. *Law and Human Behavior, 20*(3), 289–311. doi:10.1007/BF01499025

Dale, P. (2004). "Like a fish in a bowl": Parents' perceptions of child protection services. *Child Abuse Review, 13*(2), 137–157.

Davies, J., & Wright, J. (2008). Children's voices: A review of the literature pertinent to looked-after children's views of mental health services. *Child and Adolescent Mental Health, 13*(1), 26–31. doi:10.1111/j.1475-3588.2007.00458.x

DeGarmo, D. S., & Forgatch, M. S. (1999). Contexts as predictors of changing maternal parenting practices in diverse family structures: A social interactional perspective of risk and resilience. In E. Hetherington (Ed.), *Coping with divorce, single parenting, and remarriage: A risk and resiliency perspective* (pp. 227–252). Mahwah, NJ: Lawrence Erlbaum Associates Publishers.

Dickens, J. (2006). Care, control and change in child care proceedings: Dilemmas for social workers, managers and lawyers. *Child and Family Social Work, 11*(1), 23–32. doi:10.1111/j.1365-2206.2006.00386.x

Dickens, J. (2007). Child neglect and the law: Catapults, thresholds and delay. *Child Abuse Review, 16*(2), 77–92. doi:10.1002/car.975

Dumbrill, G. C. (2006). Parental experience of child protection intervention: A qualitative study. *Child Abuse and Neglect, 30*(1), 27–37. doi:10.1016/j.chiabu.2005.08.012

Emery, R. E., Matthews, S. G., & Wyer, M. M. (1991). Child custody mediation and litigation: Further evidence of the differing views of mothers and fathers. *Journal of Consulting and Clinical Psychology, 59*(3), 410–418.

Emery, R. E., Otto, R. K., & O'Donohue, W. T. (2005). A critical assessment of child custody evaluations: Limited science and a flawed system. *Psychological Science in the Public Interest, 6*(1), 1–29. doi:10.1111/j.1529-1006.2005.00020.x

Emery, R. E., Sbarra, D., & Grover, T. (2005). Divorce mediation: Research and reflections. *Family Court Review, 43*(1), 22–37. doi:10.111/j.1744-1617.2005.00005.x

Emery, R. E., & Wyer, M. M. (1987). Child custody mediation and litigation: An experimental evaluation of the experience of parents. *Journal of Consulting and Clinical Psychology, 50,* 179–186.

Epstein, D. (1999). Effective intervention in domestic violence cases: Rethinking the role of prosecutors, judges, and the court system. *Yale Law Journal, 11,* 3–39.

Farmer, E. (2009). How do placements in kinship care compare with those in non-kin foster care: Placement patterns, progress and outcomes? *Child and Family Social Work, 14,* 331–342.

Farmer, E., & Moyers, S. (2008). *Kinship care: Fostering effective family and friends placement.* Philadelphia, PA: Jessica Kingsley Publishers.

Fischer, T. (2007). Parental divorce and children's socio-economic success: Conditional effects of parental resources prior to divorce, and gender of the child. *Sociology, 41*(3), 475–495. doi:10.1177/0038038507076618

Fluke, J. D., Shusterman, G. R., Hollinshead, D. M., & Yuan, Y. T. (2008). Longitudinal analysis of repeated child abuse reporting and victimization: Multistate analysis of associated factors. *Child Maltreatment, 13*(1), 76–88. doi:10.1177/1077559507311517

Fostering Connections to Success and Increasing Adoptions Act, 42 U.S.C. §§ 621 *et seq.* (2008).

Frame, L., Berrick, J., & Brodowski, M. (2000). Understanding reentry to out-of-home care for reunified infants. *Child Welfare: Journal of Policy, Practice, and Program, 79*(4), 339–369.

Garbarino, J., & Kostelny, K. (1995). Parenting and public policy. In M. H. Bornstein (Ed.), *Handbook of parenting, Vol. 3: Status and social conditions of parenting* (pp. 419–436). Hillsdale, NJ: Lawrence Erlbaum Associates.

Garwood, F. (1989–1990). Involving children in conciliation. *Children and Society, 3,* 311–324.

Glover, R. L., & Glenwick, D. S. (2009). Stressful life events experienced by clinically referred foster care and nonfoster care children. *Journal of Early Childhood and Infant Psychology, 5,* 5127–5140.

Goltsman, S. (1992). Recognizing children and families in the design of a children's court. *Children's Environments, 9*(1), 72–76.

Green, B. L., Rockhill, A., & Furrer, C. (2006). Understanding patterns of substance abuse treatment for women involved with child welfare: The influence of the Adoption and Safe Families Act (ASFA). *American Journal of Drug and Alcohol Abuse, 32*(2), 149–176. doi:10.1080/00952990500479282

Hardy, F., & Darlington, Y. (2008). What parents value from formal support services in the context of identified child abuse. *Child and Family Social Work, 13*(3), 252–261. doi:10.1111/j.1365-2206.2008.00545.x

Hetherington, E. M., & Kelly, J. (2002). *For better or for worse: Divorce reconsidered.* New York, NY: W. W. Norton.

Hetherington, E. M., & Stanley-Hagan, M. (2002). Parenting in divorced and remarried families. In M. H. Bornstein (Ed.), *Handbook of parenting: Vol. 3: Being and becoming a parent* (2nd ed., pp. 287–315). Mahwah, NJ: Lawrence Erlbaum Associates Publishers.

Humphrey, K., Turnbull, A., & Turnbull, H. (2006). Impact of the Adoption and Safe Families Act on youth and their families: Perspectives of foster care providers, youth with emotional disorders, service providers, and judges. *Children and Youth Services Review, 28*(2), 113–132. doi:10.1016/j.childyouth.2005.02.011

Jackson, B. L., & Donovan, R. L. (1990). Psychological assessment in contested child custody cases. *TACD Journal, 18*(1), 47–54.

James, A. L., & James, A. (1999). Pump up the volume: Listening to children in separation and divorce. *Childhood: A Global Journal of Child Research, 6*(2), 189–206. doi:10.1177/0907568299006002003

Jee, S. H., Conn, A., Szilagyi, P. G., Blumkin, A., Baldwin, C. D., & Szilagyi, M. A. (2010). Identification of social-emotional problems among young children in foster care. *Journal of Child Psychology and Psychiatry, 51*(12), 1351–1358. doi:10.1111/j.1469-7610.2010.02315.x

Johnson, D. R., & Wu, J. (2002). An empirical test of crisis, social selection, and role explanations of the relationship between marital disruption and psychological distress: A pooled time-series analysis of four-wave panel data. *Journal of Marriage and Family, 64*(1), 211–224. doi:10.1111/j.1741-3737.2002.00211.x

Johnson, P., Yoken, C., & Voss, R. (1995). Family foster care placement: The child's perspective. *Child Welfare: Journal of Policy, Practice, and Program, 74*(5), 959–974.

Johnson, S. P., & Sullivan, C. M. (2008). How child protection workers support or further victimize battered mothers. *Affilia: Journal of Women and Social Work, 23*(3), 242–258. doi:10.1177/0886109908319113

Kaltenborn, K. (2001a). Children's and young people's experiences in various residential arrangements: A longitudinal study to evaluate criteria for custody and residence decision making. *British Journal of Social Work, 31*(1), 81–117. doi:10.1093/bjsw/31.1.81

Kaltenborn, K. (2001b). Individualization, family transitions and children's agency. *Childhood: A Global Journal of Child Research, 8*(4), 463–498. doi:10.1177/0907568201008004004

Kaltenborn, K. (2005). Parent-child contact after divorce: The need to consider the child's perspective. In G. W. Peterson, S. K. Steinmetz, & S. M. Wilson (Eds.), *Parent-youth relations: Cultural and cross-cultural perspectives* (pp. 239–260). New York, NY: Haworth Press.

Kernan, E., & Lansford, J. E. (2004). Providing for the best interests of the child?: The Adoption and Safe Families Act of 1997. *Journal of Applied Developmental Psychology, 25*(5), 523–539. doi:10.1016/j.appdev.2004.08.003

Kurki-Suonio, K. (2000). Joint custody as an interpretation of the best interests of the child in critical and comparative perspective. *International Journal of Law, Policy and the Family, 14*, 183–205.

Lee, R., & Whiting, J. (2007). Foster children's expressions of ambiguous loss. *American Journal of Family Therapy, 35*(5), 417–428.

Leeson, C. (2007). My life in care: Experiences of non-participation in decision-making processes. *Child and Family Social Work, 12*(3), 268–277. doi:10.1111/j.1365-2206.2007.00499.x

Leite, R., & Clark, K. (2007). Participants' evaluations of aspects of the legal child custody process and preferences for court services. *Family Court Review, 45*(2), 260–273. doi:10.111/j/1744-1617.2007.00142.x

Lorenz, F. O., Simons, R. L., Conger, R. D., Elder, G. H., Johnson, C., & Chao, W. (1997). Married and recently divorced mothers' stressful events and distress: Tracing change across time. *Journal of Marriage and Family, 59*(1), 219–232. doi:10.2307/353674

Martindale, D. A., Martin, L., Austin, W. G., Drozd, L., Gould-Saltman, D., Kirkpatrick, H. D., et al. (2007). Model standards of practice for child custody evaluation. *Family Court Review, 45*(1), 70–91. doi:10.1111/j.1744-1617.2007.129_3.x

McKay, K., Ross, L. R., & Goldberg, A. E. (2010). Adaptation to parenthood during the post-adoption period: A review of the literature. *Adoption Quarterly, 13,* 125–144. doi:10.1080/10926755.2010.481040

McLeod, A. (2007). Whose agenda? Issues of power and relationship when listening to looked-after young people. *Child and Family Social Work, 12*(3), 278–286. doi:10.1111/j.1365-2206.2007.00493.x

McWey, L. M., Henderson, T. L., & Tice, S. N. (2006). Mental health issues and the foster care system: An examination of the impact of the Adoption and Safe Families Act. *Journal of Marital and Family Therapy, 32*(2), 195–214. doi:10.1111/j.1752-0606.2006.tb01600.x

Metzger, J. (2008). Resiliency in children and youth in kinship care and family foster care. *Child Welfare, 87,* 115–140.

Mitchell, M. B., & Kuczynski, L. (2010). Does anyone know what is going on? Examining children's lived experience of the transition into foster care. *Children and Youth Services Review, 32*(3), 437–444. doi:10.1016/j.childyouth.2009.10.023

Mitchell, M. B., Kuczynski, L., Tubbs, C. Y., & Ross, C. (2010). We care about care: Advice by children in care for children in care, foster parents and child welfare workers about the transition into foster care. *Child and Family Social Work, 15*(2), 176–185.

Munro, E. (2001). Empowering looked-after children. *Child and Family Social Work, 6*(2), 129–137. doi:10.1046/j.1365-2206.2001.00192.x

Munro, E. R., & Ward, H. (2008). Balancing parents' and very young children's rights in care proceedings: Decision-making in the context of the Human Rights Act 1998. *Child and Family Social Work, 13*(2), 227–234. doi:10.1111/j.1365-2206.2007.00542.x

Nebraska Revised Statutes, Caregiver Information Form 43-1314.02 (2007).

Noonan, K., & Burke, K. (2005). Termination of parental rights: Which foster care children are affected? *Social Science Journal, 42*(2), 241–256. doi:10.1016/j.soscij.2005.03.012

Ohio Department of Job and Family Services. (2011). *Ohio resource guide for relatives caring for children.* http://www.odjfs.state.oh.us/forms/file.asp?id=1779&type=application/pdf

Orderly and Timely Interstate Placement of Foster Children Act of 2004, 42 USC § 675 (5)(G).

Pears, K. C., Fisher, P. A., Bruce, J., Kim, H. K., & Yoerger, K. (2010). Early elementary school adjustment of maltreated children in foster care: The roles of inhibitory control and caregiver involvement. *Child Development, 81*(5), 1550–1564. doi:10.1111/j.1467-8624.2010.01491.x

Powell, M. B., & Lancaster, S. (2003). Guidelines for interviewing children during child custody evaluations. *Australian Psychologist, 38*(1), 46–54. doi:10.1080/00050060310001707017

Pruett, M., & Barker, R. (2009). Children of divorce: New trends and ongoing dilemmas. In J. H. Bray & M. Stanton (Eds.), *The Wiley-Blackwell handbook of family psychology* (pp. 463–474). Wiley-Blackwell. doi:10.1002/9781444310238.ch31. Oxford, UK.

Pruett, M. K., Insabella, G. M., & Gustafson, K. (2005). THE COLLABORATIVE DIVORCE PROJECT: A court-based intervention for separating parents with young children. *Family Court Review, 43,* 38–51. doi:10.1111/j.1744-1617.2005.00006.x

Pruett, M. K., & Jackson, T. D. (2001). Perspectives on the divorce process: Parental perceptions of the legal system and its impact on family relations. *Journal of the American Academy of Psychiatry and the Law, 29*(1), 18–28.

Quas, J., Wallin, A., Horwitz, B., Davis, E., & Lyon, T. (2009). Maltreated children's understanding of and emotional reactions to dependency court involvement. *Behavioral Sciences and the Law, 27*(1), 97–117. doi:10.1002/bsl.836

Ryan, J. P., Hong, J. S., Herz, D., & Hernandez, P. M. (2010). Kinship foster care and the risk of juvenile delinquency. *Children and Youth Services Review, 32*(12), 1823–1830.

Saposnek, D. T. (2004). Working with children in mediation. In J. Folberg, A. L. Milne, & P. Salem (Eds.), *Divorce and family mediation: Models, techniques, and applications* (pp. 155–179). New York, NY: Guilford.

Schoffer, M. J. (2005). Bringing children to the mediation table: Defining a child's best interest in divorce mediation. *Family Court Review, 43*(2), 323–338. doi:10.1111/j.1744-1617.2005.00032.x

Scott, E. S., Reppucci, N. D., & Aber, M. (1988). Children's preferences in adjudicated custody decisions. *Georgia Law Review, 22,* 1035–1078.

Shaw, T. V. (2006). Reentry into the foster care system after reunification. *Children and Youth Services Review, 28*(11), 1375–1390. doi:10.1016/j.childyouth.2006.02.006

Smith, A. B., & Gollop, M. M. (2001). What children think separating parents should know. *New Zealand Journal of Psychology, 30*(1), 23–31.

Starnes, C. (2003). Swords in the hands of babes: Rethinking custody interviews after *Troxel. Wisconsin Law Review, 2003,* 115–169.

Szaj, C. M. (2002). The fine art of listening: Children's voices in custody proceedings. *Journal of Law and Family Studies, 4,* 131–150.

Taussig, H. N., Clyman, R. B., & Landsverk, J. (2001). Children who return home from foster care: A 6-year prospective study of behavioral health outcomes in adolescence. *Pediatrics, 108,* e10. doi:10.1542/peds.108.1.e10

Taylor, H., Beckett, C., & McKeigue, B. (2008). Judgements of Solomon: Anxieties and defences of social workers involved in care proceedings. *Child and Family Social Work, 13,* 23–31. doi:10.1111/j.1365-2206.2007.00507.x

Tyler, T. R., & Blader, S. L. (2003). The group engagement model: Procedural justice, social identity, and cooperative behavior. *Personality and Social Psychology Review*, *7*(4), 349–361. doi:10.1207/S15327957PSPR0704_07

UK Parliament. (1998). *Human Rights Act.* Retrieved from http://www.opsi.gov.uk/acts/acts1889/ukpga_19980042_en_1

Uniform Marriage and Divorce Act, 9A Uniform Laws Annotated, Sec. 316 (1979).

Wallace, S. R., & Koerner, S. (2003). Influence of child and family factors on judicial decisions in contested custody cases. *Family Relations, 52*(2), 180–188. doi:10.1111/j.1741-3729.2003.00180.x

Wallerstein, J. S., Lewis, J., & Blakeslee, S. (2000). *The unexpected legacy of divorce: A 25 year landmark study.* New York, NY: Hyperion.

Waterhouse, L., & McGhee, J. (2009). Anxiety and child protection: Implications for practitioner–parent relations. *Child and Family Social Work, 14*(4), 481–490. doi:10.1111/j.1365-2206.2009.00631.x

Weisz, V., Wingrove, T., Beal, S., & Faith-Slaker, A. (2011). Children's participation in foster care hearings. *Child Abuse and Neglect, 35*(4), 267–272.

Weisz, V., Wingrove, T., & Faith-Slaker, A. (2007–2008). Children and procedural justice. *Court Review, 44,* 36–42.

Winokur, M. A., Crawford, G. A., Longobardi, R. C., & Valentine, D. P. (2008). Matched comparison of children in kinship care and foster care on child welfare outcomes. *Families in Society: The Journal of Contemporary Social Services*, *89*(3), 338–346.

Winter, K. (2010). The perspectives of young children in care about their circumstances and implications for social work practice. *Child and Family Social Work*, *15*(2), 186–195.

5

Child Witnesses' Experiences of Distress in Criminal Court: Sources, Consequences, and Solutions

Elizabeth Rush, Jodi A. Quas, and Bradley D. McAuliff

When courts intervene on behalf of children alleging victimization, one of the many pressing issues, both in the United States and abroad, is how best to accommodate children's needs while maintaining a fair judicial process for the accused. Debates have arisen as to how much children should be informed about the case, whether children should take the stand, what procedural accommodations should be made to facilitate children's testimony, and the consequences of legal involvement and the use of procedural innovations on children and legal decision makers. These debates have emerged in dozens of legal cases, and varying perspectives are evident in divergent policy recommendations, state and federal statutes, and international doctrines (*Connecticut v. Aroyo*, 2007; Hall & Sales, 2008; *Kennedy v. Louisiana*, 2008; *Maryland v. Craig*, 1990; Office of the United Nations High Commissioner on Human Rights, 1990; Schudson, 1987; Section 1, Article 6[3] in the European Convention on Human Rights, 1953).

Unfortunately, these debates have not always relied on the most up-to-date information available from social scientific research, despite a small but important body of work devoted to understanding how children who have experienced or witnessed crime react to legal involvement. The purpose of the current chapter is to provide a synopsis of the main findings from this research. We specifically focus on which aspects of legal participation are especially distressing to children, both initially and over time, and on the potential utility of methods designed to reduce this distress, which itself can affect not only children but also the case itself. Our hope is that this review can inform legal professionals and policymakers as they grapple with the challenging and critical question of how best to pursue justice for crimes against children.

Our chapter is organized into two main sections. First, we describe extant research concerning the experiences of children who come into contact with the legal system as alleged victims of crime and the consequences of that involvement on their wellbeing. Second, we describe several alterations to standard legal procedures, often referred to as "innovative practices," for use with child victims. Our discussion of these alterations is not designed to be a comprehensive review of all possible innovative practices that have been proposed and used, but instead, we describe practices that have received the most attention in social scientific research, that are most likely to be implemented, and that hold the most promise for facilitating children's legal participation and the pursuit of justice. We close with recommendations for practice and policy regarding how best to pursue justice in cases involving child witnesses.

Before turning to our review, we should note that our focus concerns children's experiences and participation in criminal court. The purpose of these cases concerns the innocence or guilt of the defendant, and if guilty, how the defendant should be punished. The cases do not directly concern the *wellbeing* of a child who experienced or witnessed a crime, which is of central concern in family or dependency cases (see Quas & Sumaroka, 2011, for a discussion of how children's reactions may vary across different systems; see also chapter 4 of this volume for a description of the experiences of children in dependency and divorce cases). A child involved in a criminal case is simply a witness who has been asked to provide evidence on behalf of the defense or prosecution. Some efforts may be made to facilitate the child's involvement, but, because the child's needs are not the central purpose for the case (again, unlike for dependency cases), the child's needs are secondary to the main purpose of determining the defendant's innocence or guilt. Moreover, the legal standards, rules of evidence, and procedures are quite rigid and afford considerable rights to a defendant, which is critical given that his or her liberty is at stake in a criminal case. Accordingly, any accommodations made on behalf of a child must be made within these constraints.

It is also important to note that, because a vast majority of children involved in criminal cases were not merely bystander witnesses but experienced abuse, violence, or assault (Goodman, Quas, Bulkley, & Shapiro, 1999; Plotnikoff & Woolfson, 2009), the children are not likely representative of normative populations or community samples of children, but instead constitute an at-risk population (Quas & Sumaroka, 2011). At issue, therefore, is whether legal involvement serves to exacerbate the risk of trauma in these already highly vulnerable children, and if so, what can be done about it that does not infringe upon a defendant's right to a fair trial.

Distress and Legal Involvement

When a child witness is involved in a criminal case, legal professionals face the difficult challenge of balancing the fact-finding goals of the adversarial legal system with children's special needs. This balance is not an easy one to strike. Several aspects of criminal legal proceedings necessary for gathering information and ensuring a fair trial may be potentially harmful to children, as reflected in high levels of emotionality, overt distress, self-reported anxiety, or behavioral problems displayed by children during the case. Immediate or short-term displays of distress or anxiety may impact not only children's longer term wellbeing but also the trial's fact-finding function by influencing the quality of children's testimony (Goodman et al., 1992; Saywitz & Nathanson, 1993) and jurors' evaluations of that evidence. That said, simply participating in a criminal case does not necessarily increase children's distress, and children can often serve as important and effective witnesses without undue harm. Instead, certain aspects of children's experiences during an ongoing criminal case have the *potential* to increase distress for some children. Determining how best to intervene and facilitate children's participation while reducing this distress requires a clear understanding of which aspects are potentially the most problematic.

That said, it is imperative we first define "distress" before moving to a more detailed discussion of its potential causes and remedies. Researchers studying children in legal contexts have operationally defined this construct in a myriad of ways across studies. A few studies have utilized sensitive, sophisticated measures of internal physiological states indicative of distress such as increased heart rate, breathing, and cortisol levels (Saywitz, Nathanson, Snyder, & Lamphear, 1993; Yim, Quas, Cahill, & Hayakawa, 2010). However, obtaining such measures is often impractical, especially when examining naturally occurring events (Peterson & Warren, 2009), as is often the case in studies pertaining to children's legal experiences. Thus, most other studies have utilized self- or observer-report measures or behavioral indicators such as crying (Cashmore, 1992; Murray, 1995). Despite their clear differences, these measures all share a common purpose: to detect a child's negative emotional response to legal involvement. Thus, in this chapter, we conceptualize distress more broadly to refer to a general sense of anxiety, fear, or generalized negative emotion, as perceived by children themselves, other individuals closely involved, or neutral observers.

Testifying. Testifying in court is perhaps the most well-documented aspect of criminal court involvement that affects children's experiences of distress. Indeed, both the courts and scientific research have emphasized that testifying is likely to be particularly distressing for children (e.g., *Coy v. Iowa*, 1988; *Danner v. Kentucky*, 1998; Goodman et al., 1992; *Maryland v. Craig*, 1990; Oates & Tong, 1987; Quas et al., 2005; Sas, Austin, Wolfe, & Hurley, 1991), with distress typically defined according to overt (e.g., crying) or self-reported indices of intense negative emotions. For one, in order to testify, children must discuss events that were likely arousing, frightening, painful, and potentially highly personal and embarrassing, which is quite distressing for any witness, including children (Batterman-Faunce & Goodman, 1993; Henry, 1997). Additionally, in situations of abuse, children may feel some degree of culpability for the alleged offense (Feiring, Taska, & Chen, 2002; Quas, Goodman, & Jones, 2003), which may further exacerbate their distress. Children must also testify in an austere, formal context with numerous unfamiliar adults observing (Hall & Sales, 2008). Anecdotal reports from victims of child sexual abuse (CSA) indicated that their feelings ranged from "minor anxiety" to "dread and terror" when on the stand (Back, Gustafsson, Larsson, & Bertero, 2011). They reported feeling confused and disillusioned because of a perception that they had done something wrong, or they took offense to the public nature of the discussions.

Second, not only must children answer questions about sensitive topics, but also the questions are often posed via cross-examination. Children have described cross-examination in particular as "confusing, complex, rushed, repetitive, bullying and frightening" (Plotnikoff & Woolfson, 2004) and appear far more distressed during cross-examination than direct (Goodman et al., 1992). Although the goal of all questioning during criminal proceedings should be to uncover the truth, often the operational goal of cross-examination is to discredit witnesses at all costs. This may include using accusatory language or leading and confusing questions containing complex syntactic structure and legal jargon (Brennan & Brennan, 1988; Davies, Henderson, & Seymour, 1997; Davies & Seymour, 1998; Ghetti, Alexander, & Goodman, 2002; Hall & Sales, 2008; Zajac, Jury, & O'Neill, 2009). Anecdotal evidence indicates that such strategies are effective. Children express fears of being "screamed at" by attorneys (Sas, 1991) and report being doubtful of their own testimony because of defense attorneys' aggressive questioning (Back et al., 2011).

Third, facing the defendant can be quite distressing. This individual may be someone who threatened or actually harmed the child and, accordingly and understandably, children fear for their wellbeing. Potentially even worse are situations in which the defendant is a loved one, for whom a child still has feelings. Facing the accused is often cited by children as the most salient stressor they face when preparing to testify (Brannon, 1994; Goodman et al., 1992; Henry, 1997; Sas et al., 1991). In support of this notion, Goodman et al. (1992) found that among a sample of children who testified in court, many felt more positively about testifying after the experience was over than before they gave testimony, but they often still expressed negative feelings about having had to face the defendant.

Although some have argued that all witnesses, not only children, may experience some distress while testifying (e.g., *Coy v. Iowa,* 1988), there are several reasons to be concerned about the consequences of this distress specifically on children. One is directly relevant to the fact-finding mission of the courts. High levels of distress can affect children's ability to provide clear, accurate responses. In a comprehensive, longitudinal examination of 218 child victims involved in sexual assault cases, Goodman et al. (1992) documented features of children's courtroom experiences and testimony and collected measures of children's feelings about testifying and observer ratings of the children's fearfulness and anxiety. Several findings emerged, suggesting that stress associated with testifying affected children's testimonial competency. Children who did not have a loved one present in the courtroom appeared more frightened, provided less consistent testimony, and were less able to answer the prosecutor's questions than children who had a loved one present for support. In addition, higher levels of precourt anxiety and negative feelings about facing the defendant during their testimony predicted poorer ability to answer the prosecutor's questions. Experimental studies have confirmed the trends evident in Goodman et al.'s study: Overt distress, as well as high reported arousal, while testifying in court decreases children's accuracy. Researchers exposed children to a play event and later interviewed children about what happened in either a courtroom context or a less intimidating location (private room, Nathanson & Saywitz, 2003; classroom, Saywitz & Nathanson, 1993). Children questioned in the mock courtroom evidenced greater anxiety and impaired memory performance compared to children questioned in the alternative location. These patterns are similar to other research that reveals that heightened stress, according to several types of indices, including physiological, while recounting a prior experience adversely impacts memory (Het, Ramlow, & Wolf, 2005; Quas, Bauer, & Boyce, 2004; Quas & Lench, 2007).

Two final points are worth noting regarding children's testimonial distress and their memory and communication abilities. First, any adverse effects of heightened arousal at retrieval on memory may be exaggerated when children are recalling a prior event that itself was distressing (Peters, 1991; Quas et al., 2004; Quas & Lench, 2007). Second, given that distress while testifying is likely to be highest during cross-examination, adverse effects of that distress on children's performance are likely to be greatest as well. Children often change their answers in response to cross-examination (Zajac, Gross, & Hayne, 2003), and these changes occur regardless of the accuracy of their original statements (Zajac & Hayne, 2003). Closed-ended, leading questions; "loaded" questions that imply the response desired (Davies & Seymour, 1998); and complicated legalese terms and sentence structures (Brennan & Brennan, 1988; Perry et al., 1995) are especially likely during cross-examination and are known to reduce children's accuracy, regardless of stress level (Ceci & Bruck, 1993; Ceci, Kulkofsky, Klemfuss, Sweeney, & Bruck, 2007). Heightened distress may reduce children's ability to attend to the complex features of questions and answer correctly, and the difficult questions themselves may actually exacerbate children's distress, leading to further difficulties in their ability to answer (Almerigogna, Ost, Bull, & Akehurst, 2007).

Not only can testifying be distressing as it is taking place and hence potentially affect children's ability to recount their experiences, but also testifying, and the concomitant anxiety, may lead to adverse effects that persist well after the testimony is complete. Several studies have documented negative associations between testifying and maladaptive outcomes (Bill, 1995; Oates & Tong, 1987). One study compared CSA victims who testified and who did not testify on several personality variables, behavioral characteristics, and school performance 4 years after the case (Bill, 1995). Testifiers evidenced lower scores on measures of self-concept, self-control, and discipline than nontestifiers and exhibited more problem behaviors at home, although testifiers and nontestifiers may have differed in other key ways (e.g., in age, abuse duration, or severity of abuse) before testifying that may also explain the evident differences. Similar results, though, were obtained by Goodman et al. (1992), who matched testifiers to nontestifiers on demographic (e.g., age, socioeconomic status) and case characteristics (e.g., severity of abuse), as well as parent-reported behavior problems, at the outset of the case. Seven months after testifying, testifiers continued to experience high levels of problems, whereas nontestifiers' problems decreased. These patterns were primarily due to continued problems among children who testified repeatedly, whose cases lacked corroborative evidence, and who had nonsupportive caregivers (see Whitcomb, Goodman, Runyon, & Hoak, 1994, for similar trends). Even 12 to 14 years later, testifying repeatedly continued to predict increased problems, as reported in a follow-up study of the original participants who were now adolescents and young adults (Quas et al., 2005).

As a whole, the evidence reviewed thus far does not favor having children take the stand, at least repeatedly, when they are required to face the defendant directly and answer questions via cross-examination. Answering questions while in front of the defendant, especially questions posed during cross-examination, can be quite distressing to children. This distress may adversely affect their ability to communicate and answer questions accurately. Moreover, testifying repeatedly, particularly when cases rely quite heavily on children's statements (due to lack of corroborative evidence) or when children do not have caregiver support, may affect children's adjustment over time. However, results of a few studies do not support uniform bans on children taking the stand or at least suggest that some children may fare better if they have their day in court. Specifically, Runyan, Everson, Edelsohn, Hunter, and Coulter (1988) found that children who testified in juvenile court had faster declines in anxiety and conduct problems than children who did not testify. Goodman et al. (1992) observed that children who did not testify felt worse about not testifying when the case resulted in a not guilty verdict as opposed to a guilty verdict. These feelings were maintained over time, as reported in the follow-up study (Quas et al., 2005). Additionally, among former victims who had experienced less severe sexual abuse, not testifying was associated with poorer functioning years later. Consistent with these findings, theories of adults' evaluations of justice emphasize a lack of participation in decision-making processes as an important antecedent to negative perceptions of procedural justice (Tyler, 2003; Tyler & Huo, 2002).

In summary, there is consistent empirical evidence that testifying can be distressing for children, especially when it is repeated, involves answering questions posed by hostile attorneys, and is done without the support of a caregiver. This distress can negatively impact children's abilities to provide accurate testimony and may lead to longer term negative mental health consequences. However, when it is done only once with a supportive caregiver, testifying, even if somewhat distressing at the time, may help empower child victims, allowing them to feel that their voice has been heard and that they did all they could to help achieve justice in the case (Berliner & Conte, 1995; Goodman et al., 1992; Runyan et al., 1988). The precise conditions under which testifying is harmful versus beneficial, and how best to reduce children's distress while taking the stand, still need to be specified more clearly. As we discuss shortly, some legal procedures are attempting to facilitate children's ability to provide accurate, complete testimonial accounts.

Legal knowledge. Another aspect of children's legal experiences that contributes to heightened distress is children's lack of understanding of the legal system, including general understanding and understanding in relation to their case specifically. Children often fail to understand fully the purpose of the legal system and the functions of its personnel. They also often misunderstand procedures and decisions, including decisions made in their case. Certainly children's understanding improves with age, but even older children and adolescents remain somewhat limited in their knowledge (Flin, Stevenson, & Davies, 1989; Peterson-Badali, Abramovitch, & Duda, 1997; Saywitz, Jaenicke, & Camparo, 1990; Warren-Leubecker, Tate, Hinton, & Ozbek, 1989). Adolescents' difficulties in understanding legal concepts are especially noteworthy for technical (e.g., jury, prosecute) and uncommon terms (e.g., perjury, motion; Burnett, Noblin, & Prosser, 2004; Grisso et al., 2003). Moreover, children's limited knowledge is not simply a function of their lack of experience in the legal system. Comparisons between children with and without direct contact with the legal system typically reveal few differences in understanding (Cooper, Wallin, Quas, & Lyon, 2010; Grisso et al., 2003; Saywitz et al., 1990).

Of course, the more relevant question in the current chapter is not whether children understand the legal system, but rather whether their lack of understanding is related to their distress, ability to participate, and/or functioning. Several lines of research suggest that a lack of understanding does affect these others aspects of children's legal involvement. Poorer legal understanding is related to greater anticipatory distress about testifying in a mock trial (Goodman et al., 1998) and more negative feelings about participation in dependency court hearings (Quas, Wallin, Horwitz, Davis, & Lyon, 2009). These findings are similar to those obtained in medical contexts that indicate children are more anxious about procedures when they have less knowledge than when they know what will happen (Goodman, Quas, Batterman-Faunce, Riddlesberger, & Kuhn, 1997; Harbeck-Weber & McKee, 1995; Zeltzer, Fanurik, & LeBaron, 1989).

Insufficient understanding may also undermine children's ability to participate effectively. Children may be uncertain of their responsibility or not fully understand the reasons they must endure multiple interviews or testify repeatedly and answer the same questions posed multiple times by different professionals. Nor may children understand the adversarial nature of cross-examination or attorneys' intentions when asking complex questions (Zajac et al., 2003;

Zajac & Hayne, 2003). All of this can contribute to errors, increases in "don't know" responses, or inconsistencies in children's responses. Finally, children who are confused while answering questions may feel less comfortable refuting suggestions from attorneys and interviewers (Almerigogna et al., 2007).

Lack of legal understanding may further increase children's fears of testifying or disclosing information to multiple legal personnel or may create feelings of self-blame or fear of punishment (Perry et al., 1995; Sas, 1993; Saywitz, Goodman, & Lyon, 2002; Saywitz et al., 1993; Zajac et al., 2003). Children express fears of being in trouble or of being on trial themselves (e.g., Back et al., 2011). To the extent that such misunderstandings lead children to perceive negative consequences of disclosing information or otherwise participating, they are less likely to be forthcoming in answering questions posed by professionals in interviews and in court (Lyon & Ahern, 2011; Wagland & Bussey, 2005), which can compromise the progression of a case. Finally, lack of legal knowledge may affect children's understanding of a decision or case outcome, including their role in that decision. Case outcome is strongly related to children's attitudes about their legal experiences, initially and over time (Goodman et al., 1992; Quas et al., 2005). Insofar as children do not understand decisions, they may fail to recognize those that are positive, or perhaps less negative. Children may also assume more responsibility than is warranted for unwanted outcomes. Any self-blame for the outcome may contribute to negative perceptions of the legal system or perhaps reduced likelihood of reporting crimes in the future.

Repeated interviews. Repeated interviews have received much criticism because of concerns about children's distress and because of their potential to bias children's reports (see the Council of Europe, 2007; Goodman & Quas, 2008; *Kennedy v. Louisiana*, 2008; Quas & Sumaroka, 2011). Unfortunately, though, some degree of interview repetition is unavoidable. Children's initial reports may be incomplete or ambiguous, requiring clarification and additional details, and both the defense and prosecution are entitled to question witnesses. However, being asked to divulge details about distressing or embarrassing events can itself be stressful to children, even when not repeated (Back et al., 2011; Henry, 1997; Hershkowitz, Lanes, & Lamb, 2007), and as such, even enduring one interview is likely distressing. This distress may be exacerbated across multiple interviews, especially with multiple unfamiliar adults, which is often the norm in cases involving child victims (Cross, Jones, Walsh, Simone, & Kolko, 2007; Goodman et al., 1992; Malloy, Lyon, & Quas, 2007). For instance, in a survey of children who were seen at a standard investigative center or a child advocacy center because of alleged abuse, most reported that they had to recount details of their abuse too often to too many people (Jones, Cross, Walsh, & Simone, 2007), confirming that repeated interviews do represent a source of distress for child victims. Moreover, this distress is not short lived. Henry (1997) reviewed case files and interviewed 90 CSA victims about trauma symptoms and distress associated with the legal case. The number of interviews was negatively related to children's trauma symptomatology.

Similarly, experiencing a greater number of interviews was associated with more mental health problems for sexual abuse victims over a decade after the completion of their case (Quas et al., 2005).

Although repeated interviews appear to increase children's distress, as yet, it is unclear whether this distress is due to the number of interviews per se or the number of *interviewers*. For example, Tedesco and Schnell (1987) found that the number of different interviewers who questioned children was negatively related to victims' ratings of perceived helpfulness of the legal system after the case had ended. Berliner and Conte (1995) found that increased contact with legal professionals (e.g., detectives, prosecutors) was related to increased distress for children. Because these variables are undoubtedly highly correlated with number of interviews, it is difficult to establish the precise cause of children's distress. Speaking with multiple people may be a more salient predictor of children's distress than multiple interviews. When speaking about intensely personal events, child victims and witnesses may need to establish a trusting relationship with an adult interviewer over time before they feel comfortable divulging certain details (Carnes, Nelson-Gardell, Wilson, & Orgassa, 2001; DeVoe & Faller, 1999), and thus repeated interviews by a single individual may actually lead to more complete reports (Elliot & Briere, 1994; Quas & Schaaf, 2002) and decreased distress over time. Additional research examining these variables in isolation, especially separate from specific interview strategies that can increase errors (see Ceci, Loftus, Leichtman, & Bruck, 1994), could better inform interventions to decrease the number of times children must repeat their accounts, possibly to different individuals, while maximizing information gleaned.

Case length. Continuances and delays in legal cases constitute an additional source of distress for children. First, the average length of criminal cases in the United States is 1 to 2 years (Walsh, Lippert, Cross, Maurice, & Davison, 2008). Similar lengths of time for cases have been reported in other countries. In England, the average time between the referral of a case involving a child witness and the start of the trial in the Crown's Court is approximately 1 year, and the start of a trial in the Magistrate's Court is about 10 months (Plotnikoff & Woolfson, 2004). Delays, date changes, and continuances contribute to the time spans, and children are often directly affected by these alterations.

Plotnikoff and Woolfson (2004, 2009) surveyed several hundred children participating in legal proceedings in England, Wales, and Northern Ireland and found that only 44% of the children who testified did so on the first scheduled date. About 25% of the children had to return two or three times because of rescheduling before taking the stand, and 30% of trials were rescheduled one or more times. Waiting and rescheduling is a source of considerable apprehension for children (Goodman et al., 1992), who experience all of the anticipatory preparation and stress regarding testifying, only to be sent home to prepare again at a later date. Delays and continuances also keep children's anxiety at relatively high levels (Runyan et al., 1988), precluding them from fully recovering from their experiences (Goodman et al., 1992).

It is encouraging that several jurisdictions in the United States, as well as other countries such as England, have enacted legislation that expedites processing in cases involving child witnesses, for example, legislation calling for priority scheduling (Crown Prosecution Service, 2008; National Center for the Prosecution of Child Abuse, 2011; Plotnikoff & Woolfson, 2009). However, much of this legislation is somewhat vague and does not provide standards or goals for length of time to case resolution. Moreover, a direct comparison between children who took part in legal cases in the United Kingdom in the early 2000s versus 5 years later revealed that, although a slight decrease in the overall case length emerged, delays and continuances remained common, with one-third of all trials being rescheduled one or more times (Plotnikoff & Woolfson, 2009). Further, in Northern Ireland, a mere 8% of children testified on their first scheduled appearance (Plotnikoff & Woolfson, 2004, 2009). Thus, continued efforts must be directed toward not only reducing the overall length of legal cases but also, and perhaps more important, reducing the number of continuances when children are scheduled to testify.

Case outcome. A final potential source of distress for children concerns the outcome of the case. Unfavorable case outcomes are largely out of children's control, and given that children's ability to cope with uncontrollable stressors develops across childhood and into adolescence (Altshuler & Ruble, 1989), it is not surprising that outcomes can be distressing. Whether this distress is linked to longer term negative outcomes is not entirely clear, however. Sas (1993) reported poorer adjustment among children whose cases ended in not guilty rather than guilty verdicts. Yet neither Goodman et al. (1992) nor Quas et al. (2005) found similar links, shortly after the case concluded or after many years, although links between case outcome and legal attitudes did emerge (children whose cases resulted in not guilty or lenient sentences felt substantially more negative about the legal system and their own case). Some of the variability in links between case outcome and children's distress may be related to individual differences in children's ability to employ successful coping strategies after receiving an unfavorable case decision, such as cognitive distraction or seeking support from appropriate adults (Altshuler & Ruble, 1989; Rudolph, Dennig, & Weisz, 1995; Skinner & Zimmer-Gembeck, 2007). Children also may not fully understand the lack of control they have over the case outcome and blame themselves for a not guilty verdict. Self-blame is evident even in some adults who endure negative experiences (e.g., assault, rape; Anderson, Miller, Riger, Dill, & Sedikides, 1994; Frazier, 1990) and is linked to increases in negative mental health consequences. Self-blame is especially relevant in cases involving child victims because, particularly in sex abuse cases (Kaufman et al., 1998; Kogan, 2004; Quas et al., 2003), and insofar as some children feel responsible for their abuse, self-blame could moderate links between unfavorable verdicts and negative outcomes.

Despite inconsistent links between case outcome and psychological distress, as mentioned, case outcome is consistently related to children's feelings about the legal system. Children feel more negative about the legal case, their legal experiences, and the legal system generally when the case is dropped, the defendant is acquitted, or the defendant receives a lenient rather than a guilty or relatively severe sentence (Goodman et al., 1992; Sas, 1991). Similarly, parents often feel that not enough was done to help their children's case (Goodman et al., 1992). These associations are evident shortly after a case ends, as well as many years later (and even when controlling for initial mental health, age, abuse characteristics, and testifying; Quas et al., 2005), demonstrating remarkable consistency over time. Additionally, case outcomes may serve as an important moderator between children's perceptions of other potential stressors, namely, testifying, and negative attitudes. Goodman et al. (1992) found that children who did not testify in court felt worse about not testifying when the defendant was found not guilty as opposed to guilty. It is possible that these children perceived a missed opportunity for exerting control over the outcome of the case. Thus, although testifying is perceived to be distressing at the time, in terms of longer term outcomes, it may serve a protective function by allowing children to feel that their voice was heard, reducing negative attitudes associated with a not guilty verdict.

Summary. Various aspects of children's participation in criminal proceedings can be quite distressing, which can affect children's memory completeness and accuracy, reporting, communication, and short- and long-term wellbeing and legal attitudes. These aspects include testifying repeatedly, not understanding the legal system generally and one's own case specifically, multiple continuances and delays, and case outcome. Of importance, and as we have alluded to throughout, the effects of specific components of children's legal experiences are likely to affect children symbiotically. For instance, limited knowledge of the legal system may underlie or heighten children's distress about testifying, bewilderment about the case outcome, or anxiety about responding to repeated questions—each of which appears to also exert its own effects on children's feelings and ability to participate. Children's ability (or inability) to participate may affect the progression and outcome of the case, which in turn may influence children's feelings. Delays and continuances, similarly, may exacerbate or prolong distress associated with other aspects of legal involvement. Although the apparent interdependency of these components makes it difficult to tease apart direct contributors to children's distress, the interdependency also potentially provides opportunities to implement interventions that target broad-based, underlying constructs related to multiple potentially stressful aspects of legal involvement, thereby potentially ameliorating distress and improving children's effective participation.

Distress and Innovative Practices

Given the potential for considerable stress endured by children during their participation in a criminal case and the potential for this distress to affect their ability to communicate during the case, it is not surprising that various procedural and evidentiary innovations have been introduced to facilitate children's involvement. The innovations can be heuristically divided into several types. One set targets the pretrial phase of a legal case and focuses on either increasing children's comfort and familiarity with the progression of the case or streamlining the investigative and legal process. Another set targets the trial itself and focuses on enhancing children's understanding or comfort or reducing their need to testify repeatedly or in open court (see Hall & Sales, 2008; Malloy, Mitchell, Block, Quas, & Goodman, 2007; McAuliff & Kovera, 2002; Sandler, 2006). Here, we discuss a select group of these innovations. Extensive discussion of the range of innovations, including empirical research that has examined their utility, as well as research that has examined perceptions of their use, already exists (Goodman et al., 1999; Malloy et al., 2007; Quas & McAuliff, 2009).

Pretrial education and preparation. Perhaps the most feasible and least controversial of procedural innovations designed to facilitate children's participation in legal proceedings are programs that increase children's understanding of the legal process and comfort with respect to their role in that process. The formality and comprehensiveness of these programs vary widely, both within the United States and abroad, ranging from informal instructions given by a child protection worker or courtroom staff to well-structured, intensive, multisession trainings (Sas 1991, 1993; Saywitz & Snyder, 1993, 1996).

Informal preparation programs typically include brief court tours or summaries of generic information about court, legal personnel, or the process of a legal case. In U.S. jurisdictions, investigators, attorneys, or victim advocates may review basic facts of the case or prepare children for testimony by giving them a courtroom tour (Goodman et al., 1999). Similarly, in some English courts, child witnesses are often given the opportunity to participate in a "familiarization visit" during which they tour the courtroom and can ask questions about court (Plotnikoff & Woolfson, 2009). In English High Courts, children and their parents are also often provided with informational booklets orienting them to the court and trial process.

More formal programs employ specialized organizations or trained individuals who assist child victims during the legal process. These individuals provide children with general knowledge or materials regarding the trial process, as well as case-specific information. One particularly comprehensive program, the Child Witness Project in Ontario, Canada, overseen by the Ministry of the Attorney General, is a five-component program specifically designed to help prepare children to take the stand in criminal court. The first component is an education component, which familiarizes child witnesses with the rules of the courtroom, the roles of various legal personnel, and important legal terminology. A role-playing component allows children to practice answering questions and prepares them to cope with cross-examination. A third component provides relaxation training and anxiety management techniques. A courtroom orientation allows children to tour the courtroom and learn what they can expect when they come to court. Finally, after the conclusion of the trial, children are provided with a debriefing and follow-up assessment, during which they are debriefed about the outcome of the case, reassured about their performance, and asked to give feedback about their experience in the preparation program (Cunningham & Hurley, 2007). A similar program, the Court Education for Young Witnesses Program, has been developed in New Zealand. Like the Ontario Child Witness Project program, this program is multifaceted and provides education and support for child witnesses from well before trial to its completion (Davies, Devere, & Verbitsky, 2004).

Formal pretrial preparation programs in the United States are often facilitated by child advocacy centers (CAC), organizations that bring together child welfare professionals in a given region to promote interagency coordination and provide services to children and families. As an example, the Safe Passage CAC in Colorado Springs provides individual court preparation for children and court orientation for caregivers. The agency also provides a support person to children during their trial. In Huntsville, Alabama, child witnesses have the opportunity to participate in a series of structured sessions to address questions about the roles of legal personnel and fears about testifying in court (e.g., facing the defendant and answering prosecutors' and defense attorneys' questions; Keeney, Amacher, & Kastanakis, 1992).

The various education programs represent easily implementable and fairly cost-effective procedures that may enhance children's legal understanding, reduce their anxiety, and facilitate their meaningful participation. Few scientific investigations have rigorously evaluated the effects of the programs (formal or informal) on children's wellbeing or on the progression of the case, although anecdotal evidence and one empirical study are suggestive of several benefits. Specifically, Sas (1991) evaluated an early version of the Child Witness Project in Ontario just mentioned. Her research benefited from random assignment of children to receive either in-depth preparation or standard practices. The prepared children exhibited better adjustment following the case outcome and were rated as more well behaved by attorneys. Additionally, guilty verdicts were more prevalent in cases involving prepared children. Anecdotal evidence from Plotnikoff and Woolfson's (2009) survey revealed similar trends. The child witnesses and their parents generally reported preparation programs as being helpful. Given that these patterns have emerged only in unpublished governmental reports, however, further empirical research is needed to examine preparation programs more carefully. Research should also identify which components are the most effective and whether components vary in developmental appropriateness so that programs can be targeted most effectively.

Recently, a few jurisdictions and child welfare organizations have utilized emerging technologies to help prepare children for court. In England, Plotnikoff and Woolfson (2009) noted that a minority of children who completed their survey were provided with a DVD about the experience of testifying in court. Those who received the DVD largely reported that it was helpful. A similar DVD has been developed by the National Children's Advocacy Center in Huntsville, Alabama. The Canadian Society for the Investigation of Child Abuse (http://csicainfo.com/) developed an interactive court preparation computer game within which children navigate around "Superhero Island" to learn information about court. Although empirical studies have not addressed the effectiveness of these types of technologies in preparing children for court, these novel approaches may represent promising and cost-effective avenues given that children are becoming increasingly accustomed to instructional technologies in school settings.

Finally, unlike other innovative practices (discussed shortly), pretrial preparation programs appear to be well received by the legal community, particularly because such programs do not change the trial process itself. In a national survey of U.S. prosecutors, preparatory techniques including courtroom tours and preparing children for testifying were reported as the most frequently utilized, most effective, and least controversial innovation for child witnesses (Goodman et al., 1999). Less is known regarding how child witness preparation affects jurors' perceptions and decisions because no studies have systematically explored children's preparation within the context of a real or simulated trial.

Future research should examine in a comprehensive fashion whether preparation programs actually reduce children's distress and facilitate their participation, and if so, which aspects of preparation are most beneficial. Such research should incorporate recent technologies such as DVDs and interactive computer games that are being used to prepare children for their day in court to determine what, if any, effects these have on children and how those effects compare to traditional preparation programs. Studies must consider the broader context in which preparation occurs by including measures of jurors' perceptions of prepared versus unprepared children. Limited evidence indicates that children who undergo preparation programs are less anxious and are better witnesses than unprepared children (Sas, 1991); however, jurors may perceive children who are not anxious or upset as less credible witnesses (Kovera, Gresham, Borgida, Gray, & Regan, 1997; McAuliff & Kovera, 2002), an issue we return to later.

Use of support persons and intermediaries. In the United States, both federal and state statutes allow for the appointment of support persons for child witnesses in legal proceedings. Trial judges have a fair amount of discretion when determining whether a support person should be allowed and who is qualified to serve as such a person. Like pretrial preparation, legal professionals view support person use fairly favorably and implement it frequently in cases involving children. Forty-one percent of state trial court judges surveyed by Hafemeister (1996), for instance, had allowed children to testify while on an adult's lap. A national survey of prosecutors revealed that over 90% of respondents indicated they always or frequently used a support person with children (Goodman et al., 1999). McAuliff, Nicholson, Amarilio, and Ravashenas (2012) conducted a national survey of victim/witness assistants (VWAs) and found that use of a support person was extremely common with children of all ages in cases involving child sexual abuse, physical abuse, neglect, and adult domestic violence. Support persons are also commonly used in countries outside the United States. For example, both Canada and England have enacted legislation allowing the appointment of support persons to child witnesses (§486.1, *Criminal Code of Canada*; Plotnikoff & Woolfson, 2009).

Of note, the precise relationship between the support person and the child witness and what this individual does to provide support varies considerably, across and within countries. In the United States, for instance, prosecutor-based VWAs or parents/guardians most frequently serve as support persons, with these individuals being selected by the courts. In Canada, however, children are permitted to choose someone to serve as their support person (Bala, 1999). In England, the support person again could be either a witness care officer (similar to a VWA) appointed by the court or someone known to the child. Whether a child has any say in who the person is varies across jurisdictions (Plotnikoff & Woolfson, 2009). Variability in the support person's role was strikingly evident in a national survey of U.S. VWAs conducted by McAuliff et al. (2012). Most support persons provide informational support (e.g., referrals to community resources, conducting the courtroom visit, and disseminating procedural information), with relatively fewer providing emotional support. When emotional support was provided, though, it typically consisted of simply attending court and being near the child during testimony. In Canada, however, the definitional role of a support person is explicitly to accompany the child while testifying (§486.1, *Criminal Code of Canada*), and thus, the support person's role is limited to actual trial proceedings. In England, support organizations at times provide children with the opportunity to meet a supporter before trial who then helps prepare them for giving testimony. Children are also provided with a support person to wait with them before giving testimony and are given the option to have a support person with them while giving testimony (Plotnikoff & Woolfson, 2009). Across all countries, though, the support person is not allowed to question the child directly.

Despite the widespread use of support persons with children, only two studies have examined the effects of this innovation on children's emotional reactions to and communication during legal proceedings. Goodman et al.'s (1992) analysis of children's testimony during preliminary hearings and at trial suggested that certain forms of social support were indeed associated with positive outcomes, at least in terms of children's performance and ability to communicate. Children who had a nonoffending parent or loved one present in the courtroom during preliminary hearings were rated as being less frightened during their testimony and were less likely to provide inconsistent testimony about certain crime details. Moreover, children testifying in the presence of a nonoffending parent or loved one at trial were able to answer a larger number of the prosecutor's questions. Somewhat more recently, Santtila, Korkman, and Sandnabba (2004) analyzed investigative interviews of suspected child abuse victims in Finland and found that use of support persons in forensic interviews affected both children and interviewers. Surprisingly, the presence of a support person was associated with longer, more suggestive interviewer utterances and shorter, less detailed responses from children. It is unclear why the results varied from those of Goodman et al., but the different goals of the two formats (trials vs. forensic interviews), combined with differential preparation of children and possibly the support persons for each, may be important. Overall, the varying findings, in concert with limitations inherent in correlational research (i.e., inability to make causal inferences or to control for confounds), highlight the need for additional research to clarify the precise nature of the associations between support person use and children's reports and experiences (e.g., emotions, stress) in court.

A few studies have also examined how legal professionals and jurors view support person use. Goodman et al. (1999) surveyed prosecutors nationwide about their perceptions of innovations for child witnesses. Respondents reported that the presence of a support person in court was especially useful in reducing children's trauma but somewhat less useful in promoting guilty outcomes. More recently, McAuliff et al. (2012) surveyed VWAs nationwide. They appeared to share prosecutors' enthusiasm for support person use, indicating that it decreases children's stress and increases their accuracy and perceived credibility. Somewhat contrasting views were found, however, among prospective jurors: McAuliff and Kovera (2012) surveyed jury-eligible community members about their expectations regarding child witness behavior and credibility in the presence of a support person. Prospective jurors felt that, while a support person may reduce children's distress, the children's truthfulness would be more difficult to ascertain when a support person was present relative to not. Prospective jurors also believed that support person use was fairer to children than traditional testimony, but no different from prerecorded videotape testimony or closed-circuit television testimony (CCTV, which involves a child testifying live, but from a remote location outside of the courtroom, and the child's testimony is projected into the courtroom via television). Finally, no differences emerged in perceived fairness to the defendant between support person use versus traditional or any other alternative form of testimony.

In a separate investigation, McAuliff and colleagues (Nefas, Duckworth, & McAuliff, 2008) experimentally tested the effects of support person use on jurors' perceptions. Jury-eligible community members viewed a DVD depicting an 11-year-old professional actress hired to play the role of a child testifying from the witness stand in open court. The researchers systematically varied the presence of a support person seated next to the child on the witness stand. Other than making occasional eye contact, the support person did not interact with or touch the child in any way. Participants rated the accuracy and trustworthiness of the 11-year-old girl in the simulation more negatively when she testified with a support person than when she did not. Participants who viewed the support person also expressed concern that she may have coached and spent a great deal of time with the child prior to testifying. These data provide preliminary evidence that support person use, even if positive for children, may have unintended consequences on jurors' perceptions of child witnesses. Of course, because the child's behavior and testimony in the study were held constant, any effects of support person presence on children's actual testimonial performance (e.g., stress, accuracy, demeanor) was not manipulated in the study and this performance itself could affect jurors' perceptions in important ways. These unanswered questions are critical to address given the apparent prevalence and positive perceptions of support person use among legal professionals.

Relatively recently, a novel approach related to the use of support persons has been introduced in some countries. Specifically, intermediaries have been included, typically in trials, to relay questions to children. In South Africa and England, for instance, prosecutors can apply for a court-appointed intermediary to help communicate attorneys' questions to children (Hanna, Davies, Henderson, Crothers, & Rotherham, 2010). These intermediaries stand beside child witnesses in court or, in the case of testimony via closed-circuit television, are present with children in their alternative location. The intermediaries rephrase attorneys' questions in developmentally appropriate language so that they are understandable to children. These individuals may be particularly effective in conveying the meaning of questions without any possible corresponding accusatory tone that may be embedded in attorneys' questions, especially those posed by defense attorneys. Thus, in addition to facilitating children's understanding of the questions, intermediaries may alleviate the accusatory atmosphere that often causes distress for children (Back et al., 2011; Hanna et al., 2010; Sas, 1991). Although research has not directly examined the effects of intermediary use on children's distress or the quality of their reports, research concerning training procedures to help children identify and respond to confusing questions (e.g., by stating that they do not understand) indicates that such training can increase children's accuracy (Saywitz, Snyder, & Nathanson, 1999).

We are not aware of any use of intermediaries in the United States, and no evaluations of the effects of their use exist. However, in countries (e.g., South Africa, England) where intermediaries are frequently used, they are generally well received and are perceived by both witnesses and criminal justice personnel to be effective in reducing children's distress and improving their testimonial competence (Hanna et al., 2010; Plotnikoff & Woolfson, 2007). Controversy still exists, nonetheless, regarding what the precise role of intermediaries should be, for instance, whether intermediaries can comment on the intelligibility of questions or on the child's understanding of them, which is not allowed in South Africa (Jonker & Swanzen, 2007), or whether intermediaries should be able to comment on question sequencing or highly problematic (e.g., suggestive) questions, which is explicitly forbidden in England. Thus, although intermediary use may hold some promise, research needs to test how best to utilize intermediaries and the potential effects of their behavior on children (e.g., stress, accuracy) and the case itself.

Alternative forms of testimony. A third general method of accommodating child witnesses involves having a child testify via some form of alternative media (e.g., CCTV, with a shield limiting their ability to view the defendant, or via videotaped statements) rather than live in open court while facing the defendant. Although alternative testimony formats are used only rarely in the United States and remain highly controversial (Goodman et al., 1999), they are widely used in many other countries (e.g., England, Wales, Canada, Sweden), which are unhampered by constitutional constraints (Landström, Granhag, & Hartwig, 2005; Myers, 1998; Wilson & Davies, 1999). Moreover, given the potential of alternative forms of testimony to infringe on a defendant's constitutional rights, the use of these innovations has been the subject of a substantial amount of empirical research on their utility and effects.

In the United States, some states allow videotaped depositions, which offer attorneys from both sides an opportunity to examine and cross-examine the witness in lieu of testifying, effectively eliminating the need for the child to take the stand during the actual trial. In other states, children are required to give in-person testimony or undergo cross-examination in the courtroom in addition to taking part in a videotaped deposition (Hall & Sales, 2008; Quas & McAuliff, 2009). In more limited cases, a videotaped forensic interview may be admitted as testimony in a trial. However, because this type of testimony constitutes hearsay, its use is much more controversial, and courts must determine admissibility in light of legal standards regarding hearsay exceptions (*Crawford v. Washington,* 2004; Lyon, 2007; Quas & McAuliff, 2009; Sawicki, 2009). Further, in most states, videotaped testimony is only permitted in cases of physical or sexual child abuse (Hall & Sales, 2008), rather than in all types of prosecutions in which children testify.

Insofar as children who testify in a traditional format have to appear in court and experience the preparatory anxiety associated with testifying (Goodman et al., 1992; Henry, 1997; Nathanson & Saywitz, 2003; Sas, 1991, 1993), certainly testifying via videotape should benefit children by eliminating that distress. Wilson and Davies (1999) found that children who provided testimony via previously recorded videotape were rated as less anxious by naïve observers than were children who testified via CCTV, although the quality of interviews also varied across the two modes of testimony, making it unclear which contributed to the seeming reduction in children's anxiety. Also, it is not clear whether children feel as though their "voice has been heard," so to speak, and feel as though they were active participants when they videotaped statements in lieu of testifying directly. In many cases, though, particularly in Europe, children are required to be available for cross-examination even when videotaped testimony is presented. Thus, it may be that videotaped testimony reduces some of the distress or perhaps reduces the need for children to testify repeatedly, which still may lead to considerable benefits for children.

Closed-circuit television testimony (commonly called "Live Link" outside of the United States) involves utilizing a one-way or two-way TV link to transmit a child's live testimony during the trial. Depending on state law, attorneys may be present in the testimony room with the child or may remain in the courtroom to pose questions over the television link (Hall & Sales, 2008;

Quas & McAuliff, 2009). Like videotaped testimony, CCTV is permitted in most states (Hall & Sales, 2008), and the U.S. Supreme Court conditionally approved its use in the landmark case of *Maryland v. Craig* (1990), but concerns about its constitutionality and difficulties in implementation (discussed later) continue to severely limit its actual use.

Other countries use CCTV much more regularly, and a sizeable body of work has examined the effects of CCTV in actual cases and mock trial studies (e.g., Burton, Evans, & Sanders, 2006; Davies & Noon, 1991, 1993; Davies & Westcott, 1995; Goodman et al., 1998; Murray, 1995; Westcott, Davies, & Clifford, 1991). Overall, these studies indicate that giving testimony via CCTV is perceived to be less distressing to children than testifying in a traditional manner, both by outside observers and by legal professionals, including criminal justice personnel (Burton et al., 2006; Davies & Noon, 1991, 1993; Hamlyn, Phelps, Turtle, & Sattar, 2004). Some studies have also found that the quality of children's testimony is enhanced by the use of CCTV, with children who testify via CCTV being more confident, consistent, forthcoming, and audible than children who testify in open court (Davies & Noon, 1991, 1993; Davies & Westcott, 1995). Additionally, in a sophisticated mock trial study, Goodman et al. (1998) exposed children to a laboratory play event and, 2 weeks later, had them testify about that event either via CCTV or in court during a mock trial. Compared to children who testified in open court, children who testified via CCTV were less anxious before trial, according to their own report, and were rated by mock jurors as less stressed while testifying. Finally, the CCTV testifiers, especially those who were slightly younger, were more accurate.

Importantly, despite the fairly consistent benefits in terms of children's comfort and accuracy, and despite legal professionals' somewhat favorable stance toward the use of CCTV, jurors' perceptions of children's accuracy and credibility are much more variable. Some research has found no differences in jurors' perceptions of the quality of children's testimony based on medium of presentation (Clifford, Davies, Westcott, & Garratt, 1992, as cited in Davies, 1999; Ross et al., 1994). However, other studies, most noteworthy the comprehensive mock trial simulation conducted by Goodman et al. (1998) just described, have found that mock jurors perceive CCTV testifiers as less accurate and believable than traditional testifiers. This pattern is similar to other findings that tend to indicate jurors react more favorably to a child witness when they are able to view the child directly rather than indirectly (Goodman et al., 1998; Goodman et al., 2006).

Despite evidence indicating potential benefits of CCTV and videotaped testimony, the use of such procedures presents problems in adversarial justice systems like that of the United States. Specifically, the confrontation clause of the Sixth Amendment to the U.S. Constitution guarantees defendants the right to confront witnesses against them. Insofar as videotaped testimony or CCTV (or any other form of alternative testimony format for that matter) prevents children from facing the defendant, violations of defendants' Sixth Amendment rights are of concern (Hall & Sales, 2008). The pervasive effects of these concerns can be observed by comparing statutes regarding the use of such innovative techniques with legal professionals' reports of their actual use. While most states, federal law, and U.S. Congress have enacted legislation permitting the use of CCTV or videotaped testimony (Hall & Sales, 2008), prosecutors report rarely using these procedures (Goodman et al., 1999; Hamill, Graham, Thomason, & Huerta-Choy, 2011), often citing fears of defense challenges or appeals. A recent survey of members of the National District Attorney's Association (Hamill et al., 2011) revealed that many prosecutors did not use televised testimony because of legal restrictions. Even if televised testimony was not barred outright, many respondents indicated that it was exceedingly difficult to meet legal standards for its inclusion.

Interestingly, although most criticisms of videotaped testimony and CCTV revolve around the assumption that accommodations for children could bias jurors by increasing presumptions of the defendant's guilt, much of the research that has directly examined the effect of videotaped testimony and CCTV on jurors' perceptions of child witnesses and case outcomes indicates the opposite (Eaton, Ball, & O'Callaghan, 2001; Swim, Borgida, & McCoy, 1993; Troxel, Ogle, Cordon, Lawler, & Goodman, 2009). When effects of the innovations emerge, they virtually always favor defendants and reduce guilty verdicts (Eaton et al., 2001; Goodman et al., 1998; Orcutt, Goodman, Tobey, Batterman-Faunce, & Thomas, 2001; Swim et al., 1993). Specifically, in some studies, the mode of testimony presentation (e.g., CCTV or videotape vs. open court) has not been found to predict case outcomes or jurors' perceptions of trial fairness. In others, however, significant differences in case outcomes favoring defendants have been found based on testimony presentation mode, with alternative testimony formats reducing rather than increasing guilty verdicts (Eaton et al., 2001; Ross et al., 1994; Swim et al., 1993). For example, Eaton and colleagues (2001) showed mock jurors a videotape of a simulated child sexual abuse trial, varying child testimony format (videotaped, CCTV, or live in court). Mock jurors rendered more guilty verdicts when children testified in court versus the other formats. Thus, the use of videotaped and CCTV testimony appears to either have no effect on case outcomes or, if anything, to favor defendants.

Further evidence that videotaped and CCTV testimony do not bias jurors against defendants (and may in fact bias jurors against children instead) comes from studies examining the perceived credibility of children who receive accommodations versus those who do not. Some research examining jurors' reactions to videotaped and CCTV testimony (Lindsay, Ross, Lee, & Carr, 1995; Ross et al., 1994; Swim et al., 1993) has found that jurors' perceptions of children do not vary as a function of testimony mode. However, somewhat more ecologically valid studies suggest otherwise. In the Goodman et al. (1998) study detailed previously, children were randomly assigned to testify live in court or via CCTV. Jury-eligible community members were recruited to participate in a mock trial held at a real courthouse. In striking contrast to previous studies, jurors perceived CCTV testifiers more negatively than live testifiers along several dimensions, including believability and accuracy (see also Tobey, Goodman, Batterman-Faunce, Orcutt, & Sachsenmaier, 1995). Similar results were found in a more recent mock trial study (Goodman et al., 2006), in which children were rated by jurors as more credible when they testified live versus on videotape or via hearsay testimony of a social worker. In turn, jurors' credibility judgments were positively related to their confidence in the defendants' guilt. A series of studies conducted in Sweden obtained similar results: Children who testified about a laboratory event live were rated by observers in more positive terms (e.g., pleasant, forthcoming; Landström & Granhag, 2010; Landstrom, Granhag, & Hartwig, 2005) and their statements were judged to be more convincing (Landström, Granhag, & Hartwig, 2007) than children whose testimony was viewed on videotape (or, in some cases, CCTV).

One potential explanation for these findings concerns the possibility of the differential emotional impact of viewing children's testimony live versus on videotape. Observers may, for example, pay greater attention to live testimony because it is more vivid, emotional, and interesting than testimony presented via videotape (Landström & Granhag, 2010). Another possibility, though, focuses more on children's behavior while testifying. McAuliff and Kovera (2002, 2012) have speculated that accommodated children may change their verbal and/or nonverbal behavior in ways that negatively affect jurors' perceptions. Specifically, according to expectancy violation theory (Burgoon & Hale, 1988), people have expectancies for others' behavior based on what they perceive to be typical for a particular setting and purpose. Expectancy violations attract attention and often result in an interpretation/evaluation process in which people assess the expectancy violation, assign to it a positive or negative valence, and then react accordingly. Applying this theory to child witnesses, jurors may evaluate children's testimony differently depending on whether or not their testimonial behavior confirms or violates jurors' expectancies for how a child victim should behave or would typically behave while testifying.

In child sexual abuse cases, jurors may well expect children to appear emotional, distressed, and anxious, similar to jurors' expectations of such behaviors from rape victims (Calhoun, Cann, Selby, & Magee, 1981; Hackett, Day, & Mohr, 2008). Alternative forms of testimony, such as CCTV and videotaped interviews, are designed to reduce children's distress (and are effective at doing so). Children who provide evidence via these alternate mediums may thus appear less upset while testifying, potentially violating jurors' expectations and leading to their lower evaluations. Evidence somewhat consistent with such a possibility was obtained by McAuliff and Kovera (2012) in a survey of jury-eligible adults' perceptions of children's testimonial capabilities. Respondents did not expect children who received some sort of accommodation before or while testifying (e.g., support person presence) to appear more rehearsed or less spontaneous than children testifying in a traditional manner. Their view thus contrasts with actual research, which indicates children often are less distressed as a result of accommodations. How this discrepancy between accommodated children's behavior and jurors' expectations may impact assessments of children's credibility has implications for the broad utility of alternative testimony in improving the overall fact-finding mission of the court.

Summary. Numerous procedural innovations have been proposed for and used to accommodate child victims who participate in legal cases. Those that target the pretrial phase tend to be less or minimally controversial, especially in the United States, and are the most cost-effective methods of enhancing children's understanding of what arguably is a complex, confusing process. Pretrial preparation programs, formal and informal, fall into this category. They are, however, in need of more systematic empirical research designed to evaluate which aspects of preparation programs are most helpful to children and best facilitate the system's ability to pursue justice. The more controversial innovations affect the trial process itself. Those reviewed here concern varying with whom or how children provide testimony in court. Despite controversies surrounding the use of these innovations in terms of their effects on case progress and outcome, evidence fairly consistently indicates that such innovations reduce children's distress. What is less clear, however, is how the use of those innovations, by both directly and indirectly affecting children's distress, may influence the progression and potential outcome of the case. Of note, the innovations we discussed here are not the only procedures that may facilitate children's participation, and new technologies and practices are being developed and tested, both in the United States and abroad. The use of intermediaries in South Africa and England represents one type of practice, and, in the United States, the increased use of dogs, rather than adults, as support for children represents another. Of course, these procedures also pose challenges and can, at times, be quite controversial. It is imperative, though, that any broad implementation of a new innovative practice be done with a strong empirical basis regarding its effects on children and on the case itself.

Future Directions and Conclusions

Unfortunately, children, like adults, at times endure or witness crime and as a result may become involved in legal proceedings. This involvement may range from simply answering questions in a single interview, to enduring multiple evaluations and examinations, to testifying, possibly repeatedly, in multiple hearings or at trial. On the one hand, involvement at each of these junctures may be stressful for children, at least at the time. On the other hand, however, it is unrealistic and legally impermissible to assume that children's participation can be eliminated entirely. Moreover, discouraging or eliminating children's participation may actually be detrimental to the children themselves, who, at least in the long term, may need to have some acknowledgment of the wrongdoing and have a voice in the legal process. How best to ensure that children have some voice while reducing the potential for harmful longer term effects remains challenging.

Fortunately, however, scientific research has identified several of the facets of children's legal experiences most likely to increase their distress, to affect their ability to communicate, and to lead to longer term adverse outcomes. Future research must continue to examine how best to enhance children's legal understanding without increasing distress. That is, evidence consistently indicates that at least some of the distress children experience during the progression of a legal case stems from children's inability to understand their situation fully, including what information about the case is relevant to them, their role in the case, and how the case is progressing. At the same time, older children, especially adolescents, who are presumably more knowledgeable about the legal system, also exhibit high levels of distress and often react quite negatively when asked about their legal experiences. They are questioned more harshly in court and are more likely than younger children to have their credibility challenged. Legal professionals need to be informed about developmental changes in children's cognitive and linguistic capabilities and how these changes may influence their legal knowledge, communication, and emotional reactions to legal involvement. What strategies are most effective in providing legal professionals this information, though, have never been tested directly. Training programs could include, for example, simply the dissemination of information regarding basic changes in cognitive development across childhood and the implications of those changes for legal understanding; more direct teaching of professionals of how to explain the legal process in developmentally appropriate terms, phrase questions in a developmentally appropriate manner, and assess children's comprehension; or increased use of intermediaries with expertise talking to children by rephrasing or reinterpreting questions and answers. Investigations of the effectiveness of the different possible programs will reveal which type or types of training lead to the strongest benefits for children and also best promote the pursuit of justice (Hall & Sales, 2008).

Research has also tested several procedures and innovative approaches that appear effective in reducing distress. Some of these approaches (e.g., CCTV, videotaped, or hearsay testimony) face considerable challenges in the United States because of concerns about infringement of defendants' constitutional rights. Others, though, such as preparation programs, do not raise these concerns to as great of an extent. Additional research is needed to determine which aspects of less controversial innovations are most critical to reducing children's distress. This research also needs to be directed toward testing newly emerging innovative practices, especially instructional media (e.g., DVDs or computer-based games), given that their use may become increasingly popular with technologically savvy youth. Of importance, though, among innovations most commonly cited for possible use, most appear to have either no effect on case outcome or have slightly negative effects on perceptions of child witnesses. At the same time, concerns still remain about the potential prejudicial effects of the innovations on jurors' perceptions of a defendant. An incredibly important direction for future research may thus be to explore different methods of instructing jurors about potential effects of innovations, for instance, on children's demeanor, as well as the objective quality of their testimony to ensure that innovations' benefits are being actualized and unanticipated harms are being eliminated.

In conclusion, despite the need for continued research on the important topic of children's emotional reactions to criminal court involvement, a small but influential body of work already exists. This work highlights both what aspects of children's legal experiences are most likely to lead to harm and what can be done about it in terms of altering standard legal procedures via innovative practices. Broad dissemination of findings from this body of work will encourage the implementation of the most helpful, legally acceptable, and ethical innovations, thus allowing for fair and equitable representation to all those involved in a legal case.

References

Almerigogna, J., Ost, J., Bull, R., & Akehurst, L. (2007). State of high anxiety: How non-supportive interviewers can increase the suggestibility of child witnesses. *Applied Cognitive Psychology, 21,* 963–974. doi:10.1002/acp.1311

Altshuler, J. L., & Ruble, D. N. (1989). Developmental changes in children's awareness of strategies for coping with uncontrollable stress. *Child Development, 60,* 1337–1349. doi:10.2307/1130925

Anderson, C. A., Miller, R. S., Riger, A. L., Dill, J. C., & Sedikides, C. (1994). Behavioral and characterological attributional styles as predictors of depression and loneliness: Review, refinement, and test. *Journal of Personality and Social Psychology, 66,* 549–558. doi:10.1037/0022-3514.66.3.549

Back, C., Gustafsson, P. A., Larsson, I., & Bertero, C. (2011). Managing the legal proceedings: An interpretative phenomenological analysis of sexually abused children's experience with the legal process. *Child Abuse and Neglect, 35,* 50–57. doi:10.1016/j.chiabu.2010.08.004

Bala, N. (1999). Child witnesses in the Canadian criminal courts: Recognizing their capacities and needs. *Psychology, Public Policy, and Law, 5,* 323–354. doi:10.1037/1076-8971.5.2.323

Batterman-Faunce, J. M., & Goodman, G. S. (1993). Effects of context on the accuracy and suggestibility of child witnesses. In G. Goodman & B. Bottoms (Eds.), *Child victims, child witnesses: Understanding and improving testimony* (pp. 301–330). New York, NY: Guilford Press.

Berliner, L., & Conte, J. R. (1995). The effects of disclosure and intervention on sexually abused children. *Child Abuse and Neglect, 19,* 371–384. doi:10.1016/S0145-2134(94)00138-3

Bill, D. F. (1995). *The effect of testifying in court on children who have been sexually abused.* Dissertation Abstracts International: Section B: The Sciences and Engineering, 5558.

Brannon, L. C. (1994). The trauma of testifying in court for child victims of sexual assault v. the accused's right to confrontation. *Law and Psychology Review, 18,* 439–460.

Brennan, M., & Brennan, R. E. (1988). *Strange language: Child victims under cross-examination* (3rd ed.). Wagga Wagga, New South Wales: Charles Sturt University-Riverina.

Burgoon, J. K., & Hale, J. L. (1988). Nonverbal expectancy violations: Model elaboration and application to immediacy behaviors. *Communication Monographs, 55,* 58–79. doi:10.1080/03637758809376158

Burnett, D. M., Noblin, C. D., & Prosser, V. (2004). Adjudicative competency in a juvenile population. *Criminal Justice and Behavior, 31,* 438–462. doi:10.1177/0093854804265175

Burton, M., Evans, R., & Sanders, M. (2006). *Are special measures for vulnerable and intimidated witnesses working? Evidence from the criminal justice agencies.* London: Home Office.

Calhoun, L. G., Cann, A., Selby, J. W., & Magee, D. L. (1981). Victim emotional response: Effects on social reactions to victims of rape. *British Journal of Social Psychology, 20,* 17–21. doi:10.1111/j.2044-8309.1981.tb00468.x

Carnes, C. N., Nelson-Gardell, D., Wilson, C., & Orgassa, U. C. (2001). Extended forensic evaluation when sexual abuse is suspected: A multisite field study. *Child Maltreatment, 6,* 230–242. doi:10.1177/1077559501006003004

Cashmore, J. (1992). *The use of closed-circuit television for child witnesses in the A.C.T.* (Children's Evidence Research Paper 1). Sydney, NSW, Australia: Australian Law Reform Commission.

Ceci, S. J., & Bruck, M. (1993). Suggestibility of the child witness: A historical review and synthesis. *Psychological Bulletin, 113,* 403–439. doi:10.1037//0033-2909.113.3.403

Ceci, S. J., Kulkofsky, S., Klemfuss, J. Z., Sweeney, C. D., & Bruck, M. (2007). Unwarranted assumptions about children's testimonial accuracy. *Annual Review of Clinical Psychology, 3,* 311–328. doi:10.1146/annurev.clinpsy.3.022806.091354

Ceci, S. J., Loftus, E. F., Leichtman, M. D., & Bruck, M. (1994). The possible role of source misattributions in the creation of false belies among preschoolers. *International Journal of Clinical and Experimental Hypnosis, 42,* 304–320. doi:10.1080/00207149408409361

Connecticut v. Arroyo, 935 A.2d 975 (Conn—Supreme Court 2007).

Cooper, A., Wallin, A. R., Quas, J. A., & Lyon, T. D. (2010). Maltreated and nonmaltreated children's knowledge of the juvenile dependency system. *Child Maltreatment, 15,* 255–260. doi:10.1177/1077559510364056

Council of Europe. (2007). *Convention on the protection of children against sexual exploitation and sexual abuse report.* Lanzarote: Council of Europe Treaty Series No. 201.

Coy v. Iowa, 487 U.S. 1012 (1988).

Crawford v. Washington, 541 U.S. 36 (2004).

Cross, T. P., Jones, L. M., Walsh, W. A., Simone, M., & Kolko, D. (2007). Child forensic interviewing in children's advocacy centers. *Child Abuse and Neglect, 31,* 1031–1052. doi:10.1016/j.chiabu.2007.04.007

Crown Prosecution Service. (2008). *Safeguarding children: Guidance on children as victims and witnesses.* London: Crown Prosecution Service.

Cunningham, A., & Hurley, P. (2007). *A full and candid account: Using special accommodations and testimonial aids to facilitate the testimony of children.* Ontario: Centre for Children and Families in the Justice System.

Danner v. Kentucky, 525 U.S. 1010 (1998).
Davies, E., Devere, H., & Verbitsky, J. (2004). Court education for young witnesses: Evaluation of the pilot service in Aotearoa, New Zealand. *Psychiatry, Psychology and Law, 11*, 226–235. doi:10.1375/1321871042707179
Davies, E., Henderson, E., & Seymour, F. (1997). In the interests of justice? The cross-examination of child complaints of sexual abuse in criminal proceedings. *Psychiatry, Psychology and Law, 4*, 217–229. doi:10.1080/13218719709524912
Davies, E., & Seymour, F. (1998). Questioning child complainants of sexual abuse: Analysis of criminal court transcripts in New Zealand. *Psychiatry, Psychology and Law, 5*, 47–61. doi:10.1080/13218719809524919
Davies, G. (1999). The impact of television on the presentation and reception of children's testimony. *Journal of Law and Psychiatry, 22*, 241–256. doi:10.1016/S0160-2527(99)00007-2
Davies, G., & Noon, E. (1991). *An evaluation of the live link for child witnesses.* London: Home Office.
Davies, G., & Noon, E. (1993). Video links: Their impact on child witness trials. *Issues in Criminological and Legal Psychology, 20*, 22–26.
Davies, G., & Westcott, H. (1995). The child witness in the courtroom: Empowerment or protection? In M. S. Zaragoza, J. R. Graham, G. C. N. Hall, R. Hirschman, & Y. S. Ben-Porath (Eds.), *Memory and testimony in the child witness* (pp. 199–213). Thousand Oaks, CA: Sage.
DeVoe, E. R., & Faller, K. C. (1999). The characteristics of disclosure among children who may have been sexually abused. *Child Maltreatment, 4*, 217–227. doi:10.1177/1077559599004003003
Eaton, T. E., Ball, P. J., & O'Callaghan, M. G. (2001). Child-witness and defendant credibility: Child evidence presentation mode and judicial instructions. *Journal of Applied Social Psychology, 31*, 1845–1858. doi:10.1111/j.1559-1816.2001.tb00207.x
Elliot, D. M., & Briere, J. (1994). Forensic sexual abuse evaluations of older children: Disclosures and symptomatology. *Behavioral Sciences and the Law, 12*, 261–277. doi:10.1002/bsl.2370120306
European Convention on Human Rights, Section 1, Article 6[3] (1953).
Feiring, C., Taska, L., & Chen, K. (2002). Trying to understand why horrible things happen: Attribution, shame, and symptom development following sexual abuse. *Child Maltreatment, 7*, 26–41. doi:10.1177/1077559502007001003
Flin, R. H., Stevenson, Y., & Davies, G. M. (1989). Children's knowledge of court proceedings. *British Journal of Psychology, 80*, 285–297. doi:10.1111/j.2044-8295.1989.tb02321.x
Frazier, P. A. (1990). Victim attributions and post-rape trauma. *Journal of Personality and Social Psychology, 59*, 298–304. doi:10.1037/0022-3514.59.2.298
Ghetti, S., Alexander, K., & Goodman, G. S. (2002). Legal involvement in child sexual abuse cases: Consequences and interventions. *International Journal of Law and Psychiatry, 25*, 235–251. doi:10.1016/S0160-2527(02)00104-8
Goodman, G. S., Myers, J. E. B., Qin, J., Quas, J. A., Castelli, P., Redlich, A. D., & Rogers, L. (2006). Hearsay versus children's testimony: Effects of truthful

and deceptive statements on jurors' decisions. *Law and Human Behavior,* 363–401. doi:10.1007/s10979-006-9009-0

Goodman, G. S., & Quas, J. A. (2008). Repeated interviews and children's memory: It's more than just how many. *Current Directions in Psychological Science, 17,* 386–390. doi:10.1111/j.1467-8721.2008.00611.x

Goodman, G. S., Quas, J. A., Batterman-Faunce, J. M., Riddlesberger, M. M., & Kuhn, J. (1997). Children's reactions to and memory for a stressful event: Influences of age, anatomical dolls, knowledge, and parental attachment. *Applied Developmental Science, 1,* 54–75.

Goodman, G. S., Quas, J. A., Bulkley, J., Shapiro, C. (1999). Innovations for child witnesses: A national survey. *Psychology, Public Policy, and Law, 5,* 255–281. doi:10.1037/1076-8971.5.2.255

Goodman, G. S., Taub, E. P., Jones, D. P. H., England, P., Port, L. K., Rudy, L., & Prado, L. (1992). Testifying in criminal court. *Monographs of the Society for Research in Child Development, 57*(5, Serial No. 229), 1–142. doi:10.2307/1166127

Goodman, G. S., Tobey, A. E., Batterman-Faunce, J. M., Orcutt, H., Thomas, S., Shapiro, C., & Sachsenmaier, T. (1998). Face-to-face confrontation: Effects of closed circuit-technology on children's eyewitness testimony and jurors' decisions. *Law and Human Behavior, 22,* 165–203. doi:10.1023/A:1025742119977

Grisso, T., Steinberg, L., Woolard, J., Cauffman, E., Scott, E., Graham, S., et al. (2003). Juveniles' competence to stand trial: A comparison of adolescents' and adults' capacities as trial defendants. *Law and Human Behavior, 27,* 333–363. doi:10.1023/A:1024065015717

Hackett, L., Day, A., & Mohr, P. (2008). Expectancy violation and perceptions of rape victim credibility. *Legal and Criminological Psychology, 13,* 323–334. doi:10.1348/135532507X228458

Hafemeister, T. L. (1996). Protecting child witnesses: Judicial efforts to minimize trauma and reduce evidentiary barriers. *Violence and Victims, 11,* 71–92.

Hall, S. R., & Sales, B. D. (2008). *Courtroom modifications for child witnesses: Law and science in forensic evaluations.* Washington, DC: American Psychological Association. doi:10.1037/11808-000

Hamill, S. B., Graham, E. S., Thomason, E., & Huerta-Choy, R. (2011). Current practices in the use of televised child testimony: Questions of constitutionality and personal biases. *Criminal Justice Policy Review, 12,* 282–294.

Hamlyn, B., Phelps, A., Turtle, J., & Sattar, G. (2004). *Are special measures working?* London: Home Office.

Hanna, K., Davies, E., Henderson, E., Crothers, C., & Rotherham, C. (2010). *Child witnesses in the New Zealand criminal courts: A review of practice and implications for policy.* Auckland, New Zealand: Institute of Public Policy, AUT University.

Harbeck-Weber, C., & McKee, D. H. (1995). Prevention of emotional and behavioral distress in children experiencing hospitalization and chronic illness. In M. Roberts (Ed.), *Handbook of pediatric psychology* (2nd ed., pp. 167–184). New York, NY: Guilford Press.

Henry, J. (1997). System intervention trauma to child sexual abuse victims following disclosure. *Journal of Interpersonal Violence, 12,* 499–512.

Hershkowitz, I., Lanes, O., & Lamb, M. (2007). Exploring the disclosure of child sexual abuse with alleged victims and their parents. *Child Abuse and Neglect, 31,* 111–123. doi:10.1016/j.chiabu.2006.09.004

Het, S., Ramlow, G., & Wolf, O. (2005). A meta-analytic review of the effects of acute cortisol administration on human memory. *Psychoneuroendocrinology, 30,* 771–784. doi:10.1016/j.psyneuen.2005.03.005

Jones, L. M., Cross, T. P., Walsh, W. A., & Simone, M. (2007). Do Children's Advocacy Centers improve families' experiences of child sexual abuse investigations? *Child Abuse and Neglect, 31,* 1069–1085. doi:10.1016/j.chiabu.2007.07.003

Jonker, G., & Swanzen, R. (2007). Intermediary services for child witnesses testifying in South African Criminal Courts. *SUR International Journal of Human Rights, 3,* 95–119.

Kaufman, K. L., Holmberg, J. K., Orts, K. A., McCrady, F. E., Rotzien, A. L., Daleiden, E. L., & Hilliker, D. R. (1998). Factors influencing sexual offenders' modus operandi: An examination of victim-offender relatedness and age. *Child Maltreatment, 3,* 349–361. doi:10.1177/1077559598003004007

Keeney, K. S., Amacher, E., & Kastanakis, J. A. (1992). The court prep group: A vital part of the court process. In H. Dent & R. Flin (Eds.), *Children as witnesses* (pp. 201–209). Oxford: Wiley.

Kennedy v. Louisiana, 128 S. Ct. 2641 (2008).

Kogan, S. M. (2004). The role of disclosing child sexual abuse on adolescent adjustment and revictimization. *Journal of Child Sexual Abuse, 14,* 25–47. doi:10.1300/J070v14n02_02

Kovera, M. B., Gresham, A. W., Borgida, E., Gray, E., & Regan, P. C. (1997). Does expert testimony inform or influence juror decision-making? A social cognitive analysis. *Journal of Applied Psychology, 82,* 178–191. doi:10.1037/0021-9010.82.1.178

Landström, S., & Granhag, P. A. (2010). In-court versus out-of-court testimonies: Children's experiences and adults' assessments. *Applied Cognitive Psychology, 24,* 941–955. doi:10.1002/acp.1606

Landström, S., Granhag, P. A., & Hartwig, M. (2005). Witnesses appearing live versus on video: Effects on observers' perception, veracity assessments and memory. *Applied Cognitive Psychology, 19,* 913–933. doi:10.1002/acp.1131

Landström, S., Granhag, P. A., & Hartwig, M. (2007). Children's live and videotaped testimonies: How presentation mode affects observers' perception, assessment and memory. *Legal and Criminological Psychology, 12,* 333–347. doi:10.1348/135532506X133607

Lindsay, R. C. L., Ross, D. F., Lea, J. A., & Carr, C. (1995). What's fair when a child testifies? *Journal of Applied Social Psychology, 25,* 870–888. doi:10.1111/j.1559-1816.1995.tb02650.x

Lyon, T. D. (2007). History of children's hearsay: From old Bailey to post-Davis. *Indiana Law Journal, 82,* 1029–1058.

Lyon, T. D., & Ahern, E. C. (2011). Disclosure of child sexual abuse: Implications for interviewing. In J. E. B. Myers (Ed.), *APSAC handbook on child maltreatment* (3rd ed., pp. 233–252). Thousand Oaks, CA: Sage.

Malloy, L. C., Lyon, T. D., & Quas, J. A. (2007). Filial dependency and recantation of child sexual abuse allegations. *Journal of the American*

Academy of Child and Adolescent Psychiatry, 46, 162–170. doi:10.1097/01.chi.0000246067.77953.f7

Malloy, L. C., Mitchell, E., Block, S., Quas, J. A., & Goodman, G. S. (2007). Children's eyewitness memory: Balancing victim's needs and defendant's rights when seeking the truth. In M. P. Toglia, J. D. Read, D. F. Ross, & R. C. L. Lindsay (Eds.), *The handbook of eyewitness psychology, Vol. 1: Memory for events* (pp. 545–574). Mahwah, NJ: Erlbaum.

Maryland v. Craig, 497 U.S. 836 (1990).

McAuliff, B. D., & Kovera, M. B. (2002). The status of evidentiary and procedural innovations in child abuse proceedings. In B. L. Bottoms, M. B. Kovera, & B. D. McAuliff (Eds.), *Children, social science, and the law* (pp. 412–445). New York, NY: Cambridge University Press. doi:10.1017/CBO9780511500114.016

McAuliff, B. D., & Kovera, M. B. (2012). Do jurors get what they expect? Traditional versus alternative forms of children's testimony. *Psychology, Crime and Law, 18,* 27–47.

McAuliff, B. D., Nicholson, E., Amarilio, D., & Ravanshenas, D. (2012). Supporting children in U.S. legal proceedings: Descriptive and attitudinal data from a national survey of victim/witness assistants. *Psychology, Public Policy, and Law.* doi:10.1037/a0027879

Murray, K. (1995). *Live television link: An evaluation of its use by child witnesses in Scottish criminal trials.* Edinburgh, Scotland: Scottish Office, Central Research Unit.

Myers, J. E. B. (1998). *Legal issues in child abuse and neglect* (2nd ed.). Beverly Hills, CA: Sage.

Nathanson, R., & Saywitz, K. J. (2003). The effects of courtroom context on children's memory and anxiety. *Journal of Psychiatry and Law, 31,* 67–98.

National Center for the Prosecution of Child Abuse. (2011). *Speedy trial statutes for child victims and witnesses.* Retrieved from http://www.ndaa.org/pdf/NCPCA%20Speedy%20Trial%202011.pdf

Nefas, C., Duckworth, T., & McAuliff, B. D. (2008). *Support person use and child victim testimony: Believe it or not.* Paper presented at the annual meeting of the American Psychology-Law Society, Jacksonville, FL.

Oates, R. K., & Tong, L. (1987). Sexual abuse of children: An area with room for professional reforms. *Medical Journal of Australia, 147,* 544–548.

Office of the United Nations High Commissioner on Human Rights. (1990). *Convention on the rights of the child.* Retrieved from http://www2.ohchr.org/english/

Orcutt, H. K., Goodman, G. S., Tobey, A. E., Batterman-Faunce, J. M., & Thomas, S. (2001). Detecting deception in children's testimony: Factfinders' abilities to reach the truth in open court and closed-circuit trials. *Law and Human Behavior, 25,* 339–372. doi:10.1023/A:1010603618330

Perry, N. W., McAuliff, B. D., Tam, P., Claycomb, L., Dostal, C., & Flanagan, C. (1995). When lawyers question children: Is justice served? *Law and Human Behavior, 19,* 609–629. doi:10.1007/BF01499377

Peters, D. (1991). The influence of stress and arousal on the child witness. In J. Doris (Ed.), *The suggestibility of children's recollections* (pp. 60–76). Washington, DC: American Psychological Association.

Peterson-Badali, M., Abramovitch, R., & Duda, J. (1997). Young children's legal knowledge and reasoning ability. *Canadian Journal of Criminology, 39,* 145–170.

Peterson, C., & Warren, K. L. (2009). *Emotion and memory in development: Biological, cognitive, and social considerations* (pp. 60–85). New York, NY: Oxford University Press.

Plotnikoff, J., & Woolfson, R. (2004). *In their own words: The experiences of 50 young witnesses in criminal proceedings.* London: NSPCC.

Plotnikoff, J., & Woolfson, R. (2007). *The 'go-between': Evaluation of the intermediary special measure.* London: Ministry of Justice Research Summary No. 1.

Plotnikoff, J., & Woolfson, R. (2009). *Measuring up? Evaluating implementation of government commitments to young witnesses in criminal proceedings.* London: NSPCC.

Quas, J. A., Bauer, A., & Boyce, W. T. (2004). Physiological reactivity, social support, and memory in early childhood. *Child Development, 75,* 797–814. doi:10.1111/j.1467-8624.2004.00707.x

Quas, J. A., Goodman, G. S., Ghetti, S., Alexander, K. W., Edelstein, R., Redlich, A. D., et al. (2005). Childhood sexual assault victims: Long-term outcomes after testifying in criminal court. *Monographs of the Society for Research in Child Development, 70*(2, Serial No. 280), 1–128. doi:10.1111/j.1540-5834.2005.00337.x

Quas, J. A., Goodman, G. S., & Jones, D. P. H. (2003). Predictors of attributions of self-blame and internalizing behavior problems in sexually abused children. *Journal of Child Psychology and Psychiatry, 44,* 723–736. doi:10.1111/1469-7610.00158

Quas, J. A., & Lench, H. C. (2007). Arousal at encoding, arousal at retrieval, interviewer support, and children's memory for a mild stressor. *Applied Cognitive Psychology, 21,* 289–305. doi:10.1002/acp.1279

Quas, J. A., & McAuliff, B. D. (2009). Accommodating child witnesses in the criminal justice system: Implications for death penalty cases. In R. Schopp, R. Weiner, B. Bornstein, & S. Willborn (Eds.), *Mental disorder and criminal law: Responsibility, punishment and competence* (pp. 79–102). New York, NY: Springer.

Quas, J. A., & Schaaf, J. M. (2002). Children's memories of experienced and nonexperienced events following repeated interviews. *Journal of Experimental Child Psychology, 83,* 304–338. doi:10.1016/S0022-0965(02)00150-9

Quas, J. A., & Sumaroka, M. (2011). Consequences of legal involvement on child victims of maltreatment. In M. E. Lamb, D. J. La Rooy, L. C. Malloy, & C. Katz (Eds.), *Children's testimony: A handbook of psychological research and forensic practice* (pp. 323–350). Oxford: Wiley.

Quas, J. A., Wallin, A. R., Horwitz, B., Davis, E., & Lyon, T. (2009). Maltreated children's understanding of and emotional reactions to dependency court involvement. *Behavioral Sciences and the Law, 27,* 97–117. doi:10.1002/bsl.836

Ross, D. F., Hopkins, S., Hanson, E., Lindsay, R. C. L., Hazen, K., & Eslinger, T. (1994). The impact of protective shields and videotape testimony on conviction rates in a simulated trial of child sexual abuse. *Law and Human Behavior, 18,* 553–566. doi:10.1007/BF01499174

Rudolph, K. D., Dennig, M. D., & Weisz, J. R. (1995). Determinants and consequences of children's coping in the medical setting:

Conceptualization, review, and critique. *Psychological Bulletin, 118,* 328–357. doi:10.1037/0033-2909.118.3.328

Runyan, D. K., Everson, M. D., Edelsohn, G. A., Hunter, W. M., & Coulter, M. L. (1988). Impact of legal intervention on sexually abused children. *Journal of Pediatrics, 113,* 647–653. doi:10.1016/S0022-3476(88)80373-1

Sandler, J. C. (2006). Alternative methods of child testimony: A review of law and research. In C. R. Bartol & A. M. Bartol (Eds.), *Current perspectives in forensic psychology and criminal justice* (pp. 203–214). Thousand Oaks, CA: Sage.

Santtila, P., Korkman, J., & Sandnabba, K. (2004). Effects of interview phase, repeated interviewing, presence of a support person, and anatomically detailed dolls on child sexual abuse interviews. *Psychology, Crime, and Law, 10,* 21–35. doi:10.1080/10683160210000030559

Sas, L. D. (1991). *Reducing the system-induced trauma for child sexual abuse victims through court preparation, assessment and follow-up* (Final Report, Project No. 4555-1-125, National Welfare Grants Division, Health and Welfare Canada). London, Ontario: London Family Court Clinic.

Sas, L. D. (1993). *Three years after the verdict: A longitudinal study of the social and psychological adjustment of child witnesses referred to the child witness project* (Final Report, Project No. 4887-06-91-026, Family Violence Prevention Division of Health Canada). London, Ontario: London Family Court Clinic.

Sas, L. D., Austin, G., Wolfe, D., & Hurley, P. (1991). *Reducing the system induced trauma for child sexual abuse victims through court preparation, assessment, and follow-up.* Ottawa: National Welfare Grant Division, Health and Welfare Canada.

Sawicki, M. E. (2009). The Crawford v. Washington decision—Five years later: Implications for child abuse prosecutors. *National Center for Prosecution of Child Abuse: Update, 21,* 1–8.

Saywitz, K., Goodman, G. S., & Lyon, T. D. (2002). Interviewing children in and out of court: Current research and practice implications. In J. E. B. Myers, L. Berliner, J. Briere, T. Hendrix, C. Jenny, & T. Reid (Eds.), *APSAC handbook on child maltreatment* (2nd ed., pp. 349–377). Thousand Oaks, CA: Sage.

Saywitz, K., Jaenicke, C., & Camparo, L. (1990). Children's knowledge of legal terminology. *Law and Human Behavior, 14,* 523–535. doi:10.1007/BF01044879

Saywitz, K. J., & Nathanson, R. (1993). Children's testimony and their perceptions of stress in and out of the courtroom. *Child Abuse and Neglect, 17,* 613–622. doi:10.1016/0145-2134(93)90083-H

Saywitz, K. J., Nathanson, R., Snyder, L., & Lamphear, V. (1993). *Preparing children for the investigative and judicial process: Improving communication, memory, and emotional resiliency* (Final Report to the National Center on Child Abuse and Neglect, Grant No. 90-CA-1179). Los Angeles, CA: University of California.

Saywitz, K. J., & Snyder, L. (1993). Improving children's testimony with preparation. In G. S. Goodman & B. L. Bottoms (Eds.), *Child victims, child witnesses: Understanding and improving testimony* (pp. 117–146). New York, NY: Guilford.

Saywitz, K. J., & Snyder, L. (1996). Narrative elaboration: Test of a new procedure for interviewing children. *Journal of Consulting and Clinical Psychology, 64,* 1347–1357.

Saywitz, K. J., Snyder, L., & Nathanson, R. (1999). Facilitating the communicative competence of the child witness. *Applied Developmental Science, 3,* 58–68. doi:10.1207/s1532480xads0301_7

Schudson, C. B. (1987). Making courts safe for children. *Journal of Interpersonal Violence, 2,* 120–122. doi:10.1177/088626087002001011

Skinner, E. A., & Zimmer-Gembeck, M. J. (2007). The development of coping. *Annual Review of Psychology, 58,* 119–144. doi:10.1146/annurev.psych.58.110405.085705

Swim, J. K., Borgida, E., & McCoy, K. (1993). Videotaped versus in-court witness testimony: Does protecting the child witnesses jeopardize due process? *Journal of Applied Social Psychology, 23,* 603–631. doi:10.1111/j.1559-1816.1993.tb01105.x

Tedesco, J. F., & Schnell, S. V. (1987). Children's reactions to sex abuse investigation and litigation. *Child Abuse and Neglect, 11,* 267–272. doi:10.1016/0145-2134(87)90066-4

Tobey, A. E., Goodman, G. S., Batterman-Faunce, J. M., Orcutt, H. K., & Sachsenmaier, T. (1995). Balancing the rights of children and defendants: Effects of closed-circuit television on children's accuracy and jurors' perceptions. In M. S. Zaragoza, J. R. Graham, G. C. N. Hall, R. Hirschman, & Y. S. Ben-Porath (Eds.), *Memory and testimony in the child witness* (pp. 214–239). Thousand Oaks, CA: Sage.

Troxel, N. R., Ogle, C. M., Cordon, I. M., Lawler, M., & Goodman, G. S. (2009). Child witnesses in criminal court. In B. Bottoms, C. Najdowski, & G. Goodman (Eds.), *Children as victims, witnesses, and offenders: Psychological science and the law* (pp. 150–166). New York, NY: Guilford Press.

Tyler, T. R. (2003). Procedural justice, legitimacy, and the effective rule of law. *Crime and Justice, 30,* 283–357.

Tyler, T. R., & Huo, Y. J. (2002). *Trust in the law.* New York, NY: Russell-Sage.

Wagland, P., & Bussey, K. (2005). Factors that facilitate and undermine children's beliefs about truth telling. *Law and Human Behavior, 29,* 639–655. doi:10.1007/s10979-005-7371-y

Walsh, W. A., Lippert, T., Cross, T. P, Maurice, D. M., & Davison, K. S. (2008). How long to prosecute child sexual abuse for a community using a children's advocacy center and two comparison communities? *Child Maltreatment, 13,* 3–13. doi:10.1177/1077559507307839

Warren-Leubecker, A., Tate, C. S., Hinton, I. D., & Ozbek, I. N. (1989). What do children know about the legal system and when do they know it? First steps down a less traveled path in child witness research. In S. J. Ceci, D. F. Ross, & M. P. Toglia (Eds.), *Perspectives on children's testimony* (pp. 158–183). New York, NY: Springer-Verlag.

Westcott, H. L., Davies, G. M., & Clifford, B. R. (1991). Adults' perceptions of children's videotaped truthful and deceptive statements. *Children and Society, 5,* 123–135. doi:10.1111/j.1099-0860.1991.tb00378.x

Whitcomb, D., Goodman, G., Runyon, D., & Hoak, S. (1994). *The emotional effects of testifying on sexually abused children.* Washington, DC: National Institute of Justice.

Wilson, J. C., & Davies, G. M. (1999). An evaluation of the use of videotaped evidence for juvenile witnesses in criminal courts in England and Wales. *European Journal on Criminal Policy and Research, 7,* 81–96.

Yim, I. S., Quas, J. A., Cahill, L., & Hayakawa, C. M. (2010). Children's and adults' salivary cortisol responses to an identical psychosocial laboratory stressor. *Psychoneuroendocrinology, 35,* 241–248. doi:10.1016/j.psyneuen.2009.06.014

Zajac, R., Gross, J., & Hayne, H. (2003). Asked and answered: Questioning children in the courtroom. *Psychiatry, Psychology and Law, 10,* 199–209. doi:10.1375/pplt.2003.10.1.199

Zajac, R., & Hayne, H. (2003). I don't think that's what really happened: The effect of cross-examination on the accuracy of children's reports. *Journal of Experimental Psychology: Applied, 9,* 187–195. doi:10.1037/1076-898X.9.3.187

Zajac, R., Jury, E., & O'Neill, S. (2009). The role of psychosocial factors in young children's responses to cross-examination style questioning. *Applied Cognitive Psychology, 23,* 918–935. doi:10.1002/acp.1536

Zeltzer, L. K., Fanurik, D., & LeBaron, S. (1989). The cold pressor pain paradigm in children: Feasibility of an intervention model: II. *Pain, 37,* 305–313. doi:10.1016/0304-3959(89)90195-4

6

Civil Plaintiffs, Trauma, and Stress in the Legal System

Mary White Stewart and Steven M. Wood

A consideration of the stressors and the potential for trauma in the justice system is built on widely held concerns about our civil justice system and provides the backdrop for addressing how plaintiffs experience the justice system, what their experiences are, and how those experiences might be improved. It is clear that Americans believe people are too quick to sue and that juries are too willing to hand out large awards (Howell, 1998). Thomas Ehrlich (1976) introduced the term *legal pollution* to express concerns with the overreliance on the legal system, and Bayless Manning (1977) used the word *hyperlexis* to describe the "national disease" overloading the U.S. justice system. Although medical malpractice lawsuits suffer the greatest condemnation, there is significant concern with the more general "glut of litigators" (Faria, 1993) and the overall "litigation explosion" (Olson, 1991). While research does not support the existence of such a glut or explosion (Merry & Silbey, 1984; Vidmar, 1997), this public perception remains firmly entrenched in minds of U.S. citizens (Meinhold & Neubauer, 2001). These perceptions may have significant financial and personal consequences for those involved in or reacting to legal decisions in civil cases (Wayte, Samra, Robbennolt, Heuer, & Koch, 2002).

Another frequent criticism of the civil justice system is that a dramatic rise in lawsuits has led to skyrocketing insurance rates, sometimes driving doctors out of certain practices (e.g., obstetrics), although some contend that this increase is inflated by the number of "repeat offenders" filing suits (Public Citizen Congress Watch, 2005). Others express concerns that doctors are fleeing certain states because of the high number of medical malpractice lawsuits (see Faria, 1993; Olson, 1991; Vidmar, 2005). However, in some states where there is concern about losing doctors as a result of frivolous lawsuits (e.g., Oklahoma, New Jersey, Mississippi, Nevada), the number of doctors is increasing even as the public and legislative concern over the medical crisis grows (U.S. General Accounting Office, 2003). Another more general complaint is that frivolous lawsuits are clogging the courts, leading to expensive delays and denying the potential for justice. Still another complaint is that jury awards are not only exorbitant but also ridiculous—for example, as in the oft-cited McDonald's coffee case. Attorneys and their plaintiffs who bring medical malpractice cases are often blamed for the increase in lawsuits, as well as the spiraling health care costs (Budeti, 2005; Gibeaut, 2005). The plaintiff's bar is concerned about the efforts under way in many states to address these perceived abuses through restricting pain and suffering and other noneconomic damages in civil cases, as illustrated by President George Bush's call in 2003 to cap noneconomic damages at $250,000 (*Medical Malpractice*, 2003). They are also concerned that media publicity about rare and misunderstood cases such as "the McDonald's case"—what Susan Saladoff (Casavant, 2011) calls the "most infamous case in the world"—poisons juries against their plaintiffs, resulting in a jury system that favors the defendant.

The experience of plaintiffs in the civil justice system takes place within a cultural and political milieu characterized by significant disagreement about whether the justice system operates the way it was intended or whether it is being abused by "sue happy" plaintiffs and their "greedy attorneys" seeking "jackpot justice" (see Susan Saladoff's [2011] HBO documentary "Hot Coffee"). A report conducted for the U.S. Chamber Institute for Legal Reform (2009) indicated that the cost of the U.S. tort system was $254.7 billion ($838 per citizen) in 2008. It seems that these high costs have not established confidence in the justice system. A 2008 election night poll indicated that 83% of voters believed that frivolous lawsuits are a serious problem, and only 4% believed that the victims benefited from lawsuits (U.S. Chamber Institute for Legal Reform, 2012). Meinhold and Neubauer (2001) expand this finding, showing that African Americans have slightly more faith in the justice system than Whites, but they too agree that people are too quick to sue and that there are too many frivolous lawsuits.

Despite the oft-cited perception that America is a "sue happy society," some authors (e.g., Felstiner, Abel, & Sarat, 1980–1981) conclude that Americans are relatively reluctant to sue, particularly when compared with other societies. Galanter (1974) provides reports on the plethora of "spite" suits in Yugoslavia, as reported in the *New York Times* (October 16, 1966), giving as an example the 53 suits tenants in one building brought against one another. In another example, Frake (1957) reports that suits are so common among the Lipay of the Philippines that they are almost expected. Individuals from these societies often question why Americans are so slow to perceive injury and reluctant to litigate (Felstiner et al., 1980–1981). In addition, Nader and Singer (1976) suggest that the study of the emergence and transformation of disputes may lead to the conclusion that Americans perceive and pursue too few wrongs, rather than too many. Galanter (1974) even suggests that the low level of litigiousness in some societies, such as Japan, may flow from an "underdeveloped sense of justiciable rights" (p. 106). While litigiousness cannot be measured only by the number of trials that occur, between 1992 and 2002, the number of civil trials decreased by 43% (from 8,029 to 4,569) in U.S. district courts and 32% (from 712,676 to 487,200) in 22 state courts (Galanter, 2004).

These concerns, as Merry and Silbey (1984) suggest, may reflect a deeper belief about the general breakdown of society rather than being specifically focused on the details of lawsuits. However, they serve as the backdrop against which lawsuits are brought and defended and provide the underlying context within which attorneys shape their cases and juries hear them.

Our purpose in this chapter is to investigate the ways in which the civil litigation process and the legal system affect the experience of the plaintiff. The focus of this chapter will be on the entire process—from the initial stages during which a potential plaintiff is deciding whether to sue and how to select an attorney through the verdict or settlement and the plaintiff's subsequent response. We will address the many factors in civil cases that shape the experience of the plaintiff, particularly as these factors influence the stress and trauma that accompany the litigation process, and will conclude by offering suggestions for ways in which the wellbeing of civil plaintiffs may be improved.

While the focus is more heavily on the plaintiff, this is not to deny the stress experienced by the defendant, particularly the individual defendant. Indicative of the awareness of such stress is the existence of several Web sites designed for physicians who have been sued for malpractice. The Physicians Litigation Stress Support Center helps doctors address their emotional responses (e.g., fear, guilt, and anger) while adhering to the advice of their attorneys and counsel for the insurance companies defending them. Articles on the World Wide Web such as "Medical Malpractice Litigation: Coping with the Stress of Malpractice Litigation" (Controlled Risk Insurance Company/ Risk Management Foundation, n.d.) and "Litigation Stress" (Andrew, n.d.) are indicative of the recognition that defendants experience stress as well. Our focus on the plaintiff is a recognition that civil cases are likely to be ones in which a corporation or company rather than an individual is the defendant. Nonetheless, as we suggest throughout this chapter, the experience of a lawsuit is unavoidably stressful for everyone involved, from plaintiffs to witnesses to attorneys to jurors.

Deciding to Sue

People who bring civil suits are often not motivated by monetary desires, but by the desire to be heard or to tell their story (e.g., Conley & O'Barr, 1988; Tyler, 1990). Although plaintiffs want to prove that the party being sued is responsible for the harm or damage, they may not be as interested in financial remuneration as they are in an opportunity to tell their story in their own words. Relis (2002) suggests that plaintiffs are responding to feelings of distress, frustration, or disappointment. They are agitated, tense, or upset (Felstiner & Sarat, 1992). Their subjective interpretations of their experiences are unsettling to the point that they are willing to endure the public scrutiny, discomfort, inconvenience, and potential expense of filing and pursuing a lawsuit. Moreover, many plaintiffs view the ability to tell their story to a sympathetic listener (i.e., judge)—who acknowledges and appreciates the gravity of the situation—as therapeutic (Conley & O'Barr, 1988).

Different plaintiffs may perceive the same dispute differently. Some plaintiffs focus on feelings of being wronged or mistreated, some stress fairness, and others focus on responsibility (Relis, 2002). Regardless of the focus of the litigation, plaintiffs have one or a combination of goals (Vidmar, 1990), including righting a wrong, asserting their rights, achieving moral vindication (Galanter, 1983; Strasburger, 1999), expressing the desire for revenge (Genn, 1999), or seeking accountability (Strasburger, 1999). A significant number of these plaintiffs never intend to go to court; however, they may sue in order to express their feelings, particularly to a person in a position of authority (Relis, 2002) or in hopes that a suit may lead to an apology (Conley & O'Barr, 1988).

Transforming a Personal Injury Into a Legal Dispute

In deciding to sue, an individual must transform a sense of injury into a determination that someone is responsible and that it is worth pursuing compensation from that person in a court of law as opposed to alternative means of compensation. Felstiner et al. (1980–1981) point out in their classic article that individuals transform only a small proportion of injuries or wrongs into legal cases and tend to tolerate substantial stress and injury without transforming this into a grievance or dispute. The question then becomes, "What processes facilitate or hamper the transformation of a perceived wrong into an injury or grievance?"

Felstiner et al. (1980–1981) refer to the process of legal transformations as "naming," "claiming," and "blaming." They suggest that each stage requires the conceptual involvement of the injured person and others in the construction of a discrete event or series of events as a particular type of phenomenon. From the perspective of these individuals, experiences may be perceived as either injurious or not (naming). If these individuals perceive the experience as injurious, it may or may not move to the next step of becoming a grievance (claiming). Finally, the grievance becomes a dispute (blaming) through the involvement of a third party. To clarify, an individual can identify an event as injurious and present that injury to a party perceived as either responsible or in the position to respond. If the wronged individual believes the offending party has responded appropriately to the named injurious experience, then it may not become a dispute. However, there are other reasons besides the response of the perceived offender that lead a person to decide whether to transform an injury into a dispute, such as the anticipated cost of litigation or the potentially negative impact on the relationships between the parties involved either directly or indirectly.

Considerations about relationships are particularly pertinent in cases in which there is a long-standing or ongoing relationship between parties, such as in the workplace or in situations involving contract disputes. As Galanter (1974) concludes, bringing an employment suit almost guarantees that the person will not return to work, since it creates such an uncomfortable environment for all participants. Likewise, Dziech and Weiner (1984), as well as Giuffre and Williams (1994), note that women often fail to report sexual harassment, despite established legal protections, because doing so negatively affects their work relationships and the overall work environment. Other risks associated with reporting include retaliation, isolation, shunning, and psychological suffering. Fear of the legal process and publicity, as well as self-blame, which threatens the individual's sense of competence and self-worth, may also discourage the transformation of an injury into a grievance or dispute. For example, in sexual harassment cases, not only may others see the claimant as "asking for it" through her behavior, demeanor, or dress, but also she is likely to incorporate their judgments into her own self-assessment (Stewart, 2002).

The breast implant litigation studied by one of the authors (Stewart, 1998) serves as a useful illustration of the factors influencing the transformation of a personal injury into a legal dispute. The women who sued the Dow Corning Corporation for their injuries resulting from faulty breast implants reveal that a number of related, but separable, factors went into their decision to go forward. Their actual physical condition was the initial, critical factor, yet they had to identify their problem as being not just a physical one, but also one caused by the breast implants rather than by something else such as hormonal and other changes accompanying menopause. This initial step was fraught with difficulty for the women, given the vociferous debate in the media about the safety of the implants and the hesitation on the part of doctors to attribute the women's symptoms to the breast implants. The women operated within a "climate of disbelief" (Stewart, 1998) in which little support existed for their claim that the implants had caused their problems.

A related consideration for the women and their doctors was the compilation of the varied, often elusive symptoms into one coherent illness. The difficulty experienced by the women during this stage was related not only to the media's denial of a problem but also to the doctors' suspicions of the symptoms presented by the women and the doctors' confusion about whether they were seeing a bona fide illness, "malingering," or "complaints of menopause." Further, medical records sometimes either carried more credibility than the words of the women on which they were initially based or misrepresented their problems—causing the women's complaints to be "lost in translation." In addition, the potential plaintiff faced practical problems of access to records and other necessary information requested by the attorney for use in the trial.

This process was particularly trying for women whose injuries occurred over a number of years, had no clear pattern, and were difficult to relate to the implants (Stewart, 1998).

A third concern was the fact that entering into litigation meant the women were going to have to "relive the experience" not only in discussions with their attorneys and the defense but also during the trial itself. "Reliving the experience" leads some plaintiffs to experience psychological retraumatization and delays in the emotional healing process (Fulcher, 2004). Moreover, this retraumatization may lead to litigation-induced trauma sensitization (LITS), a scenario in which plaintiffs dissociate themselves from the injurious event and thereby give a false impression that their psychological injuries have dissipated (Fulcher, 2004).

Another consideration for many plaintiffs, as illustrated in the breast implant litigation, was mistrust of attorneys, fear that a better attorney could have been hired, concern about their attorney's competency or ethics, or concern that their attorney would be too busy or would not pay enough attention to their particular case (Felstiner & Sarat, 1992). Such concerns are no doubt shared by defendants in criminal cases, as approximately 80% of defendants charged with a felony in the nation's largest counties during 2004 and 2006 reported having public defenders or assigned counsel (Cohen, 2011).

A final consideration, in this and other cases, is the reaction of the family. Families may not want the notoriety or the disruption that sometimes accompanies a trial and, as in the case of the breast implant litigation, may be reluctant to have sensitive or personal topics discussed in public by strangers. They also might not want the stress and attention that such a lawsuit may bring to them or other members of their family. Most important, the stress of the litigation proceedings may cause "burnout" on the part of family members as the plaintiffs' need for telling their story exceeds the family members' tolerance and patience for listening, leaving the plaintiffs socially isolated and left to handle the lawsuit on their own (Strasburger, 1999).

Pretrial

The next critical steps in this process are selecting an attorney, establishing a relationship with the attorney and staff, and engaging in pretrial conferences, depositions, and other activities necessary to prepare a case and oneself for trial or eventual settlement. Several factors can influence the amount of anxiety and discomfort plaintiffs experience during this pretrial phase, influencing their level of satisfaction with the legal process and the outcome.

Attorney–Plaintiff Relationships

Plaintiffs are correct in assuming that they need an attorney to have successful access to the justice system and to resolve the kinds of legal problems that they have encountered (Genn, 1999). Even the most sophisticated of plaintiffs do not have the education or experience needed to handle a lawsuit without representation (Strasburger, 1999). Plaintiffs approach the attorney–plaintiff relationship with little experience, have little familiarity with the process or the laws governing the case, and have little knowledge about how to access the system on their own, or may not be able to do so (e.g., in a class action suit). This unfamiliarity and uncertainty can cause stress.

While securing an attorney is critical, plaintiffs are surprisingly careless about the attorney they select. Bogart and Vidmar (1990) suggest that, while plaintiffs may say that factors such as integrity and competence are important, they are likely to choose the first attorney they approach or the first one recommended to them. While plaintiffs are not particularly careful about the selection of an attorney, they nonetheless have expectations for and concerns about the attorney and the legal process itself. Some factors taken into consideration by plaintiffs as they approach an attorney are the reputation of the attorney; the cost of the attorney and the entire suit; the loyalty of the attorney; the supportiveness of the attorney's staff; the ability of the attorney to listen, empathize, and understand; and the attorney's competence and reputation. Many plaintiffs will also be concerned about whether the merits of their case are strong enough to convince the attorney to pursue legal action (Cohen & Vesper, 2001).

Plaintiffs want the attorney to take their case, but they also want the case to reflect their experience. While some legal scholars (e.g., Freedman, 1987) suggest that attorneys must forgo their individual autonomy to accommodate and ensure their plaintiff's autonomy, a more likely scenario is that plaintiffs must give up control of their story and may lose significant pieces of their story as the attorney reshapes it for legal purposes. Yet, plaintiffs may be reluctant to tell their full story to their attorney for a number of reasons, including feeling responsible, looking silly, being ashamed about their behavior or their involvement in the situation, feeling embarrassed, or because certain elements of the case may make them look bad or weaken their case (see also Felstiner & Sarat, 1992).

While the plaintiff "owns" the story (i.e., the injury), once told, it is no longer the plaintiff's. Perhaps the very pieces of the story that have the most significance to the plaintiff become irrelevant or secondary. This is particularly troubling since it reveals a discrepancy between the "reality" experienced by the plaintiff and the "reconstructed logic" used by the attorney in shaping the case (Kaplan, 1964). This is also troubling because the ability to or desire to tell their story may well be the motivation for the lawsuit (Conley & O'Barr, 1988).

The attorney translates the broader goals of the plaintiff into the narrower legal issues and purposes of the law and courts and, further, often redefines the case, deflating the plaintiff's expectations (Bogart & Vidmar, 1990) and redefining the plaintiff's goals and underlying "problem." This transformation involves both content and language. Certain facts that are of importance to the plaintiff may be legally irrelevant; the attorney is seeking legally pertinent information while the plaintiff may be seeking to express the personally relevant details of the case, leading to a "dialogue of the deaf" (Knowles, 2006).

The language used by the attorney establishes the reality that will be put forward and in the process sometimes constrains, ignores, or even, from the plaintiff's perspective, disregards the plaintiff's story. Several authors (e.g., Matruglio, 1994; Tomasic, 1978) suggest that attorneys' use of legal or technical language can hamper understanding and communication and leave plaintiffs feeling confused or frustrated. Despite their best attempts, attorneys may not be able to explicate the legal technicalities to their plaintiffs in an understandable way (Cohen & Vesper, 2001). Communication may also be hampered by other factors such as social class differences, cultural differences, failure on the part of plaintiffs to provide adequate information, confusion on the part of plaintiffs, or insensitivity on the part of attorneys. The almost unavoidable lack of control plaintiffs can feel over their case can lead to unhappiness and frustration (Matruglio, 1994). The fact that attorneys bill by the hour may also present a conflict to some plaintiffs who desire a relationship with their attorney and the ability to confide and explain themselves freely but who, at the same time, may feel a need to truncate their conversations and contact in order to limit costs.

In addition to all of the problems plaintiffs may experience, there are often large differences between the objectives, values, tactics, and views of attorneys and plaintiffs, and many attorneys pay little attention to the goals or feelings of their plaintiffs (Relis, 2002). While plaintiffs may want to be heard or have their feelings acknowledged, attorneys are more likely to want to protect their plaintiff's financial position (Sarat & Felstiner, 1986). In attempting to protect their plaintiff's position, attorneys may work to avoid delays, as well as the time and expense of preparation, and settle early (Galanter, 1974). They may prefer to settle cases rather than go to trial, a decision that may reflect the best interests of plaintiffs or attorneys, or both, but which, in either case, results in the outcome that plaintiffs will never have a chance to achieve other goals from the litigation, such as telling their story in public and gaining vindication. Perhaps due to their anxieties about the case or their inexperience, plaintiffs are likely to be heavily influenced by their attorney's interpretations of the case (Redmount, 1961; Yngvesson, 1989) and eventually move closer to or fully accept their attorney's interpretation of "reality" (Hosticka, 1979; Morris 1987).

The lack of correspondence between the objectives and views of attorneys and their plaintiffs parallels those reported by researchers studying doctor–patient relationships. In their study of reasons patients give for suing their doctors, Vincent, Young, and Phillips (1994) concluded that patients want their doctors to be accountable, honest, and appreciative of the severity of the trauma experienced by the patients. Just as a doctor who assumes the patient who feels wronged only wants compensation, an attorney who assumes the plaintiff's main goal is compensation for loss of past and future earnings, or pain and suffering, may miss the real reason the plaintiff is there. This can reduce plaintiff satisfaction and ignore the motivation for the suit. Lind et al. (1990) make it clear that plaintiffs' satisfaction with their attorney and the legal process is correlated with their expectations for the outcome of the case—not the actual outcome. This suggests that the communication between attorney and plaintiff is particularly vulnerable to misinterpretation and requires sensitive communication and clarification of the plaintiff's goals and the attorney's position.

Interestingly, despite the fact that there has been a good deal of scholarly attention paid to legal topics such as impediments to justice and problems with the legal system, plaintiffs' satisfaction with the process as a whole has not improved (Relis, 2002). Further, even though most plaintiffs indicate that they were satisfied with their attorney (Genn, 1999), this does not mean the attorney actually provided adequate advice (Relis, 2002). Rosenthal (1974) found that 66% of the plaintiffs he interviewed were satisfied with their attorney, even though, in 77% of the cases, the plaintiffs received less compensation than they should have. As Zuckerman (1996) and Harris (1994) suggest, plaintiffs have to trust that their best interest will be served since they are in no position to judge the adequacy of the advice or representation. Their lack of experience may lead them to have inordinately high expectations for their attorney if they are what Sarat and Felstiner (1995) call "one-time users" as opposed to persons who have more familiarity with the legal system. Those who have more experience in the legal system are also likely to be more aware of the necessity of giving up control and allowing the attorney to frame the story, thereby changing their expectations of what the attorney can accomplish.

The range of concerns expressed by plaintiffs seeking civil redress is led by money and time, including delays in their case. Some plaintiffs even believe that their attorney is delaying a case in order to get more money (Davis, 1988, as cited in Relis, 2002), although in civil litigation, the attorney often takes the case on a contingency basis, thereby reducing the financial concern. Genn (1999) reports that plaintiffs often feel that legal fees are unreasonably high or unfair, although interestingly, Matruglio (1994) finds that there is no correlation between costs actually paid to attorneys and the plaintiffs' beliefs about whether these charges are reasonable. Although there is some variation by type of case, plaintiffs are actually likely to feel that fees are too high in any case (Bogart & Vidmar, 1990; Genn, 1999). Matruglio reports that only 43% of Australian plaintiffs in personal injury cases thought they were getting their money's worth. Even those plaintiffs who did not think that attorney fees were unreasonable were still not sure that the value they received was worth the amount they paid. Some suggest (e.g., Galanter, 1983) that this may be because much of the work of attorneys is invisible and therefore difficult to gauge in terms of benefit. Zuckerman (1996) offers that this may be in part because the plaintiff does not understand the legal process or complexities and therefore cannot gauge the value of the service being provided.

Matruglio (1994) found that 78% of the plaintiffs he interviewed thought their case would go to trial, while only 8% actually did. The negotiation process is extremely stressful for plaintiffs who may not feel competent to judge the offers being made by their adversary and who may feel pressured into accepting an offer or feel that they have lost their voice in the negotiation process (see Morris et al., 1973, in Relis 2002). In fact, Harris et al. (1984) report that attorneys do not always get the best settlement for their plaintiff, with 42% to 77% of the cases being ones in which the plaintiffs should have received more money than they did.

Structural Issues

Social class may have an impact on the plaintiff–attorney relationship, as well as the overall stress level of the plaintiff. We know that therapists prefer to work with and feel more successful working with middle-class plaintiffs than lower class plaintiffs (Dowds, Fontana, Russakoff, & Harris, 1977). Perhaps it is also true that attorneys communicate better with or are more comfortable with persons from backgrounds similar to their own. This may depend on the type of case usually brought by people in these different social categories. Galanter (1974) shows that the capacity to use the law to their own benefit is distributed by personal characteristics, and that these personal characteristics are systematically situated in social structure. For example, attorneys are reluctant to represent plaintiffs with low to moderate incomes or to accept cases without large settlement potential (Maute, 1992). Further, those individuals unable to afford attorneys from larger or more prestigious firms are often given overworked, overstressed legal service attorneys (Maute, 1992). Therefore, before these disenfranchised plaintiffs ever enter a courtroom, they may be at a distinct disadvantage for achieving success and may be at a higher risk for psychological stress.

Galanter (1974) has suggested that the basic architecture of the legal system creates limits to civil plaintiffs' satisfaction. He suggests that there are certain structural elements that can predict not only one's success in the system but also one's satisfaction. For example, those who use the system on a regular basis (i.e., "repeat players") have a built-in advantage, for the most part, over those who are one-time users (i.e., "one-shotters"). Their advantage comes in the form of experience with the system and its participants. Perhaps the only advantage held by the "one-shotters" is the willingness to "burn bridges," knowing they are unlikely to be engaged in litigation in the future. Galanter believes that litigation is skewed in favor of the "repeat players" and questions whether litigation can be redistributed to provide more equality for those who are "one-shotters." Since most plaintiffs are "one-shotters," attorneys can prove particularly useful because they are familiar with the justice system, the process, and the players. Attorneys often know one another and the various court personnel. While this may benefit plaintiffs, plaintiffs may actually feel more comfortable with a more adversarial stance on the part of their attorney, expressing discomfort when there is too much familiarity, particularly when this familiarity is interpreted as diminishing the seriousness of their case or the dignity with which it is treated.

There are other problems related to differential familiarity with the legal process that may have an impact on plaintiffs. One of these is the stress that accompanies the unfamiliarity plaintiffs have with the process. The novelty of the situation can introduce a certain amount of stress on its own at least for some plaintiffs, but that, coupled with the powerlessness and dependence plaintiffs experience, exacerbates the stress. It is not clear whether the stress accompanying unfamiliarity, dependence, and powerlessness would be greater for persons accustomed to having power and prestige in other arenas or for those who are relatively powerless, but this would be a good research question. Perhaps this question is tied to the larger question of the potential impact of social class, race, or gender on the experience of persons who bring civil suits. Relying on Galanter's (1974) work on structural inequality, one would assume that lower class plaintiffs are relatively disadvantaged in a number of ways, increasing the possibility of stress they experience at all stages in the litigation process.

Depositions

In addition to the experience plaintiffs have with their attorney, as the case proceeds toward trial (or settlement), plaintiffs experience other phases such as depositions that can create a significant amount of stress. Some plaintiffs view the deposition hearings as akin to being "stripped naked" (Strasburger, 1999). The stress-inducing aspects of the deposition may occur because of a series of firsts for civil plaintiffs. It is most likely the first time the plaintiffs have discussed their case with unsympathetic strangers (e.g., court reporters) and enemies (e.g., opposing counsel and defendants; Winick, 2000). Second, while plaintiffs may have discussed the precipitating events with their own attorneys or medical personnel, the deposition is the first time plaintiffs must interact with and answer questions from the opposing party (Dickerson, 1998; U.S. Supreme Court, 2009). The deposition may be the first time plaintiffs are attacked by opposing counsel. This attack may be exacerbated if it is initiated by a "Rambo lawyer," an attorney who, during depositions, may verbally abuse witnesses and opposing counsel, make physically intimidating gestures (e.g., clenching a fist) to opposing counsel, curse, and yell (Cary, 1996). Third, it may be the first time plaintiffs are asked certain questions about the event. While the plaintiffs may have told their attorney a majority of the case facts, as previously discussed, they may not have divulged all of the case information (Felstiner & Sarat, 1992) or they may have forgotten some parts. Regardless of the intentionality of this omission, during the deposition the opposing counsel will likely expose parts of the case (if they exist) that the plaintiffs have not told their attorney. Making this situation worse, some jurisdictions do not allow plaintiffs to converse with their attorney during questioning

(Dickerson, 1998). Therefore, if the plaintiffs are asked a question that they or their attorney are not prepared for, there is little, if anything, that can be done.

Further, since depositions are not court supervised and there is no judicial oversight regarding the line of questioning, opposing counsel may ask plaintiffs senseless and inappropriate questions (Cary, 1996; Dickerson, 1998). This becomes problematic in light of the fact that plaintiffs being deposed are not allowed to ask questions of opposing counsel, cannot speak until spoken to, and, when speaking, must answer questions in a specified format (e.g., "yes" or "no" instead of offering a full explanation; Dickerson, 1998). Therefore, when plaintiffs are being verbally attacked by opposing counsel there is little they can do—aside from having their own counsel object to the line of questioning. These "Rambo lawyer" tactics may then lead to another first for plaintiffs: becoming acutely aware that they have lost a good deal of control over the situation, resulting in a sense of helplessness and fear. These interactions during depositions highlight why some plaintiffs view these proceedings as demoralizing and humiliating (Cary, 1996).

Mental Health Issues

One of the most ironic parts of the litigation process is that plaintiffs may suffer psychological injury from involvement in the very system they approached for compensation for their injuries (Strasburger, 1999). While these mental health problems can arise at any time throughout the life of the case (e.g., depositions, independent medical examinations, trial), the pretrial proceedings offer the first opportunity for the symptoms to manifest themselves. Researchers have labeled the mental and emotional symptoms that arise as a result of the stress induced by the trial process itself as forensic stress disorder (FSD; Cohen & Vesper, 2001) and litigation response syndrome (LRS; Lees-Haley, 1988). Both are distinguished from the related posttraumatic stress disorder (PTSD) because they result not from the incident or injury but from the trial process itself. The existence of such disorders as actual disorders or syndromes and the distinction between them and PTSD needs further clarification, but it is noteworthy that researchers have acknowledged the extreme stress that can result from the litigation process.

According to Cohen and Vesper (2001) and Lees-Haley (1988), a diagnosis of FSD or LRS includes symptoms such as recurrent and intrusive recollections of the investigation, inquiry, deposition, or interrogation involving obsessive thoughts, panic attacks, and distressing nightmares or dreams, as well as intense psychological distress at exposure to cues symbolizing or resembling an aspect of the traumatic event (Cohen & Vesper, 2001). While these mental health problems may begin for plaintiffs as early as when they decide to sue, this condition is exacerbated during pivotal points in the case such as independent evaluations, depositions, and trial. These symptoms usually last until the trial is over, but may last longer. The duration of the symptoms reflects the interplay of several factors including (1) the length of the case; (2) the degree of humiliation, hopelessness, and helplessness the plaintiff feels; (3) the nature of the relationship between the attorney and the plaintiff; and (4) whether the plaintiff receives treatment for these symptoms (Cohen & Vesper, 2001).

While FSD and LRS share many characteristics of PTSD, they are differentiated from PTSD on two accounts. First, with FSD and LRS, the litigation process itself triggers the symptoms, while PTSD occurs when an individual is exposed to (1) a traumatic event that involves actual or threatened death or serious injury or (2) a threat to the physical integrity of self or others (American Psychiatric Association, 1994). Second, FDS and LRS only influence the plaintiffs' perceptions of their legal experience, whereas PTSD tends to interfere with all aspects of the individuals' lives (Cohen & Vesper, 2001). It would seem, however, that this distinction is somewhat lacking in clarity, given that persons are unlikely to successfully compartmentalize their lives in ways that completely isolate the present from the past.

The Trial

Most civil cases in the United States settle out of court either through an agreement by both parties or ratification by the courts (Galanter, 1983). Although settlements may be the norm, plaintiffs will sometimes choose to take the case to trial. Trials afford plaintiffs an opportunity to face the defendant in court and present evidence concerning the harm the defendant has caused and allow the courts to make a finding of wrongdoing (Thibaut & Walker, 1975).

Several studies assess the relative satisfaction of plaintiffs with traditional legal proceedings compared with alternative dispute resolution methods such as arbitration and mediation (see chapter 13 in this volume for more information about alternative dispute resolution). Lind et al. (1990) found that the important factor in determining plaintiffs' evaluation of fairness and satisfaction with different processes was whether the procedure met the plaintiffs' own personal standards for fairness and their expectations on outcomes and costs rather than any objective outcome, cost, or delay. The centrality of subjective expectations carries the risk that plaintiffs could expect less than they should gain from the process and thereby conclude that the trial or proceeding was fair and the outcome positive (Lind et al., 1990) even if it was not.

Plaintiffs who choose not to settle and instead proceed with a trial view coming to court as the most important part of the litigation process (Relis, 2002). However, the American court system is relatively professionalized and impersonal (Galanter, 1983) and does not necessarily lend itself to the kind of vindication or sense of having "won" that plaintiffs may seek.

Within the litigation process, it is indeed *the process*, the procedural justice factors, that is, for plaintiffs, as important as or more important than substantive concerns, including even the outcome of the case (Relis, 2002). Further, the symbolic features of the courtroom experience, such as how dignified the proceedings are and how respectful and polite the interactions are, are important to plaintiffs' feelings about outcome (Lind et al., 1990). Plaintiffs' evaluations of their court experiences are related to their expectations, and often, the experience does not measure up to those expectations. Plaintiffs often do not fully comprehend the process, do not believe that they have an opportunity to participate as fully as they wanted, and do not feel they were treated as respectfully or with as much sensitivity as they deserved (Genn, 1999). In particular, plaintiffs often believe they did not receive the personal attention they expected or the justice they thought litigation would bring (Burger, 1982; Relis, 2002). Overall, as indicated by Relis's literature review, there were only a small number of instances in which plaintiffs expressed positive feelings toward their experience in formal court proceedings (including Burger, 1982; Kritzer, 1990; Sarat, 1977; Tyler, 1988).

This suggests that efforts to alter court procedures may not result in desired improvement in plaintiffs' perception of the experience. For example, reduced cost and delay may not result in increased satisfaction on the part of plaintiffs, particularly if this diminishes the respectfulness and dignity of the process from the plaintiffs' perspective. Plaintiffs' subjective expectation of the process and their personal standards of procedural fairness are of paramount importance in their assessment of the litigation experience (Lind et al., 1990).

Stress Related to Stages of the Trial

Despite its perceived importance, participating in court causes many plaintiffs to panic (Relis, 2002). As discussed previously, there are a number of reasons for this, including the unfamiliarity of the proceedings and the level of dependence the plaintiff experiences. During the trial phase in particular, there is the added stress caused by unfamiliar language, legal maneuvers, and the structure of the trial itself, all of which may make plaintiffs feel uncomfortable or alienated (Lind et al., 1990). During Genn's (1999) study of the courtroom experience in England and Wales, a participant told her:

> It was all absolutely new. I have never been to a court in my life in any offence, I never wanted to see the courts. I'm just scared of court basically.... I was worrying about legal fees and it was scaring me up that I literally couldn't fight the case against [the large company] and me a small Asian person trying to take them to court.... Though my case was genuine... I was very nervous. I was a nervous wreck. (p. 223)

Many plaintiffs also believe that the court proceedings are rushed, the judge is bored, and they lose their individuality (Merry, 1990). These perceptions arise from four separate points in the trial proceedings—the opening and closing statements, direct examinations, and cross-examinations—with each one exerting its own unique stressors on plaintiffs.

Opening statements. Opening statements are an integral part of attorneys' courtroom performance (Pyszczynski & Wrightsman, 1981). Although attorneys may not present any actual evidence in their opening statements (Garner, 2009), these initial statements afford the plaintiff attorneys an opportunity to offer jurors a preview of the case and the evidence they plan to present. Despite not being able to present evidence, the attorney must attempt to create a coherent, narrative framework around the events leading to the lawsuit. While the goal of the opening statements is for the attorneys to persuade the jury into believing their story is the "true story" (Kadoch, 2000), the question remains, "Is the 'true story' really the story plaintiffs want the jury to hear?" Since plaintiffs are prohibited from telling their story through opening statements, they must rely on the attorney to tell the story. The attorney, in turn, constructs the story within the constraints of both the law and the framework within which the attorney wants jurors to hear the evidence, and in the process may not satisfy the plaintiffs' underlying and driving desire to "tell their story," nor accurately reflect the plaintiffs' view of the case they have against the defendant.

Not only do plaintiffs lose control of their story, but also they must occupy the passive role of listener while their attorney reveals an important and critical aspect of their life in front of strangers. Most of the actors in the courtroom are strangers, and plaintiffs are likely to perceive these actors as "insiders" while viewing themselves as "outsiders." The feelings of powerlessness and dependence that characterize the earlier stages of the legal process would seem equally or more applicable here. It is important to acknowledge that the ability to control the story and to have one's voice heard may have more of an influence on the way plaintiffs assess the process than on how the decision is evaluated (see Wayte et al., 2002).

Closing statements. Similar to the opening statements, closing statements do not allow the introduction of evidence, but give attorneys the opportunity to speak directly to the fact finders to request that the judge or jury consider the evidence and apply the law in a way that is beneficial to their clients (Garner, 2009). Closing statements are also the attorneys' final attempt to persuade the jury to believe that the evidence supports the story they put forth during opening statements and to convince them that it is consistent with their thematic narrative. Just like the opening statements, attorneys create the closing statements and espouse only the information they believe is pertinent to the case, again relegating plaintiffs to the position of spectator.

Direct examination. Similar to criminal proceedings, civil proceedings involve direct examination of witnesses by their attorney and cross-examination of these witnesses by the opposing attorney. Although plaintiffs do not always choose to take the witness stand, their direct testimony is often a central part of the case. Taking the stand to testify at trial is one of the most stressful emotional aspects of a lawsuit (Winick, 2000). The courtroom is a public place and plaintiffs give their testimony in the presence of strangers and enemies (Winick, 2000). In order to help reduce the amount of stress that accompanies testifying in open court, attorneys and trial consultants often coach plaintiffs prior to attending court, providing them with a rehearsal of the questioning they will experience during trial and giving them instruction on how to respond effectively (Relis, 2002). Although done with the best intentions, there is some evidence that this coaching may actually increase a plaintiff's sense of powerlessness and vulnerability (Pitman, Sparr, Saunders, & McFarlane, 1996). At the same time, these feelings must be weighed against the alternative situation in which the plaintiff's response to questions could be confusing, conflicting, or in other ways detrimental to the case.

Cross-examination. Although the direct examination is considered by plaintiffs to be stress inducing, cross-examination by opposing counsel can be worse. Plaintiffs are often required to recount sensitive information by answering questions that may be personally invasive or asked in an accusatory or condescending way (Relis, 2002). Plaintiffs view having to answer such questions as highly degrading and deeply humiliating (Relis, 2002). In addition, cross-examination increases the plaintiffs' perception of victimization by placing them, rather than the defendant, on trial (Pitman et al., 1996). For example, repeated questioning by attorneys causes some plaintiffs to feel hurt and/or angry because they can view the repeated questioning as an attempt to impugn their credibility (Weissman, 1990). Overall, a plaintiff who is unfamiliar with the litigation process, unaccustomed to the process of cross-examination, or unaware of the purpose of cross-examination may even begin to believe that the system is protecting the defendant rather than helping the plaintiff (Pitman et al., 1996).

Other Stress-Inducing Aspects of Trial

Aside from the negative emotional effects of opening and closing statements, direct examinations, and cross-examinations, other trial-related issues may have a detrimental impact on plaintiffs. First, plaintiffs report that loss of time at work, sleeplessness, negative health consequences, and disrupted personal relationships are all likely to accompany the litigation process, dramatically affecting their quality of life (Relis, 2002). Second, attending court each day costs plaintiffs time and money (Merry, 1986). For plaintiffs with children, an added cost of litigation may be securing and paying for childcare they may not have otherwise needed. Finally, litigation does not remain a peripheral engagement for those involved in it, but is likely to be the centerpiece of their lives, during the preparation for trial, during the trial itself, and subsequent to it as they deal with the outcome (Matruglio, 1994). For some, the litigation proceedings take over their lives (Relis, 2002).

Posttrial

Following the physical, psychological, and emotional stress of the pretrial and courtroom proceedings, a new stress begins for plaintiffs during the posttrial process. During this time, plaintiffs may find themselves asking, "Was it all worth it?" Based on research and interviews of plaintiffs, from a nonmonetary perspective, the answer to this question is often no. Many plaintiffs indicate that, regardless of results, they wish they had never started the litigation process (Relis, 2002). Also, some plaintiffs indicated that had they known about the stress and anguish litigation entails, they would have decided against pursuing their case.

Receiving Payments From Judgment

An examination of the psychological wellbeing of civil plaintiffs as they traverse the process of receiving settlement payments appears to be an area of interest that could benefit from future research. While much of the research on civil litigation has focused on plaintiffs' psychological wellbeing during the pretrial and trial phases, little is known about the stress involved following a judgment against the defendant or, for that matter, for the defendant. What is known is that a finding in favor of the plaintiff does not necessarily mean that the plaintiff will receive any compensation. As one judgment enforcer suggests, 80% of all U.S. plaintiffs will not receive their trial-mandated settlements (Crane, 2007). The remaining 20% of plaintiffs will more than likely receive compensation only after a lengthy appeals process that may eventually exhaust the emotional and financial resources of plaintiffs.

Regaining "Normalcy"

Return to a semblance of "normalcy" after months, sometimes years, of preparation and concentrated focus on the trial is often not as smooth or easy as plaintiffs may have anticipated, and relief may be replaced by other feelings, including a sense of purposelessness. Marshall, Picou, and Schlichtmann (2004) studied individuals involved in litigation stemming from the 1989 Exxon Valdez oil spill. They found that the level of intrusive stress (i.e., occurrence of event-related, intrusive recollections over time) was higher for plaintiffs in 2000 than in 1991 and 1992. Furthermore, being involved in litigation concerning the oil spill was a strong predictor of intrusive stress over time from 1992 to 2000. Compared to plaintiffs, nonplaintiffs' intrusive stress levels were significantly lower in 1991, 1992, and 2000 (Marshall et al., 2004).

Blanchard et al. (1998) found similar results in their study involving motor vehicle accident (MVA) victims. These authors administered several initial psychological distress (Clinician Administered PTSD Scale [CAPS], Beck Depression Inventory [BDI], Impact of Event Scale [IES], and State-Trait Anxiety Inventory) and role performance (e.g., work performance and relationship with family members) measures to nonlitigating MVA victims, as well as litigating MVA victims who had either settled their lawsuits or whose lawsuits were still pending. Initial assessments of these three groups indicated that nonlitigants had significantly lower CAPS, BDI, State Anxiety, and IES scores; better relationships with friends; and more involvement in recreational activities than either of the litigating groups.

Blanchard et al. (1998) then followed up with these three groups 1 year later. After 1 year, all three groups had significantly lower CAPS scores than they had initially, but those victims who had not initiated a lawsuit had significantly lower CAPS scores than litigants whose lawsuits were still pending, with the group who settled in between the two. Regarding State Anxiety, Trait Anxiety, and IES scores, nonlitigants were lower on all three measures than either of the litigating groups, who did not differ. Individuals who had litigation pending had significantly higher BDI scores, poorer relations with friends, and lower participation in recreational activities than nonlitigants. Individuals with pending litigation were also less likely to be working at the 12-month follow-up. Litigants who settled had intermediate BDI, relationship with friends, and participation in recreation scores and were not different from either of the other two groups.

Overall, these findings suggest that the process of litigation impedes the postaccident recovery of plaintiffs (Marshall et al., 2004), but Relis (2002) concludes that more information is needed on the long-term impact of litigation on plaintiffs. However, from what is known, the stress, worry, and other losses the plaintiffs experience during the process were not compensated for by the outcome, even if they prevailed.

Policy Recommendations

Many of the recommendations to follow come not as suggestions for legislation or changes in the court system itself or even as formal policies. Rather, they are, for the most part, suggestions designed to alert attorneys, judges, and others involved in the litigation process to the stressors and trauma that might accompany litigation and to suggest ways of ameliorating those. It is clear from a review of the literature that there are some misunderstandings and some areas of confusion that could be remedied. It is also clear that there are aspects of the process that are simply bound to be troublesome, stressful, or anxiety producing due to the adversarial nature of the process and because so much is at stake. Most of our suggestions are for attorneys since first, it would be relatively easy for attorneys to make the changes we suggest, and second, complaints from plaintiffs often center on their experience with attorneys. Our suggestions are as follows:

- Attorneys should develop good listening skills whereby they learn to actually listen to their plaintiffs' stories before translating them into a legal case. Attorneys should communicate an understanding of what plaintiffs have to say and what they are concerned about, which may have the result of increasing plaintiffs' faith in themselves (Freeman &

Weihofen, 1972), thereby making the plaintiffs more convincing and credible.

- Attorneys should allow plaintiffs to express *feelings* and to tell their story in their own words. Then, they should explain why it has to be translated into legal language to achieve the plaintiffs' goals.
- Attorneys should acknowledge the stress that is likely to accompany the entire litigation experience. Attorneys should provide plaintiffs with a realistic picture of the trial and the experiences plaintiffs will have during the process, including the potential for feeling powerless, confused, uncomfortable, or even threatened.
- Attorneys should learn how to deal with legal irrelevancies such as plaintiffs' feelings (e.g., anger and frustration; Zander, 1978) without offending the plaintiffs for whom these "irrelevancies" may be a central part of the case and the underlying reason they are suing. Attorneys can caution plaintiffs that certain aspects of their story, while very important to the plaintiffs, are irrelevant in the narrow confines of the legal system.
- Attorneys should take into account what plaintiffs often think is the most important element in their dispute—their desire for moral vindication and a desire to highlight the importance of upholding social norms (Merry & Silbey, 1984)—and communicate to them that litigation may not be the best way to achieve this goal.
- Attorneys should provide information to plaintiffs to indicate their competence, such as a law school degree and association and bar memberships, in order to assure plaintiffs that their choice of an attorney is a good one and that their attorney is eminently qualified to pursue their case.
- Attorneys should provide indicators of commitment to the case (e.g., sending information to the plaintiff, having staff contact the plaintiff on a regular basis) to overcome plaintiffs' feelings that they are not very important to the attorney, either because the attorney is too busy or because their case is insignificant (Steele & Nimmer, 1976).
- Attorneys should provide a welcoming and professional office—Harris (1994) points out that few plaintiffs view attorneys' offices as welcoming, which contributes to their lack of satisfaction with their attorney and the experience.
- Attorneys should specifically acknowledge the stressors that will accompany the trial, including worry, impact of sleep and health, economic consequences, and potential destructiveness to personal relationships. Attorneys should forewarn plaintiffs that there is the potential for short-term or long-term emotional or psychological consequences, including feelings of being misunderstood, unheard, or disappointed in the outcome. Attorneys may want to suggest that plaintiffs might benefit from therapy during this period.

- Attorneys should forewarn plaintiffs that the benefits of trial, even with a win, might not outweigh the economic, personal, and social costs plaintiffs may experience. In addition, attorneys should weigh the potential emotional cost to their plaintiff when they are making a determination about taking the case forward.
- Attorneys should forewarn plaintiffs that there might be difficulty in collecting compensation even with a win in court.
- The courtroom demeanor of judges, attorneys, and court staff should be monitored for professionalism to increase plaintiffs' satisfaction.

In reviewing these suggestions, it seems clear that a process of mediation might well enhance plaintiff satisfaction, particularly if the mediation is structured in such a way that the parties can confront one another and have the opportunity to express their position. Since the purpose of mediation is to assist the parties to resolve a dispute, it allows for open communication between parties, a freedom that is clearly lacking in the more formal setting of the courtroom. This process allows an opportunity for the participants to be heard and to feel understood, reflecting the need expressed by many plaintiffs: the desire to be heard. While attorneys may perceive mediation as a process allowing for a more rapid or efficient solution to or settlement of a case, the purpose for clients may be to improve relationships between parties or to allow for understanding of issues instead (Gabel, 2003). These qualities of mediation may be more useful to plaintiffs who feel wronged than the courtroom setting and such alternative dispute resolution methods should occupy a higher profile place in the legal community (see chapter 13 for more discussion of alternative dispute resolution).

Litigation, by its very nature, is a stressful process. It is clear, however, that some of the stressors of the process and much of the trauma could be reduced through relatively simple changes. One of the central changes would be to improve the process of communication between attorney and client, clarifying the relationship between the plaintiff's goals and the legal process. More specifically, one should not assume that plaintiffs understand the legal system in any sophisticated manner, nor should one assume that plaintiffs understand the way in which their needs can or cannot be met through litigation. Attorneys should make clear to plaintiffs the limitations of the legal system in the achievement of their goals and should clarify for plaintiffs the unavoidable emotional risks they will face. Such steps will help reduce stress and promote wellbeing among plaintiffs.

References

American Psychiatric Association. (1994). *Diagnostic and statistical manual of mental disorders* (4th ed.). Washington, DC: Author.

Andrew, L. (n.d.). *Litigation stress.* Retrieved from http://www.black-bile.com/resources/eMedicine+Litigation+Stress.pdf

Blanchard, E. B., Hickling, E. J., Taylor, A. E., Buckley, T. C., Loos, W. R., & Walsh, J. (1998). Effects of litigation settlements on posttraumatic stress symptoms in motor vehicle accident victims. *Journal of Traumatic Stress, 11*(2), 337–354.

Bogart, W. A., & Vidmar, N. (1990). Problems and experience with the Ontario civil justice system: An empirical assessment. In A. C. Hutchinson (Ed.), *Access to civil justice* (pp. 1–51). New York, NY: Carswell.

Budeti, P. P. (2005). Tort reform and the patient safety movement: Seeking common ground. *Journal of the American Medical Association, 293*(21), 2660–2662.

Burger, W. E. (1982). Isn't there a better way? *American Bar Association Journal, 68*, 274–277.

Cary, J. M. (1996). Rambo deposition: Controlling an ethical cancer in civil litigation. *Hofstra Law Review, 25*, 561–606.

Casavant, M. A. (2011, January 18). "Hot coffee" director Susan Saladoff. *Filmmaker.* Retrieved from http://www.filmmakermagazine.com/news/2011/01/hot-coffee-director-susan-saladoff-2/

Cohen, L. J., & Vesper, J. H. (2001). Forensic stress disorder. *Stress: The International Journal on the Biology of Stress, 25*(1), 1–21.

Cohen, T. H. (2011). *Who's better at defending criminals? Does type of defense attorney matter in terms of producing favorable case outcomes.* Retrieved from http://ssrn.com/abstract=1876474

Conley, J. M., & O'Barr, W. M. (1988). Hearing the hidden agenda: The ethnographic investigation of procedure. *Law and Society Review, 51*(4), 181–197.

Controlled Risk Insurance Company/Risk Management Foundation. (n.d.). *Medical malpractice litigation: Coping with the stress of malpractice litigation.* Retrieved from http://www.rmf.harvard.edu/files/documents/Coping_with_Stress.pdf

Crane, A. B. (2007, March 6). How to collect court judgments. *Bankrate.* Retrieved from http://www.bankrate.com/brm/news/advice/20070306_how_to_collect_court_judgments_a1.asp

Dickerson, A. D. (1998). The law and ethics of civil depositions. *Maryland Law Review, 57*, 273–379.

Dowds, B. N., Fontana, A. F., Russakoff, L. M., & Harris, M. (1977). Cognitive mediators between patients' social class and therapists' evaluations. *Archives of General Psychiatry, 34*(4), 917–920.

Dziech, B. W., & Weiner, L. (1984). *The lecherous professor: Sexual harassment on campus.* Boston, MA: Beacon Press.

Ehrlich, T. (1976, February 18). Legal pollution. *New York Times Magazine.* Retrieved from http://select.nytimes.com/gst/abstract.html?res=F10910FC3E5F117688DDA10894DA405B868BF1D3&scp=1&sq=legal+pollution&st=p

Faria, M. (1993). On the liability crisis and the glut of litigators. *Journal of the Medical Association of Georgia, 82*(4), 155–156.

Felstiner, W. L. F., Abel, R. L., & Sarat, A. (1980–1981). The emergence and transformation of disputes: Naming, blaming, claiming... *Law and Society Review, 15*(3/4), 631–654.

Felstiner, W. L. F., & Sarat, A. (1992). Enactments of power: Negotiating reality and responsibility in lawyer-plaintiff interactions. *Cornell Law Review, 77*, 1447–1498.

Frake, C. O. (1957). Litigation in Lipay: A study in Subanun law. In *Proceedings of the Ninth Pacific Science Congress* (Vol. 3, pp. 217–222). Bangkok, Thailand: Ninth Pacific Science Congress.

Freedman, M. H. (1987). Brendan F. Brown and commentary: Legal ethics and the suffering plaintiff. *Catholic University Law Review, 36*, 331–336.

Freeman, H. A., & Weihofen, H. (1972). *Clinical law training: Interviewing and counseling.* St. Paul, MN: West Publishing Company.

Fulcher, G. (2004). Litigation-induced trauma sensitisation (LITS)—A potential negative outcome of the process of litigation. *Psychiatry, Psychology and Law, 11*(1), 79–86.

Gabel, S. (2003). Mediation and psychotherapy: Two sides of the same coin? *Negotiation Journal, 19*(4), 315–328.

Galanter, M. (1974). Why the "haves" come out ahead: Speculations on the limits of legal change. *Law and Society Review, 9*(1), 95–160.

Galanter, M. (1983). Reading the landscape of disputes: What we know and don't know (and think we know) about our allegedly contentious and litigious society. *UCLA Law Review, 4*, 5–71.

Galanter, M. (2004). The vanishing trial: An examination of trials and related matters in federal and state courts. *Journal of Empirical Legal Studies, 1*(3), 459–470.

Garner, B. A. (Ed.). (2009). *Black's law dictionary* (9th ed.). St. Paul, MN: West Publishing Company.

Genn, H. (1999). *Paths to justice: What people do and think about going to law.* Portland, OR: Hart Publishing.

Gibeaut, J. (2005, March 28). The med-mal divide. *American Bar Association Journal.* Retrieved from http://www.abajournal.com/magazine/article/the_med_mal_divide/

Giuffre, P. A., & Williams, C. L. (1994). Boundary lines: Labeling sexual harassment in restaurants. *Gender and Society, 8*, 378–401.

Harris, D., Maclean, M., Genn, H., Lloyd-Bostock, S., Penn, P., Corfield, P., & Brittan, Y. (1984). *Compensation and support for illness and injury.* New York, NY: Oxford University Press.

Harris, N. (1994). *Solicitors and plaintiff care: An aspect of professional competence.* London: National Consumer Council.

Hosticka, C. (1979). We don't care about what happened, we only care about what is going to happen: Lawyer-plaintiff negotiations of reality. *Social Problems, 26*(5), 599–610.

Howell, S. E. (1998). *Citizen evaluation of the Louisiana courts.* Retrieved from http://scholarworks.uno.edu/cgi/viewcontent.cgi?article=1026&context=src_pubs&sei-redir=1#search=%22Citizen+Evaluation+of+the+Louisiana+Courts%22

Kadoch, L. C. (2000). Seduced by narrative: Persuasion in the courtroom. *Drake Law Review, 49*, 71–123.

Kaplan, A. (1964). *The conduct of inquiry: Methodology for behavioral science.* San Francisco, CA: Chandler.

Knowles, E. (2006). Dialogue of the deaf. *The Oxford dictionary of phrase and fable.* Retrieved from http://www.encyclopedia.com/doc/1O214-dialogueofthedeaf.html

Kritzer, H. (1990). *The justice broker: Lawyers and ordinary litigation*. New York, NY: Oxford University Press.
Lees-Haley, P. R. (1988). Litigation response syndrome. *American Journal of Forensic Psychology, 6*(1), 3–12.
Lind, E. A., Maccoun, R. J., Ebener, P. A., Felstiner, W. L. F., Hensler, D. R., Resnik, J., & Tyler, T. R. (1990). In the eye of the beholder: Tort plaintiffs' evaluations of their experiences in the civil justice system. *Law and Society Review, 24*(4), 953–996.
Manning, B. (1977). Hyperlexis: Our national disease. *Northwestern University Law Review, 71*(6), 767–782.
Marshall, B. K., Picou, J. S., & Schlichtmann, J. R. (2004). Technological disasters, litigation stress, and the use of alternative dispute resolution mechanisms. *Law and Policy, 26*(2), 289–307.
Matruglio, T. (1994). *Plaintiffs and the process of litigation: An analysis of the perceptions of plaintiffs following their experience of litigation*. Sydney: Civil Justice Research Centre.
Maute, J. L. (1992). Balanced lives in a stressful profession: An impossible dream? *Capital University Law Review, 21*, 797–819.
Medical malpractice. (2003, January 16). Retrieved from http://www.pbs.org/newshour/bb/ white_house/jan-june03/malpractice_01-16.html
Meinhold, S., & Neubauer, D. W. (2001). Exploring attitudes about the litigation explosion. *Justice System Journal, 22*(2), 105–115.
Merry, S. E. (1986). Everyday understandings of the law in working-class America. *American Ethnologist, 13*(2), 253–270.
Merry, S. E. (1990). *Getting justice and getting even: Legal consciousness among working-class Americans*. Chicago, IL: University of Chicago Press.
Merry, S. E., & Silbey, S. S. (1984). What do plaintiffs want? Reexamining the concept of dispute. *Justice System Journal, 9*, 151–178.
Morris, J. (1987). Power and responsibility among lawyers and plaintiffs: Comment on Ellmann's lawyers and plaintiffs. *UCLA Law Review, 34*, 781–810.
Nader, L., & Singer, L. R. (1976). Law in the future: What are the choices? *California State Bar Journal, 51*, 281–320.
Olson, W. (1991). *The litigation explosion: What happened when America unleashed the lawsuit*. New York, NY: E. P. Dutton.
Pitman, R. K., Sparr, L. F., Saunders, L. S., & McFarlane, A. C. (1996). Legal issues in posttraumatic stress disorder. In B. A. van der Kolk, A. C. McFarlane, & L. Weisaeth (Eds.), *Traumatic stress: The effects of overwhelming experience on mind, body, and society* (pp. 378–397). New York, NY: Guilford Press.
Public Citizen Congress Watch. (2005). *Fewer lawsuits and more doctors: The myth of Washington State's medical malpractice "crisis."* Washington, DC: Author.
Pyszczynski, T. A., & Wrightsman, L. S. (1981). The effects of opening statements on mock jurors' verdicts in a simulated criminal trial. *Journal of Applied Social Psychology, 11*(4), 301–313.
Redmount, R. (1961). Attorney personalities and some psychological aspects of legal consultation. *University of Pennsylvania Law Review, 109*, 972–990.

Relis, T. (2002). Civil litigation from plaintiffs' perspectives: What we know and what we don't know about the litigation experience of individual plaintiffs. *Studies in Law, Politics, and Society, 25*, 151–212.

Rosenthal, D. (1974). *Lawyer and plaintiff: Who's in charge?* New York, NY: Russell Sage Foundation.

Saladoff, S. (Producer & Director). (2011). *Hot coffee* [motion picture]. United States: Home Box Office.

Sarat, A. (1977). Studying American legal culture: An assessment of survey evidence. *Law and Society Review, 11*, 427–488.

Sarat, A., & Felstiner, W. (1986). Law and strategy in the divorce lawyer's office. *Law and Society Review, 20*, 93–134.

Sarat, A., & Felstiner, W. (1995). *Divorce lawyers and their plaintiffs*. New York, NY: Oxford University Press.

Steele, E. H., & Nimmer, R. T. (1976). Lawyers, plaintiffs, and professional regulation. *American Bar Foundation Research Journal, 1*(3), 917–1019.

Stewart, M. W. (1998). *Silicone spills: Breast implants on trial*. Westport, CT: Praeger.

Stewart, M. W. (2002). *Ordinary violence: Everyday assaults against women*. Westport, CT: Bergin & Garvey.

Strasburger, L. H. (1999). The plaintiff-patient: Mental health consequences of civil litigation. *Journal of the American Academy of Psychiatry and the Law, 27*(2), 203–211.

Thibaut, J., & Walker, L. (1975). *Procedural justice: A psychological analysis*. Hillsdale, NJ: Lawrence Erlbaum Associates.

Tomasic, R. (1978). *Lawyers and the community*. Sydney: Law Foundation of New South Wales.

Tyler, T. R. (1988). What is procedural justice?: Criteria used by citizens to assess the fairness of legal procedures. *Law and Society Review, 22*(1), 103–136.

Tyler, T. R. (1990). A psychological perspective on the settlement of mass tort claims. *Law and Contemporary Problems, 53*(4), 199–205.

U.S. Chamber Institute for Legal Reform. (2009). *2009 update on U.S. tort cost trends*. Retrieved from http://www.towersperrin.com/tp/getwebcachedoc?webc=USA/2009/200912/2009_tort_trend_report_12-8_09.pdf

U.S. Chamber Institute for Legal Reform. (2012). *Lawsuit abuse is having a devastating impact on our society*. Retrieved from http://www.facesoflawsuitabuse.org/facts/

U.S. General Accounting Office. (2003, August). *Medical malpractice: Implications of rising premiums on access to health care*. Retrieved from http://www.gao.gov/assets/240/239263.pdf

U.S. Supreme Court. (2009). *Federal rules of civil procedure*. Retrieved from http://www.uscourts.gov/uscourts/RulesAndPolicies/rules/CV2009.pdf

Vidmar, N. (1990). Review: The origins and consequences of procedural fairness. *Law and Social Inquiry, 15*, 877–892.

Vidmar, N. (1997). *Medical malpractice and the American jury: Confronting the myths about jury incompetence, deep pockets, and outrageous damage awards*. Ann Arbor, MI: University of Michigan Press.

Vidmar, N. (2005). Medical malpractice and the tort system in Illinois. *Illinois Bar Journal, 93*, 340–348.

Vincent, C., Young, M., & Phillips, A. (1994). Why do people sue doctors? A study of patients and relatives taking legal action. *Lancet, 343*(8913), 1609–1613.
Wayte, T., Samra, J., Robbennolt, J. K., Heuer, L., & Koch, W. J. (2002). Psychological issues in civil law. In J. R. P. Ogloff (Ed.), *Taking psychology and law into the twenty-first century* (pp. 323–369). New York, NY: Kluwer.
Weissman, H. N. (1990). Distortions and deceptions in self presentation: Effects of protracted litigation in personal injury cases. *Behavioral Sciences and the Law, 8*, 67–74.
Winick, B. (2000). Therapeutic jurisprudence and the role of counsel in litigation. *California Western Law Review, 37*, 105–120.
Yngvesson, B. (1989). Inventing law in local settings: Rethinking popular legal culture. *Yale Law Journal, 98*(8), 1689–1709.
Zander, M. (1978). *Legal services for the community*. London: Temple Smith.
Zuckerman, A. A. S. (1996). Lord Woolf's access to justice: Plus ca change... *Modern Law Review, 59*, 773–796.

7

The Experiences of Older Adults in the Legal System

Edie Greene and Sheri C. Gibson

Between 2000 and 2010, the number of people in the United States under age 18 increased by 2.6%, and the 18 to 44 age group grew by a mere 0.6%. By contrast, the 65-and-older population increased by 15.1% (U.S. Census Bureau, 2011). By the year 2030, there will be 70 million older Americans, including almost 9 million people age 85 and older; the latter now constitutes the fastest growing segment of the U.S. population (U.S. Census Bureau, 2008).

Although one tends not to think of older adults as active participants in the legal system, their sheer number means that they will have increasingly important and visible interactions with the law in years to come. The elderly are already enmeshed with the legal system on issues as diverse as health care; end-of-life decisions; Social Security, Medicaid, and Medicare entitlements; estate planning, wills, trusts, and probate; cognitive impairment and guardianship; and elder abuse. A number of professional organizations address the legal issues of older adults, including the National Academy of Elder Law Attorneys (http://www.naela.org), the Center for Elders and the Courts (http://www.eldersandcourts.org), the National Center on Elder Abuse (http://www.ncea.aoa.gov), and the American Bar Association Commission on Law and Aging (http://www.abanet.org/aging).

In this chapter, we examine what psychologists and other social scientists have learned about the impact on older adults of involvement in three areas of the law: (1) as aging inmates in correctional facilities in the United States, (2) as victims of intimate partner and financial abuse, and (3) as individuals with impaired cognitive abilities involved in guardianship proceedings. We chose these issues because researchers and scholars have paid relatively more attention to them than to other issues involving the elderly, although empirical scrutiny of capacity issues in the context of guardianship is still sorely lacking, as we note.

Older adults are generally not willing participants in the system—whether it is the correctional, criminal, or probate system. This fact enables us to discern the negative ramifications (as well as some positive outcomes) on individuals who are brought into the fold of the legal system involuntarily. It also allows us to assess the success of interventions developed to enhance the wellbeing of older adult prisoners, crime victims, and those with cognitive impairments and suggest possibilities for future policy refinement and revision. For the purposes of discussing the impact on older adults of involvement in the legal system, we occasionally use the terms *elder* and *elderly* where they seem most appropriate, recognizing the potential for derogatory undertones (American Psychological Association, 2010).

Incarceration

Inmate populations are growing older. In 2002, 8% of the total U.S. prison population was composed of individuals age 50 or older, nearly doubling the figure of the previous decade (Aday, 2003). Alarmingly, between 1995 and 2003, the percentage of growth in the population of inmates age 55 and older was larger than for any other cohort (Harrison & Beck, 2004). Women over age 50 constituted 12% of the female prison population in 1989 (Kratcoski & Babb, 1990), and the population of incarcerated women age 55 and older doubled between 1990 and 2001 (Harrison & Beck, 2002). This shift in the overall prison age composition will continue into the foreseeable future (Caldwell, Jarvis, & Rosenfield, 2001).

The "graying" of prisons is the result of two converging trends. First, prison inmates, like people who are not incarcerated, are tending to live longer. Second, sentencing practices of the past several decades have meant that vastly more offenders have received lengthy or lifelong sentences with little chance of parole. As a result, people who committed crimes when relatively young are aging in prison, developing chronic conditions and diseases of old age, and dying behind bars.

The increase in the number of aging prisoners is especially acute in California, where three-strikes laws mandate that offenders who are convicted of a third violent or serious crime must be sentenced to between 25 years and life in prison. Offenders eligible to be sentenced under three-strikes laws tend to be older than other inmates because they need time to accumulate two prior serious offenses. As a result, the population of California inmates over age 55 has increased 500% in the past 15 years (California Department of Corrections, 2007).

Ironically, aging inmates are far less likely to recidivate than their younger counterparts. According to national data, the recidivism rate for inmates ages 18 to 29 is above 50% but is only 2% for those over 55 (Beck, Hughes, & Wilson, 2001). By the time people reach old age, the major sources of reinforcement for criminal activity (e.g., money, prestige, sex, power, settling disputes, righting perceived wrongs) have largely dissipated. And yet, elderly prisoners languish behind bars, at significant risk for health and psychological problems and at substantial cost to taxpayers. In this section, we describe some of the health and socioemotional issues that impact aging prisoners.

Effects of Incarcerating Older Adults

Health effects. Older inmates experience accelerated aging in prison, suffering from serious health problems at an earlier age than older adults in the general population (Yorston & Taylor, 2006). An inmate's physiological age averages 7 to 10 years older than his or her chronological age (Mitka, 2004). This stems in part from the already poor health history of impoverished inmates, a high prevalence of substance abuse, and lack of access to high-quality health care. But the stressors and rigors of incarceration also negatively affect inmates' physical and mental wellbeing.

Imprisonment results in low levels of self-care (Beckett, Peternelj-Taylor, & Johnson, 2003) that increase the incidence of serious health problems. Over the course of their lives, inmates have experienced higher rates of alcohol and substance abuse and addiction and a higher incidence of conditions related to risky behaviors (e.g., HIV/AIDS, hepatitis B and C, liver disease) than the general aging population (Linder, Enders, Craig, Richardson, & Meyers, 2002). A comprehensive review of 21 research articles on the health status of older inmates determined that the most commonly reported health issues were psychiatric conditions, cardiovascular disease, arthritis and/or back problems, respiratory diseases, endocrine disorders, and vision and hearing problems (Loeb & AbuDagga, 2006). Yet these conditions are also commonly reported by older adults in the general population. So what evidence exists that incarceration exacerbates or compounds the ailments of old age? Data come from three sources: information about health conditions that go untreated in prison, prisoners' self-reports on changes in their health status after being incarcerated, and a study that compared major illnesses recorded in medical records among elderly male prisoners, younger male prisoners, and community-dwelling older men.

Psychiatric disorders are the most common untreated condition in prisons. Rates of mental illness are high among prison inmates, and one study indicated that only 18% of older inmates with psychiatric diagnoses were given psychotropic medications. In contrast, 85% of elderly inmates with cardiovascular disease received medication for this condition (Fazel, Hope, O'Donnell, Piper, & Jacoby, 2004), indicating that mental illness often goes untreated.

Researchers have assessed self-reported changes in health in male inmates from a geriatric facility (mean age of 69 years) and a comparable group of younger inmates in the general prison population at the same correctional institution (mean age of 51 years; Marquart, Merianos, & Doucet, 2000). Both groups rated their preincarceration health as good to excellent and reported declines in physical wellbeing after a 5-year period of incarceration. But data showed that the health of older inmates deteriorated faster than that of younger inmates, implying that the combination of imprisonment and advanced age contributes to declining health.

Perhaps the clearest evidence of the compounding effects of aging and incarceration comes from a study that compared medical records and reception health screenings of 233 male prisoners 60 years and older with the self-reported health status of 992 male prisoners ages 18 to 49 and 895 community-dwelling men ages 65 to 74 (Fazel, Hope, O'Donnell, Piper, & Jacoby, 2001). The differences were apparent: 45% of elderly prisoners suffered from psychiatric disorders as compared to only 1% of community-dwelling elderly men (admittedly, this condition was likely underreported in the latter group); 35% of elderly prisoners had cardiovascular disease as compared to 3% of younger prisoners and 29% of community-dwelling older men; and 13% of elderly prisoners had genitourinary problems as compared with 1% of younger prisoners and 4% of community dwellers. In general, findings indicated high rates of morbidity in a population of older inmates and obvious differences in the health status of this population, a group of younger prisoners, and elderly men who are not incarcerated.

The psychiatric problems of elderly inmates merit special attention. It is widely accepted that long-term incarceration has negative effects on mental wellbeing, and several studies have documented the prevalence of psychiatric disorders in elderly male prisoners. For example, Fazel, Hope, O'Donnell, and Jacoby (2001) conducted diagnostic testing and interviewed 203 inmates (mean age 65.5) in correctional institutions in England and Wales. They also examined medical records to learn about major illnesses and current medications. On the basis of these data, they diagnosed depressive disorder in 30% of the sample and noted that only 12% were being treated with antidepressant medication. In an assessment of depression in a group of 121 male prisoners age 55 and over serving life or indeterminate sentences in English prisons, Murdoch, Morris, and Holmes (2008) found that nearly half (48%) of the sample scored above the mildly depressed threshold and an additional 3% were severely depressed. These rates of depression are higher than rates found in samples of younger inmates (e.g., Brink, Doherty, & Boer, 2001) and community-dwelling men of comparable age (Fiske, Wetherell, & Gatz, 2009). Surprisingly, Murdoch et al. concluded that the prevalence of depression was unrelated to the amount of time an inmate had been incarcerated or the length of his sentence but *was* related to physical health morbidity. The burden of chronic ill health seems to impact adversely on an elderly inmate's mood (or vice versa).

Fazel et al. (2001) also diagnosed personality disorder in 30% of their sample of 203 elderly male inmates. This rate is lower than that of a group of younger inmates (ages 18 to 65), 64% of whom, according to Singleton,

Meltzer, and Gatward (1998), had personality disorders. But it is higher than the rate of personality disorders in samples of community-dwelling older adults, with nearly all studies reporting prevalence rates ranging from 3% to 15% (Molinari & Segal, 2010).

Social and emotional effects. Given their lifelong experiences in criminal activity and advancing age, older prisoners historically had high status in institutional hierarchies. But with the influx of gang members in prison, older criminals no longer wield the power they once had and many experience or are fearful of victimization by younger, stronger inmates (U.S. Department of Justice, 2004). Fear of being victimized means that older prisoners may not exercise and may restrict their movements in other ways, leading to further isolation.

As inmates age or are separated from family and friends over an extended period, their social support tends to erode. Visitors are few, and letters and phone calls decrease and in some instances cease altogether (Lynch & Sabol, 2001; Travis, 2005). Some data suggest that isolation from outside support may be purposeful. According to a group of 80 prisoners ages 65 to 84 interviewed by Crawley and Sparks (2006), prisoners sometimes cut off contact in order to reduce their suffering and the suffering of others. One elderly inmate noted, "Prison life is more bearable and easier to cope with if you have nobody to care about beyond the walls" (p. 69). Yet many inmates with no hope of release described prison life itself as a lonely, almost unbearable struggle. Some of these men felt resentment that they were still imprisoned for crimes carried out more than half a lifetime before.

When questioned about the stressors that accompany long-term confinement, many prisoners identified the fear of physical and mental deterioration and the possibility (often, the reality) of dying in prison (Crawley & Sparks, 2006). Concerns about physical deterioration were most acute in those who suffered from chronic illnesses, given that access to immediate medical care in the prison—especially at night—seemed problematic at best. These men lived with intense fears of suffering a heart attack, stroke, asthma attack, or debilitating fall. Although nearly all interviewees expressed a dread of dying in prison, several inmates with life sentences articulated a deep desire to die in order to "escape." According to one: "Every night I hope I don't see the morning because there is no life for me. I am depressed 24 hours a day, and I know I'm going to die in prison. I hope I don't wake up..." (p. 74).

Perhaps the biggest concern of these elderly prisoners was their realization that, on reviewing their lives—most older adults look back over and reassess their lives at some point—they would see failures, missed opportunities, and botched relationships. Such a negative evaluation tends to fill people with regret, anxiety, and despair and makes the prospect of an impending death much more difficult to endure. According to Crawley and Sparks, this sense that time has run out makes an elderly prisoner's experience of incarceration vastly different from that of a younger inmate who still has "sufficient years left to try to re-make (and re-write) his life when he is released" (pp. 77–78).

Effects of incarceration on older women. The concerns of incarcerated older women differ in some ways from those of male inmates. Almost half of female inmates rated their health as poor or terrible, compared to only 12% of older men (Kratcoski & Babb, 1990). In prisons, older women have higher rates of comorbid conditions and greater use of medical care than men (Baillargeon, Pulvino, & Dunn, 2000). Older female prisoners experience higher rates of hypertension, asthma/chronic obstructive pulmonary disease, and arthritis than older women living in the community (Williams et al., 2006).

They also report high rates of functional impairment: 69% of geriatric female prisoners questioned by Williams et al. reported at least one impairment in prison activities of daily living (PADLs) such as hearing orders from staff, dropping to the floor for alarms, standing for head count, getting to dining halls for meals, and climbing on and off the top bunk. Functional impairment is associated with more adverse experiences such as falling, feeling unsafe, or being physically abused by other inmates.

Older female inmates also report a high need for privacy and safety, and many are intimidated by prison violence and the threat of violence. According to one inmate: "There are some older women who can't take care of themselves, so to be in a room with eight women and...with aggressive women is not a very safe place for them to be....What happens is you see a lot of older women with black eyes" (Williams et al., 2006, p. 705).

Concerns about release. Although desirous of release, many of the elderly men studied by Crawley and Sparks (2006) were also anxious about that eventuality. In fact, only those with supportive families were enthusiastic about release. Prisoners without such support voiced concerns about how they would fare on the outside. They expressed worry about "starting from scratch," given that they had no relatives or friends, personal possessions, or housing. Understandably, some expressed the desire to simply stay put. "They had insufficient years left in life (or the energy) to 'start over'" (Crawley & Sparks, 2006, p. 75). Those with chronic medical conditions who had become dependent on some formal care from prison staff and on informal care provided by other inmates were especially concerned about access to health care upon release.

But tens of thousands of aging prisoners *are* being released every year (Williams & Abraldes, 2007) with significant psychosocial and medical needs that probation, parole, and health care agencies are ill equipped to handle. The stressors associated with adjustments to nonprison life are significant for nearly all former inmates but are especially problematic for older people. Some have lived behind bars for decades, others for more time than they have spent on the outside. They are often released into unsafe neighborhoods in which elderly, frail individuals are particularly vulnerable. Many lack family ties, employment and housing options, and financial resources. Significant medical and psychiatric needs and the stigma associated with having been imprisoned further compound their difficulties (Williams & Abraldes, 2007).

Analysis of Current Interventions

Given the multiple issues surrounding aging inmates, including their growing numbers and complex medical and psychiatric problems, various interventions have been implemented to address the issues. These include decarceration (releasing elderly inmates before their full sentences have been served), designing programming and housing to meet the needs of older prisoners, and developing hospice facilities within prison walls.

Decarceration. As prisons became overcrowded, corrections officials showed increasing interest in using scarce resources and space for high-risk offenders and selectively releasing, or decarcerating, inmates whom they consider to be a low risk to society. Because many older inmates tend to be both low risk and costly to house, and because most prisons were not designed to house inmates with limited mobility and chronic health problems, prison officials began transferring them to less expensive community-based programs including group homes, state nursing facilities, and congregate care institutions (Krebs, 2000).

Though unavailable to most prisoners, the Project for Older Prisoners (POPS) is a model re-entry program that identifies prisoners who have already served the average sentence for their offense, are deemed unlikely to recidivate, and whose victims have agreed to the release. Operating in five states (Louisiana, Maryland, Michigan, North Carolina, and Virginia) and the District of Columbia, the program assists older prisoners in transitioning back into the community. Evaluation data show that as of 2002, POPS had counseled more than 500 older inmates and assisted attorneys in winning the release of approximately 100, with no instances of recidivism (Rikard & Rosenberg, 2007). Another model, the Senior Ex-Offender Program, uses federal Office of Aging funding to provide housing, work opportunities, and financial, medical, and mental health services to newly released, older offenders (Williams & Abraldes, 2007). Data are needed on the effectiveness of the program to help offenders make a successful transition to living in the community.

Programming and housing to meet the needs of aging prisoners. Aging prisoners have different educational, recreational, and emotional needs and abilities than younger prisoners. Basic education courses should be paced more slowly, recreation programs should take into account the physical limitations of older inmates, and counseling programs should focus on issues of isolation, loss, and impending death, rather than on the rehabilitation and re-entry concerns of younger inmates. A number of programs now follow these dictates (Snyder, van Wormer, Chadha, & Jaggers, 2009), and some older inmates get programmatic assistance with Social Security, Medicare, and Medicaid applications and with writing wills.

As the population of older inmates has grown, some facilities have also begun to provide separate housing units that can accommodate wheelchairs and walkers, have wide aisles and handrails, and include assisted living areas and a central dining hall. Prison officials are divided on whether older inmates should be integrated with or segregated from the general population of inmates (Rikard & Rosenberg, 2007). Some favor integration because they believe that older inmates have a calming effect on the general population and because integration allows better access to educational and vocational programs and to visitors (Yates & Gillespie, 2000). On the other hand, segregation minimizes safety concerns for older prisoners and allows them to forge support networks and friendships with people their age, reducing feelings of desperation and loneliness (Yates & Gillespie, 2000).

End-of-life issues. Though highly controversial, a few states have statutory provisions for compassionate release programs, sometimes referred to as medical parole, in which a dying inmate is released to a community health care facility or home care. In some states, an inmate whose health has improved must return to the correctional facility (Rikard & Rosenberg, 2007). More commonly, prisons rely on hospice programs to care for terminally ill inmates. Qualification requirements are the same as those in the community: a life-ending condition and a prognosis of 6 months or less to live. Hospice staff sometimes report that their services are at odds with the strict security procedures in place in most prisons (Granse, 2003). For example, corrections officers are often wary of prisoners' needs for medications to manage pain and continue to subject inmates to demeaning body cavity searches after visits to medical providers.

But some patient-friendly models of hospice care within correctional settings now exist; the program at the maximum-security unit at the Louisiana State Penitentiary at Angola is one example (Snyder et al., 2009). In this program, other inmates function as volunteers, and an unexpected salutary consequence is that in addition to filling in for absent family members and providing comfort to dying inmates, many volunteers have been transformed by those experiences. Other hospice programs ease prison rules for dying inmates by allowing extended visitations, honoring food requests, and providing different clothing.

Policy Recommendations

Given the significant problems of prison overcrowding and diminished state coffers, and the reality that elderly inmates tend not to recidivate, policymakers should be advocating for reform in sentencing statutes and the creation of alternatives to incarceration for older adult offenders. According to Krebs (2000), the time is right to reevaluate existing sentencing practices, including three-strikes laws that put people behind bars for life, statutes that require life sentences without the possibility of parole and that carry very long-term mandatory minimum terms, and laws that eliminate the possibility of granting early release for good behavior. Alternatives to prison include diversion programs for first-time offenders and house arrest and electronic monitoring programs that keep the offender in the community.

Inside prisons, staff should be trained to understand and address the unique needs of older inmates and to become knowledgeable about normal aging processes. Simulated exercises that involve the use of glasses that blur vision, earplugs that reduce hearing acuity, and wheelchairs, walkers, and other props can increase empathy, and instruction on effective modes of communicating with the elderly can enhance staff interactions with older inmates (Snyder et al., 2009). Staff should be trained on the types of programming that will be accessible and useful to the elderly.

Finally, significant resources should be directed to re-entry and reintegration programs like POPS that benefit older adults. Community-based programs that historically have been unwilling or unable to accommodate older individuals with multiple health problems should be reformed. Day treatment centers, residential treatment programs, and nursing homes should be made available to recently released offenders, and social service agencies should be able to provide services and referrals of use to this population. Clearly, the need for trained professionals to work with older adults both inside and out of prison is essential, and just as obviously, resources to address these needs are lacking. Perhaps most obviously, as the cohort of baby boomers enters into the latter years of life, the problems associated with graying in prison will only become more acute, requiring that even more resources be directed their way.

Victimization

One consequence of increased longevity is a concomitant increase in the number of elderly people with frailties, chronic medical conditions, dementias, functional disabilities, and loss of decision-making capabilities. The erosion of social support and income that come with aging predispose the elderly to isolation and vulnerability. Elderly individuals who are isolated and no longer able to care for themselves or for their property are at risk of self-neglect, abuse, or exploitation by others.

Although elder mistreatment and victimization are not new phenomena, reported cases of elder abuse are increasing rapidly, and various studies have attempted to capture the size of the problem. In 1991, researchers estimated that 2.5 million Americans were victims of various forms of elder abuse, and by 1996, that number increased by 150% (National Center on Elder Abuse, 1998). Since that time, Adult Protective Services (APS), a social service agency responsible for investigating claims of elder abuse and neglect, has reported a 19.7% increase in elder abuse (Teaster, 2006).

The most recent report on prevalence rates of elder abuse comes from the National Elder Mistreatment Study (Acierno et al., 2010), in which 5,777 cognitively intact older adults provided self-reported data about frequency, type, and duration of abuse. Analyses revealed that 1 in 10 respondents reported some form or combination of physical, sexual, or emotional abuse or neglect occurring during a 1-year period. Over half of the respondents (55%) reported sharing a residence with the perpetrator, providing valuable information about the interpersonal complexities of elder abuse.

For many years, older adults silently tolerated these crimes, sometimes perpetrated by nameless criminals, but often by trusted caregivers and family members. Only within the last 25 years have elder abuse and neglect been given proper attention in policy circles and within the criminal justice system. It was not until 1993 that the American Medical Association published guidelines for dealing with the diagnosis and treatment of elder abuse and neglect victims (Aravanis et al., 1993). In this section, we explore the effects on elderly victims of neglect; intimate partner violence, a surprising and often misunderstood form of elder abuse; and financial abuse, an increasingly common form of elderly victimization yet largely hidden from public view. We briefly evaluate interventions and provide recommendations for further research.

Impact of Abuse and Neglect on Older Adults

Elder neglect. Elder neglect is defined as the "refusal or failure to fulfill any part of a person's obligations or duties to an elderly person" (National Center on Elder Abuse, 1998) and has been identified as the most common form of elder mistreatment in a domestic setting (National Center on Elder Abuse, 2005). The dependency of an older adult on a caregiver not only increases the vulnerability of the older person but also poses an environmental risk for neglect.

The caregiver stress theory, one model of elder abuse and neglect (Burnight & Mosqueda, 2011), posits that elder mistreatment and neglect occur when an adult caregiver assisting an impaired older person is unable to manage his or her caregiving responsibilities (Wolf, 2000). Due to the older adult's dependence on the caregiver, the caregiver becomes frustrated, overwhelmed, and abusive vis-à-vis the unremitting needs of the care recipient. Critics of the caregiver stress theory argue against this explanation because it places responsibility for abuse and neglect on the elder rather than on the responsible party (Brandl, 2002).

While caregiver stress has been linked to elder mistreatment and neglect, research has not shown that caregiver stress *alone* is a strong predictor of elder abuse (Hudson, 1986). Rather, it should be considered a risk factor that must not be overlooked (Burnight & Mosqueda, 2011). In a recent convenience sample of care recipients with dementia and their caregivers, 47.3% of the care recipients experienced some form of mistreatment, but only 29.5% experienced neglect by their caregiver (Wiglesworth et al., 2010). An earlier descriptive study of U.S. hospitalizations with elder mistreatment diagnostic codes revealed that the largest percentage (47%) of inpatient stays of adults age 60 and older was associated with a diagnosis of nutritional neglect (Rovi, Chen, Vega, Johnson, & Mouton, 2009).

Intimate partner violence. Intimate partner violence (IPV) is a serious problem affecting the wellbeing of millions of people (Krug, Dahlberg, Mercy, Zwi, & Lozano, 2002). Although more commonly reported in younger cohorts, this form of abuse is a significant concern for older populations given their age-specific risk factors such as frailty and isolation (Krug et al., 2002). Intimate partner violence among older adults can be persistent throughout marriages or initiated by late-life changes or transitions that affect the relationship, such as a chronic disease or cognitive decline (Brandl & Meuer, 2000). In some instances, IPV can ensue with new relationships or second marriages (Brandl & Raymond, 1997), but in all cases IPV includes sexual, physical, and psychological abuse between two people in an intimate relationship. Risk factors for men and women who experience physical IPV include poor health, depression, substance use, and the development of a chronic disease, chronic mental illness, or injury (Coker et al., 2002).

Gender-biased assumptions that stem from feminist theories of power and control posit that women are always the victims and men always perpetrators (Dutton & Nicholls, 2005). But the empirical and theoretical literature on IPV in older age shows that women are as likely as men to be perpetrators (Reeves, Desmarais, Nicholls, & Douglas, 2007), and the belief that older women are not aggressors deleteriously impacts help-seeking behaviors in older men (Reeves et al., 2007). The implications for detection, assessment, and intervention in cases of IPV are far-reaching and require professionals to adopt new ways of identifying older victims and perpetrators.

Physical and mental health effects of intimate partner violence. As in other areas of elder victimization, there is scant understanding of the long-term effects of IPV among older adults. Identifying the long-term consequences of IPV is complicated by poorly defined terms of abuse, inconsistencies in research methodologies, limited screening and risk assessment instruments, and underutilization of health care diagnostic coding in U.S. community hospitals (Desmarais & Reeves, 2007; Rovi et al., 2009). Most research conducted on the physical and mental health effects of IPV includes small sample sizes consisting primarily of female victims.

The long-term health and psychological repercussions associated with *early* experiences of intimate partner abuse are somewhat better understood. These include depression, posttraumatic stress disorder, headache, irritable bowel syndrome, chronic pain, suicidality, and substance abuse (Campbell, 2002; Coker et al., 2002; Nelson, Nygren, McInerney, & Klein, 2004). In a poll of 995 partnered women over the age of 55 in primary care offices, Zink, Fisher, Regan, and Pabst (2005) found significantly higher rates of self-reported depression and chronic pain among IPV victims than nonvictims. Consistent with studies of younger victims (Campbell et al., 2002; Coker et al., 2000), Zink et al. found that older victims of IPV also had lower physical and mental health scores and more reports of digestive problems than nonvictims. Their findings support a growing need for additional training of physicians to recognize and inquire with sensitivity about comorbid symptoms that may be indicative of IPV among older patients.

Elder financial mistreatment. Elder financial abuse (EFA) is the illegal or improper use of an elder's funds, property, or assets. Examples include cashing a check without authorization or permission, forging a signature, misusing or stealing money or possessions, coercing or deceiving a victim into signing a document (e.g., contract or will), and improperly using conservatorship, guardianship, or power of attorney. Some experts speculate that elders are ripe targets because they are more trusting and less sophisticated about financial matters than younger people (Kemp & Mosqueda, 2005) and relatively naïve about digital methods of handling financial transactions.

Whereas physical abuse and neglect can be more easily identified by those in medical and mental health fields, financial abuse is a difficult crime to detect. It leaves no physical mark, is largely hidden from public view, and typically occurs over years and in the context of family relationships that involve issues of entitlement and obligation. It is often difficult to distinguish from well-intentioned but misguided advice (Hafemeister, 2003; Rabiner, O'Keeffe, & Brown, 2006). Many older adults are quite unaware that it has occurred. Others hesitate to report because they are embarrassed or ashamed, lack understanding of protective and legal processes, are reluctant to inform on family members for fear of reprisal, or are concerned that reporting may lead to their loss of independence (Rabiner et al., 2006).

Most professionals who have contact with older victims (e.g., physicians, nurses, bankers, attorneys, mental health providers) have not been properly trained to recognize the signs and are not required to report the abuse (Quinn & Tomita, 1997). As a result, it is difficult to estimate the exact prevalence and incidence of such cases, although data from the National Center on Elder Abuse (2005) suggest that there may be at least 5 million victims of EFA per year.

A critical distinction between EFA and other types of financial crimes (e.g., fraud) is the close and trusting relationship between the elder and the exploiter, often a professional caregiver, family member, neighbor, or trusted professional. Although historically associated with child or spousal abuse, the concept of undue influence—the misuse of one's role and power to exploit the trust of another—also applies to EFA. Undue influence is typically accomplished by using subtle pressure and coercion to gain control over a weaker person's decision making (Brandl et al., 2007).

Older adults who are isolated, have cognitive impairments such as dementia, or are in a major life transition such as widowhood are particularly susceptible to undue influence (Choi & Mayer, 2000; Nievod, 1992; Quinn, 2000). For example, widowed women who were once accustomed to having financial affairs handled by a husband may find themselves trusting another (typically younger) man to assume that role. Widowers may fall victim to younger women posing in need of money in exchange for domestic chores and companionship (Nerenberg, 1996). In both scenarios, the perpetrator infiltrates the elder's home, preys upon his or her weaknesses, and consequently abuses the relationship for financial gain. Undue influence is not exclusive to nonfamilial caregivers; the situation is played out just as frequently among family members. In fact, the majority of reported cases of EFA have occurred between an elderly person and his or her adult child, grandchild, or other relative (National Center on Elder Abuse, 1998).

What Is Not Known About the Impact of Abuse

Because elder abuse is a largely hidden form of victimization, has been identified as a social problem only relatively recently, and is complex and multifaceted, the scope of the problem is just beginning to emerge. Difficulties in estimating incidence and prevalence are related to varying definitions and measurement techniques and to the lack of comparison groups in large-scale surveys (Lowenstein, 2009).

An understanding of cultural influences on abuse perpetration and on the reactions of victims is in its infancy. The issues include a differential focus among cultures on the individual versus the family and community, cultural variations in rights and privileges of females and males, and complexities related to culturally sensitive means of data collection and interpretation (Newman, 2006).

Information on the etiology of intimate partner violence is conflicting; some data suggest that aggression may be symptomatic of dementia because delusions of spousal infidelity are common in individuals suffering from dementia (Greene, Bornstein, & Dietrich, 2007; Mirakhur, Craig, Hart, McIlroy, & Passmore, 2004), and other data suggest that intimate partner abuse in old age reflects patterns of power dominance and control that were present throughout the relationship (Desmarais & Reeves, 2007). Scientists have yet to discern the circumstances in which each explanation applies, and without a thorough understanding of the causes of abuse, it is difficult to create solutions. Given the multifaceted nature of elder abuse, several theoretical explanations are likely to emerge (Connolly, 2010).

There is also sparse research on the formal and informal services and resources that older victims—particularly victims of intimate partner abuse—avail themselves of and whether they are well served by those interventions. Little is known about how abuser-focused concerns of the criminal justice system and victim-focused concerns of APS work independently or in combination to enhance victim safety and reduce reoffending. In some jurisdictions, if the police arrest an alleged abuser, APS will provide fewer resources to the victim, assuming that the source of the violence has been controlled; and if the police know that a case has been referred to APS, they are less likely to arrest and prosecute, assuming that the referral will effectively stem the abuse.

Finally, little is known about how courts can best accommodate elderly victims and perpetrators. The American Bar Association has recommended that prosecutors be given latitude in how they question older abuse victims, be allowed to film victims' testimony before capacity is lost or the victim dies, and be able to offer evidence from collateral sources, as is done in cases involving allegations of child abuse (American Bar Association, 2008). How fact finders will react to any of these practices is largely unknown.

Analysis of Current Interventions

Among the interventions currently in place or proposed to address the problem of elder abuse, three seem particularly noteworthy. These include mandatory reporting, advancing state and federal responses to elder abuse as authorized by the Elder Justice Act, and developing elder abuse forensic centers that streamline responses to cases of suspected abuse.

Mandatory reporting laws. One reason that elder abuse is so rarely prosecuted is that many cases go unreported (Dessin, 2000; Hafemeister, 2003). Whether mandatory reporting increases the number of investigated and prosecuted cases is unclear, in part because of variability among states in the threshold for what constitutes abuse and who is considered a reporter. Some states mandate that any person with knowledge of abuse should report it, whereas other states require reporting only by persons with certain qualifications, and still others designate certain professionals as mandatory reporters.

In a survey of state officials from aging and APS agencies, less than 10% ranked mandatory reporting as the most effective way to maximize the number of elder abuse cases brought to the attention of authorities (U.S. General Accounting Office, 1991). Many respondents perceived that mandatory reporting laws do not directly influence the processing of valid cases but agreed that reporting requirements have led to additional resources and services.

Elder Justice Act. Enacted in March 2010, the Elder Justice Act (EJA)—part of the Patient Protection and Affordable Care Act—delineates plans to advance state and federal efforts to prevent and respond to elder abuse, neglect, and exploitation (National Health Policy Forum, 2010). Although appropriations have not yet been approved by Congress, several grant programs have been authorized by the EJA to fund state programs that emphasize training in detection and/or prevention of elder abuse and exploitation; enforcement of mandatory reporting requirements in suspected abuse in long-term care facilities; and the development of two elder abuse advisory boards to propose legislation on issues of elder abuse, neglect, and exploitation.

Elder abuse forensic centers. In response to an overwhelming increase in suspected cases of elder abuse and a decrease in state funding and resources (American Association of Retired Persons [AARP] Public Policy Institute, 2011), a new approach to investigating cases has been realized through the development of elder abuse forensic centers. Multidisciplinary teams consisting of professionals working within APS, law enforcement, long-term care, geriatric medicine, and neuropsychology have come together to collaborate on intervention. In 2003, California opened the first elder abuse forensic center, the Elder Abuse Forensic Center of Orange County.

In a recent examination of seven different multidisciplinary teams in California, all funded by the Archstone Foundation through its Elder Abuse and Neglect Initiative, Twomey et al. (2010) addressed the challenges faced by elder abuse forensic centers. These include issues of client confidentiality, cross-training of different disciplines, and group dynamics (Twomey et al., 2010). Some challenges were specific to managing complex cases of elder abuse. For example, team members from different mandatory reporting agencies and jurisdictions were challenged to navigate the elder abuse reporting system while learning about other disciplines' cultures, systems, and roles.

Complicated group dynamics prompted the development of "ground rules" for the Financial Abuse Specialist Team (FAST) in Solano County, which encouraged mutual respect for fellow team members and recognition of the challenges faced by their disciplines.

Despite these unique challenges, elder abuse forensic centers have largely been successful (Twomey et al., 2010). They play a critical role in increasing collaboration and efficiency among several disciplines in handling complicated cases of elder abuse, raising awareness and providing education through community outreach efforts, and protecting vulnerable adults from potential abuse.

Policy Recommendations

In her article "Where Elder Abuse and the Justice System Collide," Marie-Therese Connolly (2010) sets out recommendations for improving justice system responses to elder abuse. Given the comprehensive nature of these recommendations and for purposes of brevity, we list some of them here and recommend her article to readers who seek more detailed information. Connolly suggests the following: (1) form a national blueprint advisory committee to identify the most serious problems, promising solutions, and crucial next steps to redress elder abuse; (2) increase research and evaluation efforts; (3) develop theoretical models to explain elder abuse; (4) evaluate the effectiveness of mandatory reporting laws and criminal background checks to reduce elder abuse; (5) assess ways to prosecute cases when victim capacity is an issue; (6) evaluate, modify, and replicate successful multidisciplinary elder abuse forensic programs; (7) provide advocates to promote and maintain the wellbeing of victims through investigations and prosecutions; (8) train law enforcement, prosecutors, court personnel, and judges to recognize elder abuse and respond to it in effective ways; and (9) establish a clearinghouse of elder abuse resources.

Decision-Making Autonomy

Increased longevity also raises questions about what should happen when older adults begin to make decisions that are not in their best interest or that put themselves and others in danger, and how two core principles—autonomy and protection—can be optimized in responding to these issues. Psychologists and other clinicians address these concerns when they assess whether an individual has the cognitive and procedural skills necessary to function effectively in a particular domain. Moye and Marson (2007) identified eight major capacity domains that are relevant to older adults, including medical decision making and financial capacity.

Although most judgments about capacity are made in an informal manner by a network of family members, clinicians, attorneys, caregivers, and social service personnel, capacity judgments sometimes become legal decisions made in an adversarial context by judges and informed by clinical assessments. This may occur when someone seeks to assume control over an elder's decisions (e.g., concerning driving) against the older person's will. It may occur when family members disagree about how best to care for an older adult who is believed or determined to lack capacity. In recent years, the large-scale transfer of wealth from the World War II generation to the baby boomer generation and the fragmentation of families have resulted in a marked increase in intrafamilial conflict about older adults' intentions and decisional capacity (Moye & Marson, 2007). Probate judges resolve these disputes.

The mechanism that the law has devised to deal with these issues is the establishment of guardianships and conservatorships by which judges appoint surrogate decision makers to handle the personal and financial affairs of the incapacitated elderly person. There are no federal laws governing guardianship; hence, policies and practices related to the duties and responsibilities of courts and guardians are determined by state regulations. In general, guardianship statutes are based on the doctrine of *parens patriae* that gives the government both the right and the duty to protect people who are no longer able to care for themselves. Thus, if a probate judge deems it in the best interest of the older adult or of society, the state may authorize surrogates to make decisions about an incapacitated person's care and protection, even over that person's objections (Grisso, 2003). In practical terms, guardianship can result in the loss of the right to make choices about living arrangements; health care; the purchase, use, or disposal of property; travel; making or revoking a will; getting married or divorced; spending money; and driving.

The National Health Interview Survey's 1995 Supplement on Disability (National Center for Health Statistics, 1999), a household survey of noninstitutionalized individuals in the United States, questioned adults age 60 and older (n = 13,784) about the factors associated with having a guardian (Reynolds, 2002). Those factors included having a small family network (additional family members decreased the probability of having a guardian by 42%), not living with a spouse (living with a spouse decreased the probability of having a guardian by 58%), and having functional impairments, confusion, disorientation or forgetfulness, and Alzheimer's disease. The decreasing size of families and increasing rate of divorce among future cohorts of older adults foreshadow the important role of guardianships in the future.

What Is Known About the Effects of Guardianship on Older Adults

Personal control enhances life satisfaction among the elderly (Berg, Hassing, McClern, & Johansson, 2006; Kunzmann, Little, & Smith, 2002; Langer & Rodin, 1976), and many older adults want to maintain their own authority for making decisions for as long as possible. According to one survey, they desire to have "the last word" about their care (Boisaubin, Chu, & Catalano, 2007).

Some evidence suggests that wards have felt angry, resentful, agitated, and upset by guardianship proceedings and the removal of decision autonomy (Bulcroft, Kielkopf, & Tripp, 1991).

Yet many adults who are made wards of guardians probably fare better with some assistance than they would without (Moye, 2003). Empirical evidence on surrogates' ability to represent the health care preferences of elderly and disabled people showed that surrogates can enhance the chances that the best interests of the other person are taken into account (Shah, Farrow, & Robinson, 2009), although a meta-analysis on how accurately surrogates can predict patients' end-of-life treatment preferences showed that predictions were incorrect in one-third of cases (Shalowitz, Garrett-Mayer, & Wendler, 2006).

The value of guardianship was made apparent by interviews of a random sample of 50 individuals under guardianship in Los Angeles County (Wilber, Reiser, & Harter, 2001). The interviews documented high levels of confusion and significant limitations in interviewees. When asked how they felt about their guardianship arrangements, 40% indicated that they did not understand or remember that they had appointed guardians. When one interviewee "learned" from the interviewer what guardianship/conservatorship entailed, she responded, "I'm sure I would not like that." Twelve percent of interviewees expressed satisfaction with their guardians, whereas 24% had lingering reservations and concerns, including the possibility that assets would be depleted and the ward placed in a skilled nursing facility.

On the basis of their data, Wilber et al. concluded that the most severe impact on the wards was not the appointment of a guardian per se, but rather preexisting impairments and problems (e.g., a long-standing psychiatric disorder, physical limitations, cognitive impairment) that probably resulted in the provision of protective services in the first place. These data imply that although there is some lingering distrust and confusion in a significant minority of cases, the appointment of a guardian to make decisions on behalf of an incapacitated elderly person can yield satisfactory outcomes in a large number of cases.

What Is Not Known About the Effects of Guardianship on Older Adults

It is difficult to assess how at-risk older adults under guardianship compare with similar individuals without guardians on measures of longevity, physical and emotional health, and self-reported wellbeing, and equally difficult to quantify the costs of removing autonomy on wards who are not seriously incapacitated (Wright, 2010). With the exception of a unique early study in which researchers randomly assigned older adults who were incapable of self-care to an experimental group that received a variety of medical, financial, legal, and social services or to a control group that did not (and found negligible differences between the two on measures of survival, contentment, and functional competence; Bleckner, Bloom, Nielsen, & Weber,

1974), researchers have been unwilling or unable to conduct studies of this sort because of concerns related to denying care to those in need. As a result, questions still loom about the effects of the loss of autonomy on wellbeing.

Based on her experiences representing elders in guardianship proceedings and borrowing the concepts of therapeutic jurisprudence, Professor Jennifer Wright has provided a comprehensive and nuanced analysis of the putative therapeutic and antitherapeutic effects of guardianship on the wellbeing of respondents and wards (Wright, 2010; for further discussion of therapeutic jurisprudence, see chapter 2, this volume). Although her observations may hold up to empirical scrutiny, as yet the rigorous research that can systematically examine her suspicions is lacking. Still, her analysis provides an exceptionally clear blueprint for moving the field forward and elucidating the real consequences of intervention in the lives of older, infirmed adults.

Wright suggests that there are many negative implications of guardianship, including the fact that because medical and social service personnel pressure families to take protective action, painful discussions between family members and elders with diminishing capacity are shut down. The all-or-nothing adversarial nature of guardianship proceedings results in a hardening of positions among family members, attorneys, and respondents that does little to further compromise. She also suggests that guardianship hearings demean and shame the respondent because he or she must listen to others testify about the loss of decision-making ability and difficulties related to self-care. This cruel public portrayal of the infirmed older adult can, according to Wright, lead to loss of self-esteem and serious depression. Finally, Wright opines that a contested guardianship proceeding can fracture family relationships, result in a ward feeling hostile and resentful toward the guardian, and reduce the likelihood that treatments that might slow or reverse the decline are sought out.

Wright also offers a litany of putative therapeutic effects, including the possibility that the filing of a petition will force the older adult to confront the realities of the situation and discuss, perhaps for the first time, the need for additional care. These conversations can help elders to understand the high costs associated with their insistence on self-sufficiency, both for themselves and for care providers. Wright also suggests that the petition for guardianship is often the catalyst for a series of physical, mental, and functional assessments that can lead to treatments or other accommodations to enhance safety and comfort. Finally, in the best of circumstances, guardianship proceedings can enable older adults to speak on their own behalf and, when supported by counsel, experts, and other witnesses familiar with the situation, to feel empowered by the experience. Although Wright articulates these possibilities in a compelling and reasoned way, most of her observations still await empirical confirmation.

Analysis of Current Interventions

Clearly, some older adults are so incapacitated and lacking in functional abilities that they would be unable to care for themselves or their assets under almost any independent living situation or structured financial arrangement. For these individuals, a formal or informal transfer of decision-making powers is imperative. Short of this extreme, some assistance in bill paying and money or asset management can keep an older adult solvent and protect his or her estate. Attention to the physical aspects of one's environment (e.g., wheelchair access, potential hazards) can also enhance the chances of successful independent living.

Simply changing some aspect of an individual's environment may provide sufficient support to allow that person to continue to function independently and make his or her own decisions. In these situations, remedies short of full guardianships (e.g., case or care managers, durable powers of attorney for property or health care, living wills, community advocacy systems, and money management programs) are appropriate. Indeed, there is growing pressure on probate judges to move away from full guardianship that rescinds decision making in a wide variety of domains and, instead, to appoint surrogates to narrowly constrained tasks (e.g., making decisions about driving or medical treatment; National Guardianship Network Members, 2004). As capacity assessment improves, clinicians will be increasingly able to suggest alternatives to guardianship that support independent living, and judges and other legal professionals will be increasingly able to tailor their interventions to the specific needs of a particular individual (Moye & Marson, 2007), with the ultimate goal to maximize both autonomy of the elderly and protection of those who are most vulnerable.

Policy Recommendations

In her thoughtful analysis of the guardianship system, Wright (2010) also suggested ways to reshape the system to maximize the therapeutic effects of intervention and minimize its antitherapeutic consequences. She borrowed two concepts—problem-solving courts and mediation—from other contexts and proposed ways they might fit into guardianship reform (for more on the therapeutic component of problem-solving courts, see chapter 2, this volume). She suggested that rather than focusing on the traditional litany of questions such as whether the respondent is legally incapacitated, whether a guardian is needed, and who the guardian should be, problem-solving courts would ask about the underlying reasons that the parties entered into guardianship proceedings and how various medical, social service, and counseling providers could work with the parties to reach a solution that is acceptable to all.

Since 1991, the Center for Social Gerontology, a nonprofit research, training, and policy institute in Ann Arbor, Michigan, has been conducting field research of various guardianship mediation programs that involve the use of trained, neutral facilitators to work with disputing parties to resolve conflicts related to protective intervention (Butterwick, Hommel, & Keilitz, 2001). Although lacking a rigorous study that randomly assigns some cases to mediation and others to traditional probate court proceedings, the center has ascertained that participants believe mediation can be effective in reaching satisfactory resolutions and are generally satisfied with their experiences. Whether this reform is a practical alternative to traditional proceedings and whether it can address some of the presumed negative effects of those proceedings await further study (see chapter 13, this volume, for more on alternative dispute resolution).

Although both of these reforms offer attractive ways to resolve immediate problems and improve the wellbeing of petitioners and respondents in the short term, the fact that many mental faculties typically continue their downward slide suggests that they may not be cost-effective solutions for the long term. Empirical research will be needed to assess the viability of each.

Conclusion

As the population of older adults grows, elders' involvement in the legal system will increase as well. A variety of issues—only a few of which we have elaborated on in this chapter—bring them into contact with the law: loss of capacity, entitlements, abuse and neglect by caregivers and "trusted" others, age discrimination, estate planning and probate, health care reform, disability rights, and end-of-life decisions. Many older prisoners have been "in contact with" the law for decades. In this admittedly selective analysis, we have documented that a large number of elderly prisoners, unlikely to recidivate and costly to taxpayers, are languishing behind bars waiting to die in prison. We have also shown that older adults are increasingly likely to be victimized, often by relatives and friends who prey on victims' declining faculties, and that these declining capabilities raise concerns about how to optimize both self-determination and protection in old age. We have discussed the ability of mental health professionals to assess decision-making capacity, as well as the willingness of guardians to make decisions on behalf of vulnerable older adults with diminished decision-making capacity.

Each of these situations demands unique and nuanced responses, predicated on knowledge of the physical and psychosocial determinants of aging and the complexities of elder law. This will obviously require infusions of resources to support research, training, and advocacy efforts and to develop innovative ways to enhance elders' involvement in the legal system. Time will tell whether those resources will flow. The need is surely present.

References

Acierno, R., Hernandez, M., Amstadter, A., Resnick, H., Steve, K., Muzzy, W., et al. (2010). Prevalence and correlates of emotional, physical, sexual, and financial abuse and potential neglect in the United States: The national elder mistreatment study. *American Journal of Public Health, 100*, 292–297.

Aday, R. (2003). *Aging prisoners: Crisis in American corrections.* Westport, CT: Praeger.
American Association of Retired Persons (AARP) Public Policy Institute. (2011). *Weathering the storm: The impact of the great recession on long-term services and supports.* Retrieved from http://www.aarp.org
American Bar Association, Criminal Justice Section, Senior Lawyers Division Commission on Domestic Violence, Commission on Law and Aging. (2008). *Report to the House of Delegates.* Retrieved from http://www.americanbar.org/content/dam/aba/publishing/criminal_justice_section_newsletter/crimjust_policy_crimeselderly.authcheckdam.pdf
American Psychological Association. (2010). *Publication manual of the American Psychological Association* (6th ed.). Washington, DC: Author.
Aravanis, S. C., Adelman, R. D., Breckman, R., Fulmer, T. T., Holder, E., Lachs, M., et al. (1993). Diagnostic and treatment guidelines on elder abuse and neglect. *Archives of Family Medicine, 2,* 371–388.
Baillargeon, J., Pulvino, J., & Dunn, K. (2000). The disease profile of Texas prison inmates. *Annals of Epidemiology, 10,* 74–80.
Beck, A., Hughes, T., & Wilson, D. (2001). *Trends in state parole, 1990–2000.* Washington, DC: Bureau of Justice Statistics. Retrieved from http://bjs.ojp.usdoj.gov/index.cfm?ty=pbdetail&iid=822
Beckett, J., Peternelj-Taylor, C., & Johnson, R. (2003). Growing old in the correctional system. *Journal of Psychosocial Nursing and Mental Health Services, 41,* 12–18.
Berg, A., Hassing, L., McClern, G., & Johansson, B. (2006). What matters for life satisfaction in the oldest-old? *Aging and Mental Health, 10,* 257–264.
Bleckner, M., Bloom, M., Nielsen, M., & Weber, R. (1974). *Final report: Protective services for older people. Findings from the Benjamin Rose Institute Study.* Cleveland, OH: Benjamin Rose Institute.
Boisaubin, E., Chu, A., & Catalano, J. (2007). Perceptions of long-term care, autonomy, and dignity, by residents, family and caregivers: The Houston experience. *Journal of Medicine and Philosophy, 32,* 447–464. doi:10.1080/03605310701626414
Brandl, B. (2002). Power and control: Understanding domestic abuse in later life. *Generations, 24,* 39–45.
Brandl, B., Dyer, C. B., Heisler, C. J., Otto, J. M., Stiegal, L. A., & Thomas, R. W. (2007). *Elder abuse detection and intervention: A collaborative approach.* New York, NY: Springer Publishing Company.
Brandl, B., & Meuer, T. (2000). Domestic abuse in later life. *Elder Law Journal, 8,* 297–335.
Brandl, B., & Raymond, J. (1997). Unrecognized elder abuse victims: Older abused women. *Journal of Case Management, 6,* 62–68.
Brink, J., Doherty, D., & Boer, A. (2001). Mental disorder in federal offenders: A Canadian prevalence study. *International Journal of Law and Psychiatry, 24,* 339–356.
Bulcroft, K., Kielkopf, M., & Tripp, K. (1991). Elderly wards and their legal guardians: Analysis of county probate records in Ohio and Washington. *Gerontologist, 31,* 156–164.
Burnight, K., & Mosqueda, L. (2011). *Theoretical model development in elder mistreatment.* Report submitted to the U.S. Department of Justice, Document No. 234488. Washington, DC: Department of Justice.

Butterwick, S., Hommel, P., & Keilitz, I. (2001). *Evaluating mediation as a means of resolving adult guardianship cases.* Ann Arbor, MI: Center for Social Gerontology.

Caldwell, C., Jarvis, M., & Rosenfield, H. (2001). Issues impacting today's geriatric female offenders. *Corrections Today, 63,* 110–113.

California Department of Corrections. (2007). *Prison census data as of December 31, 2007.* Sacramento, CA: Data Analysis Unit.

Campbell, J., Jones, A. S., Dienemann, J., Kub, J., Schollenberger, J., O'Campo, P., et al. (2002). Intimate partner violence and physical health consequences. *Archives of Internal Medicine, 10,* 1157–1163.

Campbell, J. C. (2002). Health consequences of intimate partner violence. *Lancet, 359,* 1331–1336.

Choi, N. G., & Mayer, J. (2000). Elder abuse, neglect, and exploitation: Risk factors and prevention strategies. *Journal of Gerontological Social Work, 33,* 5–25.

Coker, A. L., Davis, K. E., Arieas, I., Sujata, D., Sanderson, M., Brandt, H. M., et al. (2002). Physical and mental health effects of intimate partner violence for men and women. *American Journal of Preventative Medicine, 23,* 260–268.

Coker, A. L., Smith, P. H., Bethea, L., King, M. R., & McKeown, R. E. (2000). Physical health consequences of physical and psychological intimate partner violence. *Archives of Family Medicine, 5,* 451–457.

Connolly, M. (2010). Where elder abuse and the justice system collide: Police power, *parens patriae,* and 12 recommendations. *Journal of Elder Abuse and Neglect, 22,* 37–93. doi:10.1080/08946560903436338

Crawley, E., & Sparks, R. (2006). Is there life after imprisonment? How elderly men talk about imprisonment and release. *Criminology and Criminal Justice, 6,* 63–82. doi:10.1177/1748895806060667

Desmarais, S., & Reeves, K. (2007). Gray, black, and blue: The state of research and intervention for intimate partner abuse among elders. *Behavioral Sciences and the Law, 25,* 377–391.

Dessin, C. L. (2000). Financial abuse of the elderly. *Idaho Law Review, 36,* 203–226.

Dutton, D. G., & Nicholls, T. L. (2005). The gender paradigm in domestic violence research and theory: Part 1—The conflict of theory and data. *Aggression and Violent Behavior, 10,* 680–714.

Fazel, S., Hope, T., O'Donnell, I., & Jacoby, R. (2001). Hidden psychiatric morbidity in elderly prisoners. *British Journal of Psychiatry, 179,* 535–539.

Fazel, S., Hope, T., O'Donnell, I., Piper, M., & Jacoby, R. (2001). Health of elderly male prisoners: Worse than the general population, worse than younger prisoners. *Age and Aging, 30,* 403–407.

Fazel, S., Hope, T., O'Donnell, I., Piper, M., & Jacoby, R. (2004). Unmet treatment needs of older prisoners: A primary care survey. *Age and Aging, 33,* 396–398.

Fiske, A., Wetherell, J., & Gatz, M. (2009). Depression in older adults. *Annual Review of Clinical Psychology, 5,* 363–389. doi:10.1146/annurev.clinpsy.032408.153621

Granse, B. (2003). Why should we even care? Hospice social work practice in a prison setting. *Smith College Studies in Social Work, 73,* 359–376.

Greene, E., Bornstein, B., & Dietrich, H. (2007). "Granny, (don't) get your gun." Competency issues in gun ownership by older adults. *Behavioral Sciences and the Law, 25,* 405–423.

Grisso, T. (2003). *Evaluating competencies: Forensic assessments and instruments.* New York, NY: Kluwer Academic/Plenum Publishers.

Hafemeister, T. L. (2003). Financial abuse of the elderly in domestic situations. In R. J. Bonnie & R. B. Wallace (Eds.), *Elder mistreatment: Abuse, neglect, and exploitation in an aging America* (pp. 382–445). Washington, DC: National Academies Press.

Harrison, P., & Beck, A. (2002). *Prisoners in 2001.* (Publication no. 195189). Washington, DC: Department of Justice, Bureau of Justice Statistics.

Harrison, P., & Beck, A. (2004). *Prisoners in 2003.* (Publication no. 205335). Washington, DC: Department of Justice, Bureau of Justice Statistics.

Hudson, M. (1986). Empirical and theoretical perspectives on elder abuse. In K. Pillemer & R. Wolf (Eds.), *Elder abuse: Conflict in the family* (pp. 126–166). Dover, MA: Auburn House Publishing Co.

Kemp, B. J., & Mosqueda, L. A. (2005). Elder financial abuse: An evaluation framework and supporting evidence. *Journal of the American Geriatrics Society, 53,* 1123–1127.

Kratcoski, P., & Babb, S. (1990). Adjustment of older inmates: An analysis by institutional structure and gender. *Journal of Contemporary Criminal Justice, 6,* 264–281.

Krebs, J. (2000). Arguments and strategies for the selective decarceration of older prisoners. In M. Rothman, B. Dunlop, & P. Entzel (Eds.), *Elders, crime, and the criminal justice system* (pp. 229–249). New York, NY: Springer.

Krug, E., Dahlberg, L. L., Mercy, J. A., Zwi, A. B., & Lozano, R. (Eds.). (2002). *World report on violence and health.* Geneva: World Health Organization.

Kunzmann, U., Little, T., & Smith, J. (2002). Perceiving control: A double-edged sword in old age. *Journal of Gerontology: Psychological Science and Social Science, 57B,* 484–491.

Langer, E., & Rodin, J. (1976). The effects of choice and enhanced personal responsibility for the aged: A field experiment in an institutional setting. *Journal of Personality and Social Psychology, 34,* 191–198.

Linder, J., Enders, S., Craig, E., Richardson, J., & Meyers, F. (2002). Hospice care for the incarcerated in the United States: An introduction. *Journal of Palliative Medicine, 5,* 549–552. doi:10.1089/109662102760269788

Loeb, S., & AbuDagga, A. (2006). Health-related research on older inmates: An integrative review. *Research in Nursing and Health, 29,* 556–565. doi:10.1002/nur.20177

Lowenstein, A. (2009). Elder abuse and neglect—"Old phenomenon": New directions for research, legislation, and service developments. *Journal of Elder Abuse and Neglect, 21,* 278–287. doi:10.1080/08946560902997637

Lynch, J., & Sabol, W. (2001, September). *Prisoner reentry in perspective.* Crime Policy Report Vol. 3. Washington, DC: Urban Institute.

Marquart, J., Merianos, D., & Doucet, G. (2000). The health-related concerns of older prisoners: Implications for policy. *Aging and Society, 20,* 79–96.

Mirakhur, A., Craig, D., Hart, D., McIlroy, S., & Passmore, A. (2004). Behavioural and psychological syndromes in Alzheimer's disease. *International Journal of Geriatric Psychiatry, 19,* 1035–1039.

Mitka, M. (2004). Aging prisoners stressing health care system. *Journal of American Medical Association, 292,* 423–424. doi:10.1001/jama.292.4.423.

Molinari, V., & Segal, D. (2010). Personality disorders: Description, aetiology, & epidemiology. In M. Abou-Saleh, C. Katona, & A. Kumar (Eds.), *Principles and practice of geriatric psychiatry* (3rd ed., pp. 649–654). New York, NY: John Wiley & Sons.
Moye, J. (2003). Guardianship and conservatorship. In T. Grisso (Ed.), *Evaluating competencies: Forensic assessments and instruments* (pp. 309–389). New York, NY: Kluwer Academic/Plenum Publishers.
Moye, J., & Marson, D. (2007). Assessment of decision-making capacity in older adults: An emerging area of practice and research. *Journal of Gerontology: Psychological Sciences, 62B,* P3–P11.
Murdoch, N., Morris, P., & Holmes, C. (2008). Depression in elderly life sentence prisoners. *Internation Journal of Geriatric Psychiatry, 23,* 957–962.
National Center for Health Statistics. (1999). *National health interview survey on disability, 1995: Phase I, person and condition data.* Hyattsville, MD: U.S. Department of Health and Human Services.
National Center on Elder Abuse. (1998). *National elder abuse incidence study.* Washington, DC: Author.
National Center on Elder Abuse. (2005). *Elder abuse prevalence and incidence.* Retrieved from http://www.ncea.aoa.gov
National Guardianship Network Members: National Academy of Elder Law Attorneys, National Guardianship Association, National College of Probate Judges. (2004). *National wingspan implementation session: Action steps on adult guardianship progress.* Retrieved from http://www.ncsconline.org/famviol/elderabuse/pdf/Nat'l%20Wingspan%20Implementation%20Session_Action%20Steps%20on%20Adult%20Guardianship%20Progress.pdf
National Health Policy Forum. (2010). *The Elder Justice Act: Addressing elder abuse, neglect, and exploitation.* Retrieved from http://www.nhpf.org
Nelson, H. D., Nygren, P., McInerney, Y., & Klein J. (2004). Screening women and elderly adults for family and intimate partner violence: A review of the evidence for the U.S. Preventive Services Task Force. *Annals of Internal Medicine, 5,* 387–396.
Nerenberg, L. (1996). *Financial abuse of the elderly.* Washington, DC: National Center on Elder Abuse.
Newman, M. (2006). International/cultural perspectives on elder abuse. In R. W. Summers & A. M. Hoffman (Eds.), *Elder abuse: A public health perspective* (pp. 65–75). Baltimore, MD: United Book Press.
Nievod, A. (1992). Undue influence in contract and probate law. *Journal of Questioned Document Examination, 1,* 14–26.
Quinn, M. J. (2000). Undoing undue influence. *Journal of Elder Abuse and Neglect, 12,* 9–17.
Quinn, M. J., & Tomita, S. K. (1997). *Elder abuse & neglect: Causes, diagnosis, and intervention strategies.* New York, NY: Springer Publishers.
Rabiner, D. J., O'Keeffe, J., & Brown, D. (2006). Financial exploitation of older persons: Policy issues and recommendations for addressing them. *Journal of Elder Abuse and Neglect, 16,* 65–84.
Reeves, K. A., Desmarais, S. L., Nicholls, T. L., & Douglas, K. S. (2007). Intimate partner abuse of older men: Considerations for the assessment of risk. *Journal of Elder Abuse and Neglect, 19,* 7–27.

Reynolds, S. (2002). Guardianship primavera: A first look at factors associated with having a legal guardian using a nationally representative sample of community-dwelling adults. *Aging and Mental Health, 6,* 109–120.
Rikard, R., & Rosenberg, E. (2007). Aging inmates: A convergence of trends in the American criminal justice system. *Journal of Correctional Health Care, 1,* 150–162.
Rovi, S., Chen, P., Vega, M., Johnson, M. S., & Mouton, C. P. (2009). Mapping the elder mistreatment iceberg: U.S. hospitalizations with elder abuse and neglect diagnoses. *Journal of Elder Abuse and Neglect, 21,* 346–359.
Shah, S., Farrow, A., & Robinson, I. (2009). The representation of healthcare end users' perspectives by surrogates in healthcare decisions: A literature review. *Scandinavian Journal of Caring Sciences, 23,* 809–819. doi:10.1111/j.1471-6712.2008.00674.x
Shalowitz, D., Garrett-Mayer, E., & Wendler, D. (2006). The accuracy of surrogate decision makers. *Archives of Internal Medicine, 166,* 493–497.
Singleton, N., Meltzer, H., & Gatward, R. (1998). The prevalence of dementia, depression and neurosis in later life: The Liverpool MRC-ALPHA study. *International Journal of Epidemiology, 22,* 838–847.
Snyder, C., van Wormer, K., Chadha, J., & Jaggers, J. (2009). Older adult inmates: The challenge for social work. *Social Work, 54,* 117–124.
Teaster, P. (2006). *The 2004 survey of adult protective services: Abuse of adults 60 years of age and older.* Washington, DC: National Center on Elder Abuse.
Travis, J. (2005). *But they all come back: Facing the challenges of prisoner reentry.* Washington, DC: Urban Institute.
Twomey, M., Jackson, G., Li, H., Marino, T., Melchior, L., Randolph, J., et al. (2010). The successes and challenges of seven multidisciplinary teams. *Journal of Elder Abuse and Neglect, 22,* 291–305. doi:10.1080/08946566.2010.490144
U.S. Census Bureau. (2008). *Demographic data 2000.* Retrieved from http://www.census.gov
U.S. Census Bureau. (2011). *2010 census shows nation's population is aging.* Retrieved from http://2010.census.gov/news/releases/operations/cb11-cn147.html
U.S. Department of Justice. (2004). *Correctional health care: Addressing the needs of elderly chronically ill and terminally ill inmates.* Washington, DC: National Institute of Corrections.
U.S. General Accounting Office. (1991). *Elder abuse: Effectiveness of reporting laws and other factors.* Report to the Chairman, Subcommittee on Human Services, Select Committee on Aging, House of Representatives. Retrieved from http://www.popcenter.org/problems/crimes_against_elderly/PDFs/USGAO_1991.pdf
Wiglesworth, A., Mosqueda, L., Mulnard, R., Liao, S., Gibbs, L., & Fitzgerald, W. (2010). Screening for abuse and neglect of people with dementia. *Journal of the American Geriatrics Society, 3,* 493–500.
Wilber, K., Reiser, T., & Harter, K. (2001). New perspectives on conservatorship: The views of older adult conservatees and their conservators. *Aging, Neuropsychology and Cognition, 8,* 225–240.
Williams, B., & Abraldes, R. (2007). Growing older: Challenges of prison and reentry for the aging population. In R. Greifinger (Ed.), *Public health behind bars: From prisons to community* (pp. 56–72). New York, NY: Springer.

Williams, B., Lindquist, K., Sudore, R., Strupp, H., Willmott, D., & Walter, L. (2006). Being old and doing time: Functional impairment and adverse experiences of geriatric female prisoners. *Journal of the American Geriatrics Society, 54,* 702–707. doi:10.1111/j.1532-5415.2006.00662.x

Wolf, R. S. (2000). Elder abuse: An introduction. *Generations, 20,* 301–305.

Wright, J. (2010). Guardianship for your own good: Improving the wellbeing of respondents and wards in the USA. *International Journal of Law and Psychiatry, 33,* 350–368. doi:10.1016/j.ijlp.2010.09.007

Yates, J., & Gillespie, W. (2000). The elderly and prison policy. *Journal of Aging and Social Policy, 11,* 167–175.

Yorston, G., & Taylor, P. (2006). Commentary: Older offenders—No place to go? *Journal of the American Academy of Psychiatry and Law, 34,* 333–337.

Zink, T., Fisher, B. S., Regan, S., & Pabst, S. (2005). The prevalence and incidence of intimate partner violence in older women in primary care practices. *Journal of General Internal Medicine, 10,* 884–888. doi:10.1111/j.1525-1497.2005.0191.x

Part III

LEGAL PROFESSIONALS

8

Stress and Cardiovascular Disease in Law Enforcement

Warren D. Franke and Sandra L. Ramey

Introduction

It is almost axiomatic within the law enforcement profession that police work and cardiovascular disease (CVD) go hand in hand. Indeed, many states codify this relationship with a heart-lung presumption, which provides disability retirement benefits for officers stricken with CVD. Even at the federal level, laws presume that police and their families need to be protected from the pervasive threat of CVD; the U.S. Department of Justice's Hometown Heroes Survivors Benefits Act (2003) provides "a statutory presumption that public safety officers who die from a heart attack or stroke following a non-routine stressful or strenuous physical public safety activity or training, died in the line of duty for benefit purposes." These facts beg the question: Is this very expensive presumption well founded, or is it based on anecdotal evidence? This chapter reviews the research assessing the association between CVD and the law enforcement profession and examines factors that might contribute to this association. The primary focus here will be stress, because a widespread assumption is that the stress of police work is a major contributor to CVD.

The Prevalence of Cardiovascular Disease in Law Enforcement

The most common way to evaluate the relationship between law enforcement and CVD has been to determine if officers have higher CVD mortality than

Table 8.1. Cardiovascular Disease Mortality in U.S. Law Enforcement Cohorts

Locale	Odds Ratio	95% CI	How Compared	Outcome	Ref
Nationally					
50 states	1.58	$p < 0.05$	Standardized mortality ratio (SMR)	↑ mortality	Guralnick, 1962
27 states			Proportionate mortality rate (PMR)	↑ mortality	Calvert, Merling, & Burnett, 1999
Sheriffs, bailiffs, etc.	1.26	1.11–1.43			
Correctional officers	1.21	1.07–1.36			
Police and detectives	1.14	1.06–1.21			
States					
Connecticut	1.32	1.16–1.48	SMR	↑ mortality	Sardinas, Miller, & Hansen, 1986
Rhode Island	1.7	1.2–2.5	Summary odds ratio (SOR)	↑ mortality	Dubrow, Burnett, Gute, & Brockert, 1988
Utah	1.6	1.1–2.4	SOR	↑ mortality	Dubrow et al., 1988
Washington	1.15	$p < 0.05$	PMR	↑ mortality	Milham, 1983
New Jersey	1.07	$p > 0.05$	PMR	= mortality	Feuer & Rosenman, 1986
Municipalities					
Buffalo	1.05	0.93–1.19	SMR	= mortality	Vena, Violanti, Marshall, & Fiedler, 1986
Buffalo	1/06	0.96–1.18	SMR	= mortality	Violanti, Vena, & Petralia, 1998
Seattle, Tacoma, and Portland	0.86	0.75–0.98	SMR	↓ mortality	Demers, Heyer, & Rosenstock, 1992

a control population. Six of 10 published studies (shown in Table 8.1) found that a law enforcement cohort suffered a statistically significant increase in mortality. Given that three studies did not find a significant difference and one found police officers to have reduced mortality, the evidence from these studies was not clear-cut. However, overall, the data suggest that law enforcement officers experience a higher CVD mortality rate.

Nevertheless, these studies suffer an inherent weakness: In solely assessing CVD *mortality*, by definition they ignore CVD *morbidity*. During the past 30 years, CVD mortality has declined while morbidity has increased (Roger et al., 2011). Thus, assessing solely mortality may skew interpretation of the relationship between CVD and the law enforcement profession.

A handful of studies assessed CVD morbidity in police in reference to a nonpolice cohort (Franke, Collins, & Hinz, 1998; Franke, Ramey, & Shelley, 2002; Ramey, Downing, & Franke, 2009; Sparrow, Thomas, & Weiss, 1983). These studies examined police in a range of ages—from officers at midcareer to those well into their retirement. Cardiovascular disease typically takes considerable time to become clinically overt, and the effects of risk factors on CVD progression may go unnoticed until after years of exposure. Thus, exploring the CVD–law enforcement relationship over a wide range of ages may provide insight that cannot be gleaned otherwise.

Figure 8.1 reveals a trend showing that, compared to civilian peers, young officers do not have an increased prevalence of CVD but that, as officers age, their rates of CVD become as much as 70% higher. Although several conventional CVD risk factors contributed to this increase, it is noteworthy that in studies of older officers (Franke et al., 1998; Ramey et al., 2009), the law enforcement profession remained a "risk factor" even after statistically controlling for age. The odds ratio was 1.70 (95% confidence interval [CI] = 1.03–2.79) for retired officers who were, generally, in their 50s (Ramey et al., 2009) and 2.34 (95% CI = 1.5–3.6) for retired officers in their 60s and older (Franke et al., 1998). On the other hand, studies assessing younger, active-duty officers may underreport

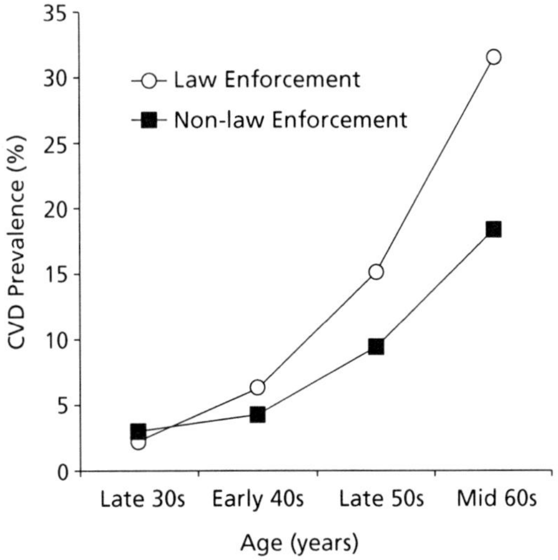

Figure 8.1 Differences in prevalence of cardiovascular disease (CVD) in cohorts of law enforcement officers and nonofficers.

group differences. The aforementioned favorable disability retirement policies probably induce younger officers with clinically significant CVD to leave the department. This may have excluded them from the studied cohorts. Such is a valid shortcoming in the cross-sectional study by Franke et al. (2002), but not for Sparrow et al. (1983), who employed a longitudinal design.

These complicating factors prompted studies that used an alternative approach: testing whether law enforcement officers have an increased prevalence of *subclinical* CVD. To that end, Joseph and colleagues compared active-duty police officers to a civilian control group on several relevant measures: brachial artery flow–mediated dilation (Joseph et al., 2010), common carotid intima–media thickness, and mean maximum carotid intima–media thickness (Joseph et al., 2009). Brachial artery flow–mediated dilation assesses endothelial function via determining how greatly this peripheral artery dilates in response to the accumulation of local metabolites. A reduction in this dilatory response is suggestive of endothelial dysfunction due to atherosclerosis. Rather than reflecting functional changes, alterations in carotid intima–media thickness reflect structural changes in the peripheral vasculature ascribable to atherosclerosis. The results showed that, although both the control and police officer groups were free of clinically overt CVD, the officers had reduced endothelial function and increased structural changes (i.e., increased intima–media thickness) in their peripheral vasculature. Joseph and colleagues (2009, 2010) controlled for group differences in age, gender, depression, and conventional CVD risk factors. Thus, these differences suggest that officers have an earlier presence of atherosclerosis, estimated to be the equivalent of 3 to 4 years of plaque progression (Joseph et al., 2010). This study, however, did not attempt to measure the mechanisms underlying this subclinical CVD.

To date, the literature strongly suggests that law enforcement officers are at an increased risk of developing CVD and, as will be described further in the next section, this risk remains after controlling for conventional CVD risk factors. Thus, the analogy of the law enforcement profession as a "risk factor" is valid.

Conventional Cardiovascular Disease Risk Factors in Law Enforcement

The published literature is replete with studies suggesting police work is linked to well-known CVD risk factors: physical inactivity, hypercholesterolemia, hypertension, tobacco use, obesity, and hyperinsulinemia (Kales, Tsismenakis, Zhang, & Soteriades, 2009; Peter & Siegrist, 1983; Pollock, Gettman, & Meyer, 1978; Thomas, Cady, O'Connell, Bischoff, & Kershnar, 1979; Williams et al., 1987). Studies comparing officers and nonofficers have consistently found several CVD risk factors to be more prevalent in officers, thereby putting them at an increased risk for CVD (Franke et al., 1998; Franke et al., 2002; Joseph et al., 2009; Pyörälä, Miettinen, Halonen, Laakso, & Pyörälä, 2000; Ramey, 2003; Ramey et al., 2009). Nevertheless, simply comparing the prevalence of individual risk factors across populations does not describe the relative influence of these risk factors. For example, how can one determine the net effect on CVD risk if officers are at higher risk than controls in one factor but at lower risk in another?

Identifying the combined and interactive influence of a set of risk factors better assesses the "gestalt" of these risk factors. Accordingly, prediction equations, developed through the ongoing Framingham study, can estimate the probability of developing CVD (Wilson et al., 1998; current algorithms are available at http://www.framinghamheartstudy.org/risk/index.html). Indeed, in the United States, the Framingham algorithm offers the best model (Eichler, Puhan, Steurer, & Bachmann, 2007). As such, we used a Framingham algorithm to compare the 10-year risk of developing clinically significant CVD, comparing law enforcement officers and a reference population. No difference was found using either cross-sectional (Franke, Cox, Schultz, & Anderson, 1997; Franke et al., 2010) or longitudinal comparisons (Franke et al., 1997). To the best of our knowledge, no one else has made a similar comparison. Thus, our study suggests the CVD–law enforcement relationship is complex because police officers' increased CVD risk arises from something other than conventional CVD risk factors. Of course, individual officers may have an increased risk for CVD due to conventional risk factors, but this is true for anyone regardless of occupation.

These prediction models are limited, however, because they only considered a subset of known risk factors: age, gender, total cholesterol, high-density lipoprotein, systolic blood pressure, tobacco use, diabetes status, and presence of left ventricular hypertrophy. The studies did not include obesity or physical inactivity, which are CVD risk factors that can be particularly problematic for police. For example, while not universally seen (e.g., Joseph et al., 2009), most evidence suggests officers tend to be more overweight than the general population (Franke et al., 2002; Ramey et al., 2009; Ramey, 2003; Ramey, Downing, Franke, Perkhounkova, & Alasagheirin, 2011; Ramey, Perkhounkova, Downing, & Culp, 2011). Over time, officers also appear to gain fat faster than the general population (Franke & Anderson, 1994). The mechanisms underlying this difference have not been definitively identified. Officers' eating habits, especially while on duty, may contribute to this weight gain. For example, some departments require officers to eat in public places, such as restaurants, rather than in their official vehicle. Moreover, in some communities, fast food establishments have a booth reserved for officers to encourage them to eat there. Law enforcement is also a relatively sedentary occupation (data unpublished). However, excessive body fat is ultimately the result of a caloric imbalance and obesity is an epidemic in the U.S. population. Thus, while considerable anecdotal evidence exists, to the best of our knowledge, the extent to which these habits differ from other occupational groups has not been extensively assessed in law enforcement.

Recall that a number of studies that found an increased CVD prevalence in officers did so after statistically controlling for the presence of conventional risk factors (Franke et al., 1998; Franke et al., 2002; Ramey et al., 2009; Joseph et al., 2009, 2010). Thus, while conventional risk factors likely contribute to CVD, for police officers, they do not fully explain the increased prevalence. The increased risk must be caused by other occupationally relevant factors.

Stress as a Cardiovascular Disease Risk Factor in Law Enforcement

Despite the concerted effort of many researchers, the mechanism(s) linking police work to CVD remain unidentified. The most commonly hypothesized contributor is job stress. Most recent reviews agree that psychosocial stress and CVD are related (Hemingway & Marmot, 1999; Krantz & McCeney, 2002; Rozanski, Blumenthal, & Kaplan, 1999), yet these reviews offer no consensus on which psychosocial variables reliably increase the risk of CVD or, of those that do, which are most important. Some evidence supports the idea that stress indirectly affects CVD risk by increasing the prevalence of conventional risk factors (Franke et al., 2002; Violanti et al., 2006), presumably because stress alters an individual's lifestyle. It is noteworthy that, for officers, high levels of physical activity do not appear to buffer the effects of stress on either CVD risk (Yoo, Eisenmann, & Franke, 2009) or perceived health (Gerber, Kellmann, Hartmann, & Pühse, 2010). Limited evidence also suggests that, for officers, neither chronic stress (Franke et al., 2010) nor posttraumatic stress disorder (McCanlies et al., 2011) is associated with a proatherogenic inflammatory vascular environment. Thus, the mechanisms by which stress exerts its deleterious effects—either in general or in law enforcement, in particular—remain uncertain.

Although the unique and pronounced effects of stress in policing are well recognized (Finn & Tomz, 1996; Havassey, 1994; Violanti, 1992), the sources of this stress can be difficult to categorize but are certainly multifactorial (Abdollahi, 2002). The unique stress of police work can be characterized by its duration (e.g., acute vs. chronic) and whether the source of stress is external, operational, or organizational. For police, *external stress* includes issues such as public criticism of police and conflicts between the demands of professional commitments and family (Garcia, Nesbary, & Gu, 2004). *Operational stress* refers to the stress associated with the actual duties of law enforcement (e.g., making on-the-spot decisions, apprehending potentially dangerous suspects, or critical incidents such as officers being assaulted). *Organizational stress* refers to issues such as dealing with the criminal justice system or the bureaucracy of a police department. The governance structure in many police agencies likely contributes to organizational stress, because it is frequently hierarchical, paramilitaristic, and often with a top-down style of management.

When large samples of police officers are assessed, studies consistently conclude that operational stressors are the most intense (Berg, Hem, Lau, Haseth, & Ekeberg, 2005; Garcia et al., 2004). For example, interviews with officers in the Milwaukee Police Department suggest that traffic control is a very stressful activity (Ramey, unpublished observations). Critical incidents are perhaps the most severe operational stressor and can markedly affect perceived work stress (Gershon, Lin, & Li, 2002; Violanti & Aron, 1994). However, critical incidents are typically acute, short term, and, in many police departments, relatively infrequent. For example, in a survey of 2,800 Norwegian police officers, work injuries (e.g., officer hurt in the line of duty) were rated the most severe stressor but also the least frequent (Berg et al., 2005). In contrast, job pressure was the least severe stressor but the most frequent. Job pressure is typical of an organizational stressor—less injurious in the short term but more chronic in the long term.

Evaluating operational stress as a contributor to CVD risk might be done best by assessing officers with posttraumatic stress disorder (PTSD), because the nature of police work puts officers at an increased risk for developing PTSD. (PTSD results from a traumatic event that involved the threat of injury or death; it may occur shortly after the event or months afterward.) To assess psychological symptoms of PTSD, Violanti and colleagues used the Impact of Event Scale (Horowitz, Wilner, & Alvarez, 1979) in 115 police officers and explored whether PTSD was linked to conventional CVD risk factors (Violanti et al., 2006), inflammatory markers (McCanlies et al., 2011), and subclinical CVD (Violanti et al., 2006). These studies found that officers with low versus high PTSD symptomatology did not differ statistically in these measures, suggesting that the operational stress of police work contributes little to their increased risk of CVD.

In contrast, officer health appears to be greatly affected by organizational stress. Interestingly, organizational stress appears to be more deleterious not because it is extreme, but because it is chronic. Indeed, of all types of stressors, organizational stress is generally considered to be the most hazardous (Brown & Campbell, 1990; Crank, Regoli, Hewitt, & Culbertson, 1995; Grier, 1982; Kirkcaldy, Cooper, & Ruffalo, 1995; Kroes, Margolis, & Hurrell, 1974; Storch & Panzarella, 1996; Violanti, 1981). Among police, chronic organizational stressors predict psychological distress, including PTSD, more strongly than cumulative exposure to critical incidents (Liberman et al., 2002). Moreover, officers who view organizational stress as being more stressful than operational stress are at higher risk for impaired mental health (Collins & Gibbs, 2003). Organizational stress can contribute to vital exhaustion, an outcome of occupational stress that has been previously associated with CVD (Appels, 1997; Appels & Mulder, 1989; Cole, Kawachi, Sesso, Paffenbarger, & Lee, 1999; Kopp, Falger, Appels, & Szedmak 1998; Prescott et al., 2003). Vital exhaustion is characterized by feelings of excessive fatigue and a lack of energy, increasing irritability, and feelings of demoralization (Appels, 1997).

Organizational stressors can take many forms (Ayres & Flanagan, 1992; Biggam, Power, MacDonald, Carcary, & Moodie, 1997; Collins & Gibbs, 2003; Hartsough, 1991; Malone, Denny, Dalton, & Addley, 1997; Miller & Monge, 1986, 1987; Storch & Panzarella, 1996; Violanti & Aron, 1994), but no clear consensus exists on which organizational stressors are most detrimental

(Liberman et al., 2002). Many notable organizational stressors, however, center on time constraints, as well as poor communication between officers and their superiors. For example, in a survey of over 850 officers (Collins & Gibbs, 2003), nine organizational stressors were indicated as being the most severe:

1. Work demands impinging on home life
2. Lack of consultation/communication
3. Not enough support from senior officers
4. Pressure to get results
5. Urgent requests preventing completion of planned work
6. Deadlines or time pressures
7. Too much work
8. Paperwork
9. Working in shifts

Likewise, in another review of the literature, Stinchcomb (2004) summarized organizational stressors into four categories:

1. Lack of consultation and communication
2. Not enough guidance or support from administrators
3. Inadequate feedback
4. Inadequate input into department policies, especially felt as an imbalance between too many responsibilities and too little authority, and felt particularly by senior officers, meaning those with more work experience

These studies were largely survey-based, quantitative assessments. To "flesh out" such findings, individual interviews and focus groups can provide informative qualitative assessments. To that end, sworn officers of the Milwaukee Police Department were asked to describe workforce supports and barriers to optimal health (Ramey et al., 2009). (In terms of sworn officers, the Milwaukee Police Department is one of the 20 largest departments in the United States; Reaves, 2010.) Approximately 30% of the officers voiced lack of control over their job as a problem, and more than half cited the example of not being able to use their judgment in responding to "call-backs" to public inquires because, in this department, the decision when to respond is made by the dispatcher rather than the officers. Moreover, officers reported experiencing a heavy workload, fatigue, lack of a routine, irregular hours, excessive overtime, and working different shifts in 1 week. They frequently expected to work shifts longer than 8 hours because of unpredictable events. In addition, the officers said that it was not uncommon, after working a night shift, to be required to return midmorning for a court appearance after sleeping only a few hours. All mentioned that shift work contributed to their fatigue and exhaustion. Officers also attributed fatigue, in part, to what they referred to as "hypervigilance," meaning they are constantly on the lookout for something out of the ordinary, even during off hours. Thus, they have difficulty "letting down" or relaxing, even when they are off duty. Fifty-four percent of interviewees mentioned negative health consequences, which they attributed to exhaustion, job demands, and lack of time. Specifically, they felt that irregular hours, lack of routine, and fatigue made it difficult to get enough sleep and establish healthy eating patterns, and left little time for physical activity; 42% of interviewees mentioned weight gain as an issue related to their job. Officers linked job constraints to frequent family conflicts and strained relationships with partners. Although some of these stressors are operational in nature, clearly most are organizationally mediated.

Such evidence, considered as a whole, suggests that the most significant contributors to officers' risk for CVD are organizational stressors. Indeed, organizational factors are four (Brown & Campbell, 1990) to six times (Vena, Violanti, Marshall, & Fiedler, 1986) more stressful than nonorganizational factors. Organizational stressors are also likely context dependent; the frequency, duration, and intensity of these stressors will differ depending on the organizational practices of each different department. Thus, the negative health effects on employees likely will also differ. Nevertheless, based on the extant research, it appears that much of the organizational stress in policing could be attenuated with careful attention to the work structure and climate of police departments. While much easier said than done, a close appraisal of organizational structure might lead to a sustained, robust attenuation of a considerable proportion of police officer stress.

An often overlooked aspect of the stress–law enforcement relationship is that most officers are *not* markedly stressed. This has been seen in several studies of police officers from quite disparate police departments. In studies of over 2,800 officers spanning nine different state-level police agencies (Franke et al., 2002), over 670 officers from one of the 20 largest municipal police departments in the United States (Ramey, Downing, & Knoblauch, 2008), and 336 officers (Ramey, Perkhounkova, et al., 2011) from one of the 200 largest departments (Reaves, 2010), the mean stress levels were not appreciably different from other large samples of nonofficers (Cohen & Williamson, 1988) and were similar to college-age cohorts (Cohen, Kamarck, & Mermelstein, 1983). So, although police work can certainly be stressful, for most officers on most days, it is not. A caveat to this is that the most distressing part of the job according to officers (Ramey et al., 2008) can be the chronic, albeit modest, exposure to organizational stress within the job. Furthermore, an issue that has yet to be considered fully in the literature is the extent to which the health effects of officer stress are due to the job per se, such that all officers are at an increased risk, or due to the officer's response to the stress, meaning only susceptible officers will be affected. For example, Collins and Gibbs (2003) found organizational stressors to be a significant health issue in a large police department. However, they also noted that affected officers tended to differ in several personality traits and coping behaviors from officers who were not appreciably affected.

Nevertheless, for officers who do view their job as stressful, the effects can be deleterious. In the aforementioned sample of 2,800+ active-duty officers (Franke et al., 2002), regardless of their age, CVD was directly associated with both perceived stress and duration of employment. Most striking was the comparison between the officers in the lowest and highest quintile of stress scores. The most stressed officers had a markedly higher prevalence of CVD, compared to the least stressed officers (odds ratio [OR] = 2.54; 95% CI = 1.07–6.01; unpublished data on file with author). Moreover, a recent study of active-duty male officers found the link between CVD, stress, and vital exhaustion to be statistically significant (Ramey, Perkhounkova, et al., 2011). A unit change in either perceived stress or vital exhaustion increased the odds of CVD by 20% or 31%, respectively (Ramey, Downing, et al., 2011). As seen with Franke and colleagues' study of active-duty officers (2002), the overall prevalence of CVD was lower than expected for these police officers. Again, however, for these two studies, heart-lung presumption laws likely caused the rate of CVD to be underestimated, because officers with diagnosed CVD may have self-selected out of the sample via disability retirement.

Despite considerable evidence linking CVD and the law enforcement profession (especially law enforcement–related stress), the biological mechanisms underlying this association are unknown. In a study published in 2010, we assessed the association between job-related stress, conventional CVD risk factors, and inflammatory mediators in law enforcement (Franke et al., 2010); the latter are increasingly being implicated in atherogenesis. As a group, the officers in this study displayed a relatively proatherogenic inflammatory profile that could not be attributed to differences in conventional CVD risk factors or to differences in stress. In fact, the affected officers were not greatly stressed and had chronic stress levels (including vital exhaustion) below that of the control cohort. On the other hand, we recently performed similar assessments in officers working in a large metropolitan police department and found statistically significant, albeit modest, associations between inflammatory mediators and both traumatic stress and work stress (Ramey, Downing, et al., 2011). This study was performed in a small group of officers ($n = 71$), making generalizability somewhat limited. Thus, although these studies do not define the job-related factors contributing to CVD in law enforcement officers, they do provide clues about the underlying biological mechanism.

Suggestions for Reducing Chronic Disease in Law Enforcement

The increased risk for CVD experienced by law enforcement officers can be attributed to forces that are both intrinsic and extrinsic to the profession itself. As with the U.S. population as a whole, some of this CVD risk is attributable to conventional CVD risk factors. In this context, the processes of risk factor reduction are the same for both law enforcement and civilians and usually entail promoting lifestyle changes such as increases in physical activity and healthier eating habits. For example, a recent published review assessed worksite-based health/lifestyle programs promoting the common, modifiable risk factors of tobacco use, sedentary lifestyle/inactivity, alcohol use, and poor dietary patterns associated with overweight and obesity (Soler et al., 2010). Combining health risk appraisal with health education reduced the prevalence of risk factors and improved outcomes. Programs were most effective when they were offered for at least an hour and repeated several times over the course of a year. Additionally, the best programs were accompanied by a variety of health promotion activities, including health education and awareness. This methodology could be readily employed in law enforcement, because most departments have mandatory, annual, in-service training sessions. During such mandatory sessions, officers could be informed of their health risks and receive evidence-based health education on risk and disease morbidity awareness. This type of training has the potential to reach the personnel employed by the almost 18,000 law enforcement agencies functioning in the United States.

Unfortunately, promoting physical activity in law enforcement agencies can be challenging. While fitness standards are common for new hires in most law enforcement agencies, many departments do not have ongoing fitness requirements or required annual medical examinations. In departments that are unionized, the decision to embrace a fitness standard often involves extensive negotiation among union and department leadership. If fitness standards are considered, common issues are whether (1) these standards are either job specific (i.e., all officers must meet the same standard) or if age- and gender-specific standards are used; (2), depending on how this issue is resolved, whether senior, or veteran, officers will be "grandfathered" in; (3) whether officers can exercise while on duty; and (4) what incentives will be used to encourage the adoption of physical activity.

Part of the CVD risk associated with law enforcement is uniquely due to the occupation. Because some of the stressors involved in police work are unique to that profession (e.g., operational stressors), some risk reduction techniques must also be tailored to the environment in which police officers work. For example, while lifestyle choices affect CVD risk in all individuals, the effects of job stress may be manifested in unhealthy lifestyle choices that susceptible officers make. For example, the number of officers who commit suicide is three times more than the number who die in the line of duty (Miller, 2005; Violanti & Aron, 1995). For most officers, the psychological, emotional, physical, social, and spiritual stressors of their daily work environment may contribute to unhealthy lifestyles and poor living habits (Tanigoshi, Kontos, & Remley, 2008). These habits likely underlie the increased prevalence of conventional CVD risk factors often found in officers. Clearly, programs are needed to maintain wellbeing among police.

One such program offered a psychological intervention termed the "Badge of Life" (Levenson, O'Hara, & Clark, 2010). Initiated in 2008, the Badge of Life aimed to reduce the number of police officer suicides via the Emotional Self-Care Program, which emphasizes that voluntary, confidential, annual mental health checks promote officers' emotional wellbeing. The program employs teaching and mentoring of younger officers by older ones. The program focuses on each officer's ability and responsibility to care for his or her own emotional wellbeing—an idea based on the premise that credible officers (from all levels) can "set an example" and encourage fellow officers to get involved in their own annual in-service training. The program is founded on the principles of peer support in policing, research on suicide prevention, and the work of Jeffery T. Mitchell's critical incident stress management (CISM; see also chapter 11, this volume, for use of CISM in juror innovations). According to Levenson et al. (2010), departments that embrace CISM have less absenteeism, greater cohesiveness among officers, greater job satisfaction, and more acceptance of mental health personnel in general (R. Levenson, personal communication, June 1, 2011). Assessing program efficacy is complicated by the observation that, in many police agencies, the measurement of outcomes does not usually involve the scholarly methods researchers would identify. Rather, the goal and primary interest of programs like the Badge of Life are to educate and promote positive mental health approaches within law enforcement and to be a resource for officers, police administrators, researchers, and planners (R. Levenson, personal communication, June 1, 2011). This program is currently in use and available within the United States and Canada.

In the past, the efficacy of health promotion interventions for police officers has been assessed only infrequently; those that were developed and tested employed small sample sizes and usually only collected outcome data at one time point. Most types of interventions either were based on exercise or used psychological approaches such as social skills training and befriending. In these studies, physical activity, including cardiovascular exercise and strength training, was effective for reducing the rate of clinical depression (Penalba, McGuire, & Leite, 2008); even in older officers, exercise appeared to enhance mood and improve cognitive function (Penalba et al., 2008). Cognitive behavioral therapies and similar approaches aim to help officers deal with anxiety and stress disorders by focusing on how to recognize distorted thoughts and replace them with realistic ideas (Penalba et al., 2008).

Consistently, authors have identified the police department *environment* as "stressful" and further suggest that daily encounters may contribute to a sense of negative affect, which has consequences on general health. To that end, programs have been designed to address the stress and bereavement associated with deaths that occur in the line of duty (Miller, 2007). For example, to foster "mental toughness and resilience" and to facilitate recovery from critical incidents, programs have applied methods used in sports psychology (Miller, 2008) that conceptually apply to police and can be carried over to law enforcement. Because organizational stress appears to be pervasive in most law enforcement agencies and detrimental to officer health, efforts to reduce these stressors should be made. These changes could range from the modest (e.g., adjusting work scheduling procedures) to the dramatic (e.g., changing leadership style and governance structures), depending on the nature of the stressor. Poor communication practices and top-down administrative styles are recurring stressors identified in the relevant literature. To the extent it is practical, participatory management practices would likely improve job satisfaction (Wycoff & Skogan, 1994) and, in our opinion, reduce CVD risk in many officers by reducing officer stress. Examples of such principles within existing management models include transformational leadership and giving voice to officers regarding agency improvements like upgrading computer software used by the membership. There are also opportunities to give more autonomy to officers regarding decision making. In interviews with the authors, officers in a large metropolitan police department noted that the dispatcher sends all calls to the officers and agency policy is that all calls require immediate response regardless of the nature of the call. Allowing officers to triage calls is a simple method of increasing autonomy. In addition, in this department, it is not uncommon for officers who have worked the night shift to be required to be in court early in the morning. Working with the local judicial system and judges would make it possible to consider the officer's work schedule when assigning court appearance times. These changes in administrative style would entail short-term expenses but, if they became permanent, would likely also yield long-term benefits without any ongoing expense. Given the fiscal constraints imposed upon most law enforcement agencies, the latter is a potent argument for making these changes.

Gaps in Our Knowledge and Needed Research

Concerted effort by the research community has expanded our understanding of the relationship between CVD, stress, and the law enforcement profession. Nevertheless, the largest gap in our understanding of this relationship remains our ignorance of the underlying mechanisms. The causal mechanisms are almost certainly multifactorial and likely include lifestyle activities as well as job-specific activities. Our best guess is that organizational stress is a primary component of the job-specific activities.

One difficulty in identifying the job-specific stressors is that much of the existing research is somewhat piecemeal. Comprehensively assessing the sources of stress in a law enforcement agency could be a mammoth undertaking. These stressors are complex and likely interact; they can include organizational sources, operational stress, and external stressors such as job–family conflicts. Moreover, the relative influences and the interactive effects of these different stressors likely vary across law enforcement agencies; officers within a well-managed police department may be less stressed than their peers in a poorly run department, despite similar levels of crime in their municipalities. Thus, even if one were able to quantify all the stressors in a police department, one would need to be cautious in generalizing the findings from one police department to the broader law enforcement community. Consequently, while distinguishing the different sources and types of stress is critical for developing effective targeted interventions, these sources and types likely vary across police departments. Thus, a "one size fits all" approach to reducing police stress will likely not be very successful.

As alluded to previously, a second gap in understanding the CVD–stress–law enforcement relationship is a determination of the extent to which this relationship is intrinsic to the occupation or intrinsic to the individual officer. Many researchers have made the tacit assumption that police stress uniquely affects officer health. While some of these stressors are unique to the occupation, many occupations are equally stressful; a common shortcoming of the literature is that many studies assessing police officer health have not used a meaningful control group. For example, we are unaware of any studies comparing the effects of job stress on health among police officers and similarly stressful occupations. In other words, it is unclear if the police occupation is different from other stressful occupations in its effects on officers.

While police work can certainly be stressful enough to affect officer health, it is important to recognize that most officers are either not severely stressed or do not suffer adverse health consequences from the job-specific stressors. This suggests that, to a certain extent, most officers either are not susceptible to the ill effects of this stress or have appropriate coping mechanisms in place. Thus, more research is needed to tease out whether police stress should be viewed as a universal issue that affects all officers (and is uniquely different from the effects of job stress in nonofficers) or whether police stress only affects officers susceptible to the effects of stress. If the latter, then knowledge of the attributes that increase susceptibility can be used when screening applicants for employment as police officers. Unfortunately, concerted efforts to identify these attributes in police officers have not been performed.

Finally, the biological mechanisms underlying the association between CVD and law enforcement remain unclear. In studies controlling for conventional CVD risk factors, limited evidence suggests officers are more prone to a proinflammatory vascular environment than nonofficer peers. While these studies did not identify the aspects of the law enforcement profession that trigger increased CVD risk, job-related stress does not appear to be a strong candidate. Thus, considerable work remains to be completed before we fully understand how the law enforcement occupation contributes to the development of CVD.

In order to close these gaps, an ideal research study would be a large, multisite, prospective, observational study. This study would include an array of police departments, varying in the number of officers, the population served, and the geographic locale. Current officers and incoming officers would be assessed on their current CVD risk factors, novel CVD risk markers (e.g., flow-mediated dilation, inflammatory mediators), lifestyle habits related to these factors, their current and past stress levels, and their responses to various forms of stress. In addition, a careful assessment of the organizational and administrative practices of each police department would be performed. Parallel assessments in other "peer" occupations would be performed. These data would be collected serially and long enough for CVD to become clinically significant, perhaps over 20 or 30 years. Thereafter, the data would be analyzed to determine the extent to which CVD prevalence differed among the different occupations, the factors that explained any differences in CVD, and whether these factors differed among the occupations, as well as among the different police departments. Such a study would be prohibitively expensive and logistically challenging; however, it is the type of research needed to gain a firm understanding of the CVD–stress–law enforcement relationship.

Conclusion

Based on the extant literature, it appears that law enforcement officers have an increased risk for CVD. Some of this risk is due to an excess of conventional CVD risk factors, such as a tendency to become relatively more overweight than nonpolice officers, while some is not, such as an increased proinflammatory vascular environment. The mechanisms underlying this increased risk remain elusive. While stress may play a role in the development of CVD in susceptible officers, it is an overstatement to suggest that police stress per se is causally or universally associated with the occupational risk for CVD. More research is needed to fully understand these relationships.

References

Abdollahi, M. K. (2002). Understanding police stress research. *Journal of Forensic Psychology Practice, 2*, 1–24.

Appels, A. (1997). Exhausted subjects, exhausted systems. *Acta Physiologica Scandinavica Supplementum, 640*, 153–154.

Appels, A., & Mulder, P. (1989). Fatigue and heart disease. The association between "vital exhaustion" and past, present and future coronary heart disease. *Journal of Psychosomatic Research, 33*(6), 727–738. doi:10.1016/0022-3999(89)90088-3

Ayres, R. M., & Flanagan, G. S. (1992). *Preventing law enforcement stress: The organization's role.* Washington, DC: U.S. Department of Justice, Bureau of Justice Assistance.

Berg, A. M., Hem, E., Lau, B., Haseth, K., & Ekeberg, O. (2005). Stress in the Norwegian police service. *Occupational Medicine (London), 55*(2), 113–120. doi:10.1093/occmed/kqi023

Biggam, F. H., Power, K. G., MacDonald, R. R., Carcary, W. B., & Moodie, E. (1997). Self-perceived occupational stress and distress in a Scottish police force. *Work and Stress, 11*(2), 118–133. doi:10.1080/02678379708256829

Brown, J. M., & Campbell, E. A. (1990). Sources of occupational stress in the police. *Work and Stress, 4*(4), 305–318.

Calvert, G. M., Merling, J. W., & Burnett, C. A. (1999). Ischemic heart disease mortality and occupation among 16- to 60-year-old males. *Journal of Occupational and Environmental Medicine, 41*(11), 960–966.

Cohen, S., Kamarck, T., & Mermelstein, R. (1983). A global measure of perceived stress. *Journal of Health and Social Behavior, 24*(4), 385–396.

Cohen, S., & Williamson, G. (1988). Perceived stress in a probability sample of the United States. In S. Spacapan & S. Oskamp (Eds.), *The social psychology of health: The Claremont symposium of applied social psychology* (pp. 31–67). Newbury Park, CA: Sage.

Cole, S. R., Kawachi, I., Sesso, H. D., Paffenbarger, R. S., & Lee, I. M. (1999). Sense of exhaustion and coronary heart disease among college alumni. *American Journal of Cardiology, 84*(12), 1401–1405. doi:10.1016/S0002-9149(99)00585-8

Collins, P. A., & Gibbs, A. C. (2003). Stress in police officers: A study of the origins, prevalence and severity of stress-related symptoms within a county police force. *Occupational Medicine (London), 53*(4), 256–264. doi:10.1093/occmed/kqg061

Crank, J. P., Regoli, R., Hewitt, J. D., & Culbertson, R. G. (1995). Institutional and organizational antecedents of role stress, work alienation, and anomie among police executives. *Criminal Justice and Behavior, 22*(2), 152–171. doi:10.1177/0093854895022002004

Demers, P. A., Heyer, N. J., & Rosenstock, L. (1992). Mortality among firefighters from three northwestern United States cities. *British Journal of Industrial Medicine, 49*(9), 664–670.

Dubrow, R., Burnett, C. A., Gute, D. M., & Brockert, J. E. (1988). Ischemic heart disease and acute myocardial infarction mortality among police officers. *Journal of Occupational Medicine, 30*(8), 650–654.

Eichler, K., Puhan, M. A., Steurer, J., & Bachmann, L. M. (2007). Prediction of first coronary events with the Framingham score: A systematic review. *American Heart Journal, 153*(5), 722–731. doi:10.1016/j.ahj.2007.02.027

Feuer, E., & Rosenman, K. (1986). Mortality in police and firefighters in New Jersey. *American Journal of Industrial Medicine, 9*(6), 517–527. doi:10.1002/ajim.4700090603

Finn, P., & Tomz, J. E. (1996). *Developing a law enforcement stress program for officers and their families.* Washington, DC: Office of Justice Programs, National Institute of Justice.

Franke, W. D., & Anderson, D. F. (1994). Relationship between physical activity and risk factors for cardiovascular disease among law enforcement officers. *Journal of Occupational Medicine, 36*(10), 1127–1132.

Franke, W. D., Collins, S. A., & Hinz, P. N. (1998). Cardiovascular disease morbidity in an Iowa law enforcement cohort, compared with the general Iowa population. *Journal of Occupational and Environmental Medicine, 40*(5), 441–444.

Franke, W. D., Cox, D. F., Schultz, D. P., & Anderson, D. F. (1997). Coronary heart disease risk in employees of Iowa's Department of Public Safety compared to a cohort of the general population. *American Journal of Industrial Medicine, 31*(6), 733–737. doi:10.1002/(SICI)1097-0274(199706)31:6<733::AID-AJIM10>3.0.CO,2-Z

Franke, W. D., Kohut, M. L., Russell, W. D., Yoo, H. L., Ekkekakis, P., & Ramey, S. P. (2010). Is job-related stress the link between cardiovascular disease and the law enforcement profession? *Journal of Occupational and Environmental Medicine, 52*(5), 561–565. doi:10.1097/JOM.0b013e3181dd086b

Franke, W. D., Ramey, S. L., & Shelley, M. C., 2nd. (2002). Relationship between cardiovascular disease morbidity, risk factors, and stress in a law enforcement cohort. *Journal of Occupational and Environmental Medicine, 44*(12), 1182–1189. doi:10.1097/01.jom.0000044128.59147.27

Garcia, L., Nesbary, D. K., & Gu, J. (2004). Perceptual variations of stressors among police officers during an era of decreasing crime. *Journal of Contemporary Criminal Justice, 20*(1), 33–50. doi:10.1177/1043986203262300

Gerber, M., Kellmann, M., Hartmann, T., & Pühse, U. (2010). Do exercise and fitness buffer against stress among Swiss police and emergency response service officers? *Psychology of Sport and Exercise, 11*(4), 286–294. doi:10.1016/j.psychsport2010.02.004

Gershon, R. R., Lin, S., & Li, X. (2002). Work stress in aging police officers. *Journal of Occupational and Environmental Medicine, 44*(2), 160–167.

Grier, K. (1982). *A study of job stress in police officers and high school teachers.* Unpublished doctoral dissertation, University of South Florida.

Guralnick, L. (1962). *Mortality by occupation and cause of death among men 20 to 64 years of age: United States, 1950.* Vital statistics—special report, Vol. 53, No. 4. Washington, DC: National Center for Health Statistics.

Hartsough, D. M. (1991). Stresses, spouses and law enforcement: A step beyond. In J. T. Reese, J. M. Horn, & C. Dunning (Eds.), *Critical incidents in policing* (Revised). Washington, DC: U.S. Department of Justice.

Havassey, V. J. (1994). Police stress in the 90s and its impact on the family. In J. T. Reese, E. Scrivner, & C. J. Lent (Eds.), *Law enforcement families: Issues and answers* (pp. 27–34). Washington, DC: U.S. Department of Justice and the Federal Bureau of Investigation.

Hemingway, H., & Marmot, M. (1999). Psychosocial factors in the aetiology and prognosis of coronary heart disease: Systematic review of prospective cohort studies. *British Medical Journal, 318*(7196), 1460–1467.

Hometown Heroes Survivors Benefits Act of 2003. Pub L. no. 108–182, 117 Stat 2649 (2003). Print.

Horowitz, M., Wilner, N., & Alvarez, W. (1979). Impact of event scale: A measure of subjective stress. *Psychosomatic Medicine, 41*(3), 209–218.

Joseph, P. N., Violanti, J. M., Donahue, R., Andrew, M. E., Trevisan, M., Burchfiel, C. M., et al. (2009). Police work and subclinical atherosclerosis. *Journal of Occupational and Environmental Medicine, 51*(6), 700–707. doi:10.1097/JOM.0b013e3181a02252

Joseph, P. N., Violanti, J. M., Donahue, R., Andrew, M. E., Trevisan, M., Burchfiel, C. M., et al. (2010). Endothelial function, a biomarker of subclinical cardiovascular disease, in urban police officers. *Journal of Occupational and Environmental Medicine, 52*(10), 1004–1008. doi:10.1097/JOM0b013e3181f4385c

Kales, S. N., Tsismenakis, A. J., Zhang, C., & Soteriades, E. S. (2009). Blood pressure in firefighters, police officers, and other emergency responders. *American Journal of Hypertension, 22*(1), 11–20. doi:10.1038/ajh.2008.296

Kirkcaldy, B., Cooper, C. L., & Ruffalo, P. (1995). Work stress and health in a sample of U.S. police. *Psychological Reports, 76*(2), 700–702.

Kopp, M. S., Falger, P. R., Appels, A., & Szedmak, S. (1998). Depressive symptomatology and vital exhaustion are differentially related to behavioral risk factors for coronary artery disease. *Psychosomatic Medicine, 60*(6), 752–758.

Krantz, D. S., & McCeney, M. K. (2002). Effects of psychological and social factors on organic disease: A critical assessment of research on coronary heart disease. *Annual Review of Psychology, 53*, 341–369. doi:10.1146/annurev.psych.53.100901.135208

Kroes, W. H., Margolis, B. L., & Hurrell, J. J. (1974). Job stress in policemen. *Journal of Police Science and Administration, 2*, 145–155.

Levenson, R. L., Jr., O'Hara, A. F., & Clark, R. S., Sr. (2010). The badge of life psychological survival for police officers program. *International Journal of Emergency Mental Health, 12*(2), 95–101.

Liberman, A. M., Best, S. R., Metzler, T. J., Fagan, J. A., Weiss, D. S., & Marmar, C. R. (2002). Routine occupational stress and psychological distress in police. *Policing: An International Journal of Police Strategies and Management, 25*(2), 421–439. doi:10.1108/13639510210429446

Malone, J., Denny, T., Dalton, P., & Addley, K. (1997). Stress at work part 1: Recognition, causes, outcomes and effects. In K. Addley (Ed.), *Occupational stress: A practical approach* (pp. 1–47). Oxford: Butterworth-Heinemann.

McCanlies, E. C., Araia, S. K., Joseph, P. N., Mnatsakanova, A., Andrew, M. E., Burchfiel, C. M., et al. (2011). C-reactive protein, interleukin-6, and posttraumatic stress disorder symptomology in urban police officers. *Cytokine, 55*(1), 74–78. doi:10.1016/j.cyto.2011.03.025

Milham, S. (1983). *Occupational mortality in Washington State 1950–1979.* DHHS [NISOSH] Publication No. 83–116. Cincinnati, OH: National Institute for Occupational Safety and Health.

Miller, K. I., & Monge, P. R. (1986). Participation, satisfaction, and productivity: A meta-analytic review. *Academy of Management Journal, 29*(4), 727–753.

Miller, K. I., & Monge, P. R. (1987). The development and test of a system of oral participation and allocation. In M. McLaughlin (Ed.), *Communication yearbook 10* (pp. 431–455). Beverly Hills, CA: Sage.

Miller, L. (2005). Police officer suicide: Causes, prevention, and practical intervention strategies. *International Journal of Emergency Mental Health, 7*(2), 101–114.

Miller, L. (2007). Line-of-duty death: Psychological treatment of traumatic bereavement in law enforcement. *International Journal of Emergency Mental Health, 9*(1), 13–23.

Miller, L. (2008). Stress and resilience in law enforcement training and practice. *International Journal of Emergency Mental Health, 10*(2), 109–124.

Penalba, V., McGuire, H., & Leite, J. R. (2008). Psychosocial interventions for prevention of psychological disorders in law enforcement officers. *Cochrane Database of Systematic Reviews, 16*(3), CD005601. doi:10.1002/14651858.CD005601.pub2

Peter, R., & Siegrist, J. (1999). Chronic psychological stress at work and cardiovascular disease: The role of effort-reward imbalance. *International Journal of Law and Psychiatry, 22*(5–6), 441–449. doi:10.1016/S0160-2527(99)00020-5

Pollock, M. L., Gettman, L. R., & Meyer, B. U. (1978). Analysis of physical fitness and coronary heart disease risk of Dallas area police officers. *Journal of Occupational Medicine, 20*(6), 393–398.

Prescott, E., Holst, C., Gronbaek, M., Schnohr, P., Jensen, G., & Barefoot, J. (2003). Vital exhaustion as a risk factor for ischaemic heart disease and all-cause mortality in a community sample. A prospective study of 4084 men and 5479 women in the Copenhagen City Heart Study. *International Journal of Epidemiology, 32*(6), 990–997. doi:10.1093/ije/dyg235

Pyörälä, M., Miettinen, H., Halonen, P., Laakso, M., & Pyörälä, K. (2000). Insulin resistance syndrome predicts the risk of coronary heart disease and stroke in healthy middle-aged men: The 22-year follow-up results of the Helsinki Policemen Study. *Arterosclerosis, Thrombosis, and Vascular Biology, 20*(2), 538–544.

Ramey, S. L. (2003). Cardiovascular disease risk factors and the perception of general health among male law enforcement officers: Encouraging behavioral change. *American Association of Occupational Health Nurses Journal, 51*(5), 219–226.

Ramey, S. L., Downing, N. R., & Franke, W. D. (2009). Milwaukee Police Department retirees: Cardiovascular disease risk and morbidity among aging law enforcement officers. *American Association Occupational Health Nurses Journal, 57*(11), 448–453. doi:10.3928/08910162-20091019-02

Ramey, S. L., Downing, N. R., Franke, W. D., Perkhounkova, Y., & Alasagheirin, M. H. (2012). Relationships among stress measures, risk factors, and inflammatory biomarkers in law enforcement officers. *Biological Research in Nursing, 14*, 16–26. Epub ahead of print. doi:10.1177/1099800410396356

Ramey, S. L., Downing, N. R., & Knoblauch, A. (2008). Developing strategic interventions to reduce cardiovascular disease risk among law enforcement officers: The art and science of data triangulation. *American Association of Occupational Health Nurses Journal, 56*(2), 54–62.

Ramey, S. L., Perkhounkova, Y., Downing, N. R., & Culp, K. (2011). Relationship of cardiovascular disease to stress and vital exhaustion in an urban, Midwestern police department. *American Association Occupational Health Nurses Journal, 59*(5), 221–227. doi:10.3928/08910162-20110418-02

Reaves, B. A. (2010). *Local police departments, 2007.* Retrieved from http://bjs.ojp.usdoj.gov/index.cfm?ty=pbdetail&iid=1750

Roger, V. L., Go, A. S., Lloyd-Jones, D. M., Adams, R. J., Berry, J. D., & Wylie-Rosett, J. (2011). Heart disease and stroke statistics 2011 update: A report from the American Heart Association. *Circulation, 123*(4), e18–e209. doi:10.116VCIR.0b013e3182009701

Rozanski, A., Blumenthal, J. A., & Kaplan, J. (1999). Impact of psychological factors on the pathogenesis of cardiovascular disease and implications for therapy. *Circulation, 99*(16), 2192–2217.

Sardinas, A., Miller, J. W., & Hansen, H. (1986). Ischemic heart disease mortality of firemen and policemen. *American Journal of Public Health, 76*(9), 1140–1141.

Soler, R. E., Leeks, K. D., Razi, S., Hopkins, D. P., Griffith, M., Aten, A., et al.; Task Force on Community Preventive Services. (2010). A systematic review of selected interventions for worksite health promotion. The assessment of health risks with feedback. *American Journal of Preventive Medicine, 38*(2 Suppl), S237–S262. doi:10.1016/j.amepre.2009.10.030

Sparrow, D., Thomas, H. E., Jr., & Weiss, S. T. (1983). Coronary heart disease in police officers participating in the Normative Aging Study. *American Journal of Epidemiology, 118*(4), 508–513.

Stinchcomb, J. B. (2004). Searching for stress in all the wrong places: Combating chronic organizational stressors in policing. *Police Practice and Research, 5*(3), 259–277.

Storch, J. E., & Panzarella, R. (1996). Police stress: State-trait anxiety in relation to occupational and personal stressors. *Journal of Criminal Justice, 24*(2), 99–107.

Tanigoshi, H., Kontos, A. P., & Remley, T. P. (2008). The effectiveness of individual wellness counseling on the wellness of law enforcement officers. *Journal of Counseling and Development, 86*(1), 64–74.

Thomas, P. C., Cady, L. D., O'Connell, E. R., Bischoff, D. P., & Kershnar, R. K. (1979). Heart disease risk factors in Los Angeles County safety personnel. *Journal of Occupational Medicine, 21*(10), 683–687.

Vena, J. E., Violanti, J. M., Marshall, J., & Fiedler, R. C. (1986). Mortality of a municipal worker cohort: III. Police officers. *American Journal of Industrial Medicine, 10*(4), 383–397. doi:10.1002/ajim.4700100406

Violanti, J. (1981). *Police stress and coping: An organizational analysis.* Unpublished master's thesis, The State University of New York, Buffalo.

Violanti, J. M. (1992). Coping strategies among police recruits in a high-stress training environment. *Journal of Social Psychology, 132*(6), 717–729.

Violanti, J. M., & Aron, F. (1994). Ranking police stressors. *Psychological Reports, 75*(2), 824–826.

Violanti, J. M., & Aron, F. (1995). Police stressors: Variations in perception among police personnel. *Journal of Criminal Justice, 23*(3), 287–294.

Violanti, J. M., Fekedulegn, D., Hartley, T. A., Andrew, M. E., Charles, L. E., Mnatsakanova, A., et al. (2006). Police trauma and cardiovascular disease: Association between PTSD symptoms and metabolic syndrome. *International Journal of Emergency Mental Health, 8*(4), 227–237.

Violanti, J. M., Vena, J. E., & Petralia, S. (1998). Mortality of a police cohort: 1950–1990. *American Journal of Industrial Medicine, 13*(4), 336–373. doi:10.1002/(SICI)1097-0274(199804)33:4<366::AID-AJIM6>3.0CO;2-S

Williams, M. A., Petratis, M. M., Baechle, T. R., Ryschon, K. L., Campain, J. J., & Sketch, M. H. (1987). Frequency of physical activity, exercise capacity and atherosclerotic heart disease risk in male police officers. *Journal of Occupational Medicine, 29*(7), 596–600.

Wilson, P. W., D'Agostino, R. B., Levy, D., Belanger, A. M., Silbershatz, H., & Kannel, W. B. (1998). Prediction of coronary heart disease using risk factor categories. *Circulation, 97*(18), 1837–1847.

Wycoff, M. A., & Skogan, W. G. (1994). The effect of a community policing management style on officers' attitudes. *Crime and Delinquency, 40*, 371–383.

Yoo, H. L., Eisenmann, J. C., & Franke, W. D. (2009). Independent and combined influence of physical activity and perceived stress on the metabolic syndrome in male law enforcement officers. *Journal of Occupational Environment Medicine, 51*(1), 46–53. doi:10.1097/JOM.0b013e31817f9e43

9

Stressors Experienced by State and Federal Probation Officers

Risdon N. Slate and W. Wesley Johnson

There is general agreement that working within the criminal justice system can be stressful. Persons under the control of the system (e.g., individuals on probation) for the most part do not want to be there, so dealing with them creates a challenge for those overseeing these individuals. As such, criminal justice professionals are often pulled in disharmonious directions, and courts, prosecutors, and defense attorneys may add to this conflict. The criminal justice system sometimes embraces incongruous values. Examples include retribution versus rehabilitation, public safety versus civil liberties, and crime control versus due process. The roles of probation officers are often unclear; workers and supervised individuals may both find themselves wondering: Are probation officers to be enforcers or social workers? This conflict partially results because the multiple goals of sentencing are not always compatible. Should the focus of sentencing be solely on the past criminal act that brings the person to the attention of criminal justice authorities, or should the focus be on the future behavior of the offender after his or her entanglement with the criminal justice system? Is the goal of sentencing to control and prevent crime, to punish, to deter, to protect the community, or to rehabilitate? It is no wonder that incompatible and conflicting goals can lead to frustration and even to role ambiguity among criminal justice practitioners (Brown, 1987; Slate, Wells, & Johnson, 2003; Whitehead, 1985, 1986).

Community supervision officers include both probation and parole officers. Probation is a front-end alternative to incarceration, and persons sentenced by the court to probation are monitored by probation officers in the community in an attempt to ensure compliance with court-imposed supervision conditions and to thwart reoffending. Parole is a back-end alternative to incarceration whereby persons re-entering society after serving time in prison are supervised in the community. The goals of supervision—primarily the reduction of reoffending and the integration of offenders into the community—are the same for both probation and parole officers, and the means for monitoring offenders and ensuring compliance are similar.

A number of states and the federal government have implemented supervised release and abolished parole (Anderson & Slate, 2011). This has resulted in eliminating parole board discretion in deciding to release offenders from prison after having served an indeterminate amount of time. Instead, under the determinate sentencing structure of supervised release, supervision by government agents continues in the community typically after an offender has completed 85% of his or her sentence in prison (Anderson & Slate, 2011). As such, the terms *community supervision officers*, *probation officers*, and *parole officers* are often used interchangeably.

Community supervision officers are required to perform a variety of duties. In the performance of those tasks, officers draw on a variety of skills. Some carry firearms; some may have specialized caseloads (consisting of sex offenders, substance abusers, or persons with mental illnesses); others may engage in intensive supervision (i.e., a high number of contacts in the field during a reporting period) and/or conduct presentence investigations (recommending a sentence to the court for offenders prior to sentencing). Community supervision officers are uniquely positioned, as noted by Lutze, Johnson, Clear, Latessa, and Slate (2011, p. 26), with "the power to coerce and to treat." This dual capacity of enforcer and social worker can certainly contribute to role conflict. This, and other factors, can contribute to the stress experienced by practitioners.

In this chapter the literature on the causes of stress for criminal justice practitioners, especially community supervision officers, is reviewed; data from original research on the effects of stress on state and federal probation officers are presented. We specifically focus on our most recent work on stress in probation officers. While there is a body of literature and research that focuses on the job of state probation officers, there is scant research on federal probation officers. The research presented in this study is among the first to compare the stressors experienced by state and federal probation officers. We employ a survey instrument that identifies the most common stressors perceived by both state and federal probation officers in the southern United States. Differences in state and federal probation officers' stressors are examined and discussed. Limitations of the study are addressed, recommendations for future exploration are offered, and issues affecting management are discussed. Specifically, recommendations are made for mitigating the effects of stress among community supervision officers.

Types of Stressors

Causes of stress (stressors) for criminal justice practitioners have been classified as being personal in nature, external to the organization, internal to the agency, and job or task related (see Spielberger, Westberry, Grier, & Greenfield, 1981; Whisler, 1994). As discussed later, the causes of stress have been examined in the research literature for police, probation, and correctional officers. Of course, some stressors apply to all of these groups, but other stressors are unique to a particular group. The present chapter focuses on probation officers (for more on stressors among law enforcement officers, see chapter 8).

Personal Stressors

Personal stressors are generally related to an officer's relationship with his or her family. Generally, police officers experience a lack of social support (Anshel, 2000), and their relationships with nonpolice, including family, can be problematic (Storch & Panzarella, 1996). Families of law enforcement officers have been touted for being a bastion of support for them, but they have also been chided for being burdens (Toch, 2002). Families of police officers often do not understand the monotony and exhilaration that comes with police work. For example, going from boring paperwork to a high-speed chase ending with fatalities in a matter of minutes is not indicative of the kind of exposure to downtime and adrenaline rushes that most people experience. Likewise, Abdollahi (2002) reported that a lack of family support for law enforcement officers has been linked to police officer suicides. Lack of familial support is a primary stressor for correctional officers (Cullen, Link, Wolfe, & Frank, 1985). Finn (2000) has recommended that counseling for correctional personnel and their families be offered after involvement in critical incidents or personal crises, due to the debilitating effects such events can have on correctional employees and their families. He also highlights the importance of engaging peers in such counseling efforts and notes that families are often the first to know when a problem is developing with their loved one but largely remain an untapped resource. Family support is strongly related to health and occupational stress (Anderson, 1994). As such, married probation officers are more likely to report being satisfied with their work and report experiencing less occupational stress than their unmarried colleagues (Simmons, Cochran, & Blount, 1997; Tabor, 1987).

In sum, families can be a much-needed source of support for officers. In many cases, the justice system could utilize this source of support to help officers deal with stressors. On the other hand, families can sometimes be a burden and perhaps even be a source of stress for officers. The importance of the role of the family in alleviating and contributing to the stress of criminal justice practitioners should not be underestimated.

Extrinsic (External) Stressors

Extrinsic stressors are sources of stress that are external to the organization. Perceived leniency on the part of judges, for example, has been identified as an extrinsic contributor to stress for both law enforcement and probation officers

(Abdollahi, 2002; Finn & Kuck, 2003; Whisler, 1994). For example, police officers who arrest offenders are sometimes not even consulted by the court on plea bargain decisions, and probation officers who must supervise offenders are sometimes not given input by the court on determining conditions of probation. There is also evidence that officers have experienced stressors related to a negative public image and inadequate pay (Finn, 2000). Other extrinsic stressors include a lack of recognition by the media and public for their job performance under difficult circumstances (Abdollahi, 2002). For example, in instances where pedophiles under supervised release in the community abduct and murder young children, there is often intense media coverage and scrutiny of the work being done by community supervision officers responsible for monitoring the behavior of sex offenders. Such events have brought about rigid laws that limit the options of probation officers in monitoring sex offenders and add to the cumulative effects of other forms of stress (see Bavir, 2007; Jessica Marie Lunsford Foundation, 2005). Thus, stressors external to the organization, while anticipated, are not easily controlled.

Intrinsic Stressors

Intrinsic stressors are those that are internal to the organization. The bureaucratic nature and organizational climate of criminal justice agencies are often identified as internal stressors contributing to stress levels of those employed in the justice system (Abdollahi, 2002; Storch & Panzarella, 1996; Violanti & Aron, 1994; Winter, 1993; Zhao, He, & Lovrich, 2002). Organizational characteristics, such as having no input into decisions in the workplace that affect workers on a daily basis, are significant sources of stress for employees in policing (Abdollahi, 2002; Slate, Johnson, & Colbert, 2007), institutional corrections (Cheek, 1984; Slate & Vogel, 1997), and community corrections (Finn & Kuck, 2003; Slate et al., 2003).

Failure to reward positive job performance and an insufficient promotion system not based on merit are also stressors for both law enforcement officers (Toch, 2002) and correctional employees (Finn, 2000). Likewise, inadequate promotional opportunities and unsatisfactory pay have been identified as significant causes of stress for community supervision officers (Simmons et al., 1997; Whisler, 1994; Whitehead, 1986). Other factors identified as stressors for community supervision officers include role conflict (Brown, 1987; Whitehead, 1985, 1986), interaction with superiors in the workplace (Simmons et al., 1997), and the perception that there is not enough time to sufficiently meet job demands (Thomas, 1988). For example, in terms of the latter concern, the courts often set deadlines for having presentence investigations completed to meet the court docket. This is typically done without consulting probation personnel for input or considering the flexibility of having such an extensive report completed on time.

For those employees desirous of having input in the workplace, the lack of an opportunity to participate in decision making is a potential intrinsic stressor in criminal justice agencies, which tend to resemble paramilitary organizations. As such, the inability to participate in workplace decision making is a primary source of stress in policing (Morash & Haarr, 1995; Patterson, 1992; Slate et al., 2007; Stinchcomb, 2004), corrections (Sims, 2001; Slate & Vogel, 1997; Slate, Vogel, & Johnson, 2001), and probation (Brown, 1986, 1987; Finn & Kuck, 2003; Holgate & Clegg, 1991; Simmons et al., 1997; Slate, Johnson, & Wells, 2000; Tabor, 1987; Whisler, 1994; Whitehead, 1981, 1986; Whitehead & Lindquist, 1985). Those organizations that support participatory management strategies are more likely to reduce the negative effects of intrinsic stressors.

Job- or Task-Related Stressors

There are other stressors for criminal justice employees that have been identified as being related to the job or task performed. The potential for dangerousness and being placed in precarious situations with threatening individuals is a possible stressor for those working in law enforcement (Abdollahi, 2002; Anshel, 2000; Zhao et al., 2002), corrections (Finn, 2000; Slate, 1993; Slate & Vogel, 1997), and probation (Finn & Kuck, 2005; Thomas, 1988). For example, Whisler (1994) reported in a survey of law enforcement officers that out of a list of 57 potential stressors, the two highest rated causes of stress for police were "fellow police officer killed in the line of duty" and "killing someone in the line of duty" (p. 36).

An abundance of paperwork has also been noted as a source of job stress for virtually all employees within the justice system (Abdollahi, 2002; Brown, 1987; Finn, 2000; Finn & Kuck, 2005; Simmons et al., 1997; Thomas, 1988; Whisler, 1994). Additionally, community supervision officers have reported experiencing stress due to large caseloads and deadlines for reports without adequate time to get the work done (Finn & Kuck, 2003, 2005; Simmons et al., 1997).

The categories of personal, external, internal, and job- or task-related stressors serve as a means for classifying factors generally related to stress for criminal justice practitioners. We now turn specifically to job challenges faced by supervision officers and consider further insights from previous studies.

Community Supervision Officers: Job Challenges

There are several types of stressors that community supervision officers experience. First, they may experience stress due to technology. Second, they may experience stress due to the nature of the job (supervising offenders). These stressors can have numerous and differential effects on officers.

In the last several decades there have been "quantum" leaps in technology and the use of risk assessment instruments that have changed the nature of community supervision for both state and federal probation officers. While much of the work of community supervision officers 20 to 30 years ago involved processing hard-copy paperwork, field work, and face-to-face interaction, utilization of digitized records has changed the nature of supervising offenders on probation and parole. Today, a greater portion of the work is done in the office. This is true of both administrative supervisors and those directly involved in offender supervision. An overemphasis on in-office supervision visits with offenders can be particularly problematic as such interactions are often sterile and artificial and not a true example of offenders' natural environments. While the work of community supervision assumes human interaction—face-to-face encounters with offenders and organizational evaluations that involve supervisors' real-time review of such encounters, changes in technology have resulted in a dehumanization of the process where both officers and administrators rely more frequently on digitized records to assess the behavior of the offender and the quality of probation officers' work than in previous decades. While officers may be effective one on one with offenders, failure to adequately document such encounters can lead to negative personnel evaluations, thus creating negative stress for the probation officers. Likewise, officers who place priority on the completion of paperwork and documentation may have fewer face-to-face interactions with offenders and be less successful in their supervision efforts. This qualitative change in the nature of "community supervision work" has altered the relationship that an officer has with the probationer and the relationship between the administrator/supervisor and the probation officer.

The most valuable organizational asset to justice organizations is their workforces. The bottom line is that humans are making decisions about other humans. The failure to recognize the role of human agency in organizational operations often drives employee turnover and reduces worker morale, job satisfaction, and organizational efficacy (Lutze et al., 2011).

The second type of stress relates to the quantity and nature of the individuals who are supervised by correctional supervision officers. Of all offenders under correctional supervision at the beginning of 2010 in the United States, 70% were monitored by probation or parole officers in the community (Glaze, 2010). Thus, the burden of supervising and facilitating the treatment of this population of offenders falls directly on the shoulders of community supervision officers. Many offenders under community supervision have been previously incarcerated and are not well equipped to deal constructively with the freedoms they experience once out of prison (Anderson & Slate, 2011; Taxman, Shephardson, & Byrne, 2004), and evidence indicates that community supervision populations continue to be very similar demographically to prison populations (Wilson & Petersilia, 2011). In comparison to previous decades, offenders under community supervision are more likely to have felony records, have fewer job-related employment skills, and have a diagnosable mental illness. Almost four out of five persons released from state prisons are said to be released to some kind of conditional community supervision. In excess of 66% of persons released from prison are rearrested for a new crime within 3 years of release from prison, with almost half of them being found guilty of a crime (Anderson & Slate, 2011). This fact ups the stakes and increases the pressure on parole officers to prevent further harmful acts from being perpetrated in the community. The average caseload is estimated to be around 70 offenders per parole officer, and around 130 per probation officer (Council of State Governments, 2005; Taxman, 2008). Such caseload sizes result in cursory supervision with brief office visits at best and a lack of supervision of offenders in the communities where they reside and work; this contributes to the probability for the individual's failure while on conditional release in the community (Council of State Governments, 2005). Such conditions are inherently stressful for officers.

Stress can have many effects on officers; one extreme effect is leaving the job entirely. Employee turnover rates have been identified as a symptom of stressful working environments in the research literature (Slate, 1993). The stress experienced by community supervision officers is reflected in employee turnover rates as high as 30% (Lee, Joo, & Johnson, 2009; Simmons et al., 1997).

Previous studies of community supervision officer stress and wellbeing have focused on individual characteristics such as age, gender, and marital status and organizational factors such as adequacy of training, opportunity for advancement, lack of job security, and the atmosphere for participation in decision making (Slate et al., 2003). The interactions among stress (internal and external), job satisfaction, and employee turnover are complex (Dial, Thompson, & Johnson, 2008; Lee et al., 2009; Slate et al., 2000). Prior research indicates that while female probation officers report greater levels of physical stress (signs and symptoms of illness) than their male counterparts, male probation officers are significantly more likely to exhibit higher levels of internal stress, job stress, and personal stress (Wells, Colbert, & Slate, 2006).

Stress levels of community supervision officers are greater than those of the general population (Tabor, 1987). Yet, there are only a few studies that have examined differences in the levels and qualities of stress experienced by state and federal community supervision officers (Lee et al., 2009; Slate et al., 2000). To our knowledge, no prior study has examined both state and federal community supervision officers' stress levels using officers primarily from the same broad geographic location.

Purpose of the Current Study

The work of federal and state probation/parole officers is similar, but there are distinct differences. This study examines and compares stress levels of both federal and state probation officers. Based on previous research, it was believed that officers' perceptions about the conduciveness of the work environment to participatory decision making would be a pivotal variable for consideration for both state and federal probation officers. It is common knowledge that state community supervision officers' caseloads are higher, and their salaries are lower, when compared to their federal counterparts. Thus, there was interest to see if either of these stressors would differ between state and federal probation officers. However, due to the exploratory nature of our study, we did not posit any specific hypotheses comparing state and federal probation officers.

Method

Participant Sample and Procedure

This study utilizes survey data collected from state and federal probation officers from a southern state and federal probation officers from three additional states. State authorities allowed researchers to e-mail surveys to all sworn officers, and the researchers provided postage-paid envelopes so respondents could mail the survey back anonymously to the researchers. A similar strategy was used with the federal officers, except the federal administrators ensured that each officer received a survey. Agencies were selected for inclusion in the study based on availability and ease of accessibility; representativeness of the sample is therefore an issue, as discussed later.

There were 925 surveys distributed to all sworn state probation officers in the southern state that was included in the research. This resulted in a total of 626 usable surveys (68.8% response rate) being completed and returned for analysis. In the four states (two southern and two midwestern) with federal probation officers included in the study, 387 surveys were disseminated, and 272 were completed and returned for analysis, resulting in a 70% response rate.

Measures

A questionnaire was utilized to measure internal stressors (including perceptions of participation in decision making), external stressors, personal stressors, and job- or task-related stressors as delineated in survey form by Whisler (1994) and previously used in probation officer stress research by Slate et al. (2003) and Wells et al. (2006). Each item on the scales developed by Whisler ranged from *not stressful* to *very stressful* on a 6-point ordinal scale. A 26-item scale was used to measure internal stress, asking respondents to indicate the degree to which they experienced stress due to potential stressors, such as being expected to do too much in too little time, inadequate salary, and lack of promotional opportunities. External stress was measured through a 14-item scale composed of such potential stressors as ineffectiveness of the judicial system, negative media accounts of probation, and not being treated like a professional by the public. Personal stress was assessed by a 7-item scale that included such potential stressors as having to take work home, demands made by family for time, and concern about making a mistake. Job- or task-related stress, focusing on specific components of the officer's job, was examined via a 14-item scale consisting of possible stressors such as due dates for reports, visiting the homes of those supervised, and excessive paperwork. Cronbach's alpha yielded high reliability for each scale included in our study, with stress internal to the organization = .94, stress external to the organization = .90, personal stress = .86, and job- or task-related stress = .88.

Physical symptoms of stress indicative of health-related problems have been associated with criminal justice practitioners working as police, correctional, and probation officers (see Wells et al., 2006; see also chapter 8, this volume). As such, the Selye Health Scale, a 54-item Likert-type scale, devised by Cheek and Miller (1982b) and used in previous research with criminal justice practitioners (Cheek, 1984; Cheek & Miller, 1982a; Slate & Vogel, 1997; Slate et al., 2001) to determine physical stress levels of criminal justice personnel, measured the severity of signs and symptoms of physical maladies reported by respondents. Subjects rated their experience with various symptoms such as "overeating," "crying," "worrying," "drinking alcohol or taking something to relax," "colitis," and "cancer" on a 6-point Likert-type scale ranging from *never* to *very often*. Cronbach's alpha measure of reliability for this scale included in the study was .95.

Job satisfaction was measured with a 6-item Likert-type scale. Respondents indicated agreement or disagreement on a 5-point scale to items such as "I believe I will remain with this agency until I retire," "I am proud of what I do for a living," and "I would recommend this job to others." This scale to assess job satisfaction has been used in previous research (Wells et al., 2006) and resulted in a Cronbach's alpha in our current study of .81.

As noted earlier, the ability to participate in workplace decision making has been a pivotal variable in prior research with criminal justice practitioners. A scale devised by Slate (1993) measured this variable, as well as the attitudes of probation officers regarding participation in workplace decision making. A 7-item Likert-type scale, with responses ranging from *strongly agree* to *strongly disagree*, constituted the atmosphere for participation variable and was composed of statements such as, "I feel comfortable offering my opinion to supervisors at work," "My supervisors ask me for input on decisions that affect me at work," and "From past experience at this agency, I feel it is a waste of time and energy to tell management anything." The variable of attitudes about workplace decision making was measured using a 5-item Likert-type scale and was composed of responses to statements such as, "The quality of decisions increases as worker participation in decision making increases," "Everyone should be allowed to participate in decision making in the workplace on matters that affect them," and "Participation in decision making tends to make individuals feel they have a stake in running the organization." The Cronbach's alpha for these two subscales on atmosphere for and attitudes about workplace decision making resulted in Cronbach alphas of .79 and .81, respectively, for the present study. Thus, the reliability coefficients for each of the scales utilized in the study were acceptable (Fox, 1981; Hair, Black, Babin, Anderson, & Tatham, 2006).

Results

In terms of demographics, 325 of the state community supervision respondents were female and 301 were male. Federal probation respondents included 168 males and 104 females. The majority of the respondents were White (n = 441 for the state probation officers and n = 156 for the federal probation officers). Non-Whites made up 28% (n = 174) of the state probation officers and 42% ($n = 113$) of the federal probation officers. This proved to be a significant difference ($t = 4.09$; $p < .001$; $df = 882$), indicating more diversity among federal probation officers. The average age of state probation officers was 36.2 years, and similarly the average age for federal probation respondents was 37.2 years. The demographics for the sample were representative of the overall population for the research project as determined by workforce information provided by probation administrators to the researchers at the time our survey was disseminated.

Table 9.1 reveals the top 10 stressors (internal, external, personal, and/or job and task related) for both federal probation and state probation officer respondents. Each stressor was ranked by participants on a 6-point ordinal scale (0 = *not stressful* to 6 = *stressful*).

As evident in Table 9.1, the means of the eight highest stressors for state probation officers in the study were greater than the highest stressor reported by federal probation officers (excessive paperwork = 3.95). Five of the top 10 stressors identified by state probation officers were internal to the organization, 5 were external to the organization, and 1 was job or task related (it should be noted that 11 stressors are actually included in the table, as the means were tied for 2 of them). For federal probation officers, 3 of the top 10

Table 9.1. Means of the Top 10 Stressors

Federal Probation Officers		State Probation Officers	
1. Excessive paperwork (J)	3.95	Inadequate salary (I)	4.93
2. Expected to do too much in too little time (I)	3.83	Courts being too lenient on offenders (E)	4.53
3. Due dates for reports (J)	3.77	Lack of promotional opportunities (I)	4.34
4. Must take work home (P)	3.33	Frustration with the criminal justice system (E)	4.19
5. Lack of community resources (E)	3.20	Excessive paperwork (J)	4.17
6. Concern that you'll make a mistake (P)	3.19	Ineffectiveness of the judicial system (E)	4.16
7. Frustration with the criminal justice system (E)	3.08	Expected to do too much in too little time (I)	4.12
8. Scheduling of court appearances (E)	3.04	Lack of recognition for good work (I)	4.06
9. Visiting probationers' homes (J)	2.95	Ineffectiveness of the correctional system (E)	3.80
10. Political pressure within the agency (I)	2.95	Inadequate support from the agency (I)	3.62
		Lack of community resources (E)	3.62

I = a stressor internal to the organization; E = a stressor external to the organization; J = a job- or task-related stressor; P = a personal stressor.

stressors were external to the organization, 3 were job or task related, 2 were internal to the organization, and 2 were personal in nature. The type of stressors experienced can have a significant impact on what approaches might be best to alleviate the stressors, as will be discussed in detail later.

Stressors common among the top 10 for both federal and state probation officers included *excessive paperwork, expected to do too much in too little time, frustration with the criminal justice system*, and *lack of community resources*. It is worth noting that the common stressors among the state and federal probation officers were two stressors external to the job, one job- or task-related stressor (excessive paperwork), and one intrinsic to the job (expected to do too much in too little time). The other stressors in the top 10 for both groups were relatively unique to each work environment. Lastly, on average, state probation officers ranked the internal stressor of inadequate salary higher than any of the other 61 stressors ($M = 4.93$ out of a possible 6), while federal probation officers' responses reflected a M of 1.93, for a significant difference between the two groups ($t = 30.28$; $p < .001$; $df = 905$).

Table 9.2 reflects the results of the t tests and reveals significant differences between state and federal probation officers on key variables. Scales include internal, external, job- or task-related, personal, and physical stressors; scale values are sums of responses to the individual items. State probation officers were significantly more likely than federal probation officers to reflect higher internal stress levels

Table 9.2. Comparison of Federal and State Probation Officers on Key Variables

	Federal Probation Officers (n = 272)		State Probation Officers (n = 626)			
Scale	Mean	SD	Mean	SD	*t*	*df****
Atmosphere for participation	21.64	5.91	20.73	5.96	−2.11*	520.2
Attitudes about participation	20.85	2.77	20.56	3.16	−1.34	581.1
External stress	37.04	10.57	48.25	13.33	13.13**	618.9
Internal stress	63.25	25.21	80.40	25.88	9.13**	528.1
Job stress	39.33	13.16	41.35	14.86	1.99	544.4
Job satisfaction	25.03	4.37	21.01	5.23	−11.90**	609.3
Personal stress	16.30	7.63	16.04	7.11	−0.486	491.6
Physical stress	218.38	72.86	230.95	73.95	2.29*	506.5

*$p < .05$.

**$p < .001$.

*** The variance in *dfs* is the result of incomplete responses by some officers, rendering inaccurate computation of some of their scales which were therefore not usable.

(federal $M = 63.25$ and state $M = 80.40$; $t = 9.13$; $p < .001$; $df = 528.1$), external stress levels (federal $M = 37.04$ and state $M = 48.25$; $t = 13.13$; $p < .001$; $df = 618.9$), and physical stress levels (federal $M = 218.38$ and state $M = 230.95$; $t = 2.29$; $p < .05$; $df = 506.5$). Federal probation officers were significantly more likely than state probation officers to report a positive atmosphere for participation in workplace decision making (federal $M = 21.64$ and state $M = 20.73$; $t = -2.11$; $p < .05$; $df = 520.2$) and to indicate that they were satisfied with their jobs (federal $M = 25.03$ and state $M = 21.01$; $t = -11.90$; $p < .001$; $df = 609.3$). The two groups did not differ significantly on their attitudes about participation, job stress, or personal stress.

Discussion

The purpose of this chapter was to expand on the literature regarding stress experienced by community supervision officers by examining and comparing levels of federal and state probation officer stress. Doing so can help identify areas for organizational reduction of stress, potentially leading to cost savings, reduction in turnover, and promotion of employee wellness.

As indicated in the literature review, stressors for community supervision officers can be categorized into four categories: personal, job or task related, and internal or external to the organization. The majority of the leading stressors found in our study for both federal and state probation community supervision respondents were internal to the respective organizations surveyed. There were also significant differences in the external stress of state community supervision officers compared to federal community supervision officers. As with previous research, the atmosphere for participation in workplace decision making and physical stress levels proved to be key variables. Our study also revealed a significant difference between the job satisfaction levels of federal and state community supervision officers and discrepancies regarding salary not previously observed in the research literature on this topic.

Seven of the top 10 stressors for the state and federal probation agencies were internal to the respective organizations. Four of the top 10 stressors for both organizations were job or task related; 2 personal stressors made the top 10 list for federal probation officers. Stressors internal to an organization may be alleviated within an organization through possibly soliciting employee input. Job- or task-related stressors might also be alleviated by employee input. As for personal stressors, referral to employee wellness programs might prove of benefit.

Certainly, stressors *external* to an organization, such as frustration with the criminal justice system, being perceived negatively by the public, or ineffectiveness of the judicial or correctional system, may not be as readily alleviated by organizational intervention strategies as stressors *internal* to an agency. Perhaps future research should address organizational strategies for addressing stressors external to the organization. Seeking collaborations between organizations and delineating agency responsibilities via memorandums of understanding between agencies can go a long way toward alleviating confusion and stressful situations. Likewise, public forums in which criminal justice personnel meet with the citizenry for input and give-and-take can serve to lessen tensions between criminal justice practitioners and the public.

The highest stressor on average was an internal stressor identified by state probation officers as inadequate salary. As noted by Herzberg (1966), an adequate salary does not serve as a motivator for enhancing employee attitudes and performance, but an inadequate salary can lead to job dissatisfaction. Correspondingly, the federal probation officers, who, on average, expressed less concern about their salaries, were significantly more satisfied with their work environments than were the state probation officers in the study. Furthermore, state probation officers were significantly more stressed on average than federal probation officers in the present study due to factors internal and external to the organization. As previously noted, a contributor to employee stress is the perception that one has a lack of input into the decisions that affect one in the workplace. Here again, federal probation officers perceived their work environment as more conducive to participating in workplace decision making and were significantly less stressed concerning this variable than state probation officers. The importance of this variable is that if utilized effectively by administrators, it could assist in allowing employees to have a voice and input into matters that affect them in the workplace, such as salaries, being expected to do too much in too little time, and lack of recognition for good work.

The inability to have input in decisions that affect one in the workplace is significantly related to physical maladies and stress (Slate & Vogel, 1997; Slate et al., 2007). Likewise, state probation officers in this study were significantly more stressed than federal probation officers about the atmosphere for participation in workplace decision making, and they were significantly more physically stressed than their federal counterparts. Of course, the federal government tends to be more apt to have access to financial resources than many states facing severe budget constraints. Likewise, the federal government seems to be more receptive to innovative management strategies such as participatory management than many of the states. Historically, in both law enforcement and in corrections, federal criminal justice agencies have often been the first to initiate innovations in offender and management practices. This trend is also evident in community corrections.

As identified by Terry (1981, 1983), three potential methods for reducing stress are (1) to help the stressed individual, (2) to increase an individual's capability to deal with stress, and (3) to eliminate the causes of stress. Terry maintains that the latter approach is the best for alleviating stress but has received the least attention. Instead, employee assistance programs are often put into place. Typically, organizations tend to focus on individuals instead of the source of the problem—the stress of the organization and job. This method has been described as absurd, and it has been recommended that the focus should not be on "bad people" but on the "bad situations" that "good people" find themselves in (Maslach, 1982). There are those who recommend that organizations should be restructured to fit people instead of trying to modify people to fit organizations (Newman & Beehr, 1979). However, the comfortable approach for interventions seems to be to attempt to change people instead of organizations (Ivancevich, Matteson, & Richards, 1985).

Study Limitations

It should be cautioned that this study was exploratory in nature and should serve as a basis for contributing to the formulation of hypotheses for future comparative research. Furthermore, only one state's probation personnel were included in this study. For example, the state probation officers included in this study were not unionized, and unionization may make a difference in employee participation in workplace decision making and in stress outcomes. Additionally, presentence reports were seldom prepared by state probation officers, and this may vary from state to state. Therefore, generalizations to such professionals in other states should be cautioned. This study also incorporated several scales. To ensure consistency in comparisons for future research in this area, we would recommend that these same scales be utilized.[1]

Implications and Future Directions

Of course, the importance of keeping physical stress in check is that health care costs can be costly not only to individuals and their families but also to organizations. Stress in the workplace has also been linked to turnover (Slate & Vogel, 1997), and having to continually train employees to replace stressed-out workers is costly.

We believe "[t]he greatest investment an organization can make is in its human capital" (Maggio & Terenzi, 1993, p. 15). Management guru Peter Drucker believed in employee empowerment (Lamdan, 2008), and, after having completed this study, we reiterate that criminal justice organizations should continue to explore opportunities for employees to participate in decisions that affect them in the workplace. We are not naïve enough to believe that all decisions within the criminal justice system can be offered up for employee input, but some can and should be. Certainly, the time for participatory management is not at the height of a crisis when bullets are whizzing overhead. Employee input should occur long before a crisis occurs. For example, when certain officers have expertise in dealing with specific types of offenders, such as sexual offenders or persons with mental health or substance

---

[1] The full questionnaire may be acquired by contacting rslate@flsouthern.edu.

abuse problems, it makes sense to develop specialized caseloads for supervision instead of general caseloads. Allowing employee input into workplace decision making can serve to identify such aptitudes and development of such caseloads. Such specialization may serve to thwart potential crises. In one of the federal probation agencies examined in our study, the administration had solicited input regarding officers performing the dual role of presentence investigations and supervision of offenders. Officers overwhelmingly responded that they would prefer to do one or the other but not both. Upon receiving this employee input, the administration allowed their employees to choose to do both or one or the other. Such practices hold much promise in reducing stress in officers. The current study may be one step in encouraging positive changes to the system.

Conclusion

Discussions of wellness and reducing community correctional officer stress have never been more important. In a time of fiscal constraint and shrinking budgets, both federal and state community supervision organizations are feeling pressure to do more with less. In the midst of what has been termed a third deinstitutionalization movement (Johnson, 2011), probation and parole caseload numbers have steadily increased. South Carolina and Mississippi are among many states that have cut the budgets of their institutional corrections systems to meet fiscal demands. In California, the U.S. Supreme Court recently upheld a three-judge panel's decision to release over 40,000 inmates due to overcrowding and the inability to provide proper care (*Brown v. Plata*, 2011). Due to mandatory sentencing laws, overcrowding, and the national fiscal crisis, other states are in similar situations (Anderson & Slate, 2011). As prisons parole and release offenders, an already overburdened probation and parole system will come under greater pressure to ensure the safety of communities. The ability to increase the productivity of probation and parole officers will depend on how the organizational cultures of federal and state probation and parole systems adjust to even greater demands for accountability.

Perhaps the most significant development in changing the work and delivery of probation and parole is the incorporation of evidence-based practices. While probation and parole agencies have made notable strides in implementing evidence-based practices, there "remains a paucity of evidence" (Mears, 2010, p. 240) to demonstrate the particular practices that actually work. Mears contends that many policy decisions are made with a "black box" that is devoid of credible evaluation and assessment, thus limiting the ability of the criminal justice system to change and adapt in a meaningful way. Employee input into what works and what does not could prove to be an integral component in ensuring such decisions are reasoned and informed. The failure of community supervision systems to adjust to evolving pressures will have ripple effects on employee morale and stress for years to come. According to some observers, community safety and the wellbeing of over 50,000 probation and parole officers are at stake (Reynolds, 2000; C. Wicklund, executive director, American Probation and Parole Association, personal communication, January 13, 2011). As we found in our study, a perceived positive atmosphere for participation was a pivotal variable for federal probation officers, and they were more likely to report that they were satisfied with their jobs than state probation officers. Previous studies that we have cited have emphasized the importance of participatory management in reducing stress. Participatory management's time in the criminal justice arena has come, as contented employees perform better than those who are discontented, and input into workplace decision making can lead to greater contentment (Slate et al., 2003).

References

Abdollahi, K. M. (2002). Understanding police stress research. *Journal of Forensic Psychology Practice, 2*, 1–24.

Anderson, E. M. (1994). *Stress and its correlates: An empirical investigation among North Dakota peace officers.* Unpublished doctoral dissertation, University of North Dakota, Grand Forks, North Dakota.

Anderson, P. R., & Slate, R. N. (2011). *The decision-making network: An introduction to criminal justice.* Durham, NC: Carolina Academic Press.

Anshel, M. (2000). A conceptual model and implications for coping with stressful events in police work. *Criminal Justice and Behavior, 27*, 375–400.

Bavir, A. (2007). When hysteria and good intentions collide: Constitutional considerations of California's sexual predator punishment and control act. *Whittier Law Review, 29*, 679–706.

Brown, P. W. (1986). Probation officer burnout: An organizational disease/an organizational cure. *Federal Probation, 50*(1), 4–7.

Brown, P. W. (1987). Probation officer burnout: An organizational disease/an organizational cure, part II. *Federal Probation, 51*(3), 17–21.

Brown v. Plata 131 S. Ct. 1910 (2011).

Cheek, F. E. (1984). *Stress management for correctional officers and their families.* College Park, MD: American Correctional Association.

Cheek, F. E., & Miller, M. D. (1982a). *Managerial stress in correctional facilities handbook.* Trenton, NJ: New Jersey Department of Corrections.

Cheek, F. E., & Miller, M. D. (1982b). *Prisoners of life.* Washington, DC: American Federation of State, County and Municipal Employees.

Council of State Governments. (2005). *Report of the Re-Entry Policy Council: Charting the safe and successful return of prisoners to the community.* New York, NY: Council of State Governments. January 2005.

Cullen, F., Link, B., Wolfe, N., & Frank, J. (1985). The social dimensions of correctional officer stress. *Justice Quarterly, 2*, 505–533.

Dial, K. C., Thompson, R. A., & Johnson, W. W. (2008). The effect of "care" from immediate supervisors on correctional employees. *Corrections Compendium, 33*(2), 1–3, 26–34.

Finn, P. (2000). *Addressing correctional officer stress: Programs and strategies.* National Institute of Justice. Retrieved July 29, 2011, from https://www.ncjrs.gov/pdffiles1/nij/183474.pdf

Finn, P., & Kuck, S. (2003). *Addressing probation and parole officer stress.* Abt Associates. Retrieved November 28, 2011, from https://www.ncjrs.gov/pdffiles1/nij/grants/207012.pdf

Finn, P., & Kuck, S. (2005). *Stress among probation and parole officers and what can be done about it.* National Institute of Justice. Retrieved November 28, 2011, from http://www.docstoc.com/docs/35645633/Stress-Among-Probation-and-Parole-Officers-and-What-Can-Be-Done-About-It

Fox, J. (1981). *Methods in quantitative criminology.* New York, NY: Academic Press.

Glaze, L. E. (2010). *Correctional populations in the United States, 2009.* Bureau of Justice Statistics. Retrieved July 29, 2011, from http://bjs.ojp.usdoj.gov/content/pub/pdf/cpus09.pdf

Hair, J., Black, W., Babin, B., Anderson, R., & Tatham, R. (2006). *Multivariate data analysis* (6th ed.). Upper Saddle River, NJ: Prentice-Hall.

Herzberg, F. (1966). *Work and the nature of man.* New York, NY: Thomas Y. Crowell Company.

Holgate, A. M., & Clegg, I. J. (1991). The path to probation officer burnout: New dogs, old tricks. *Journal of Criminal Justice, 19,* 325–337.

Ivancevich, J. M., Matteson, M. T., & Richards, E. P. (1985). Special report: Who's liable for stress on the job? *Harvard Business Review, 64,* 60–72.

Jessica Marie Lunsford Foundation. (2005). *Helping children in crisis.* Retrieved June 27, 2012, from http://www.keddiemedia.com/portfolio/jmlfoundation/faq.html

Johnson, W. W. (2011). Rethinking the interface between mental illness, criminal justice and academia. *Justice Quarterly, 28,* 15–22.

Lamdan, R. (2008, December 18). *Empowering knowledge workers for greater value.* Enterprise Innovation. Retrieved August 10, 2011, from http://www.enterpriseinnovation.net/content/empowering-knowledge-workers-greater-value

Lee, W. J., Joo, H. J., & Johnson, W. W. (2009). Turnover intention, job satisfaction, internal stress and participatory management among federal probation officers. *Federal Probation, 73*(1). Retrieved August 6, 2011, from http://www.uscourts.gov/uscourts/FederalCourts/PPS/Fedprob/2009-06/FederalProbationOfficers.html

Lutze, F., Johnson, W. W., Clear, T., Latessa, E., & Slate, R. N. (2011). *The future of community corrections is now: Stop dreaming and take action.* Presented at the Academy of Criminal Justice Sciences Annual Meeting in Toronto, Canada, March 2.

Maggio, M., & Terenzi, E. (1993). The impact of critical incident stress: Is your office prepared to respond? *Federal Probation, 57*(4), 10–16.

Maslach, C. (1982). *Burnout: The cost of caring.* Englewood Cliffs, NJ: Prentice Hall.

Mears, D. P. (2010). *American criminal justice policy: An evaluation approach to increasing accountability and effectiveness.* New York, NY: Cambridge University Press.

Morash, M., & Haarr, R. N. (1995). Gender, workplace problems, and stress in policing. *Justice Quarterly, 12*, 113–140.
Newman, J. E., & Beehr, T. A. (1979). Personal and organizational strategies for handling job stress: A review of research and opinion. *Personnel Psychology, 32*, 1–43.
Patterson, B. L. (1992). Job experience and perceived job stress among police, correctional, and probation/parole officers. *Criminal Justice and Behavior, 19*, 260–285.
Reynolds, M. O. (2000). *Privatizing probation and parole*. Dallas, TX: National Center for Policy Analysis. Retrieved July 31, 2011, from http://www.ncpa.org/pdfs/st233.pdf
Simmons, C., Cochran, J. K., & Blount, W. R. (1997). The effects of job-related stress and job satisfaction on probation officers' inclinations to quit. *American Journal of Criminal Justice, 21*, 213–229.
Sims, B. (2001). Surveying the correctional environment: A review of the literature. *Corrections Management Quarterly, 5*(2), 1–12.
Slate, R. N. (1993). *Stress levels and thoughts of quitting of correctional personnel: Do perceptions of participatory management make a difference?* Unpublished doctoral dissertation, Claremont Graduate School, Claremont, California.
Slate, R. N., Johnson, W. W., & Colbert, S. S. (2007). Police stress: A structural model. *Journal of Police and Criminal Psychology, 22*, 102–112.
Slate, R. N., Johnson, W. W., & Wells, T. (2000). Probation officer stress: Is there an organizational solution? *Federal Probation, 64*(1), 56–60.
Slate, R. N., & Vogel, R. E. (1997). Participative management and correctional personnel: A study of the perceived atmosphere for participation in correctional decision making and its impact on employee stress and thoughts about quitting. *Journal of Criminal Justice, 25*, 397–408.
Slate, R. N., Vogel, R. E., & Johnson W. W. (2001). To quit or not to quit: Perceptions of participation in correctional decision making and the impact of organizational stress. *Corrections Management Quarterly, 5*(2), 68–78.
Slate, R. N., Wells, T., & Johnson, W. W. (2003). Opening the manager's door: State probation officer stress and perceptions of participation in workplace decision-making. *Crime and Delinquency, 49*, 519–541.
Spielberger, C. D., Westberry, L. G., Grier, K. S., & Greenfield, G. (1981). *The police stress survey: Sources of stress in law enforcement*. Tampa, FL: Human Resources Institute.
Stinchcomb, J. B. (2004). Searching for stress in all the wrong places: Combating chronic organizational stressors in policing. *Police Practice and Research, 5*, 259–278.
Storch, J. E., & Panzarella, R. (1996). Police stress: State-trait anxiety in relation to occupational and personal stressors. *Journal of Criminal Justice, 24*, 99–107.
Tabor, R. W. (1987). *A comparison study of occupational stress among juvenile and adult probation officers*. Unpublished doctoral dissertation, Virginia Polytechnical Institute and State University, Blacksburg, Virginia.
Taxman, F. S. (2008). *Supervision of offenders: An untapped frontier for policy reform*. Retrieved July 31, 2011, from http://webb.senate.gov/issuesandlegislation/upload/taxman.pdf
Taxman, F. S., Shepardson, E. S., & Byrne, J. M. (2004). *Tools of the trade: A guide to incorporating science into practice*. Washington, DC: U.S. Department

of Justice, National Institute of Corrections. Retrieved November 23, 2011, from http://static.nicic.gov/Library/020095.pdf

Terry, W. C., III. (1981). Police stress: The empirical evidence. *Journal of Police Science and Administration, 9*, 61–75.

Terry, W. C., III. (1983). Police stress as an individual and administrative problem: Some conceptual and theoretical difficulties. *Journal of Police Science and Administration, 11*, 97–106.

Thomas, R. L. (1988). Stress perception among select federal probation and pretrial services officers and their supervisors. *Federal Probation, 52*(3), 48–58.

Toch, H. (2002). *Stress in policing.* Washington, DC: American Psychological Association.

Violanti, J. M., & Aron, F. (1994). Ranking police officers. *Psychological Reports, 75*, 824–826.

Wells, T., Colbert, S., & Slate, R. N. (2006). Gender matters: Differences in state probation officer stress. *Journal of Contemporary Criminal Justice, 22*, 63–79.

Whisler, P. M. (1994). *A study of stress perception by selected state probation officers.* Unpublished master's thesis, University of South Florida, Tampa, Florida.

Whitehead, J. T. (1981). The management of job stress in probation and parole. *Journal of Probation and Parole, 13*, 29–32.

Whitehead, J. T. (1985). Job burnout in probation and parole: Its extent and intervention implications. *Criminal Justice and Behavior, 12*, 91–110.

Whitehead, J. T. (1986). Job burnout and job satisfaction among probation managers. *Journal of Criminal Justice, 14*, 25–35.

Whitehead, J. T., & Lindquist, C. A. (1985). Job stress and burnout among probation/parole officers: Perceptions and causal factors. *International Journal of Offender Therapy and Comparative Criminology*, 29, 109–119.

Wilson, J. Q., & Petersilia, J. (2011). *Crime and public policy.* New York: Oxford University Press.

Winter, D. (1993). Slot rattling from law enforcement to lawbreaking: A personal construct theory exploration of police stress. *International Journal of Personal Construct Psychology*, 6, 253–267.

Zhao, J. S., He, N., & Lovrich, N. (2002). Predicting five dimensions of police officers stress: Looking more deeply into organizational settings for sources of police stress. *Police Quarterly*, 5, 43–63.

10

A Stressful Profession: The Experience of Attorneys

Krystia Reed and Brian H. Bornstein

Attorneys are an integral part of the U.S. legal system. Although no one is required to use legal counsel, the right to have the assistance of an attorney for criminal defendants is protected by the Sixth Amendment. This right has been interpreted to extend past the trial itself and is protected from the very beginning of the adversary process, such as when a criminal suspect is taken into custody (*Brewer v. Williams*, 1977). The Supreme Court has recognized that in order to protect this right fully, legal counsel must be provided to those who are unable to afford an attorney (see *Johnson v. Zerbst,* 1938, in federal prosecutions, and *Gideon v. Wainright*, 1963, in state prosecutions). Furthermore, law enforcement must inform a criminal suspect of these rights once he or she is taken into custody (*Miranda v. Arizona*, 1966). If a suspect is not informed of these rights once the adversarial process begins, the evidence obtained after that point may not be admissible in court. These protections of the right to an attorney in criminal trials emphasize the importance of providing adequate legal representation to criminal defendants. Often, attorneys in criminal trials are involved in high-stakes cases, which can mean the difference between freedom and imprisonment or life and death. In fact, having adequate legal representation is so important that if a defendant can prove that his or her attorney was not protecting his or her interests, a new trial may be ordered.

While the right to legal representation is protected only in criminal trials, the plethora of attorneys who specialize in civil matters (such as tort law, contract law, tax law, and family law) underline the importance of adequate legal representation in all areas of law. Legal representation in civil matters can be crucial, particularly when the stakes are high (e.g., class actions) or the issue is extremely complex (e.g., products liability, medical negligence). Consequently, any threat to an attorney's ability to represent his or her client can undermine the principles of fairness and justice on which the legal system depends. One such threat comes from attorneys who are too stressed to do their jobs properly.

In 1991, the American Bar Association (ABA) addressed the growing problem of the consequences of stress in the legal system at a conference entitled *At the Breaking Point.* The report produced from the conference identified the growing trend of job dissatisfaction and a decline in physical and mental health within the legal profession (ABA, 1991). The report concluded that the trend was a significant threat to the wellbeing of lawyers and law firms nationwide. The startling rates of depression, substance abuse, and burnout among lawyers, however, do not just affect those attorneys personally, but also threaten the integrity of the entire legal system, as they render attorneys less capable of performing their jobs and protecting their clients' interests adequately. Therefore, it is extremely important to understand the magnitude of the problem and its consequences for legal professionals and the community. This chapter will address the prevalence of distress in the legal system and the factors that might influence distress; it will then discuss the consequences of attorney distress for the legal system and the possible solutions to the problem of attorney distress.

The Prevalence of Stress and Distress in the Legal Profession

The legal community began to identify a problem leading to the decline in job satisfaction for attorneys in the 1980s. Commentators recognized three major underlying issues leading to legal professionals' dissatisfaction with the field: a lack of professionalism within the legal profession, low public opinion of lawyers, and low levels of job satisfaction along with high levels of distress (Daicoff, 2004). In response to these concerns, the ABA Young Lawyers Division began conducting nationwide surveys to investigate satisfaction within the legal profession. Between the first survey in 1984 and a follow-up survey in 1990, there was a 27% increase in ratings of dissatisfaction with the legal system, with 19% of the attorney sample being dissatisfied in 1990 (Elwork, 2007). Moreover, findings indicated that even attorneys who were not dissatisfied with their careers experienced high levels of daily stress due to their jobs.

There is not an agreed-upon definition of *distress* in the literature investigating attorney (dis)satisfaction. Rather, distress is a term that is used to encompass the combined emotions of unhappiness, stress, and dissatisfaction. Therefore, when discussing distress in this chapter, the term is used in a colloquial sense to mirror the literature in the field, as opposed to in a technical clinical sense—though as we discuss, it does have psychopathological ramifications. Since there is no technical definition, when comparing studies measuring attorney distress, it is important to consider that the studies might be investigating different constructs of the concept of distress.

Attorneys' high levels of reported job distress are even more significant when ratings of distress in the attorneys' personal lives are included. Distress in the legal field seems to manifest itself in a variety of ways for attorneys. For example, attorneys experience certain markers of psychological distress, such as depression, general psychological distress, and alcoholism, at a much higher rate than both the general adult population and the general professional population (Benjamin, Darling, & Sales, 1990). Attorneys' personal lives are also affected by distress, and oftentimes lawyers report failing marriages, parenting trouble, and burnout. The high prevalence of personal distress within the attorney population indicates that job distress can manifest itself in several areas in addition to ratings of job dissatisfaction. Consequently, in order fully to understand the prevalence of distress within the legal profession, it is important to understand the prevalence of psychological, physical, and social distress within members of the legal profession.

Psychological Distress

Much of the research on the consequences of stress on legal professionals has focused on the discrepancies between the rates of psychological problems for the attorney population and the national average. Studies have indicated that a large proportion of attorneys are not only dissatisfied with their careers but also suffer from some form of mental illness, such as depression or substance abuse (Benjamin et al., 1990). In fact, reported rates of depression and alcoholism are significantly higher in the attorney population than the national average. Consequently, one of the major concerns for the legal community must be addressing the psychological health problems that many legal professionals face, such as depression.

Depression

Usually when a person experiences a large amount of stress or challenges, he or she may experience a period of sadness or withdrawal. Although periods of sadness (and happiness) are part of the normal cycle of life, when a person experiences sadness for an extended period of time and it is accompanied by other symptoms such as change in appetite, problems sleeping, and loss of interest or pleasure in usual activities, he or she may be diagnosed as clinically depressed (Benjamin et al., 1990).

Attorneys are affected by depression at a rate almost three times as high as the general population (Weiss, 2007). Studies conducted nationwide consistently find that about 18% of attorneys are depressed, while only about 3% to 9% of the general population is depressed (Daicoff, 2004). Moreover, the attorney population seems to be experiencing *more severe* depression than the general population. For instance, 23.4% of Washington State lawyers and 20% of Arizona lawyers were experiencing depression at a rate exceeding two standard deviations above the general population's mean (Benjamin et al., 1990). This result was striking, since statistically only 2.7% of attorneys should score this high above the mean. In addition, 19% of the attorneys were clinically depressed, and most of that 19% were thinking about suicide (Benjamin et al., 1990). Some attorneys are even acting on these suicidal thoughts, as attorneys have been found to have significantly higher suicide rates than other professionals (Gatland, 1977).

While attorneys are suffering from depression at extreme rates, it does not seem to be based solely on the stress of a high-pressured profession. In fact, attorneys seem to be the exception to the typical professional, since professionals in general have been found to suffer from depression at rates *lower* than the general population (Elwork, 2007). In a study of 239 occupations, lawyers were found to be 70% more likely to be depressed than the rest of the populations studied (Elwork, 2007). A 1990 study of nearly 100 occupations found that 10% of attorneys met the criteria for major depressive disorder, a disease that is typically diagnosed in only 3% to 9% of the general population (Eaton, Anthony, Mandel, & Garrison, 1990). After adjusting for demographics, race, and gender, lawyers (as well as secretaries and "other teachers") were disproportionately depressed compared to the other occupations. Consequently, the high rate of depression for attorneys does not seem to be due to the law being a high-stress occupation. These findings indicate that there are stressors specific to the legal system that result in extreme consequences for attorneys.

General Psychological Distress

While much of the research on psychological distress rates for lawyers has focused on depression, attorneys are also suffering from other forms of psychological distress. In 1996, a study of a wide variety of psychological distress symptoms indicated that attorneys reported higher rates of global psychological distress (Beck, Sales, & Benjamin, 1995). Specifically, the study investigated reports of specific symptoms of anxiety, obsessive-compulsiveness, social alienation and isolation, anger, stress, insecurity, paranoia, self-consciousness, marital dissatisfaction, somatization, and depression. Between 15% and 30% of attorneys reported scores two standard deviations above the mean on measures of obsessive-compulsiveness, social alienation and isolation, interpersonal and general anxiety, and depression; statistically, only 2.27% of a population should be scoring that high (Beck et al., 1995). In fact, the results indicated that attorneys suffered from symptoms of all of the studied disorders except somatization at a rate significantly higher than the general population. Therefore, it is probable that a large proportion of the attorney population is not suffering just from depression but from other psychological disorders as well, which indicates that there are even greater psychological consequences for legal professionals.

Substance Abuse

There has been significant attention focused on the prevalence of substance abuse within the legal profession (Benjamin, Sales, & Darling, 1992; Burman, 1997; Daicoff, 2004; Robinson, 2010). Attorneys have been found to abuse alcohol at a much higher rate than the average member of the population, and the percentage of attorneys who abuse alcohol tends to increase with years of practice. Additionally, there has been concern that attorneys abuse drugs such as cocaine. Statistics indicate that legal professionals are not more likely to be addicted to cocaine, but they might experiment with drugs at a higher rate than the general population. Some evidence suggests that these substance abuse problems begin during law school (Burman, 1997; Daicoff, 2004). Consequently, it is important to consider the prevalence of substance abuse in the attorney population as another possible indication of distress.

Alcoholism

One method through which attorneys may display their distress is through alcohol abuse. Alcoholism is not an uncommon disease, and the National Clearinghouse for Alcohol and Drug Information has found that alcoholism affects about 10% of the general adult population (as cited in Benjamin et al., 1992). Attorneys, however, display rates of alcoholism at a significantly higher rate than the general population. Statistics indicate that from the second until the twentieth year of practice, attorneys abuse alcohol at a rate of 18%, which is nearly twice that of the general population (Benjamin et al., 1992). The rate of abuse tends to increase further over time, with 25% of attorneys abusing alcohol after 20 years of practice (Benjamin et al., 1992). An ABA study of attorneys in 1990 found that 13% of attorneys reported that they drank at least six alcoholic beverages daily (as cited in Daicoff, 2004). Consequently, alcoholism is a serious concern for the attorney population and may indicate high levels of underlying distress—either as a reaction to that distress or causing it.

Alcohol abuse seems to begin for legal professionals during law school. Law students tend to cope with stress by abusing alcohol and drugs and socially isolating themselves (Daicoff, 2004). Studies of law students indicate that they use alcohol as a maladaptive form of stress relief (American Association of Law Schools [AALS], 1994). A survey of law students indicated that law students believed the abuse of alcohol on campus was a common and normal part of social activities (Burman, 1997). Additionally, students reported that they often drank more than they intended and even drove drunk (which is a serious concern, particularly for law students who have to report DUIs when applying for the bar). Just as rates of alcoholism progress over years of practice, law students drink more and become increasingly concerned about their alcohol use throughout law school (Daicoff, 2004). In fact, the AALS reported that students depend on alcohol more frequently as law school progresses (AALS, 1994).

High rates of alcohol abuse and alcoholism are particularly alarming for the attorney population because alcoholism can affect job performance. Alcoholism, a chronic and progressive disease characterized by an individual losing control over drinking, can result in both behavioral changes (Benjamin et al., 1990) and cognitive impairment. Indeed, one of the criteria for diagnosing alcoholism—or any form of substance abuse—is that it interferes with one's occupational functioning (American Psychiatric Association, 2000). As with depression, attorneys suffering from alcoholism are unlikely to seek treatment, and their co-workers rarely address or recognize the problem (Robinson, 2010). Consequently, alcoholism is likely to go untreated and can result in serious repercussions for attorneys, including disciplinary action, health complications, and social isolation.

Drug Abuse

Along with concerns regarding alcohol abuse, many people in the legal community have indicated concern that attorneys react to distress through drug abuse (Elwork, 2007). Law students have been found to use drugs in conjunction with alcohol as a method of coping with stress (Elwork, 2007). Although law students were not found to use drugs in general at a higher rate than other graduate-level students, law students reported increased rates of psychedelic drugs, tranquilizers, and barbiturates compared to other graduate students (AALS, 1994). These findings indicate that, while law students may be drawn to different types of drugs than other students their age, they do not abuse drugs at a statistically different rate. Law students did, however, indicate that drug usage increased throughout law school, which may be an indication that they will be more likely to have severe substance abuse problems when they are practicing lawyers.

In a study investigating the prevalence of alcoholism and cocaine use as presumed causes of (or reactions to) attorney distress, researchers found that attorneys did not use cocaine at a significantly higher rate than the general population (Benjamin et al., 1990). In fact, only 1% of the attorney sample suffered from cocaine abuse; this is significantly less than the general population, which has a cocaine abuse rate of around 3%. Although participants did not fulfill the requirements for a clinical diagnosis of cocaine abuse, 26% of the sample had used cocaine at some point in their lives; this is significantly higher than the 12% of the general population that has used cocaine. As cocaine is an illegal drug, it is interesting that such a high rate of people who are charged with upholding the law have broken it by using cocaine. Furthermore, the results may be misleading for any one of several reasons. First, there are not sufficient data to predict whether the participants would become cocaine abusers in the future. Second, due to the self-report format, it is possible that participants were not completely honest in completing the survey. Although researchers assured participants the results would be kept confidential, participants still might not have been honest for fear of punishment for use of an illegal drug if the results became known. Therefore, it is possible that addiction affects more attorneys than this study identified based on clinical standards because people in the sample were reluctant to admit the full extent of their drug use. Even if the statistics are accurate, they still indicate an underlying drug abuse problem, since attorneys reported that they had used an illegal drug at a higher rate than the general population.

Social Distress

Although much of the research involving the consequences of attorney distress focuses on the psychological impact, attorneys also suffer from distress in their social lives. Due to the pressure to clock billable hours (working time that can be billed to a particular client rather than just time spent at the office), many attorneys spend evening and weekend hours at the office (Elwork, 2007). Since lawyers must dedicate so much of their time to work, they often have problems balancing their work and social time. Consequently, lawyers are prone to burnout or emotional exhaustion as a result of spending so many hours at the office. Burnout can lead to attorneys quitting their jobs or even leaving the legal profession altogether. Additionally, time pressures can result in attorneys neglecting their families. Often, attorneys report problems in their marriages and/or difficulties parenting.

Burnout

The high rate of dissatisfaction with the legal profession is reflected in attorney burnout and attrition. Young attorneys report that they are forced to clock many hours and take on much responsibility without sufficient guidance or mentoring (Baker, 1999). Consequently, after 2 years on the job, 25% of associates leave the firm (NALP, 1998). Forty-three percent of associates leave the firm within the first 3 years (NALP, 1998). Statistics indicate that distress is resulting in attorneys leaving one firm for another within the first few years of practice, or even leaving the legal profession completely (Elwork, n.d.).

Attorney burnout is becoming more problematic in the technological era. Law firms are pressing for a "better-faster-cheaper" work model since clients can easily seek alternate legal assistance (Rabiner, 2011). Due to technological advances in communication, such as e-mail, attorneys are almost expected to be on call 24/7. This constant pressure to focus on work is resulting in attorneys burning out more quickly. Burnout can result in attorneys feeling drained and can affect the attorney's ability to interact with his or her clients (Elwork, n.d.).

Family Problems

Lawyers cite the difficulty in striking a balance between their personal and professional lives as a source of professional dissatisfaction (e.g., Daicoff, 2004; Litowitz, 2006; Rhode, 2000; Schiltz, 1999). Since most attorneys are under substantial pressure to clock thousands of billable hours every year, lawyers often spend a majority of their time at work and therefore do not have very much time to spend with their families. Female attorneys may have greater difficulty balancing work and family than male attorneys. In fact, 10% of female attorneys are divorced, while 7% of male attorneys are divorced (Weiss, 2008). Moreover, female attorneys are three times more likely to abstain from marriage than male attorneys (Weiss, 2008). This difference has been attributed to greater work–family conflict for women than men.

Factors Producing Distress in the Legal Profession

Considering legal professionals' high ratings of distress, it is important to understand what factors cause the distress before steps can be taken to resolve the problem. One explanation for high rates of dissatisfaction within the legal profession is that certain types of people are drawn to the legal field, and those types of people are more likely to be affected by distress (Daicoff, 2004). In this case, a certain lawyer personality type or predisposition might be at fault for the discrepancies in the rates of dissatisfaction between attorneys and the general population. While research has supported the concept of a "lawyer" personality that might be partially responsible for distress, it seems that other, more job-specific factors are also influencing attorney distress (Daicoff, 2004).

The process of becoming a lawyer might be another factor influencing attorney distress, particularly because law school is known for being challenging, competitive, and stressful. There has been some support for this hypothesis also, as statistics show that entering law students are not significantly different from the general population in ratings of distress, but rates of depression increase significantly throughout law school (Benjamin, Kaszniak, Sales, & Shanfield, 1986). Within 2 years after graduating from law school, however, the number of persons still depressed has been found to decrease significantly; this explanation therefore would not explain the continued dissatisfaction with the legal profession. Thus, there is probably something about the career itself that influences attorney distress. Generic environmental stressors, such as time pressures, work overload, and competition, in combination with environmental stressors specific to law, such as the adversarial setup of the legal system and ethical dilemmas, are also possible factors influencing attorney dissatisfaction. Although it is important to understand these factors individually, it is also important to recognize that no factor works in isolation. The high rates of distress are most likely a result of persons with certain predispositions that are more susceptible to distress self-selecting law as a career in combination with triggers, such as the stressful process of attending law school and becoming a lawyer, and continued through generic work pressures in combination with law-specific stressors.

When considering the possible factors resulting in the high rates of attorney distress, it is important to keep in mind that attorneys experience distress in different ways. Although attorneys as a whole suffer from higher rates of job dissatisfaction, depression, and alcoholism than the general population, not all attorneys are distressed. Furthermore, lawyers who are suffering from distress are not necessarily experiencing all forms in combination. Although factors influencing ratings of distress might be similar, they do not affect all persons similarly.

Predisposition

One possible factor that might influence the higher ratings of dissatisfaction within the legal profession is that people who select the law as a career have a certain predisposition that makes them more susceptible to distress (Daicoff, 2004). Although it is possible that persons drawn to the legal profession share certain characteristics, very few researchers have systematically studied the "lawyer personality." Moreover, the wide variety of practice options available to persons who study law probably indicates that there is not one shared personality type for lawyers that would explain the increased rates of distress within the attorney population. Research does indicate, however, that there are certain traits that are more prominent in the legal profession. These attributes, including competitiveness, achievement orientation, and materialism, as well as a more detached decision-making style, might partially explain why attorneys are more prone to distress (Daicoff, 2004).

Competitiveness

Competitiveness has been defined as "the desire to win in interpersonal situations" (Houston, Farese, & La Du, 1992, p. 1155). Consistent with the typical stereotype of lawyers, studies suggest that attorneys are more competitive than other populations. For example, attorneys in general have been found to be more competitive than nurses, and female lawyers have been found to be more competitive than female physicians (Williams & McCullers, 1983). Additionally, Schindler (1979) found that female attorneys have higher levels of testosterone, a hormone associated with competitiveness, than female nurses, athletes, and teachers (as cited in Dabbs, Alford, & Fielden, 1998). In general, attorneys seem to have similar levels of testosterone to other professionals, but trial lawyers have significantly elevated rates of testosterone when compared to other attorneys and white-collar workers (Dabbs et al., 1998). These findings indicate that competitiveness might be one trait shared among persons attracted to law and is particularly strong in trial attorneys. Although there is no indication that competitiveness is linked with attorneys' ratings of distress, it is possible that the common trait of competitiveness might be a contributing factor to attorney distress.

Perfectionism and Achievement Orientation

Related to competitiveness, attorneys tend to be perfectionists with a high desire to achieve their goals. Perfectionism is a trait associated with people who need to be in complete control and believe that if their performance is less than perfect, then they have failed (Elwork, 2007). Similarly, the need for achievement is the desire to compete against a high internal or external standard of excellence (Chusmir, 1984). Both perfectionism and desire for achievement are associated with a desire to meet extremely high standards. Both traits can be positive and probably contribute to attorneys having high enough grades to be accepted into law school in the first place. Moreover, high standards can help attorneys be successful in their chosen occupation. Perfectionism and a need for achievement, however, can also foster feelings of distress when attorneys are unable to meet their own extremely high standards. It is highly unlikely that everything will go well all of the time—especially in a domain such as law, which has a high degree of unpredictability (e.g., trial verdicts) and routinely labels parties "winners" and "losers." Like all perfectionists, perfectionist lawyers are therefore likely to be eternally dissatisfied (Elwork, 2007).

Materialism

Another stereotype-consistent trait that lawyers tend to exhibit is materialism. Studies indicate that attorneys tend to be more focused on the economic outcome of decisions rather than noneconomic, more emotional factors (Korobkin & Guthrie, 1997). Specifically, Korobkin and Guthrie found that attorneys focused more on the economic result of an injury settlement than college students serving as mock litigants. The mock litigants, on the other hand, were more likely to consider nonmonetary aspects of the settlement, including apologies and other emotional issues. Although the Korobkin and Guthrie study does indicate that lawyers are driven by monetary motives, the results may be slightly misleading. Attorneys are paid to represent their clients vigorously, but they do not have the same emotional involvement in the case as litigants. A litigant who is involved in a lawsuit in a personal capacity may be more focused on the noneconomic components of a settlement agreement than an attorney. Therefore, the results might not actually demonstrate that lawyers are more materialistic. The study does have interesting implications, however, for the adequacy of legal counsel. If attorneys are more focused on the economic bottom line than other factors that are important to their clients, it is possible that attorneys are not appropriately representing their clients. Attorneys might be more focused on their own economic interest rather than the rule of law, integrity, and helping others; this could reduce the community's perception of attorneys and result in additional distress. Further tension between making the most logical, economically sound decision and balancing the emotional interests of the client might lead to even more distress.

Decision-Making Style

Another characteristic typically associated with attorneys is that lawyers are cold, unemotional, logical, and rational human beings. This stereotype might be due in part to the way that attorneys make decisions (Daicoff, 2004). Specifically, attorneys tend to be more likely to use impersonal reasoning and cost–benefit analyses when making decisions. In fact, in a sample of more than 1,200 attorneys, 77% of lawyers indicated that they made choices based on emotionally detached logic (Richard, 1993). Emotional detachment might particularly influence attorney distress by making them unable to understand the role of emotions in their own or their clients' behavior and by making them unable to manage their emotions in a healthy manner (Elwork, 2007). Furthermore, insensitivity to other people's feelings might result in problems in interpersonal relationships involving clients, co-workers, friends, and family, which might further exacerbate psychological distress and depression.

The Law School Experience

In addition to certain personality traits that might predispose people who self-select the legal profession to distress, the process of becoming an attorney itself could be a factor influencing attorney distress rates. In fact, one study indicated that students entering law school in Arizona experienced depression at similar rates as the general population (between 3% and 9%; Benjamin et al., 1986). By the end of the first year of law school, however, the rate of depression for law students had spiked dramatically, with 32% of the students experiencing depression. By the end of the third year of law school, 40% of law students reported elevated levels of depression. Thus, law students might be suffering from depression at a rate that is many times greater than the general population.

Law School Triggers

Since the Arizona study showed that law students were not significantly different from the general population before entering law school (Benjamin et al., 1986), it is likely that there is something inherent in the legal education process that cultivates depression and distress. One factor that might encourage depression is the characteristics of interactions with other law students. As indicated earlier, attorneys tend to be competitive and less attuned to the emotions of others. A nationwide survey of law students indicated that while entering students perceived their peers as less competitive than they had expected, law students still felt as if law school was extremely competitive (Stevens, 1973). Additionally, law students perceived aggression as a favorable trait (Stevens, 1973), which might indicate that law students are more aggressive than the general population.

In addition to competition for grades, law students compete against one another for honors (e.g., law review and honor society membership), summer clerkships, and jobs upon graduation. The knowledge that law school performance determines one's earnings and professional placement undoubtedly places pressure on law students and could trigger an underlying predisposition to mental illness.

Finally, the vast majority of law students are young adults in their early to mid-20s—an age at which many, if not most, individuals are struggling with major life choices in both their personal and professional lives. Because many students enter law school without a clear sense of why they want to become lawyers or what type of law they intend to practice, they might find themselves asking, "Why am I doing this?" These sorts of conflicts can also contribute to law students' distress (Elwork, 2007).

Deterrents to Treatment

Stress caused by competition and constant interaction with aggressive people in law school is probably exacerbated by the fact that law students are unlikely to seek help for their distress (Rothstein, 2008). The law is a profession that functions on the presumption that attorneys and people upholding the law are of sound character. Stigmas attached to mental illness and substance abuse problems might lead others within the profession to believe that a person suffering from depression or alcoholism is not of proper fitness or character as required to be a licensed attorney (Rothstein, 2008). Although in the past people may have been denied admission to the practice of law due to mental illness or alcoholism, current procedures tend to discourage discrimination based on a mental illness alone; however, misconduct that results from mental illness is not excused (Rothstein, 2008).

Despite the current trend to prohibit discrimination based on the presence of a mental illness, people in the legal community suffering from mental illnesses might still be discouraged from seeking treatment due to the general stigma associated with mental illness (e.g., Hayward & Bright, 1997). Law school applicants, for example, might be unaware that schools seldom deny admission based on mental illness without some connected form of misconduct (Rothstein, 2008). Therefore, rather than seeking treatment, which they may have to report to the school, and risk not being admitted to the bar in the future, students might not obtain the required help. Consequently, it is likely that many students are entering law school with undiagnosed and untreated illnesses. Once in law school, students still might not seek treatment due to fear of not being admitted to the bar in the future. Although law students are typically not expected to report counseling or treatment during law school, due to licensing procedures and questions that candidates must answer before being admitted to the bar, students may be deterred from seeking necessary counseling (Herr, 1997). As a result, not only do law schools provide few if any resources to students suffering from a mental illness, but there are also many deterrents that discourage prospective attorneys from seeking treatment on their own. Given that depression among law students has been found to reach rates as high as 40%, there is likely a large proportion of law students suffering from depression or other distress who are not seeking appropriate treatment (Benjamin et al., 1986).

Even if a student decides to risk seeking treatment despite the possible negative perceptions, it is possible that law students would not be able to get the necessary help. First of all, availability of treatment for law students might be limited. Unlike medical schools, law schools are not required to provide treatment to law students who need counseling (Rothstein, 2008). Even students attending law schools in larger universities that provide counseling services to students are not necessarily aware of the availability of assistance. Second, if a student is able to find treatment, it might be difficult for the student to afford it (Rothstein, 2008). Even services provided by schools are not necessarily free, and it is likely that the student's insurance will not cover the entire cost of treatment. Furthermore, the student might be more inclined to seek treatment off campus to ensure greater confidentiality; however, the cost of those services tends to be even greater and might not be covered at all by student insurance policies. This inability and unwillingness to seek treatment might persist throughout an attorney's career.

Work Pressures

While law school can be a trigger for depression and other forms of distress, it is unlikely that law school is the primary reason for elevated rates of mental distress in the legal profession. First of all, law school lasts only 3 years, and then attorneys are faced with a whole new set of challenges and stressors. Second, although Benjamin et al. (1986) found that 40% of law students were depressed during their third year of law school, 2 years after graduation only 17% of lawyers were still depressed. Although the rate of depression 2 years later was still nearly double the rate of depression in the general population, the fact that the percentage of attorneys who were experiencing depression dropped significantly seems to indicate that the law school experience does not necessarily have a permanent effect on rates of distress in the attorney population. It is likely, therefore, that work pressures interact with other factors to continue the relatively high rate of distress among attorneys past law school.

Law is an extremely stressful profession with many job pressures. These job pressures might be a partial explanation for high levels of distress in the legal system. Certain work pressures are not unique to law and can be found in a variety of professions. Time pressure, work overload, competition, and difficult co-workers/people are stressors that can be found in many working environments (Elwork, 2007). Therefore, it is unlikely that these factors in isolation explain the higher rates of distress within the legal profession specifically. Although attorneys might experience these pressures to a greater degree than other professions, there are also law-specific environmental stressors that can create a more stressful environment. Law-specific stressors include ethical dilemmas, problems balancing the role of advocate for the clients with the role of officer of the court, and the adversary system itself (Elwork, 2007). Although not much is understood about the exact influence of job stressors on attorney dissatisfaction or distress, it is probable that generic job stressors combine with law-specific pressures to perpetuate feelings of distress and dissatisfaction with the legal profession.

Time Pressures and Work Overload

One generic factor that could influence attorneys' stress levels is time pressure at work (i.e., working on tight deadlines) in combination with work overload (i.e., simply having too much work to do at one time; Elwork, 2007). While many professions experience time constraints or work overload, attorneys are probably among the top professions in terms of time pressures. Typically, lawyers working for firms are expected to log at least 1,800 billable hours per year (or 7 billable hours per day if the attorney works 5 days a week for 52 weeks a year; Elwork, 2007). Because billable hours only include working hours that can be billed to a client and not other things attorneys must do during the working day, such as eating, reading, answering e-mails, or recruiting new clients, it is estimated that in order to log 7 billable hours a day, lawyers must be at work for 9 to 12 hours (Elwork, 2007).

In order to meet the required billable hours for the year, often attorneys must stay late and work on weekends or holidays. Consequently, attorneys often complain of not having enough time to spend with their families. This complaint can result in even greater feelings of not having enough time to do what one wants or needs to do. Time pressure can even lead some attorneys to engage in ethically questionable behavior, such as padding hours or double billing (e.g., reviewing documents for one client while traveling on another client's time; see ABA Standing Committee on Ethics and Professional Responsibility, 1979).

Competition

Since the number of lawyers has increased tremendously over the past few decades, many attorneys cite increased competition as a main source of job pressure. In 1950, the ABA found that there were 200,000 practicing lawyers in the United States, or 1 lawyer for every 750 people (Elwork, 2007). By 1990, the number had more than tripled, with 700,000 practicing lawyers. As of 2008, there were over 1,180,000 licensed attorneys in the United States, which was more than 1 lawyer for every 300 people (ABA Market Research Department, 2009). This drastic growth has resulted in increased competition for jobs and an increased feeling of competitiveness even after the candidate was hired. For example, some firms let associates know that not all of them will make partner, many firms have increased the amount of time before one is eligible to become a partner, and two-tier (i.e., nonequity) partnerships have become increasingly popular (see, e.g., Hillman, 2005; Richmond, 2010). Statistics indicate that dissatisfaction is higher within large firms, which suggests that increased competition within the firm can also result in higher rates of dissatisfaction (Daicoff, 1997). Furthermore, with more lawyers available, law firms have increased competition for clients, which could create a more stressful working environment that increases competition within the firm.

In addition to an increase in the number of licensed attorneys, lawyers also report feeling increased competition due to economic downturns (Elwork, 2007). In a struggling economy, it is increasingly difficult for lawyers to make a living, and there is greater competition for available job positions, as many firms cut back on hiring or even lay off attorneys. As a result, attorneys are less satisfied with their jobs and report a decrease in morale and loyalty and greater feelings of insecurity with their position. Therefore, it is probable that competition is a major factor in attorneys' reports of (dis)satisfaction, particularly in light of the current U.S. economic situation.

Area of Practice

Although attorneys in general tend to experience elevated levels of distress, the level of distress seems to depend partially on the area of practice. Certain areas of practice appear to be more stressful than others (Elwork, 2007). Ratings of stress in different areas of practice seem to increase as the workload, the time pressures, and/or the amount of conflict with other attorneys and between opposing parties increase. Litigators, for example, are in an inherently competitive area of law. They regularly interact with other, highly competitive attorneys and argue high-stakes cases for clients who are involved in great conflict. In fact, litigators do report higher levels of stress than nonlitigators (Elwork, 2007), which can be explained by the high levels of conflict in litigation.

In addition to high levels of conflict, excessive workload can help explain why lawyers in certain areas experience more conflict than other attorneys. In general, attorneys in private practice seem to experience higher levels of stress than attorneys who work for the government or private corporations (Elwork, 2007). Public defenders, however, seem to experience higher levels of distress than other attorneys (Lynch, 1997). Public defenders typically have heavy workloads and often must go to trial without adequate preparation while facing fervent prosecutors. High levels of time pressures and conflict might explain the differences in the amount of stress attorneys experience even when they have similar training.

Another factor similar to area of practice that can result in increased levels of distress is type of payment schedule. Some attorneys, especially plaintiffs' attorneys, will take cases on a contingency basis. This means that if the plaintiff wins, the attorney receives a share of the award, usually around one-third; if the plaintiff loses, then the attorney receives nothing in exchange for his or her time and effort—which can be considerable—spent on the case. Although the contingency fee system has been hotly debated by legal ethicists (e.g., Godesky, 2009; Kritzer, 2004), it is nonetheless widespread. For present purposes, it suffices to observe that a system where one's compensation depends on the outcome of the case—no verdict, no rent money—is undoubtedly stressful.

Legal Role Conflicts

In addition to stress caused by particular areas of practice, attorneys can also experience distress caused by confusion regarding their role in the legal system. More specifically, legal role conflict arises when attorneys must balance their role as an advocate for the client with their role as an officer of the court (Elwork, 2007). Often attorneys are forced to advocate a position for their client that may seem to be an unjust result. Attorneys therefore might feel responsible for further harming the opposing party if they receive a favorable outcome, or not fulfilling the responsibility to their client if they receive an unfavorable outcome. Lawyers can also face difficult decisions when they are forced to solve their clients' problems. This pressure can be particularly stressful if the attorney makes a mistake that costs his or her client the case. As a result of the pressures attorneys face both to protect their client and to achieve just results, many attorneys indicate dissatisfaction with their roles in the legal system (Elwork, 2007). Moreover, attorneys might feel as if they are not contributing to society as they had intended when they entered the legal profession.

The adversarial system can even worsen feelings of distress due to legal role conflict. The adversarial system tends to result in parties either "winning" or "losing" without much room for compromise. As such, attorneys are forced to protect the interests of their clients even though it potentially means harming the opposing party. Consequently, the adversarial system tends to foster feelings of hostility, suspiciousness, and cynicism while promoting qualities such as aggressiveness and hostility (Elwork, 2007).

Ethical Dilemmas

Although many professionals face ethical dilemmas, there are certain ethical dilemmas that are unique to the attorney population (see, generally, Bornstein & Miller, 2009, chapter 7). Lawyers are sworn to uphold the law and must follow certain rules of conduct, such as not putting a client on the stand if the attorney knows the client is going to lie. The law, maybe more so than any other profession, is governed by strict moral principles in order to ensure just enforcement of the nation's laws. In order to protect the integrity of the system, however, lawyers are also expected to protect the interests of their clients. Protecting justice and protecting the client are two goals that do not necessarily align. In fact, attorneys often face the ethical dilemma of representing clients who they know have broken the law (e.g., confessed criminals or tortfeasors). Sometimes attorneys even represent clients who are attempting to use the law to achieve questionable ends (e.g., to avoid paying taxes or following environmental regulations), placing the client's interests and ethical behavior at odds. While lawyers may be hesitant to represent these clients, the legal system also depends on fair representation of all parties. Therefore, it is likely that attorneys sometimes feel tension between the principles of law and their own moral standards.

This tension can be particularly acute for religious attorneys, who often find themselves torn between the law of the land and a "higher" law (Bornstein & Miller, 2009). A variety of legal issues can produce conflicts between an attorney's personal religious beliefs and his or her professional obligations: family law (e.g., parental rights, surrogacy, same-sex marriage), privacy rights (e.g., abortion, assisted suicide), bioethics (e.g., end-of-life issues), and criminal law (e.g., capital punishment). For example, a devout (and antiabortion) Catholic lawyer might be appointed by the court to represent a minor seeking a waiver of parental consent for an abortion (Pearce, 2001). Here, as in many other cases, the lawyer's personal morality conflicts with his or her professional responsibility and the client's legal right. Such conflicts are difficult to resolve and are likely a significant source of stress for religious attorneys (Allegretti, 1996; Baker & Floyd, 1998; Bornstein & Miller, 2009; Schutt, 2007). Moreover, they can affect religious judges as well as practicing attorneys (Bornstein & Miller, 2009, chapter 6; Gonzalez, 1996; Greenawalt, 1995; Merz, 2004).

Overall, it almost seems that the entire structure of the legal system cultivates distress, from the basic adversarial process to everyday work pressures. Generic stressors, such as time pressure, work overload, and competition, are exacerbated through factors like billable hour demands and rapidly increasing numbers of attorneys in the profession. Legal-specific stressors combine with general work stressors to result in even greater levels of distress. In particular, concerns regarding ethical dilemmas and ambiguity in regard to the attorney's legal role can promote distress and confusion for legal professionals.

Consequences of Distress in the Legal Profession

In order to understand fully the ramifications of the high levels of distress in the legal profession, it is important to recognize the consequences of such distress. Just as distress manifests itself differently for individual attorneys, the consequences of distress differ as well. Although certain consequences, such as personal consequences for the attorney, may seem obvious, other consequences are not as apparent. In addition to affecting an individual attorney's level of mental and physical wellbeing, as discussed earlier, high levels of distress can have high costs for the attorney's employer and clients. Depression, for example, not only results in emotional and physical consequences for the depressed individual but also can impair one's job performance. When employees are unable to perform their jobs adequately, their co-workers and employers—and in the case of professionals, their clients—often suffer the consequences. Depending on the case, this can have drastic effects on the client and can even undermine the integrity of the entire legal process. While many people are probably affected by attorney distress, the three groups that are influenced the most in the legal community are the attorneys themselves, the law firms for which the attorneys work, and the clients whom the attorneys serve.

Consequences for the Attorney

In addition to the more obvious ramifications covered previously—such as mental illness, substance abuse, job dissatisfaction, and family/relationship problems—attorney distress has been linked to disciplinary actions. Often attorneys who are experiencing distress, especially in the form of depression or alcoholism, cannot complete their tasks. These problems can then result in malpractice suits against the attorney. Estimates indicate that between 27% and 100% of disciplinary cases involve drug or alcohol abuse (Daicoff, 2004). Needless to say, disciplinary action, which in its most extreme forms can include disbarment and referral to the authorities for possible prosecution, is a significant stressor itself. The shame, embarrassment, and financial consequences that ensue will only exacerbate the underlying problem.

Mental illness and drug abuse typically result in a neglect of cases or clients, which can explain a large proportion of disciplinary cases. However, other scholars suggest that inappropriate coping responses to high levels of distress can result in unprofessional behavior and ethical violations (Daicoff, 2004). For example, depression and alcoholism can result in increased rates of social isolation. The social isolation, in turn, could promote unethical behavior either because the attorney does not have social support from others or there is no peer review to keep the attorney in check (Rehnquist, 1988).

Consequences for the Law Firm

Since many of the consequences attorneys face as a result of distress are related to an inability to perform their jobs, it is probably not surprising that law firms also face ramifications from attorney distress. Since distress is linked with a large proportion of malpractice suits, many of the malpractice costs law firms face are probably linked to distress (Ramos, 1994). Distress might also be a factor in suits by afflicted attorneys against the law firm. Mental illness, or any psychological disorder such as alcoholism, anxiety disorder, or major depressive disorder, can constitute a disability under the Americans with Disabilities Act, meaning that in some instances law firms could be liable for failing to accommodate a distressed attorney's condition (Americans with Disabilities Act, 2005). Moreover, attorney distress is associated with higher insurance costs, as stress can cause various physical ailments (Elwork, 2007).

Distress can be a burden on law firms in more ways than increased malpractice and health insurance rates, however. Attorney distress is associated with high rates of absenteeism and turnover (Elwork, 2007). Many dissatisfied attorneys respond by leaving the firm or changing careers altogether (Elwork, n.d.). Absenteeism and turnover can be costly to the employer, who not only has to adjust for the days that the attorney does not show up but also has to invest time and money in training new attorneys to take over the uncompleted tasks and open job positions. In firms with extremely complex cases or long-term clients, the actual costs of turnover can be especially difficult to measure, as even more time has to be devoted to establishing relationships with the clients.

Consequences for the Clients

An attorney's inability to perform his or her job adequately can have extreme consequences for the clients whose interests the attorney is meant to serve and protect. Clients of attorneys who are reprimanded for misconduct are probably the most significantly affected by the attorney's inability to perform his or her job. As symptoms caused by distress likely account for a large proportion of disciplinary actions, a large proportion of clients whose attorneys wronged them in a way that resulted in disciplinary action were probably victims of the attorney's distress.

However, disciplinary actions likely occur only for the most noticeable or extreme mistakes. The fact that an attorney was not disciplined in any particular case does not necessarily mean that the clients were not affected by the attorney's job pressures and high levels of distress. In fact, 40% of attorneys in a survey of more than 600 lawyers indicated that they had made avoidable mistakes due to work pressure (Press, 1999). Although many of those mistakes might never be discovered or have an adverse impact on the case, it is possible that the mistakes (which attorneys recognized that they made) had significant negative effects on the clients. At a minimum, the mistakes would often diminish the attorney's efficiency and cost the client money.

Attorney distress can have a nonmonetary impact on clients as well. For example, attorneys' drive for money and pressure to achieve the greatest economic result could cause attorneys to advise their clients to make decisions that do not take into account other factors, such as emotion, which might be in the best interest of their clients (Korobkin & Guthrie, 1997). Further, the drive to produce billable hours can result in attorneys allotting their time in a manner that is not necessarily the most beneficial to the client. And finally, high levels of attorney distress could result in other social consequences, such as more unpleasant interactions between attorney and client. Less than satisfactory relationships with their attorneys could lead clients to use a different lawyer/firm for future work and to feel less satisfied with the legal process as a whole.

What to Do About Distress in the Legal Profession: Research Needs and Resources

Identifying lawyers suffering from distress is a necessary first step in addressing the problem. The ABA career satisfaction surveys have done a great service in providing national data on the issue, but additional work needs to be done focusing on various forms of mental illness and stress reactions among attorneys, risk/preventative factors, and differences across jurisdictions, types of practice, and so forth. While steps must be taken to reduce distress in the legal system to promote attorneys' wellbeing, it is also critical to understand how those steps affect the other people suffering the consequences of the distress. Given the shame and embarrassment associated with admitting one has a problem—especially among driven, successful professionals—obtaining good data on these questions is likely to be challenging. In addition to the ABA, state and local bar associations, law schools, and individual firms should get involved. Ameliorating attorney distress benefits the attorneys themselves, the profession as a whole, and society at large.

Some resources and coping mechanisms for dealing with attorney distress already exist. Some of these resources operate at the individual level, whereas others are initiatives taken by the firm or legal profession as a whole. These efforts are promising, but it is unclear how widespread they are, and data on their effectiveness is lacking.

Religious Lawyering

The "religious lawyering movement" has arisen as an approach to legal practice that provides guidelines on how career and faith can complement one another (Pearce & Uelmen, 2004, 2005–2006). Religious lawyering explores, in depth, the conflicts that can arise between religious beliefs and values and attorneys' professional obligations. In exploring these conflicts, it encourages religious lawyers to let their faith inform their work, rather than erect a dividing wall between the two domains. For example, Allegretti (1998, 2002) recommends that attorneys form a covenant with their clients. This covenant involves, among other things, valuing clients as persons, collaborating with them on decision making, and pursuing reconciliation rather than "victory."

This sort of approach can also involve raising moral objections to the client's goals or behavior in certain situations, even if it means losing the client's business (Allegretti, 1998, 2002). Of course, such a strategy is easier said than done, especially for lawyers who have few clients or have little say about who their clients are (e.g., junior associates). Nonetheless, it reflects the conviction of religious lawyering proponents that "lawyers need not shed their religious values in order to practice law" (Allegretti, 2002, p. 31). Religion is by no means the only individual resource available to aid distressed attorneys; friends, family, and psychotherapy can help as well. Nonetheless, one of religion's best known features is that it can help people, regardless of their profession, cope with life's difficulties; in that sense it can help lawyers as well. And because of its moral underpinnings, it can be particularly useful at helping attorneys deal with ethical dilemmas peculiar to their occupation.

Despite the promise shown by the religious lawyering movement, we know of no systematic data on the scope of the movement or the consequences—for either lawyers or the profession—of making a concerted effort to integrate religion into legal practice. An empirical examination of religious lawyering would be a fruitful avenue for future research.

Psychotherapy for Lawyers

Another option available to attorneys is psychological treatment. While psychotherapy is an option, it may be difficult for attorneys to seek treatment. Certain disorders are associated with a negative stigma, so seeking treatment could result in a threat to the attorney's professional reputation. In order to remain members of the bar, attorneys must meet certain standards of fitness. Seeking treatment could be taken as an indication that the attorney is not fit to be a member of the legal profession, and mentally ill attorneys might fear disbarment. Without assistance, however, the disorder could impair the attorney's ability to perform his or her job, which is a threat to the integrity of the legal system and can also lead to disbarment. Consequently, attorneys might be deterred from seeking treatment for distress when they most need it.

If an attorney does decide to find treatment for his or her disorder, there are several resources available. The ABA has attempted to help attorneys find assistance by developing programs such as the Commission on Lawyer Assistance Programs (Elwork, 2007). The Commission on Lawyer Assistance Programs publishes materials that are intended to help attorneys recognize the symptoms of psychological illness and to direct attorneys who want to seek treatment. Some state and local bar associations have also developed Lawyer Assistance Programs that can make referrals for lawyers seeking treatment, and some of the programs even provide hotlines for attorneys in need of immediate support.

Just as there are therapists who specialize in treating physicians, police officers, business executives, and members of various other professions, there are therapists who specialize in treating attorneys (a Google search we conducted turned up several). However, we know of no therapeutic organization that focuses on psychotherapy for lawyers, neither the American Psychological Association nor the American Psychiatric Association formally recognizes it as a subdiscipline, and techniques for working with lawyers (or other professionals) are not an explicit part of clinical psychology training programs. This suggests that therapists who specialize in treating attorneys are drawing on their own clinical experience, which may be substantial; nonetheless, they would benefit from training materials and a network of like-minded colleagues.

To be sure, a therapist need not have a particular interest in or experience with attorney clients to treat them effectively. However, to the extent that lawyers face some unique mental health issues—as the foregoing review suggests—specialization would have advantages. By way of analogy, consider that most general attorneys could probably provide competent representation to a client making a wrongful termination claim, but an attorney specializing in employment discrimination law would likely do better. In light of the high incidence of distress and related mental health concerns among lawyers, it behooves the mental health field to pay more attention to attorneys and to explore treatment methods that might be particularly effective with this population. Psychologists could facilitate this process by giving talks at continuing legal education programs to educate lawyers and firms on the dangers of stress, depression, and addiction. These talks could also help to reduce the stigma associated with mental illness and make attorneys aware of relevant resources.

The Comprehensive Law Movement

Although therapy and religion are good and potentially effective methods of coping with distress in the legal system, the prevalence of distress in the legal profession is an indication that it is necessary to focus on the underlying characteristics of the legal system in an attempt to prevent distress from occurring at such a high rate in the first place. Recently, there has been a trend in the legal system to use procedures that benefit all parties involved by encouraging the parties to compromise to resolve their conflict without a judge or jury. This trend has been termed the *comprehensive law movement* (Daicoff, 2004). The comprehensive law movement refers to individual methods of dispute resolution as a collective group. While the methods are distinct, included in the movement are procedures that attempt to resolve conflict in ways that are psychologically optimal for everyone. The techniques aim to promote both substantive and procedural fairness and attempt to preserve a positive relationship between the parties. Because the methods are more humanistic in nature, they can result in better psychological outcomes for everyone involved, including the attorneys. Moreover, particularly in situations in which the parties must continue to interact after the legal dispute is settled, such as divorce and child custody proceedings, these methods can promote better interactions and fewer future lawsuits.

Related to this comprehensive approach, law firms and law schools should be encouraged to become part of the solution to the problem. Stereotypically, law firms, like lawyers, have generally focused on the economic bottom line. Perhaps demonstrating to law firms the costs to the firm as a result of attorney distress could result in law firms taking steps to make the legal environment less conducive to distress. More research must be directed at the costs and benefits of the comprehensive law movement since the movement is still in its theoretical phase.

Alternative Dispute Resolution

Alternative dispute resolution (ADR) is one of the better recognized subdisciplines of the comprehensive law movement. The primary forms of ADR are arbitration and mediation. Alternative dispute resolution is an attempt to resolve conflict while avoiding litigation (Daicoff, 2004). This process was developed in the 1970s to avoid the costs of litigation and speed up the process of resolving disputes. More important for the attorneys, ADR can result in a more harmonious result and less conflict between the parties. Because conflict is one source of distress in the legal system, decreasing conflict through ADR techniques would reduce distress in the legal system.

Mediation is one form of ADR that tends to promote resolution of disputes with minimal conflict (Daicoff, 2004). In evaluative mediation, the mediator evaluates each party's position and informs the parties of their strengths and weaknesses (Daicoff, 2004). An evaluative mediator acts as an authority figure who helps influence the settlement decision by informing the parties what the result would be if the conflict were litigated. During facilitative mediation, on the other hand, the mediator helps the parties come to a resolution in which they all receive what they need (Daicoff, 2004). Facilitative mediation, therefore, does not focus on the parties' rights but on what each party needs and can result in an agreement that does not resemble what the parties would have received through litigation. Because mediation encourages parties to resolve their disputes without the conflict promoted by the adversarial system, mediation and other forms of ADR are means of reducing attorney distress in the legal system.

Preventive Law and Therapeutic Jurisprudence

Another way of reducing conflict in the legal system is preventing litigation and disputes in the first place. Preventive law is an attempt to prevent litigation by getting attorneys involved in their clients' lives before a problem arises. The lawyer and client work together to identify potential legal problems and develop a strategy to promote the client's long-term goals without legal conflict (Daicoff, 2004). Few law schools or lawyers teach or practice preventive law since it requires clients to pay for legal services before any problems arise. Although preventive law can be beneficial to attorneys in theory because it prevents conflict, more research must be done on how preventive law can be implemented and what the economic consequences of it are.

Therapeutic jurisprudence is an interdisciplinary approach to law that focuses on promoting the mental health of the people involved (Daicoff, 2004; see also chapter 2 by Sicafuse & Bornstein, this volume). Therapeutic jurisprudence was originally applied to mental health law but has been expanded to other areas of law (see, e.g., Wexler, 1992; Winick, 1994). It aims to create harmony between individuals and protect the parties' mental health. Although therapeutic jurisprudence attempts to advocate the parties' wellbeing, the goal is still to protect the parties' legal rights. Therefore, therapeutic jurisprudence can be beneficial to attorneys by minimizing conflict and protecting the parties' legal rights. While therapeutic jurisprudence is probably beneficial to the parties involved, including the attorneys, more research must be done on its application and consequences. Additionally, therapeutic jurisprudence, as a general approach to resolving legal disputes, often lacks procedures to be applied practically (Daicoff, 2004).

Due to the strengths and weaknesses of both preventive law and therapeutic jurisprudence on their own, some scholars have advocated integrating preventive law and therapeutic jurisprudence (Daicoff, 2004). This approach would begin by identifying emotional issues or social relationships that could be affected by legal action. The attorney would then be responsible for considering and evaluating the emotional consequences of legal action. Clients should be informed of the potential emotional problems and encouraged to discuss and identify other issues that could result. This combination of techniques is not well understood from a practical stance, and therefore more studies of the techniques and their consequences must be conducted. These procedures can, however, be a way to resolve legal conflicts justly and also preserve the mental health of all parties involved.

Conclusions

Attorneys are important members of the legal system entrusted with protecting the best interests of their clients by following proper legal procedures and arguing cases in a way that promotes their clients' best interests. Many lawyers, however, suffer from distress, which is demonstrated in the above-average rates of depression and substance abuse for lawyers when compared to the general population (Benjamin et al., 1990). Moreover, due to the great work demands, attorneys often report marital/family problems (Schiltz, 1999) and/or job burnout (Elwork, 2007; NALP, 1998). This distress can be extremely costly to the legal system, and therefore steps should be taken to minimize attorney distress.

In order to address attorney distress, more research must be conducted investigating the causes of attorney distress. It is possible that, because lawyers self-select the profession, the people who become attorneys are more prone to distress and have different predispositions than people who choose other professions (Daicoff, 2004; Elwork, 2007). Although certain "attorney characteristics" may exist that influence the rates of distress in the legal field, these characteristics probably interact with certain aspects of the legal system itself. Entering law students are not statistically different from the general population or students entering other high-stress professional paths such as medical school; however, by the end of law school, law students report depression at much higher rates than other populations (Benjamin et al., 1986). Furthermore, attorneys are often challenged with ethical dilemmas (Bornstein & Miller, 2009) and legal role conflict not experienced by other professional populations (Elwork, 2007), which can lead to internal conflict and distress.

Attorney distress can have a significant impact on not only the attorney personally but also the legal system as a whole. Psychological problems, such as depression and substance abuse, account for a large proportion of disciplinary proceedings within the legal field (Daicoff, 2004). The mistakes that merit the proceedings not only threaten the integrity of the legal system but also can harm the client and firm involved. Consequently, it is important for the legal system to recognize that there is a problem and begin to address it. Attorneys should be aware of the symptoms of psychological distress and should be encouraged to seek help, without repercussions, as soon as they determine that there is a problem. More research is also needed to develop methods to prevent such distress in the first place. One possibility that researchers should investigate is the comprehensive law movement, which emphasizes problem solving with a focus on the wellbeing of the parties involved. If different methods associated with the comprehensive law movement are developed beyond the movement's theoretical promise, it is possible that law schools and law firms will be encouraged to promote these more holistic approaches to law, and that attorneys will be able to develop solutions to their clients' problems with minimal stress-inducing conflict. In the end, it is necessary for the legal system to recognize that attorney distress is a significant problem and for attorneys to work with their clients and law firms to develop solutions to the problem.

References

Allegretti, J. G. (1996). *The lawyer's calling: Christian faith and legal practice.* New York, NY: Paulist Press.

Allegretti, J. G. (1998). Lawyers, clients, and covenant: A religious perspective on legal practice and ethics. *Fordham Law Review, 66*, 1101–1129.

Allegretti, J. G. (2002). The role of a lawyer's morals and religion when counseling clients in bioethics. *Fordham Urban Law Journal, 30*, 9–34.

American Association of Law Schools. (1994). Report of the AALS special committee on problems of substance abuse in the law schools. *Journal of Legal Education, 44*(1), 35–80.

American Bar Association. (1991). *At the breaking point: The report of a national conference on the emerging crisis in the quality of lawyers' health and lives, and its impact on law firms and client services.* Chicago, IL: Author.

American Bar Association Market Research Department. (2009). *Lawyer demographics.* Retrieved from http://www.americanbar.org/content/dam/aba/migrated/marketresearch/PublicDocuments/Lawyer_Demographics.authcheckdam.pdf

American Bar Association Standing Committee on Ethics and Professional Responsibility. (1979). Billing for professional fees, disbursements and other expenses. *Formal Opinion 93-379.* Retrieved from http://www.thenalfa.org/files/ABA_Formal_Opinion_93-379.pdf

American Psychiatric Association. (2000). *Diagnostic and statistical manual of mental disorders: DSM-IV-TR.* Washington, DC: Author.

Americans with Disabilities Act. (2005). *A guide to disability rights law.* Washington, DC: U.S. Department of Justice. Retrieved from http://www.ada.gov/cguide.htm

Baker, B. K. (1999). Learning to fish, fishing to learn: Guided participation in the interpersonal ecology of practice. *Clinical Law Review, 6,* 1–84.

Baker, T. E., & Floyd, T. W. (1998). *Can a good Christian be a good lawyer? Homilies, witnesses, and reflections.* Notre Dame, IN: University of Notre Dame Press.

Beck, C. J. A., Sales, B. D., & Benjamin, G. A. H. (1995). Lawyer distress: Alcohol related concerns among a sample of practicing lawyers. *Journal of Psychiatry and Law, 23,* 205–229.

Benjamin, G. A. H., Darling, E. J., & Sales, B. D. (1990). The prevalence of depression, alcohol abuse, and cocaine abuse among United States lawyers. *International Journal of Law and Psychiatry, 13,* 233–246.

Benjamin, G. A. H., Kaszniak, A., Sales, B., & Shanfield, S. B. (1986). The role of legal education in producing psychological distress among law students and lawyers. *American Bar Foundation Research Journal, 11,* 225–252.

Benjamin, G. A. H., Sales, B. D., & Darling, E. J. (1992). Comprehensive lawyer assistance programs: Justification and model. *Law and Psychology Review, 16,* 113–136.

Bornstein, B. H., & Miller, M. K. (2009). *God in the courtroom: Religion's role at trial.* Oxford: Oxford University Press.

Brewer v. Williams, 430 U.S. 387 (1977).

Burman, J. A. (1997). Alcohol abuse and legal education. *Journal of Legal Education, 47,* 39–46.

Chusmir, L. H. (1984). Law and jurisprudence occupations: A look at motivational need patterns. *Commercial Law Journal, 89,* 231–235.

Dabbs, J. M., Alford, E. C., & Fielden, J. A. (1998). Trial lawyers and testosterone: Blue-collar talent in a white-collar world. *Journal of Applied Social Psychology, 84,* 87–88.

Daicoff, S. S. (1997). Asking leopards to change their spots: Should lawyers change? A critique of solutions to problems with professionalism by reference to empirically-derived attorney personality attributes. *Georgetown Journal of Legal Ethics, 11,* 547–596.

Daicoff, S. S. (2004). *Lawyer, know thyself: A psychological analysis of personality strengths and weaknesses.* Washington, DC: American Psychological Association.

Eaton, W. W., Anthony, J. C., Mandel, W., & Garrison, R. (1990). Occupations and the prevalence of major depressive disorder. *Journal of Occupational Medicine, 32,* 1079–1087.

Elwork, A. (2007). *Stress management for lawyers: How to increase personal & professional satisfaction in the law.* North Wales, PA: Vorkell Group.
Elwork, A. (n.d.). *A lawyer's guide to dealing with burnout: Does burnout mean I should leave my job or the law altogether.* Lawyers with Depression. Retrieved from http://www.lawyerswithdepression.com/articles/a-lawyers-guide-to-dealing-with-burnout-does-burnout-mean-i-should-leave-my-job-or-the-law-altogether/
Gatland, L. (1997). Dangerous dedication: Studies suggest long hours, productivity pressures can cause serious health problems and a higher suicide rate for attorneys. *American Bar Association Journal, 83*, 28–30.
Gideon v. Wainright, 372 U.S. 335 (1963).
Godesky, L. (2009). State attorneys general and contingency fee arrangements: An affront to the neutrality doctrine? *Columbia Journal of Law and Social Problems, 42*, 587–627.
Gonzalez, R. A. (1996). Climbing the ladder of success: My spiritual journal. *Texas Tech Law Review, 27*, 1139–1157.
Greenawalt, K. (1995). *Private consciences and public reasons.* New York, NY: Oxford University Press.
Hayward, P., & Bright, J. A. (1997). Stigma and mental illness: A review and critique. *Journal of Mental Health, 6*, 345–354. doi:10.1080/09638239718671
Herr, S. (1997). Questioning the questionnaires: Bar admissions and candidates with disabilities. *Villanova Law Review, 42*, 635–722.
Hillman, R. W. (2005). Law, culture, and the lore of partnership: Of entrepreneurs' accountability, and the evolving status of partners. *Wake Forest Law Review, 40*, 793–825.
Houston, J. M., Farese, D., & La Du, T. J. (1992). Assessing competitiveness: A validation study of the competitiveness index. *Personality and Individual Differences, 13*, 1153–1156.
Johnson v. Zerbst, 304 U.S. 458 (1938).
Korobkin, R., & Guthrie, C. (1997). Psychology, economics, and settlement: A new look at the role of the lawyer. *Texas Law Review, 76*, 77–142.
Kritzer, H. M. (2004). *Risks, reputations, and rewards: Contingency fee legal practice in the United States.* Stanford, CA: Stanford Law & Politics.
Litowitz, D. (2006). *The destruction of young lawyers: Beyond one L.* Akron, OH: University of Akron Press.
Lynch, D. R. (1997). The nature of occupational stress among public defenders. *Justice System Journal, 19*, 17–36.
Merz, M. R. (2004). Conscience of a Catholic judge. *University of Dayton Law Review, 29*, 305–318.
Miranda v. Arizona, 383 U.S. 436 (1966).
NALP. (1998). Keeping the keepers: Strategies for associate retention in times of attrition. *NALP Foundation for Research and Education, 18.*
Pearce, R. G. (2001). Faith and the lawyer's practice. *St. John's Law Review, 75*, 277–281.
Pearce, R. G., & Uelmen, A. J. (2004). Religious lawyering in a liberal democracy: A challenge and an invitation. *Case Western Reserve Law Review, 55*, 127–161.
Pearce, R. G., & Uelmen, A. J. (2005–2006). Religious lawyering's second wave. *Journal of Law and Religion, 21*, 269–281.

Press, A. (1999). The good life: Law firm partners agree. *The American Lawyer.* Retrieved from http://law.com/jsp/tal/PubArticleTAL.jsp?id=900005510963

Rabiner, S. (2011). *Watch out for attorney burnout says New York Bar Association.* Strategist. Retrieved from http://blogs.findlaw.com/strategist/2011/02/watch-out-for-attorney-burnout-says-new-york-bar-assn.html

Ramos, M. R. (1994). Legal malpractice: The profession's dirty little secret. *Vanderbilt Law Review, 47,* 1657–1752.

Rehnquist, W. H. (1988). The state of the legal profession. *Legal Economics, 14,* 44–50.

Rhode, D. L. (2000). *In the interests of justice: Reforming the legal profession.* Oxford: Oxford University Press.

Richard, L. R. (1993). How your personality affects your practice: The lawyer types. *ABA Journal, 79*(7), 74–80.

Richmond, D. R. (2010). The partnership paradigm and law firm non-equity partners. *University of Kansas Law Review, 58,* 507–551.

Robinson, M. (2010). The professional cost of untreated addiction and mental illness in practicing lawyers. *Alabama Lawyer, 71,* 152–154.

Rothstein, L. (2008). Law students and lawyers with mental health and substance abuse problems: Protecting the public and the individual. *University of Pittsburgh Law Review, 69,* 531–566.

Schiltz, P. J. (1999). On being a happy, healthy, and ethical member of an unhappy, unhealthy, and unethical profession. *Vanderbilt Law Review, 52,* 871–951.

Schutt, M. P. (2007). *Redeeming law: Christian calling and the legal profession.* Downers Grove, IL: IVP Academic.

Stevens, R. (1973). Law schools and law students. *Virginia Law Review, 59,* 551–707.

Weiss, D. C. (2007). Lawyer depression comes out of the closet. *ABA Journal.* Retrieved from http://abajournal.com/news/lawyer_depression_comes_out_of_the_closet

Weiss, D. C. (2008). Women lawyers have higher divorce rates, need loving husbands, researcher says. *ABA Journal.* Retrieved from http://www.abajournal.com/weekly/women_lawyers_have_higher_divorce_rates_need_loving_husbands_researcher_say

Wexler, D. B. (1992). Putting mental health into mental health law: Therapeutic jurisprudence. *Law and Human Behavior, 16,* 27–38. doi:10.1007/BF02351047

Williams, S. W., & McCullers, J. C. (1983). Personal factors related to typicalness of career and success in active professional women. *Psychology of Women Quarterly, 7,* 343–357. doi:10.1111/j.1471-6402.1983.tb00849.x

Winick, B. J. (1994). The right to refuse mental health treatment: A therapeutic jurisprudence analysis. *International Journal of Law and Psychiatry, 17,* 99–117. doi:10.1016/0160-2527(94)90039-6

Part IV

LEGAL DECISION MAKERS: JUDGES AND JURORS

11

The Experience of Jurors: Reducing Stress and Enhancing Satisfaction

Monica K. Miller and Brian H. Bornstein

Jurors are an important part of both the criminal and civil court systems. They help uphold justice while protecting the constitutional rights of all those involved in the system. Jurors have no choice in their involvement in the court system—they are called to serve and can be disciplined for failure to comply with a jury summons. Noncompliance is a serious issue in some jurisdictions; for example, Massachusetts developed the Delinquent Juror Prosecution Program, which issued over 24,000 notices to jurors who failed to complete their civic duties between 1996 and 1999 (Office of Jury Commissioner, 2011). In this and other jurisdictions, failure to appear can result in a criminal complaint being filed against the no-show juror; if the juror fails to address the delinquency, he or she can be fined and forced to do community service.

In part because jurors are required to serve, there is some concern about the effects of jury duty (e.g., Miller & Bornstein, 2004). Jurors experience a variety of stressors, ranging from the inconvenience of having to find day-care to the upsetting experience of viewing gruesome crime photos. This wide range of stressors can negatively affect jurors' satisfaction, which could lead jurors to fail to respond to a future summons or to discourage family and friends from serving as jurors. Scholars have measured stress and well-being (e.g., Bornstein, Miller, Nemeth, Page, & Musil, 2005; National Center for State Courts [NCSC], 1998), and some courts have adopted innovations to address juror stress and satisfaction (for reviews, see Chomos et al., 2011; Miller & Bornstein, 2004). For instance, in 2010, the Alaska legislature passed

House Bill 52, which allows judges to offer up to 10 hours of counseling for jurors who experience trials "involving extraordinarily graphic, gruesome, or emotional evidence" (Alaska Legislature, 2011). Other courts are addressing mundane stressors like being unable to check in with work or check e-mail. Courts in Sacramento, California (among others), are offering free Wi-Fi Internet for jurors so they can check e-mail and/or deal with work issues during breaks (Superior Court of California, 2011), and some, like federal courts in the Western District in Washington State, even provide a laptop for jurors (U.S. District Court, Western District of Washington, 2011). Such efforts are intended to improve jurors' experiences.

The purpose of this chapter is to summarize the existing research on juror stress and satisfaction and the innovations that have been implemented or suggested to improve jurors' experiences. It then will identify gaps in existing research and suggest future research and changes in policy/procedure that could further benefit jurors. Such efforts are important to encourage jurors to do their civic duty, which has practical benefits (e.g., more efficient jury selection practices), as well as societal advantages (e.g., greater public trust and civic engagement; see Gastil, Deess, Weiser, & Simmons, 2010).

The Problem of Juror Stress and Dissatisfaction

Jurors can experience many of the same stressors as judges (see, e.g., Flores, Miller, Chamberlain, Richardson, & Bornstein, 2008–2009; Miller & Flores, 2007; for a review of judge stress, see chapter 12 by Chamberlain & Richardson, this volume). For instance, jurors (Robertson, Davies, & Nettleingham, 2009) and judges (Chamberlain & Miller, 2009) might both exhibit symptoms of vicarious trauma, which is a set of distinct stress-related symptoms that arise because a person has empathized with a victim. People who experience the victimization second-hand often experience symptoms similar to the actual victim. Even though judges and jurors likely share some stressors, jurors might experience them to a greater degree than judges. For instance, judges have self-selected to participate in the trial, which might suggest that judges have particular personality traits that make them more prepared to handle the stress that comes with the occupation they have chosen. Further, judges may have developed coping skills after years of experiencing trials. These skills would make it less burdensome for judges compared to jurors, who likely have not developed such skills (this is speculation, however; research is needed to test these ideas). Other stressors jurors experience are likely unique to their situation; for instance, jurors might have to make alternate work arrangements, and they are asked to do tasks (e.g., apply the law and decide the fate of a defendant) that are very novel experiences for which they have received no training.

In general, jurors report being generally satisfied with their experiences as jurors. Nearly all of Bornstein et al.'s (2005) jurors indicated that they felt the jury selection process and the trial were fair (98% and 99%, respectively). They reported feeling well treated by the court staff. Ninety-two percent were proud of what they had accomplished during jury duty, and 57% reported having more positive attitudes toward the justice system after their jury duty compared to how they felt before. In a survey of more than 1,400 jurors in King County, Washington, Gastil et al. (2010) found that over 60% rated their overall experience as "very good" or "excellent." Similarly, Antonio (2006) reported that jurors thought jury duty was "'... quite exciting and really enjoyed it,' 'a learning experience,' and 'very rewarding, educational'" (p. 284), and 82% of jurors found the process to be worthwhile (Young, Cameron, & Tinsley, 1999). In general, jurors have positive perceptions of jury duty, and these perceptions increase after actually serving as a juror (see, generally, Diamond, 1993a; Gastil et al., 2010; Rottman, 1998).

Even though jurors experience positive aspects of jury duty, they also might experience stress or dissatisfaction. Two main studies that have investigated juror stress are those by Bornstein et al. (2005) and the NCSC (1998). The Bornstein et al. study included 159 jurors from a variety of trial types; their survey asked jurors to rate the amount of stress they experienced from 32 potential stressors related to jury duty (e.g., receiving a summons) and to complete two mood assessments. The NCSC researchers surveyed 401 jurors, asking them to rate the amount of stress they experienced due to 50 aspects of jury duty and asking them to answer 155 questions about their experiences with stress, which were taken from or adapted from various clinical assessments. These two studies, along with a plethora of other smaller studies discussed throughout this chapter, indicate that some stressors are relatively minor—for instance, being out of one's routine, having to find alternate daycare, or being bored. Others are major stressors; for instance, some jurors experience symptoms of posttraumatic stress disorder (PTSD) or clinical depression. Bornstein and colleagues used factor analytic techniques to identify seven categories of stressors: disruption of daily life, trial complexity, evidence reaction, decision making, jury duty, jury interactions, and other external sources.

Many jurors experience stress because they have experienced a *disruption in their daily life*; this is Bornstein et al.'s (2005) first and most commonly reported category of stressors in their sample. This category also included stressors such as long days in court, length of deliberations, length of trial, and trial interruptions. This indicates that the length of time their lives are disrupted plays a role in how stressed jurors feel. Jurors in the NCSC study also indicated that trial interruptions led to juror frustration (NCSC, 1998).

Bornstein et al. (2005) found that the second most common category of stressors was *trial complexity*, which included difficulty understanding law and testimony; NCSC jurors agreed that jury instructions can be confusing, and thus stressful (NCSC, 1998). The *timing* of learning about the laws can cause stress, too; about half of Cutler and Hughes's (2001) jurors indicated that having access to the relevant laws before the trial began would have been helpful.

The third category of stressors (Bornstein et al., 2005) was labeled *evidence reactions*. Graphic photos or videos, verbal testimony, feelings for victim/plaintiff, and feelings for the defendant can lead to stress (see also NCSC, 1998). This could be particularly true for death penalty jurors, who often serve on particularly heinous murder trials (Antonio, 2006, 2008; Costanzo & Costanzo, 1994). In contrast, jurors might have a hard time following a trial if they find the evidence to be boring or uninteresting (NCSC, 1998); this could be especially true for jurors who serve on multiple trials during one jury service period (Kassin & Juhnke, 1983).

The fourth category of stressors identified by Bornstein et al. (2005) was related to jurors' *decision making*. These stressors included knowledge of what the verdict could mean and fear of making a mistake (see also Robertson et al., 2009). Bornstein et al., as well as the NCSC (1998) study, found that jurors reported stress due to not being able to discuss the trial with others. Jurors in the NCSC study also reported stress due to their inability to take notes, ask jurors questions, or ask the court for clarification.

Bornstein et al.'s (2005) next category of stressors was called *jury duty*. This category included reporting for jury duty, waiting for assignment to trial, and the jury selection process. Jurors often lack information about jury service (Munsterman, 2004; NCSC, 1998); for instance, jurors might not know where to report, where to park, what they will be asked to do, and if they are qualified to serve. Jurors also report being dissatisfied with the court's poor time management (Cutler & Hughes, 2001; NCSC, 1998), including the length of time it takes to be assigned to a trial. Answering personal questions during jury selection can also be quite stressful for jurors (NCSC, 1998; Seltzer, Venuti, & Lopez, 1991). Judge Gregory Mize conducted one-on-one interviews with prospective jurors and found that many admitted being too fearful or embarrassed to answer questions truthfully during jury selection (Mize, 1999). Some jurors also find the areas where they wait and deliberate to be uncomfortable or unpleasant (NCSC, 1998). As these examples illustrate, many items that could fit under the "jury duty" category can be stressful.

The next category of stressors involved *juror interactions* (Bornstein et al., 2005), which included stressors related to taking the minority position during deliberation, and general disagreements with other jurors (see also NCSC, 1998; Robertson et al., 2009). Jurors' interactions with court staff can also be unpleasant (NCSC, 1998).

Bornstein et al.'s (2005) final (and least stressful) category was called *external sources*; these stressors included jurors' fear of reprisal and publicity resulting from jury duty. Many NCSC jurors also reported fear of being recognized publicly as a juror, fear for safety during or after trial, and being anxious because of media presence (NCSC, 1998). Bornstein and colleagues speculated that external sources were not very stressful in their sample for the simple reason that these sources were rarely present in the trials covered by the study. It stands to reason that they would be among the most stressful aspects of certain trials, such as those involving well-known or notorious defendants or extensive media coverage.

In sum, these studies indicate that jurors experience stress at every stage of the trial process (pretrial, during trial, and posttrial). The variety of stressors range from rather mild stressors such as annoyance at trial delays and uncertainty as to their role as jurors, to more serious stressors such as viewing gruesome photos or fearing for one's safety. It is no surprise, then, that jurors can experience many symptoms related to stress.

Symptoms of Juror Dissatisfaction and Stress

The range of stressors discussed previously can produce a multitude of stress-related reactions. "Stress" is difficult to study because it can be defined in many ways, ranging from mere annoyance to clinically defined disorders such as PTSD and depression. It is also difficult to study because not all jurors experience stress at the same time or in the same way. Some symptoms are experienced during trial; some appear immediately after the trial; and others can develop days, weeks, or even months after trial has ended (Antonio, 2006; Bienen, 1993). Further, stress is not uniform across all trials. Some trials are more stressful than others (Shuman, Hamilton, & Daley, 1994); for example, jurors in murder trials almost certainly experience more stress, on average, than jurors in burglary trials. Jurors on death penalty or highly publicized trials could have an especially difficult time dealing with stress (Antonio, 2006). Finally, stress is difficult to study because not all jurors experience stress similarly. For instance, trial delays might bother some jurors but not others. Jurors who have recently experienced other stressors (e.g., divorce, family loss, illness, job loss) would likely be more susceptible to jury-related stress (Hafemeister, 1993). Women jurors tend to report more, and more extreme, stress symptoms than men (Antonio, 2008; Kaplan & Winget, 1992; Robertson et al., 2009). Indeed, an assumption that women were too delicate for jury service was one reason women historically were ineligible to be jurors, a practice that was legal until the Supreme Court's 1975 decision in *Taylor v. Louisiana* (Vidmar & Hans, 2007). Despite these difficulties associated with studying stress, various studies have revealed a number of symptoms that jurors may experience.

The most common symptoms of juror stress include trouble sleeping, nervousness, and inability to stop thinking about the trial (see Miller & Bornstein, 2004, for review). Jurors can also have fear, loneliness, isolation, and loss of appetite (Antonio, 2008). Jurors in death penalty trials who did not give the death penalty might worry that they did not deliver justice for the victim's family, whereas those who did give the death penalty could struggle with the realization that they had sentenced someone to death (Antonio, 2006). Jury duty can also lead to conflict with significant others or co-workers (Antonio, 2006) and can even lead jurors to resort to drug use to address their stress

(Antonio, 2008). After the verdict, some jurors feel regret that they reached the wrong verdict or have fears for their safety (Antonio, 2006). Additionally, some jurors in traumatic trials experience negative short-term effects, such as bouts of depression, that do not reach the level needed for a diagnosis of PTSD but that are at a level higher than in the general population (e.g., Robertson et al., 2009; Shuman et al., 1994).

In sum, juror stress can manifest itself in a variety of ways. While most jurors in most cases likely experience only mild symptoms (e.g., Bornstein et al., 2005), some can have such serious reactions that they experience significant subjective distress and intend to refuse to serve as jurors in the future (e.g., Antonio, 2006). In order to mitigate such stress and its accompanying symptoms, courts have adopted many innovations designed to improve jurors' experiences.

Methods of Addressing Juror Stress

The American Bar Association (ABA) and the NCSC are two organizations that have taken steps to address juror satisfaction and stress (as we discuss later, some individual states and courts have done so as well). Various courts have adopted a plethora of innovations to address both what we term "mundane" stressors (i.e., ones associated with the inconvenience of jury duty, such as disruption of daily routines, not having Internet access) and more serious, "clinically significant" stressors (e.g., PTSD symptoms). Mundane stressors typically occur for any trial but can be exacerbated or minimized by court practices governing jury duty, as well as by trial-specific factors such as trial duration. Clinically significant stressors occur, with rare exceptions, in only a subset of trials: those with high stakes (e.g., capital cases, class actions), charges especially likely to elicit moral outrage (e.g., child sexual abuse, terrorism), gruesome evidence, or similar unique features. Measures designed to improve juror satisfaction and/or reduce juror stress commonly focus on one or the other class of stressors, though some address both.

Trial Innovations to Address the Mundane Stressors

As noted previously, many of the stressors jurors experience are due to inconveniences and uncertainty about their role and duties. Recognizing this, courts have adopted many innovations intended to reduce these mundane stressors and improve jurors' satisfaction with the trial process. Innovations are available that address every phase of jury duty and include efforts such as jury orientation programs, private questioning during jury selection, rewriting of jury instructions, and guidance during deliberations.

Juror orientation programs can help relieve stress or dissatisfaction that results from uncertainty about what jurors will do during jury duty. Orientation can begin before the potential jurors arrive at the courthouse. Online or mailed paper orientation materials can inform jurors about issues including where to park, what to wear, how much they will be paid, and how to handle employment issues due to missing work. Once potential jurors arrive, orientation can provide information about trial procedures, their responsibilities, the basic law related to the case, and their qualifications to serve. Orientations can also help address concerns about where to get lunch, how to access the Internet, and other similar concerns (for reviews, see Chomos et al., 2011; Najdovski-Terziovski, Ogloff, Clough, & Monteleone, 2008; NCSC, 1998). One study found that jurors who were exposed to an orientation video were more knowledgeable about court procedures, were more confident, and had more positive attitudes than those who did not watch the video (Bradshaw, Ross, Bradshaw, Headrick, & Thomas, 2005). Orientation videos also increase jurors' satisfaction with the jury process (Heuer & Penrod, 1994b).

A second change some courts are making to address juror stress and satisfaction concerns limiting jury service length. Traditionally, a juror was "on call" for weeks or months, not knowing when a trial would start or how many trials he or she would serve on during that period. This uncertainty can cause stress and dissatisfaction for many jurors (Munsterman, Munsterman, Lynch, & Penrod, 1991). Further, jurors who serve on multiple trials face cumulative challenges from the ongoing disruption to their usual routine (e.g., work, school, childcare); they also begin to lose interest and have a difficult time following the procedures (Kassin & Juhnke, 1983). To address these issues, many courts have adopted a "one day/one trial" policy. This system reduces the hardships of being "on call" for an extended amount of time because it requires each juror to report to the courthouse for only one day; the juror either serves on one trial or is dismissed if not selected for a trial on the one day he or she reports. The juror has then completed jury duty.

During jury selection, jurors are sometimes asked to answer personal questions or offer private information in front of strangers (e.g., other jurors, attorneys). Because this is stressful or uncomfortable for some jurors (Hannaford, 2001; NCSC, 1998), some may decide not to respond or to answer dishonestly (Mize, 1999; Seltzer et al., 1991). This is problematic, as such information is necessary to promote a fair trial. For instance, it is important for a court to know whether any potential juror has been a victim of a crime similar to the one the current defendant is accused of; such a juror would likely be partial and thus would be excused. In order to provide comfort to jurors and obtain important information, some courts have adopted the practice of "individualized voir dire," in which judges can take a variety of steps to protect jurors. For instance, they can allow jurors to go into the judge's private chambers to answer questions, or they can allow jurors to write their answers on a piece of paper instead of vocalizing answers out loud (Chomos et al., 2011; Hannaford, 2001).

Once jurors are selected for duty, they will listen to hours—sometimes days or months—of testimony that can often be complex and confusing to the average person. Jurors might experience stress because of comprehension difficulty or simply having to remember all the details from each witness over the course of the trial. In order to assist jurors, some courts allow them to take notes during the trial and to use these notes in deliberations. Note taking can help jurors stay alert and organized (Munsterman, Hannaford-Agor, & Whitehead, 2006) and can promote more efficient deliberations (Horowitz & ForsterLee, 2001). Note taking also promotes juror satisfaction (Horowitz & ForsterLee, 2001; Munsterman et al., 2006) without substantially affecting jurors' verdicts.

Some courts also allow jurors to submit written questions of witnesses; this can help jurors who are confused about scientific terminology, timelines, or other testimony or evidence. Nearly half of the jurors in the Bornstein et al. (2005) study reported experiencing some stress because they could not ask any questions. Heuer and Penrod (1988) found that jurors who were able to ask questions felt that they understood the evidence and testimony better—and were more satisfied with jury duty—than jurors who were not allowed to do so. Despite critics' concerns, the vast majority of research indicates that there are few drawbacks to allowing jurors to ask questions (see Dodge, 2002; Jehle & Miller, 2005; and Mott, 2003, for reviews).

Another stressor jurors experience is related to instruction comprehension. Instructions for jurors are often written in "legalese" and use passive voice, double negatives, multiple phrases, and other complicated grammatical structures. As such, instructions often are very difficult to understand, and jurors' comprehension of instructions is often poor (Bornstein & Hamm, 2012; Lieberman, 2009; Marder, 2006; Reifman, Gusick, & Ellsworth, 1992). Most jurors have only a high school education (Cutler & Hughes, 2001); thus, it is no surprise that being able to read complex instructions does not necessarily lead to better comprehension than only hearing the instructions read aloud, which is the traditional method (Dumas, 2000). In order to reduce stress related to inability to understand instructions, experts have suggested that instructions be rewritten to be better understood by the general population (Charrow, 1987).

A number of empirical studies have shown that revised, simplified instructions result in better comprehension and, in many instances (though not all; see Bornstein & Hamm, 2012), better application of the law (Lieberman, 2009; Lieberman & Sales, 1997). The success of these studies led the American Bar Association to promote revising jury instructions for greater comprehensibility, and several states have recently overhauled their jury instructions to the same end (Marder, 2006). For example, Principle 14 of the American Bar Association's *Principles for Juries and Jury Trials* (2005, pp. 20–21) reads: "The court should instruct the jury in plain and understandable language regarding the applicable law and the conduct of deliberations."

The deliberation process can also be stressful for jurors (Bornstein et al., 2005); for example, there might be conflict among jurors, and they can have difficulty even deciding *how* to deliberate. Jurors might not know how to pick a foreperson, how to begin deliberations, or how to conduct the polling. To alleviate such problems, judges can offer jurors suggestions concerning the deliberation process. One study found that 80% of jurors thought that deliberation instructions helped them (Dann, Hans, & Kaye, 2004). In addition to offering instructions, some jurisdictions have sought to ease jurors' dissatisfaction with deliberations by allowing jurors to deliberate *during* the trial (Dann & Hans, 2004); this allows jurors to ask other jurors about points they did not understand (Diamond, Vidmar, Rose, Ellis, & Murphy, 2003) and ultimately helps them understand the evidence better (Hannaford, Hans, & Munsterman, 2000). Although there is a risk to early deliberation—namely, that it can lead to premature formation of a strong verdict preference, which in turn can bias jurors' interpretation of subsequent evidence—it can ease jurors' dissatisfaction with understanding evidence and can ultimately improve perceptions of jury duty.

There are many other things that courts can do to address juror stress and dissatisfaction. For instance, courts can pay jurors more for their time (Munsterman et al., 1991), allow jurors to decide when they want to serve (NCSC, 1998), provide free Internet access (Superior Court of California, 2011), implement time management techniques during trials (Chomos et al., 2011), provide daycare or reimbursement for daycare (Minnesota Judicial Branch, 2011), and take steps to ensure that the spaces where jurors wait and deliberate are safe, clean, and comfortable (Munsterman et al., 2006). While more extensive lists of jury innovations can be found elsewhere (e.g., Chomos et al., 2011; Munsterman et al., 2006), this list illustrates some major innovations that can affect juror stress and satisfaction.[1]

Innovations to Address Clinically Significant Stressors

In addition to the innovations that have been implemented to address relatively mundane stressors and annoyances, some courts have adopted more specific innovations for jurors who experience more serious stressors, such as witnessing gruesome murder trials (see Miller & Bornstein, 2004, for review). Like the strategies to address mundane stressors, these innovations can come at any point in the jury service process.

Pretrial interventions are proactive interventions that are sometimes called an "inoculation" because they are delivered *before* the jurors experience any stress (Bienen, 1993). They are typically videotaped orientations that are designed to educate jurors about stress they may experience in the upcoming trial and how to cope if they do experience stress. We know of no data about pretrial interventions in terms of how frequently they are used or whether they are effective. During trial—either during jury selection or when potentially upsetting evidence is presented—judges can similarly inoculate

---

[1] Readers interested in a general resource for jury innovations to lessen mundane stressors should see the NCSC's Jur-E Bulletin, an electronic newsletter, available at http://www.ncsc.org/Publications/Newsletters.aspx.

jurors against stress by warning them about and preparing them for it, and by explaining why such evidence is necessary. As with pretrial interventions, there is anecdotal evidence that individual judges do this, but no systematic data on the practice.

The most common interventions for dealing with case-specific, clinically significant stress take place after trial and are commonly referred to as "debriefings." Posttrial professional-led debriefings are similar to debriefings given to victims of crime or natural disasters, police officers, and others who deal with emergency crises (Feldmann & Bell, 1991, 1993). Sometimes called "critical incident debriefings," these interventions are typically group counseling sessions led by a psychologist, psychiatrist, or other professional. The sessions are designed to help jurors recognize stress, get back to normal life, and prepare for any later stress they may experience. The debriefing occurs right after trial with follow-ups as needed. The group setting helps jurors realize other jurors experienced similar stressors. Jurors generally give debriefings positive reviews, saying they were useful and helped with the coping process (Bornstein et al., 2005; Feldmann & Bell, 1991, 1993) and that the support of other jurors was positive (Feldmann & Bell, 1991, 1993; Holt, Slick, & Rayborn, 2003). Thus, professionally led debriefings have subjective benefits.

Posttrial debriefings can also be led by judges (see, e.g., Miller & Bornstein, 2004). Judges often try to reduce or prevent juror stress (NCSC, 1998), and sometimes this includes the judge talking to jurors after the trial, either formally or informally. A majority of judges think that debriefings led by judges or court officials could be effective (NCSC, 1998). Judge-led debriefings avoid the stigma of "counseling," which may be associated with professional-led debriefings, and jurors might feel more comfortable because the judge shared their trial experience (Kelley, 1994). The impact of judge-led debriefings is not well studied; however, Kelley compared jurors who did and did not get a judge-led debriefing and found no difference in stress levels between groups.

Interventions can also be videotaped, and they can be presented to jurors before or after trial. The now defunct Washington Victims and Witness Services utilized a videotape called "Jurors Are Victims Too!" The 15-minute video was a posttrial debriefing that educated jurors about stress, told them that the stress they experienced was normal, and informed them that delayed stressors could arise later (Hafemeister, 1993; Slind-Flor, 1992). Similar videos could be incorporated into a pretrial juror orientation, preparing jurors for potential stressors before they occur. Such innovations avoid the stigma of counseling and help jurors adjust to any stressors they might experience.

The most sophisticated juror stress program that has been developed is called Graduated Jury Stress Management (Nordgren & Thelen, 1999). This posttrial program requires a juror-by-juror analysis to determine which jurors need what degree of intervention. The program consists of five levels of intervention that address various levels of stress. The first level provides all jurors with written materials that describe stress and coping, which may be all that jurors with very minor stress need. The second level is designed for jurors experiencing mild stress. In this level, judges talk with jurors and tell them about stress and coping. This can be done at the same time as normal discharge instructions. The third level is intended for jurors who experience moderate stress. In a procedure called "flexible defusing," a professional talks to jurors about stress and coping for 15 to 20 minutes and determines if follow-ups are necessary. In the fourth level, jury stress debriefings help jurors with severe stress. Debriefings are interventions developed from critical incidence stress debriefings (described earlier). Finally, the most severely stressed jurors (in the fifth level) receive individual therapy from professionals for days or weeks.

As this section has noted, a variety of innovations have been developed or adopted by courts to address jurors' stress and dissatisfaction. Cutler and Hughes (2001) found that jurors were generally supportive of these innovations; however, many of them have not been tested empirically to determine whether they are effective. This gap in research, and other needed knowledge, is the topic of the next section.

Gaps in Current Knowledge of Juror Stress and Needed Research

Despite a growing awareness of the problem of juror stress, we know relatively little about either the extent of the problem or the most effective interventions. This section identifies the most pressing gaps in the existing research, discusses future research that can fill these gaps, and offers suggestions for how courts can determine what innovations would be most helpful for jurors in their jurisdictions.

Whom to Target

The most pressing need is for more systematic data on the prevalence of juror stress. Most studies to date have been case studies of jurors in particularly difficult cases or anecdotal observations by court officials. Such approaches are useful, but they run the risk of overestimating the prevalence of juror stress. Indeed, systematic studies across a broad selection of cases show that the vast majority of jurors experience little if any stress (Bornstein et al., 2005; NCSC, 1998). This is not to trivialize the problem—for certain jurors, and in certain cases, stress is clearly a significant problem—but it does suggest that many across-the-board efforts to minimize stress would be inefficient.

Some measures, especially those dealing with mundane stressors, are likely to benefit most jurors. These measures, such as juror orientation programs, one-day/one-trial systems, or providing jurors with Internet access, also tend to be relatively inexpensive, at least compared to more extensive interventions for clinically significant stress. Thus, in considering how best to deal with juror stress, it is useful to adopt a cost–benefit approach—that is, do the benefits in stress reduction outweigh the costs of implementation?

As most jurors do not experience stress, one critical component is to identify which jurors are at greatest risk (before trial) or are most upset (after trial). Bienen (1993) and Nordgren and Thelen (1999) both suggest that judges can determine which jurors should receive what level of intervention. While a case-by-case analysis is a good idea, it is difficult for judges to determine how stressed each juror is. Judges do not receive mental health training (though perhaps they should) and consequently may be unable to recognize jurors who are most at risk or stressed. Of course, judges could simply ask jurors if they anticipate (beforehand) or experienced (during or afterward) stress from trial, but this approach raises several other problems. First, judges have plenty of other things to focus on, such as seating an impartial jury and conducting a fair trial, leaving them little time to devote to jurors' wellbeing. Second, in the pretrial phase, jurors are likely poor judges of whether or not they will experience stress, especially given how little they can be told about the case beforehand. Third, jurors might deny the emotional impact of the trial. And fourth, they might experience a delayed reaction, days or weeks after the trial ends. Thus, relying on judges to identify juror stress is not a very realistic or effective strategy.

Alternatively, courts could adopt a policy that all jurors in "high stress" trials automatically receive some intervention. The difficulty here is similar to having judges identify at-risk jurors in that court personnel, who are busy doing other things, might not know which factors to look for; moreover, certain stressors, such as lengthy trials and contentious deliberations, often do not become apparent until a trial is well under way. Nonetheless, many stressors are known at the outset, such as the presence of complex or gruesome evidence, high media attention, sequestration, fear-inducing defendants (e.g., terrorists, mobsters), or the sensitive nature of certain charges (e.g., sex crimes, capital murder, child victims). A more rigorous assessment of what kinds of trials, with what kinds of characteristics, are most likely to cause stress should inform decisions about which trials have high stress potential.

In a previous article (Miller & Bornstein, 2004), we recommended the development of an assessment tool to classify jurors as experiencing low, moderate, or high stress. Such a test could be a fairly brief screening questionnaire modeled on existing measures in the psychological literature, such as the Brief Symptom Inventory (DeRogatis & Melisaratos, 1983). Thus, it would not detain jurors long after trial ended, and after being scored, debriefing personnel could follow up with jurors who indicated moderate or high stress levels.

What Jurors Want

While researchers have speculated about which innovations would help reduce stress (especially mundane stressors), and some courts have implemented various innovations to reduce stress, any particular court might have little information on what jurors in their jurisdictions think will reduce their stress. While jurors might not be the best judges of what they need to address their clinical stressors, they are likely to have a good idea of what innovations would address their mundane stressors. Courts could administer surveys asking jurors what factors caused them stress and what innovations might have prevented their stress.

While it is likely that many judges ask jurors about their experiences after trial, fewer likely have conducted formal surveys of their jurors. One exception is the U.S. District Court for the Southern District of Iowa (Sicafuse, Chomos, & Miller, 2011). After the completion of the trial, 284 jurors commented on their experience via open-ended questions. Jurors most often made comments about their perceptions of jury service, the judge, the court staff, and the courts; for instance, jurors had positive impressions of judges and staff who helped them understand the process and generally met their needs during jury service (Sicafuse et al., 2011). Jurors also discussed instructions, often stating that they did not have enough information on the first day of jury service (e.g., where to park, where the restrooms or food was located). Jurors also commented about court accommodations, for instance, expressing their appreciation for receiving lunch or commenting on the courtroom décor. Such findings suggest that courts that attend to jurors' basic comfort could help reduce jurors' stress. Some jurors felt that time management (e.g., long trial delays) or safety issues could have been better addressed, suggesting that courts make policy changes to address such stressors. Importantly, jurors offered many specific suggestions for improvement. Most commonly, they recommended that instructions could be better (including instructions for how to deliberate, instructions on the law and legal terms, and first-day instructions). Many jurors proposed improvements in the accommodations, ranging from waiting area furniture to parking.

In studies such as these, jurors provide valuable information for how that specific court can reduce stress. Courts can survey their jurors, asking what improvements could be made that may or may not be specific to that particular court (e.g., improved orientation materials, décor). More generally, a study asking specifically about a variety of innovations and given to jurors across a variety of jurisdictions would provide much more information for addressing juror stress. Whether courts ask their own jurors what might reduce their stress or read the literature about what jurors in general recommend to reduce stress, such information is an important step in making positive changes. After learning which interventions jurors want, courts have the task of deciding which interventions to use, as discussed next.

Which Interventions to Use

As the foregoing review makes clear, a variety of techniques can be used during all phases of trial. Various organizations, as well as individual courts and judges, have developed these techniques with the best of intentions. Nonetheless, there is a dearth of information on the effectiveness of these methods at reducing juror stress. Moreover, some studies that have assessed effectiveness have shown little benefit. For example, Bornstein et al. (2005) found that a posttrial debriefing did not significantly reduce jurors' stress levels, even though they perceived the debriefing as helpful. They concluded that the absence of stress reduction was due to the relatively low level of initial stress in their sample of cases. It is therefore important to study the actual effects of all stress reduction methods, including those used both prior to and following trial. It is essential for these studies to have control groups (i.e., jurors who do not receive the particular intervention). With few exceptions (e.g., Bornstein et al., 2005), most studies are unable to determine if jurors who received pretrial orientation or posttrial debriefings coped better than those who did not. For example, improvement after a debriefing is not proof that the debriefing was effective, as jurors' mental health might have improved just as much even without the debriefing. It would be particularly useful to test relatively low-cost courtroom procedural interventions for addressing mundane stressors—such as one day/one trial, improving jurors' workspace, and better time management—as these interventions could yield the greatest "bang for the buck" (see discussion of costs/benefits later).

Research on intervention efficacy must also address the issue of timing. Are pretrial interventions more or less effective than posttrial interventions? Should posttrial interventions be conducted immediately after trial or after a delay? This latter question raises both practical and psychological issues. On the practical side, our experience in working with jurors shows that many, if not most, jurors are reluctant to participate in any sort of activity immediately after trial; rather, they are impatient to leave the courthouse and get on with their lives. On the other hand, it can be difficult to convince them to return at a later date to participate in a debriefing session. On the psychological side, jurors might need a while after trial to process their emotions (Holt et al., 2003). Some symptoms, especially those of a PTSD nature, often take time to appear. Yet research also shows that the majority of stress-related symptoms diminish naturally over time (Bornstein et al., 2005). These timing issues therefore need to be explored in future research.

Benefits and Costs

An essential component in any discussion about court innovations designed to address juror stress is a cost–benefit analysis. Weighing the costs and benefits will help courts determine which innovations are likely to provide the biggest impact, while keeping costs low.

Benefits

As Miller (2008, p. 204) observes, "Other than the occasional traffic citation, jury service is one of the primary means by which the average, law-abiding citizen comes into contact with the American judicial system." Jury duty is practically a rite of passage for American adults, affecting up to one-third of citizens at some point in their lives (Gastil et al., 2010). The negative consequences of stress for the afflicted jurors themselves—and the benefits in terms of improved mental health—are obvious.

While some benefits are measurable (e.g., a reduction in scores on clinical stress measures), others are more subjective (e.g., jurors' self-reported reduction in stress after a debriefing). Even if there is no clinical stress reduction, helping jurors feel better could also help them feel better about the entire court process, and thus understanding and reducing mundane stress is important. As such, innovations that provide *subjective* stress reduction—even if they do not reduce clinical stress levels—still hold promise (Bornstein et al., 2005). Similarly, innovations designed to address mundane stressors might only make jurors' lives more convenient—but that, too, is important in shaping jurors' perceptions.

Because of the large number of citizens who go through the process, juror stress has consequences for society as well. If jury service is an unpleasant experience, people will be more likely to refuse to serve as jurors in the future, placing an additional burden on an already "stressed" justice system (Diamond, 1993b); a positive jury experience, on the other hand, fosters greater civic and political engagement (Gastil et al., 2010). Finally, and perhaps more importantly, there are potential consequences to society's interest in pursuing justice. If more citizens avoid jury service, then juries could become less representative of society; and if jurors become too stressed, then they might have trouble doing the job properly (Miller, 2008). Thus, the benefits of understanding juror stress, and lessening it, go well beyond assisting jurors themselves.

Costs

These benefits must be weighed against the costs of various procedures designed to reduce juror stress. Some of these costs are largely financial, while others are less tangible, involving time, effort, and additional personnel. In terms of financial cost, virtually any intervention to reduce stress requires a monetary investment, primarily in the form of personnel, but also in materials. The majority of pretrial innovations to address mundane stressors, such as creating a juror orientation video or improving juror space, involve an up-front cost but are then inexpensive to use (Chomos et al., 2011).

Other techniques, such as individualized, private voir dire or debriefing, would be costly each time they are used. For example, debriefings typically last between one and several hours, and they might include follow-ups days or weeks later (Bienen, 1993; Feldmann & Bell, 1991, 1993). This necessarily requires a substantial time commitment on the part of jurors and any workers involved in the process.

The largest obstacle is likely to be paying the debriefers. As discussed earlier, it is impractical to expect judges to take on this role, except on rare occasions. Paying mental health professionals to conduct the debriefings, or to train judges on how to conduct them, would be expensive. Larger jurisdictions could employ a professional debriefer, which would cost tens, and perhaps hundreds, of thousands of dollars per year. Smaller jurisdictions could hire debriefers on an ad hoc, contractual basis, but the tab could still run to thousands of dollars per trial. Government agencies often pay for interventions (Bienen, 1993), but that is not always practical, especially in tough economic times. Courts would also need to provide space for the debriefings.

There are other risks as well, which are harder to quantify but potentially more serious. Although having a jury of excessively stressed individuals could jeopardize verdicts, so could having a jury that is not stressed enough. One could argue that deciding to send a defendant to prison or make him or her pay millions of dollars *should* be stressful—in the sense of being a difficult decision that jurors really have to struggle with—at least up to a point. If jurors know they will receive a debriefing afterward, it might make it easier to give a sentence of death or be harsher in their verdict (Miller & Bornstein, 2004). Although this possibility seems to us unlikely, it is plausible and needs to be tested empirically.

Finally, debriefing—especially when led by the judge—raises ethical concerns. A judge-led debriefing could reveal juror misconduct, leading the judge to feel he or she needs to declare a mistrial. Judges are not required to investigate juror misconduct, but they might feel they need to do so (Kelley, 1994; Miller & Bornstein, 2004). Also, if there are postverdict proceedings (e.g., sentencing, retrial) in the same cause of action, judges might learn things during debriefing that would make it unethical for them to hear these later actions. These concerns are less problematic for professional-led debriefings, but even then, the debriefers might learn of juror misconduct, placing them in a difficult legal and ethical position.

On balance, then, the costs of reducing juror stress are substantial. We expect that the benefits of many, if not most, interventions would outweigh those costs, but without more data on the issue, it is impossible to say for sure.

Disseminating Knowledge

It is important that researchers address the gaps in research identified earlier in this chapter; it is also important to ensure that the information is accessible to courts that seek it. The NCSC (1998) reported that 97% of judges believed the court system has a responsibility to protect jurors from stress. Thus, many judges care about juror stress, yet many are likely uninformed as to their options. The NCSC, State Justice Institute, and American Bar Association are all charged with disseminating information to courts. Information about juror stress and stress innovations can be disseminated through judicial management programs for court personnel, judicial continuing education programs, and judicial studies programs like that at the National Judicial College in Reno, Nevada. Researchers can also publish articles in journals directed toward judges, such as *Judicature*, *The Judges' Journal*, *Court Review*, and law reviews. Researchers studying juror stress can also present information at national and state bar association meetings. Discussions among these groups must continue so that courts can access information about how to address juror stress and satisfaction effectively.

Dissemination should not be confined within the United States. While this chapter focuses on the U.S. jury system, the concern is not unique to the United States, as several countries have recently adopted or expanded jury trials (e.g., Russia, Japan, and Korea; see, e.g., Lee, 2009; Vidmar, 2000). Consequently, many countries are taking steps to study and address juror stress and dissatisfaction. For instance, Australian researchers prepared a report for the Criminology Research Council that reported on community perceptions of jury duty and jurors' experiences. They make recommendations for improving the court system, taking jurors' experiences into account (Goodman-Delahunty et al., 2008). Studies in England (Robertson et al., 2009) and New Zealand (Young et al., 1999) confirm that a minority of jurors experience stress, although it mostly falls below clinical levels. Similarly, courts in South Korea are studying jurors' reactions to jury duty. This is particularly interesting because the country has only had jury trials since 2008 (Lee, 2009). Thus, juror stress and dissatisfaction are not problems unique to the U.S. court system. Sharing knowledge with other courts around the world can help address stress in jurors worldwide. Creating collaborations and relationships that will facilitate this knowledge sharing is thus essential.

Conclusion

Juror stress has long been a concern in the legal system. As is being recognized worldwide, jurors experience both mundane and clinically significant stressors, which can be addressed with a variety of innovations. While some are quite costly, many are inexpensive and easily adopted. Although courts and other policymakers (e.g., legislatures) must conduct a cost–benefit analysis to determine which innovations to adopt, it is virtually certain that at least some innovations are worthwhile endeavors and have promise to reduce stress. While more research is clearly needed, it is still important that what is known is properly disseminated to courts. Additionally, courts can do their own research to determine what can be done in their own courts to make jurors' experiences more comfortable and rewarding. Such steps are essential in protecting the wellbeing of jurors who are performing their civic duty. Reducing juror stress can promote proper decision making and verdicts and can encourage jurors (and their families and friends) to serve in the future. As such, innovations for reducing juror stress can help protect the integrity of the legal system.

References

Alaska Legislature. (2011) House Bill No. 52. Retrieved from http://www.legis.state.ak.us/basis/get_bill_text.asp?hsid=HB0052A&session=26

American Bar Association. (2005). *Principles for juries and jury trials.* Retrieved from http://www.abanet.org/juryprojectstandards/principles.pdf.

Antonio, M. E. (2006). "I didn't know it'd be so hard": Jurors' emotional reactions to serving on a capital trial. *Judicature, 89,* 282–288.

Antonio, M. E. (2008). Stress and the capital jury: How male and female jurors react to serving on a murder trial. *Justice System Journal, 29,* 396–407.

Bienen, L. B. (1993). Helping jurors out: Post-verdict debriefing for jurors in emotionally disturbing trials. *Indiana Law Journal, 68,* 1333–1355.

Bornstein, B. H., & Hamm, J. A. (2012). Jury instructions on witness identification. *Court Review, 48,* 48–53.

Bornstein, B. H., Miller, M. K., Nemeth, R. J., Page, G. L., & Musil, S. M. (2005). Juror reactions to jury duty: Perceptions of the system and potential stressors. *Behavioral Sciences and the Law, 23,* 321–346.

Bradshaw, G. S., Ross, D. F., Bradshaw, E. E., Headrick, B., & Thomas, W. N., III (2005). Fostering juror comfort: Effects of an orientation videotape. *Law and Human Behavior, 29,* 457–467.

Chamberlain, J., & Miller, M. K. (2009). Evidence of secondary traumatic stress, safety concerns, and burnout among judges. *Journal of the American Academy of Psychiatry and the Law, 37,* 214–224.

Charrow, V. (1987). Some guidelines for clear legal writing. *University of Bridgeport Law Review, 8,* 405–408.

Chomos, J., Miller, M. K., Sicafuse, L., Richardson, J. T., Peoples, C. D., & Bremer, C. F. (2011). Increasing juror satisfaction: A call to action for judges and researchers. *Drake Law Review, 59,* 707–731.

Costanzo, S., & Costanzo, M. (1994). Life or death decisions: An analysis of capital jury decision making under the special issues sentencing framework. *Law and Human Behavior, 18,* 151–170.

Cutler, B., & Hughes, D. (2001). Judging jury service: Results of the North Carolina Administrative Office of the Courts juror survey. *Behavioral Sciences and the Law, 19,* 305–320.

Dann, B. M., & Hans, V. P. (2004). Recent evaluative work on jury trial innovations. *Court Review, 41,* 12–19.

Dann, B. M., Hans, V. P., & Kaye, D. H. (2004). *Testing the effects of selected jury trial innovations on juror comprehension of contested mtDNA evidence.* Retrieved from http://ncsconline.org/d_research/cjs/pdf/NIJ_Draft_Final_Technical_Report_Aug_4_2004.pdf

DeRogatis, L., & Melisaratos, N. (1983). The Brief Symptom Inventory: An introductory report. *Psychological Medicine, 13,* 595–605.

Diamond, S. S. (1993a). Attitude change following jury duty. *Justice System Journal, 2,* 246–257.

Diamond, S. S. (1993b). What jurors think: Expectations and reactions of citizens who serve as jurors. In R. E. Litan (Ed.), *Verdict: Assessing the civil jury system* (pp. 282–305). Washington, DC: Brookings Institution.

Diamond, S. S., Vidmar, N., Rose, M., Ellis, L., & Murphy, B. (2003). Juror discussion during civil trials: Studying an Arizona innovation. *Arizona Law Review, 45,* 1–81.

Dodge, M. (2002). *Should jurors ask questions in criminal cases? A report submitted to the Colorado Supreme Court's Jury System Committee.* Retrieved from http://www.courts.state.co.us/userfiles/File/Court_Probation/

Supreme_Court/Committees/Jury_System_Standing_Committee/dodgereport.pdf
Dumas, B. K. (2000). Communicating with juries: Jury trials: Lay jurors, pattern jury instructions, and comprehension issues. *Tennessee Law Review, 67*, 701–742.
Feldmann, T. B., & Bell, R. A. (1991). Crisis debriefing of a jury after a murder trial. *Hospital and Community Psychiatry, 42*, 79–81.
Feldmann, T. B., & Bell, R. A. (1993). Juror stress: Identification and intervention. *Bulletin for the American Academy of Psychiatry and Law, 21*, 409–417.
Flores, D. M., Miller, M. K., Chamberlain, J., Richardson, J. T., & Bornstein, B. H. (2008–2009). Judges' perspectives on stress and safety in the courtroom: An exploratory study. *Court Review, 45*, 76–89.
Gastil, J., Deess, E. P., Weiser, P. J., & Simmons, C. (2010). *The jury and democracy: How jury deliberation promotes civic engagement and political participation*. Oxford: Oxford University Press.
Goodman-Delahunty, J., Brewer, N., Clough, J., Horan, J., Ogoloff, J. R. P., Tait, D., et al. (2008). *Practices, policies and procedures that influence juror satisfaction in Australia. Report to the Criminology Research Council.* Canberra, Australia: Australian Institute of Criminology.
Hafemeister, T. L. (1993). Juror stress. *Violence and Victims, 8*, 177–186.
Hannaford, P. (2001). *Making the case for juror privacy: A new framework for court policies and procedures.* National Center for State Courts. Retrieved from http://contentdm.ncsconline.org/cgi-bin/showfile.exe?CISOROOT=/juries&CISOPTR=31
Hannaford, P. L., Hans, V. P., & Munsterman, G. T. (2000). Permitting jury discussions during trial: Impact of the Arizona reform. *Law and Human Behavior, 24*, 359–382.
Heuer, L., & Penrod, S. D. (1988). Increasing jurors' participation in trials: A field experiment with jury notetaking and question asking. *Law and Human Behavior, 12*, 231–262.
Heuer, L., & Penrod, S. D. (1994a). Juror notetaking and question asking during trials: A national field experiment. *Law and Human Behavior, 18*, 121–150.
Heuer, L., & Penrod, S. D. (1994b). Trial complexity: A field investigation of its meaning and its effects. *Law and Human Behavior, 18*, 29–51.
Holt, R., Slick, J., & Rayborn, A. (2003). Jury debriefing in Yamhill County. *Oregon State Bar Bulletin, 63*, 17–25.
Horowitz, I. A., & ForsterLee, L. (2001). The effects of note-taking and trial transcript access on mock jury decisions in a complex civil trial. *Law and Human Behavior, 25*, 373–391.
Jehle, A., & Miller, M. K. (2005). Controversy in the courtroom: Implications of allowing jurors to question witnesses. *William Mitchell Law Review, 32*, 27–57.
Kaplan, S. M., & Winget, C. (1992). The occupational hazards of jury duty. *Bulletin of the American Academy of Psychiatry and the Law, 20*, 325–333.
Kassin, S. M., & Juhnke, R. (1983). Juror experience and decision making. *Journal of Personality and Social Psychology, 44*, 1182–1191.
Kelley, J. E. (1994). Addressing juror stress: A trial judge's perspective. *Drake Law Review, 43*, 97–125.
Lee, J. (2009). Getting citizens involved: Civil participation in judicial decision-making in Korea. *Eastern Asia Law Review, 4*, 177.

Lieberman, J. D. (2009). The psychology of the jury instruction process. In J. D. Lieberman & D. A. Krauss (Eds.), *Jury psychology: Social aspects of trial process*. Burlington, VT: Ashgate Publishing.

Lieberman, J. D., & Sales, B. D. (1997). What social science teaches us about the jury instruction process. *Psychology, Public Policy, and Law, 3*, 589–644.

Marder, N. S. (2006). Bringing jury instructions into the twenty-first century. *Notre Dame Law Review, 81*, 449.

Miller, L. (2008). Juror stress: Symptoms, syndromes, and solutions. *International Journal of Emergency Mental Health, 10*, 203–218.

Miller, M. K., & Bornstein, B. H. (2004). Juror stress: Causes and interventions. *Thurgood Marshall Law Review, 30*, 237–269.

Miller, M. K., & Flores, D. (2007). Addressing the problem of courtroom stress. *Judicature, 91*, 60–69.

Minnesota Judicial Branch. (2011). *Reimbursement for daycare*. Retrieved from http://www.mncourts.gov/district/4/?page=755

Mize, G. A. (1999). On better jury selection: Spotting UFO jurors before they enter the jury room. *Court Review, 36*, 10–13.

Mott, N. L. (2003). To ask or not to ask, that is the question. *Chicago-Kent Law Review, 78*, 1099–1125.

Munsterman, G. T. (2004). What can we say in juror orientations? *Court Manager, 19*, 40.

Munsterman, G. T., Hannaford-Agor, P. L., & Whitehead, G. M. (2006). *Jury trial innovations* (2nd ed.). Williamsburg, VA: National Center for State Courts.

Munsterman, J. T., Munsterman, G. T., Lynch, B., & Penrod, S. D. (1991). *The relationship of juror fees and terms of service to jury system performance*. Williamsburg, VA: National Center for State Courts.

National Center for State Courts (NCSC). (1998). *Through the eyes of the juror: A manual for addressing juror stress*. Williamsburg, VA: Author. Retrieved from http://www.ncsconline.org/WC/Publications/Res_Juries_JurorStressPub.pdf

Najdovski-Terziovski, E., Ogloff, J., Clough, J., & Monteleone, R. (2008). What are we doing here? An analysis of juror orientation programs. *Judicature, 92*, 70–77.

Nordgren, J. C., & Thelen, M. W. (1999). Helping jurors manage stress: A multilevel approach. *Judicature, 82*, 256–263.

Office of Jury Commissioner. (2011). *Failure to appear for jury service*. Retrieved from http://www.mass.gov/courts/jury/failure.htm

Reifman, A., Gusick, S. M., & Ellsworth, P. C. (1992). Real jurors' understanding of the law in real cases. *Law and Human Behavior, 16*, 539–554.

Robertson, N., Davies, G., & Nettleingham, A. (2009). Vicarious traumatisation as a consequence of jury service. *Howard Journal, 48*, 1–12.

Rottman, D. B. (1998). On public trust and confidence: Does experience with courts promote or diminish it? *Court Review, 35*, 14–22.

Seltzer, R., Venuti, M. A., & Lopez, G. M. (1991). Juror honesty during the voir dire. *Criminal Justice, 19*, 451–462.

Shuman, D. W., Hamilton, J. A., & Daley, C. E. (1994). The health effects of jury service. *Law and Psychology Review, 18*, 267–307.

Sicafuse, L. L., Chomos, J., & Miller, M. K. (2011). *Report on federal jurors' perceptions of jury duty*. Research report for the Southern District of Iowa.

Slind-Flor, V. (1992). Countries begin to help jurors cope afterward. *National Law Journal, 14*, 3–4.

Superior Court of California. (2011). *Internet use policy.* Retrieved from http://www.saccourt.ca.gov/jury/docs/high-speed-wireless.pdf

U.S. District Court Western District of Washington. (2011). *Jury frequently asked questions.* Retrieved from http://www.wawd.uscourts.gov/juryservice/FAQ-Jury.htm#FAQh

Vidmar, N. (2000). *World jury systems.* New York, NY: Oxford University Press.

Vidmar, N., & Hans, V. (2007). *American juries: The verdict.* Amherst, NY: Prometheus Books.

Young, W., Cameron, C., & Tinsley, Y. (1999) *Juries in criminal trials, part two: A summary of research findings* (Preliminary Paper 37(2)). Wellington, New Zealand: New Zealand Law Commission.

12

Judicial Stress: A Topic in Need of Research

Jared Chamberlain and James T. Richardson

Violence against judges and their families has gained significant media attention in recent years. In 2005, the husband and mother of U.S. District Judge Joan Lefkow were murdered in a Chicago suburb (Anti-Defamation League, 2005). In the same year, a shooting spree left three people dead inside an Atlanta courtroom; among the dead was Judge Rowland W. Barnes (Brusk, Sosa, & Kaye, 2005). More recently, Darren Mack shot and wounded a family court judge in a Nevada courthouse (Associated Press, 2006), and James Ray Palmer opened fire on court workers in an Arkansas courthouse (CNN Wire Staff, 2011). In each of these cases, retribution for the judges' decisions was identified as the motive for violence. Although atypical, these incidents highlight the fact that judges make impactful decisions that could elicit aggression from those affected. The availability heuristic suggests that individuals tend to overestimate the likelihood of an event when it is particularly salient (see Tversky & Kahneman, 1973). Therefore, media attention focused on violence against judges is likely to augment such a possibility among judges and nonjudges alike. In short, these recent acts of violence against judges and their families, although rare, have likely created a tangible source of stress for many judges.

In addition to the threat of violence, judges often deal with long work hours, substantial workloads, traumatic cases, and decision-making pressures (see Chamberlain & Miller, 2008). Judges also might experience violence and trauma vicariously, and these experiences might prove stressful. For instance, family court judges are regularly exposed to child abuse and domestic violence (see Miller & Richardson, 2006). Similar to other professionals (e.g., doctors, lawyers, therapists, and emergency workers), judges might experience stress and burnout from a strenuous work schedule (see Zimmerman, 2006). Judges might also experience decision-making stress due to the direct (on themselves) and indirect (on future decisions) impact that judicial decisions can have. In the often contentious environment of the courtroom, judges might feel further pressure to make less inflammatory decisions as a way to avoid the possibility of violent retaliation. In short, judges face a unique array of occupational stressors that can dampen both professional performance and personal happiness (see Chamberlain & Miller, 2009; Miller & Flores, 2007; Miller & Richardson, 2006).

This chapter will explore existing research on judge stress, which suggests that judges experience stress from three broad sources—safety concerns, secondary traumatic stress (STS), and occupational burnout—and provides a basis and need for future research. Gaps in the literature will then be delineated to identify some specific areas of focus for future researchers. Interventions designed to prevent and/or assuage judge stress will also be outlined. Some jurisdictions have implemented policies and procedures to protect judges from stress in response to acts of violence; however, these locations appear to be in the minority, as most have not explicitly addressed the negative outcomes of a stressed judiciary. Ideas for future research will then be proposed to fill specific gaps in the literature. Finally, recommendations for policy and practice will be provided, based on logic, anecdotes, and research findings. The dearth of recommendations based on empirical findings underscores the need for further research on the topic.

Existing Research

Research investigating sources of judicial stress has become more prevalent in recent years. Chamberlain and Miller (2009) identify three sources of stress that have emerged from this area of research: safety concerns, STS, and occupational burnout. Empirical evidence of each of these sources of judicial stress will be outlined in this section.

Safety Concerns

Limited empirical evidence suggests that judges do experience stress from the threat of violence, in spite of the low base rate for such occurrences (see Fautsko, Berson, & Swensen, 2012, for statistics). A survey of 1,029 state judges in Pennsylvania revealed that judges are subject to threats of violence (Harris, Kirschner, Rozek, & Weiner, 2001). Fifty-two percent of judges reported at least one threatening incident; these incidents were lumped into four general categories: inappropriate communication (43% reported this threat), threatening communication (23% reported this threat), inappropriate approach (26% reported this threat), and physical assault (1% reported this threat). Of the judges who experienced a threat, 70% reported that the threats occurred inside the courthouse, while 44% reported that the threats occurred outside the courthouse. Follow-up interviews revealed that nearly all of the judges were fearful of violent attacks, as many expressed anxieties about the potential for violence and the lack of courtroom protection (Harris et al., 2001). In addition, all of the judges interviewed believed that their current courtroom protection was not sufficient to prevent future attacks (Harris et al., 2001).

In a qualitative investigation of judges' occupational experiences, Chamberlain and Miller (2009) revealed that judges were concerned about their personal safety, as well as the safety of their family, and some judges implied that these concerns might impact their decision-making abilities. A nationwide survey of judges revealed that judges were concerned for personal and family safety, and these safety concerns were found to be correlated with reported stress (Flores, Miller, Chamberlain, Richardson, & Bornstein, 2008–2009). The three studies investigating safety concerns among judges suggest that threats of violence create a very real stressor for members of the judiciary. A greater amount of empirical attention has been devoted to other sources of judge stress, which will be discussed in the next sections.

Secondary Traumatic Stress

Judges, especially those in family and criminal courts, are often exposed to others' trauma (e.g., stories of violence). Indeed, some high-profile cases highlight the presence of traumatic material that judges experience. For instance, the recent trial of Casey Anthony, a mother accused of killing her child, contained material that was traumatic for the family involved, as well as for other trial participants and observers (Hightower, 2011). Theories of STS indicate that judges' exposure to these troubling situations can lead to secondary trauma for many of the judges who try these cases, to the extent that judges feel empathy and compassion for those involved.

Secondary traumatic stress generally refers to stress incurred from helping another person through trauma (Salston & Figley, 2003). There are two slightly different perspectives of STS (vicarious traumatization and compassion fatigue), both of which suggest that judges are susceptible to secondary stress. From the perspective of constructivist self-development theory (CSDT; see McCann & Pearlman, 1990a, 1990b, for a description), vicarious traumatization (VT) occurs when one is indirectly exposed to the trauma of others. Constructivist self-development theory asserts, and research (Jaffe, Crooks, Dunford-Jackson, & Town, 2003; Pearlman & Mac Ian, 1995) supports, that transformations in self-concept and psychological development can occur in trauma workers as a direct result of *empathic engagement*. Vicarious traumatization can lead to changes in self-identity, spirituality, and psychological needs and can also disrupt an individual's sense of safety, trust, and control (Rasmussen, 2005).

Compassion fatigue (CF) was a concept developed for nurses in response to the significant trauma (of others) that they experienced (Joinson, 1992). Compassion fatigue is distinct from VT in that it focuses on how a compassionate connection to another individual can lead to *action* (not simply emotion) aimed at relieving pain and suffering (Koerner, 1995). Judges who are particularly compassionate toward courtroom actors are the most likely to help (or feel like they should help) alleviate trauma, and this could lead to poor or biased decisions. Compassion fatigue can also have direct and negative consequences for members of the judiciary. Cerney (1995) found that caregivers who experienced CF were susceptible to recurring thoughts and images of trauma, and Figley (1995) suggests that CF can lead to irritability, avoidance behaviors, and occupational indifference. Thus, the occurrence of CF has potentially severe implications for the personal and professional wellbeing of judges and, more generally, the integrity of judicial decision making.

Much of the research within the area of STS (e.g., Everly, Boyle, & Lating, 1999; Ortlepp & Friedman, 2002; Trippany, White Kress, & Wilcoxon, 2004) has focused on populations of professionals who consistently deal with trauma, such as emergency workers and therapists (see Osofsky, Putnam, & Lederman, 2008). The possibility of STS in the judiciary has gained limited empirical attention, in spite of the fact that judges are often exposed to the stress of others. Vicarious traumatization was examined in a survey of 105 judges (Jaffe et al., 2003). The majority (63%) of judges reported at least one symptom of work-related VT, indicating that many judges might be susceptible to VT. Females and judges with 7 or more years of experience reported more symptoms of VT than males and those with less than 7 years of experience (respectively). Thus, judges appear to be susceptible to stress stemming from the traumatic experiences of courtroom actors.

Other studies explored the prevalence and impact of STS on the judiciary using different methods. A qualitative study on the occupational experiences of judges revealed that judges believed that the courtroom is an emotional setting (Chamberlain & Miller, 2009). Further, many of the judges expressed empathy for those courtroom actors who experienced trauma (Chamberlain & Miller, 2009). Thus, judges appeared to both acknowledge the emotions of and experience an empathic connection with those who experience trauma first-hand. A survey conducted by the National Center for State Courts (2002) revealed that judges believe it is their duty to protect jurors from stress, suggesting that judges do care for courtroom actors. Similarly, Flores and colleagues (2008–2009) found that judges felt that the court has a moderate to high level of responsibility for addressing the needs of jurors in their courtrooms. Taken together, these studies suggest that judges feel empathy and assume responsibility for those who are traumatized. From the perspectives of VT and CF, experiences of empathy and compassion can have serious implications for the wellbeing of judges: Judges who feel empathy might experience changes in their self-concept, and judges experiencing compassion might be motivated to assuage the suffering of others. There is some empirical evidence (Miller, Flores, & Pitcher, 2010) to support these assertions, as judges in a jurisdiction that had been subjected to a violent event reported disruptions in their safety, intimacy, trust, and control needs.

Judges do not act as caregivers in the same way as therapists or trauma workers; however, evidence suggests that judges do experience empathy and compassion for courtroom actors, which can lead to STS. Experienced judges, and those who are female, might be particularly vulnerable to stress caused by VT, but further research is needed to draw any firm conclusions about the impact of these moderating variables. In addition to safety concerns and STS, judges also experience stress from work-related burnout.

Work-Related Burnout

Judges face challenges unique to the trial process that can add stressors to an already demanding job (see Zimmerman, 2006). In addition to the pressures of conducting courtroom procedures and protecting the welfare of courtroom actors, judges can experience stress related to decision-making pressures. Judges might also perceive occupational inequity if and when the costs of the job begin to outweigh the benefits. Elected judges experience pressures outside of their day-to-day duties (e.g., campaigning), which can be an additional source of stress (see Resnick, Myatt, & Marotta, 2011). Given the public nature of the job, judges also can experience stress from restrictions on public speech and excessive media exposure, both of which can lead to an isolated lifestyle (Zimmerman, 2000, 2006). All of these factors, paired with the potential presence of safety concerns and STS, suggest that judges are highly susceptible to work-related burnout and its resulting detrimental physical and emotional consequences.

Work-related burnout refers to physical and emotional stress stemming from occupational experiences (Salston & Figley, 2003). Burnout can result from workplace conflict, an overload of responsibilities, and the perception of inequity or inadequate awards (see Maslach, Jackson, & Leiter, 1997). Some common physical and emotional responses to burnout include headaches, hypertension, depression, insomnia, and disillusionment (Farber, 1983). Burnout can also result in a negative self-concept and negative attitudes toward work and others in general (Pines & Aronson, 1988). Work-related burnout is certainly not unique to judges, but it is particularly important to study within this population given the impact that judges can have on individuals and the legal system in general.

There is some empirical evidence that judges do experience burnout. A study investigating sources of stress among the judiciary revealed that judges experienced significant amounts of stress from poorly prepared or disrespectful counsel and from exercising judicial discretion (Eells & Showalter, 1994). Similarly, publicity surrounding judges' decisions was reported to be a significant source of stress for judges (Eells & Showalter, 1994). These findings underscore the existence of stress tied to the decision-making pressures of the position. More recent research (Chamberlain & Miller, 2009) suggests that judges demonstrate several symptoms of burnout, such as workplace conflict, perceptions of inequity, and an overload of responsibilities. The occupational stressors of judges were further delineated by Flores et al. (2008–2009). Judges reported that the highest levels of stress stemmed from attorneys' behavior, trial interruptions, and distributing evidence, suggesting that they were at risk for work-related burnout. Evidence (Lustig et al., 2008) suggests that immigration judges also experience burnout due to work overload (e.g., a high volume of cases), problems with the infrastructure (e.g., lack of resources), and challenges to esteem (e.g., scrutiny surrounding the position). Finally, several requisite experiences of burnout (e.g., an overload of responsibility and safety concerns) were reported in a small informal survey of 18 family court judges (Resnick et al., 2011). Thus, research suggests that judges suffer from work-related burnout, which can lead to serious consequences (e.g., a negative attitude toward work).

Existing research suggests that judges experience several sources of occupational stress. Although the perceived frequency of violence against judges has likely been inflated by heavy media coverage, a review of research indicates that judges *perceive* the workplace to be at least moderately unsafe. Converging evidence also suggests that judges are susceptible to STS, as judges express empathy and compassion for courtroom actors who often experience negative events. Finally, judges appear to be at risk for occupational burnout: They encounter workplace conflict, unprepared courtroom actors, and an overload of responsibility. Although these stressors are not unique to those in the judicial profession, they are especially important to understand and account for because of the instrumental role judges play in the justice system.

Gaps in the Literature

Researchers have begun to address the stress that judges face; however, many gaps exist in this line of research. Chamberlain and Miller (2009) identify a broad gap in the judge stress literature concerning deficiencies in the types of measures used. Previous studies (e.g., Chamberlain & Miller, 2009; Eells & Showalter, 1994; Harris et al., 2001) have not used complete and/or direct measures of judicial stress. For instance, Harris et al. (2001) only examined stress as it applied to threats against judges. Similarly, Eells and Showalter (1994) did not include items about burnout and safety concerns. Subsequent research has addressed problems in measurement, but these studies are not without limitations. Chamberlain and Miller (2009) used a semistructured questionnaire to investigate the experiences of judges, but they did not directly ask about secondary traumatic stress; and Flores et al. (2008–2009) used an instrument that was neither validated nor comprehensive. Future directions in this line of research (discussed in the following section) should focus on more accurate, direct, and complete measures of judge stress.

A related limitation in this area of research is that judges are not likely to disclose all symptoms and experiences due to response biases and social desirability. Judges might be unwilling to share their experiences due to the negative implications of being stressed (e.g., that stress might be viewed as a weakness). This form of response bias was acknowledged by Chamberlain and Miller (2009), as some judges were hesitant to state that they personally suffered from stress and were more likely to say that others had experienced stress. Thus, there is a need for more inventive measures that accurately determine these important connections. Existing research has also largely failed to determine whether judge stress has an adverse impact on job performance and overall wellbeing. The research conducted by Miller and colleagues (2010), which applied CSDT to the judiciary, provides some information about changes in self-development (e.g., changes in self-esteem and trust) that may occur in this population, but more research is needed on the effects of stress on a judge's personal (e.g., health) and professional performance (e.g., decision-making abilities). This will be further discussed in the following section.

The second broad gap in the literature concerns the types of samples used in previous research. Most of the extant research has relied on relatively small samples, and thus the ability to generalize to the greater population of judges in the United States is limited. Harris et al. (2001) were able to recruit a large sample of judges, but they were all from Pennsylvania, thus restricting generalizability to that state. Other studies (e.g., Flores et al., 2008–2009) have used convenience samples that were likely subject to selection biases. In these cases, it is possible that respondents were different from nonrespondents on relevant dimensions (e.g., amount of stress experienced). There is also a shortage of research examining how demographic and experiential variables impact stress among judges. Although some research (Jaffe et al., 2003) has examined gender and experiential differences in stress, more work needs to be conducted to determine what types of judges are most susceptible to stress. Flores et al. (2008–2009) found no difference between civil and criminal judges on measures of stress or safety, but more research is needed to explore other comparisons between judges (e.g., family court vs. criminal court) to determine who experiences the greatest amount of stress. In short, the majority of existing literature does not provide a broad picture of the judiciary as a whole, nor does it examine the specific moderators of stress.

In addition to gaps in measurement and sampling, there is also a need for research on intervention strategies used to assist those judges who experience stress. Specifically, intervention strategies should be informed by research investigating judge stress so that strategies are adapted to the specific types of stress that judges encounter. For example, research suggests that a Federal Judicial Center (FJC) mentoring program significantly reduced some types of stress (e.g., role overload) among new judges (Bremer, 2004). This study provides a good model for the development of intervention strategies; however, future studies are needed to investigate other techniques. Existing research has provided a basis for understanding the extent, prevalence, and impact of judge stress, but as noted, there are significant gaps in this line of work. Future research should focus on developing more valid measures of stress, using larger, more representative samples, and these results should be applied to interventions with this population.

Expanding on earlier studies, the first logical research step should be to determine the extent and prevalence of different types of stressors that judges encounter. In doing so, we challenge future researchers to examine some of the questions that remain unanswered from previous research: What factors lead to the greatest amount of stress for judges? Which type of judges are most at risk of experiencing stress? Do judges experience secondary traumatic stress similar to those in caretaking occupations (e.g., therapists, emergency workers)? Do these occupational stressors affect judges' personal lives? And what potential effects does stress have on a judge's job performance or overall well-being? Some of these and other questions have been discussed in previous reviews (Chamberlain & Miller, 2009; Miller & Richardson, 2006), and we will summarize ideas from those publications.

Miller and Richardson proposed a model of judicial stress that presents a number of issues that need to be addressed in future research (see Figure 12.1). According to the proposed model, there are three major sets of characteristics (left side of the model) that lead to stress and safety concerns: personal characteristics, job characteristics, and environmental characteristics. Personal characteristics that could affect safety concerns and stress include variables such as gender, age, amount of social support, coping ability, and amount of experience as a judge. High levels of compassion or empathy for victims can also lead a judge to experience elevated levels of stress, as predicted by previous research on CF and VT. Job characteristics that could increase safety concerns (and subsequent stress) include experiencing stress-laden trials (e.g., child abuse or murder trials), a position filled with emotional cases (e.g., family court judges), and a heavy caseload. Environmental characteristics that could lead to stress and safety concerns include having a greater awareness of violence in the general community (e.g., through media exposure), awareness of violence against other judges, and lack of faith in law enforcement personnel to protect them.

According to the model, all these characteristics can affect a judge's level of stress, which can, in turn, have negative effects on personal (e.g., negative self-esteem and anxiety about personal and familial safety) and professional (e.g., cynicism about work and compromised decision making) wellbeing. As the model depicts, there are a variety of causes of stress and safety concerns. While many of these causes have been studied in other populations (e.g., counselors or emergency workers), judges have remained largely unstudied. The model predicts many possible negative outcomes of stress for judges that have remained unexamined.

Much like other areas of research, empirical work within the realm of judicial stress has not used representative samples, nor have the measures used to establish the phenomenon been validated. Indeed, these are not easy barriers to overcome, given the significant resources needed to recruit representative samples

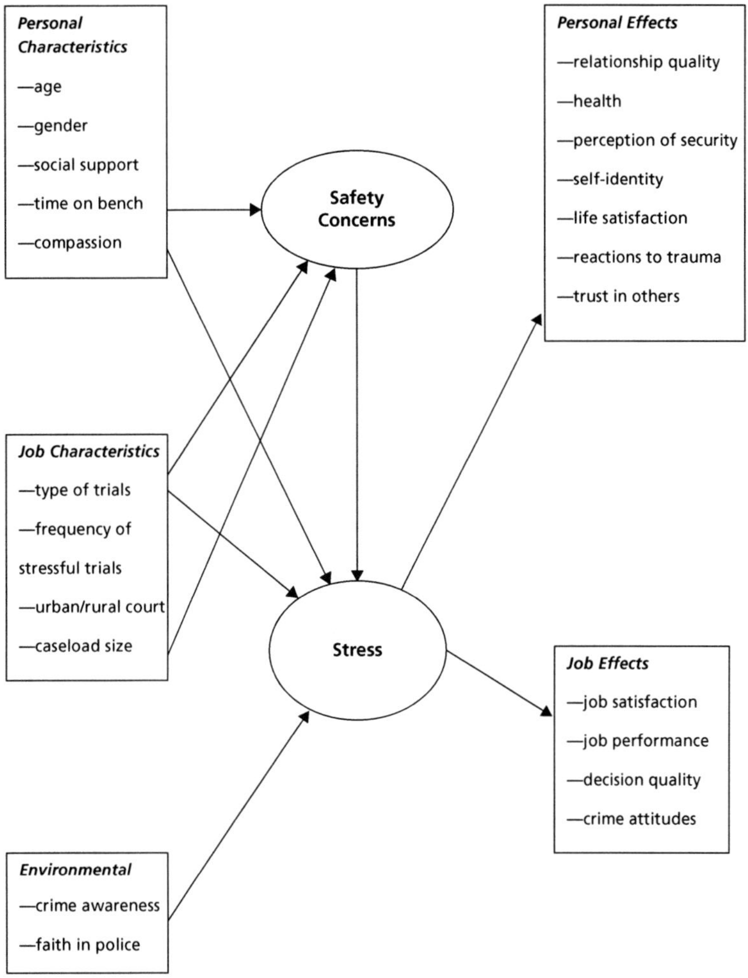

Figure 12.1 A model of judicial stress.

and validate nascent measures. The model presented by Miller and Richardson (2006) provides a wealth of research topics for future researchers to explore in the area of judicial stress. The next section will identify current interventions in the area of judge stress, most of which are focused on the safety of the judiciary.

Current Interventions

Policymakers are beginning to recognize that violence and threats of violence against judges are potentially serious issues, but there is a scarcity of research on what intervention strategies might work best to alleviate stress among members of the judiciary. Nearly all of the current interventions have focused exclusively on preventing or diminishing acts of violence against the judiciary, which only addresses one of the potential sources of stress experienced by judges. These interventions will be summarized in the following section.

Several organizations have recognized the dangers of the judicial occupation and developed strategies to prevent and/or minimize threats. A resolution supported by the Conference of Chief Justices and the Conference of State Court Administrators called for action to increase public, community, and governmental attention to the fundamental importance of court security (State Court Administrators, Conference of Chief Justices and State Court Administrators, 2005). In a joint meeting of the National Center for State Courts and National Sheriffs' Association, officials acknowledged the occupational dangers that judges face and outlined a strategic plan for addressing violence against judges (Casey, 2006). The proposed strategies included ensuring emergency preparedness, establishing effective practices and tools, building a resource center for safety information, developing an incident report database, and producing a methodology for determining security needs (Casey, 2006). Finally, the U.S. Marshals Service currently employs threat assessment, a data-driven process designed to identify, investigate, and prevent threats against the federal judiciary (Jenkins, 2001). This process provides a useful model for other jurisdictions, given that it relies on data to predict potential threats (see Jenkins, 2001; Weiner & Hardenbergh, 2001). In sum, state and national organizations have started to recognize and promote awareness of the existence of courtroom violence, and some of these organizations have put forth systems to prevent and/or diminish violent threats.

Some jurisdictions have developed specific safety measures to protect judges from violence. A somewhat ironic approach has given some judges the tools to fight back against potential threats. Specifically, judges in some New York jurisdictions were given the right to carry a concealed gun while on the bench (see Chamberlain & Miller, 2009). With the increase in violence against judges in recent years, the implementation of such a measure may be appropriate, but this approach is likely not preventive. Federal court judges were provided additional protections (e.g., home alarm systems) in response to a survey that indicated only 16% felt secure at home (see U.S. Department of Justice, Office of the Inspector General, Evaluation and Inspections Division, 2007). These systems have since been installed and they currently and continuously help to monitor the safety of these judges (U.S. Department of Justice, Office of the Inspector General, Evaluation and Inspections Division, 2007). Although increased protection and security are only two potential solutions aimed at stopping violence against judges, they may grant a sense of control to judges, which might have a positive impact on personal and professional wellbeing.

Lawmakers also have implemented measures to prevent violence against judges. For instance, the Court Security Improvement Act (2007) made it a crime to publicize personal information (e.g., a telephone number or address) of protected individuals (e.g., judges) with the intent to threaten, harm, and/or intimidate. This act is designed to deter those who might otherwise publish information about a judge with harmful intent. The act also made it a crime to make any false statements about a federal judge. Perhaps most important, the act gave the U.S. Attorney General the power to provide grant funding for the establishment and maintenance of databases that would track and predict violence against the courts. Although the grants have not yet been funded, this represents a large step in recognizing that more precise systems are needed to identify threats against judges.

With the help of the Federal Judicial Center, Bremer (2004) conducted the only known intervention designed to address general stress among new members of the judiciary. A mentoring program was developed to help newly appointed judges acclimate to the stressors of the occupation by learning from their more experienced counterparts. In an aggregate total of approximately 6 hours, distributed over a period of 6 months, experienced judges (the mentors) provided guidance in several areas, such as how to cope with stress, the impact of role changes on the family, and relaxation techniques. An evaluation of the program revealed that judges benefited from certain aspects of the program: Judges showed a significant (or marginally significant) reduction in role overload, role boundary, and psychological strain after the program was implemented (Bremer, 2004). Although this study is somewhat limited in its scope (e.g., it was focused on the federal judiciary), the results do suggest that similar mentoring programs might help to reduce stressors among judges in other jurisdictions. In sum, current interventions for judicial stress have almost exclusively focused on addressing judge safety. On one hand, this can be seen as a positive because it signifies that lawmakers, organizations, and the general public are beginning to acknowledge and address judicial safety. On the other hand, these interventions highlight the need for further recognition of other sources of stress, along with interventions designed to address these types of stress. The next section will outline areas for future research based on the aforementioned gaps in the extant literature.

Future Research

Although there have been some sound research efforts (mentioned earlier), our review of research has revealed that there is not an appropriate and well-validated measure for stress that is solely focused on judges (see Chamberlain & Miller, 2008). Most measures of "stress" either measure the causes (e.g., "Have you experienced a death in the family?") or outcomes (e.g., "Have you missed work?") of stress. In contrast, researchers should attempt to measure stress as the product of the causes and the cause of the outcomes. Other measures do not measure stress generally, but instead measure some specific stress-related condition such as anxiety, depression, compassion fatigue, vicarious trauma, and occupational burnout. While each of these measures may be helpful if researchers are interested in the specific condition, they do not individually reveal much about judges' stress in general. Thus, the first step is to build on previous work and develop a short scale that measures stress in general.

Taking potential sources of judicial stress into consideration, existing measures of stress can be incorporated into an extensive measure of judge stress. An ideal, albeit lengthy, scale might include some combination of burnout inventories, compassion fatigue scales, and various traumatic stress scales. It is also important to consider instruments specifically designed to assess judge stress. Although not based on any particular theoretical framework, the National Judges Health Stress Questionnaire (NJHSQ) and the Judicial Stress Inventory (JSI), both used by Eells and Showalter (1994), and the Pennsylvania Judges Survey (Harris et al., 2001) are potentially valuable measures of judicial stress. Unlike measures of occupational burnout, CF, and VT, these instruments include questions specifically designed for judges; thus, they may be useful in measuring occupational stressors that are specific to the judicial occupation.

Testing a new measure of stress would ideally be achieved with a pilot study, using a large representative sample of judges. Judges would be asked to complete an online or mail survey that would include several measures of the aforementioned concepts. Cooperation from the sample of judges could be sought using proven methodologies developed in other research on judges (Dobbin et al., 2001; Gatowski et al., 2001). Measures in a comprehensive study of judicial stress could include, among others, (1) the State-Trait Anxiety Inventory (STAI; Spielberger, Gorsuch, & Lusherier, 1970), a 40-item scale that was designed to assess state (e.g., transitory feelings of tension) and trait (anxiety tendencies) anxiety among adults; (2) the Beck Depression Inventory Second Edition (DBI-II; Beck, Steer, & Brown, 1996), a 21-item self-report scale intended to measure symptoms of depression; (3) the Compassion Fatigue Scale (short version; Adams, Boscarino, & Figley, 2006; Figley, 1995), a 13-item instrument developed to gauge symptoms of compassion fatigue; and (4) the Maslach Burnout Inventory (MBI-GS; Maslach et al., 1997), a 22-item scale that was designed to measure exhaustion, cynicism, and professional efficacy within an occupational setting.

A factor analysis should then be performed to identify the main components of "stress" as it manifests itself and affects judges, and the strongest items from each factor could be chosen for inclusion into a shorter scale. The goal of the pilot study should be to identify different aspects of the stress process, such as cognitive, emotional, and behavioral consequences. It is hoped that the new scale created would be significantly shorter than using all the measures listed previously, but the exact length of the refined scale would be determined by the results of the pilot study. The survey should also include a self-perceived level of stress and the Schedule of Recent Experiences (SRE; Holmes & Rahe, 1967). The latter two measures can be used for validating the scale. It might be predicted that those who score highest on the scale will also be perceived as having the most stress in their lives and reporting the largest and most severe recent life experiences. The new scale created by the aforementioned process can, of course, be used in subsequent studies as a measure of judicial stress, as efforts are made to understand the causes of stress (left side of the model in Figure 12.1) and consequences of stress (right side of model).

Other research endeavors can specifically test how judges' personal characteristics (listed in the upper left part of the model) are related to stress and safety concerns. Survey questions, which could be developed by the researcher, should be directed at determining judges' levels of social support, compassion, empathy, and idealistic view. In addition, questions about nonwork problems and personality characteristics could be asked. Judges can also be asked about the safety concerns they experience, as this construct is presumed to be an important effect of judges' personal, occupational, and environmental characteristics as well as a predictor of stress. Future research also can test the personal effects of stress (listed in the upper right part of the model). Thus, questions and scales designed to operationalize relationship quality, health, perceptions of security, self-identity, life satisfaction, reactions to trauma, and trust in others should be included.

Another study could recruit a representative national sample of judges to test the aforementioned constructs, each of which has several possible instruments available for use in such tests: (1) the Multidimensional Scale of Perceived Social Support, a 12-item measure of social support from family, friends, and significant others (Zimet, Dahlem, Zimet, & Farley, 1988); (2) an abbreviated version of the Locus of Control Scale (Rotter, 1966), a 13-item measure, which could be used as a proxy for coping skills; (3) a 28-item empathy measure (Davis, 1983), which could be used as a measure of both compassion and empathy; (4) the Midlife Development Inventory (MIDI; Lachman & Weaver, 1997), a 30-item scale, which could be used to assess judges' personality characteristics; (5) the Adult Health Concerns Questionnaire (HCQ; Spoth & Dush, 1994), a 55-item checklist, which could be used to measure overall health; and (6) the Ego Identity Scale (EIS; Tan, Kendis, Fine, & Porac, 1994), a 12-item scale designed to measure self-acceptance and sense of direction, which could be used to assess self-identity. In addition to these instruments, several other questions could be included to test constructs that lack specific instrumentation. Thus, questions might be developed to address the following constructs in the model: fear of making a mistake, idealistic view, life satisfaction, reactions to trauma, trust in others, and perceptions of security.

Yet another study could complement the aforementioned research by testing factors in the lower left part of the model in Figure 12.1. Questions about judges' job and environmental characteristics could be included. Judges could be asked to indicate the types of trials they preside over, the frequency with which they experience stressful trials, the population of their jurisdiction, and caseload size. Judges also could answer questions about crime awareness, faith in the police, how they perceive the public might respond to their decisions, and the prevalence of media coverage surrounding their cases. This complementary research also could include questions about the job effects of stress (listed in the lower right part of the model). Questions and scales could be designed to measure job satisfaction, job performance, decision quality, crime attitudes, crime attributions, missed work, job success, and professional efficacy. This study would provide valuable data about the consequences of stress for judges. However, there is still the potential for response biases (i.e., responses might imply poor occupational performance and thus judges would not answer honestly).

Another proposed study could measure the other components of the model proposed by Miller and Richardson (2006) by, yet again, surveying a representative, national sample of judges. Lacking a direct or approximate measure of many of the constructs, researchers would have to develop questions to measure the posited causes and outcomes of stress in the lower part of the model. Thus, several questions should be devised to determine how judges perceive crime, the police, the media, and the public's response to their decisions. Further, in order to test the job effects of stress and safety concerns, questions should be designed to assess judges' attitudes and attributions toward crime, as well as the amount of work they have missed. In addition, several questions should be used to measure decision quality, job success, and job performance. Job satisfaction could be assessed via the (18-item) Job in General Scale (JIG; Ironson, Smith, Brannick, Gibson, & Paul, 1989), and professional efficacy could be tapped using the (16-item) professional efficacy subscale of the Maslach Burnout Inventory.

This exploratory research would provide a solid foundation from which to form the best and most concise measures from each separate part of the Miller and Richardson (2006) model. A final study could test the entire model in one comprehensive (and no doubt expensive) study with a representative national sample of judges. This would not only allow for the testing of connections found in previous studies but also provide information about the relative influence of each construct with the overall model of judicial stress.

The research proposed herein would require significant resources, both in terms of money and time. We argue that such attention is warranted, given the key role that judges play in the legal system. The results from such research would not only provide prevalence rates of stress among the judiciary but also establish key predictors and outcomes of stress. The results of these studies could ultimately be used to develop interventions designed to prevent and minimize judge stress. The next section will outline several recommendations for policy and practice, most of which are based on the literature presented herein.

Recommendations for Policy and Practice

There are several recommended steps that judges, policymakers, and court officials can take to prevent and/or minimize the impact of judge stress. This section will summarize suggestions made in Chamberlain and Miller (2009) and Miller and Flores (2007), along with other relevant literature.

First, changes in procedures could be proposed to help minimize judge stress. Caseloads could be significantly reduced with the concept of preventive law, which relies on clients and attorneys working together to identify legal problems and strategies to prevent legal conflict (e.g., trials; Daicoff, 2004).[1] This system would likely not reduce the number of trials with high stress potential (e.g., those with gruesome evidence), but it could result in more manageable caseloads for judges. Preventive law could also be paired with alternative dispute resolution methods, which encourage collaborative, rather than adversarial, exchanges between parties. In this ideal system, clients could work with attorneys to identify solutions to any anticipated conflicts.

The approach proposed by preventive law is consistent with the therapeutic jurisprudence (TJ) approach, which views the legal system as a therapeutic agent (see Wexler, 1990; Wexler & Winick, 1991, 1996; see also Sicafuse & Bornstein, chapter 2, this volume). Those in favor of TJ argue that it is important to apply the law in a therapeutic way, such that legal decisions promote psychological and physical wellbeing. Proponents of TJ also recommend that legal actors (e.g., judges) rely on psychological research to inform decisions. The integrity of the courtroom could be protected by establishing mutual respect among judges, attorneys, plaintiffs, and defendants. Judges should set a calm example in their actions in the courtroom and always treat those appearing before them, including attorneys and parties in a dispute, with respect, making sure they are heard and their concerns acknowledged. The shift to a more collaborative and therapeutic legal system would presumably reduce judge stress by reducing the number of cases in the system and level of conflict between parties. It is important to acknowledge that the adversarial approach has a great deal of inertia (several hundred years worth) in the American justice system, and therefore systemic changes such as the ones proposed might be unrealistic. Nevertheless, any movement toward a more collaborative and therapeutic system would likely have positive implications for judges.

A second change to existing policy and procedure should focus on self-care among the judiciary, as identified by Bremer (2004). As a start, judges should be encouraged to take longer breaks (e.g., retreats, longer sabbaticals) away from work to minimize work-related burnout (see Chamberlain & Miller, 2009). Resnick et al. (2011) suggest that judges benefit greatly from attending conferences and conventions, where they can share common goals and experiences with judges from other jurisdictions. In this informal study of judges who attended the Association of Family and Conciliation Courts convention, judges reported the following stress-reducing by-products of attending such conventions: developing hobbies outside of the law, having a vacation,

[1] See also Reed and Bornstein, chapter 10, this volume, for a discussion of preventive law.

staying in touch with mentors, and collaborating with colleagues (Resnick et al., 2011). The authors suggest that the collaborative component of these conventions allows judges to normalize experiences of secondary trauma and decision-making stress. In short, the judiciary, much like any other profession, would benefit from activities designed to promote self-care, such as attending retreats and conventions.

Third, judges should be provided with the necessary opportunities, information, and skills needed to protect themselves from the effects of stress and from external threats to their wellbeing. This could involve the establishment of mentoring programs, especially for newer judges who are not aware of how lonely and stressful the role of a judge can be (see Chamberlain & Miller, 2009). Some specific interventions and therapies have been presented in the literature. Miller and Bornstein (2004) propose pretrial interventions designed to prepare jurors and judges for stress they might encounter during the trial process. During this pretrial briefing, judges would receive information about the negative effects of stress, how to recognize stress, and ways to cope with stress. Whereas pretrial interventions focus on prevention, posttrial interventions focus on dealing with stress after it has occurred. The "critical incident stress briefings" model (see Miller & Flores, 2007, p. 65) was first developed to treat those in high-stress occupations, such as law enforcement and medicine (see Feldmann & Bell, 1991), and has since been used in posttrial debriefings with jurors (Bornstein, Miller, Nemeth, Page, & Musil, 2005; see also Miller & Bornstein, chapter 11, this volume). Results from Bornstein and colleagues (2005) suggest that jurors found the debriefings to be helpful, but the efficacy of a posttrial debriefing for judges has yet to be tested. Judges might also take regular refresher courses on stress management that allow them to share their experiences and concerns with fellow judges and trained instructors in stress management (see Bremer, 2004; Miller & Flores, 2007).

Judges should also be trained to recognize symptoms of STS in themselves, especially following a trial that contains traumatic material. Osofsky and colleagues (2008) recommend that judges systematically evaluate symptoms of STS using existing measures (see Figley & Stamm, 1996; Stamm, 2002, 2009). This is not an easy task for members of the judiciary, given the nature of the job. The judicial profession is one that values impassivity and objectivity, and therefore feelings of compassion and empathy might be difficult to acknowledge. Thus, officials in judicial workplaces should foster an environment that accepts STS prevention as a necessary component of the job as a way of normalizing the experience of STS. Given the nature of the field, this will require attitudinal changes on the part of those in charge of the court system so that those experiencing stress are not stigmatized. Finally, those in charge should understand that heavy caseloads can contribute to stress, and they should make efforts to alleviate any work-related pressures. In short, future programs and policies should focus on educating judges and courtroom workers about STS and occupational burnout so that these experiences can be acknowledged and treated.

A more clinical approach to protecting judges against stress has been presented by Resnick and colleagues (2011). The proposed Psychologist Advocate Program would give judges access to a professional advocate who would be available to discuss work-related issues in a confidential setting. The program—which would utilize judges' preexisting medical coverage and thus not present additional burdens to the system—would employ cognitive behavioral therapy (CBT), which has been shown to be effective in treating stress in other populations (see Butler, Chapman, Forman, & Beck, 2006). The program would mandate monthly meeting sessions with an assigned "psychologist advocate" (creating a psychologist–judge team) to normalize CBT as a preventive measure of stress. Interventions in the 90-minute sessions, which would focus on stress management, decision making, life balance, and STS strategies, are designed to improve physical and emotional health (Resnick et al., 2011). The program also would allow judges to reassess the psychologist–judge team every 6 months to ensure the best fit for each judge. The inclusion of an intervention that uses a clinical approach (CBT) to stress prevention, management, and treatment seems appropriate for members of the judiciary, given the unique combination of occupational stressors they face. A mandated system would help to normalize the treatment for judges; however, this might not be popular among all judges, and the program might benefit from an option that would allow judges to opt out of treatment after a certain number of sessions.

A fourth general policy recommendation is related to the safety and security of the courtroom. Existing and developing interventions for courtroom safety (discussed in the previous section) highlight both the growing concern for judicial safety and existing gaps in security systems. Judges' safety concerns can be addressed, in part, by equipping courthouses with the necessary technology and personnel to deter acts of violence. This requires that those in charge are knowledgeable about potential threats to judges' wellbeing, and that these individuals take any steps necessary to ensure the safety of judges and others involved in court proceedings. Professionals should evaluate the safety procedures used in judicial buildings and use data-driven models to predict future acts of aggression. Courts should also provide safety devices such as car alarms and alarms at the homes of judges as a way to reduce stress (see previous section). All of these policy and procedure recommendations can contribute to making work and home environments safer for judges.

More research (such as the proposed work described herein) should be conducted to better understand the nature, causes, and consequences of judicial stress. Judge stress research should be a priority of funding agencies because the results of this research can be used to alleviate stress and thus increase the functioning of the judiciary. Similarly, government funding is necessary to fund research and intervention programs to ensure that judges have the resources to employ the aforementioned recommendations. Legislative responses to courtroom violence (e.g., the Court Security Improvement Act, 2007) represent important milestones for this area of research, but more is needed to address the full range of issues that judges face.

Finally, there are several recommended steps that judges and legislators can make to address judicial stress. Judges should be equipped with the necessary skills to recognize symptoms of STS and burnout, and they should be encouraged (if not required) to take time for self-care and therapeutic interventions, all of which will help to normalize their stressful experiences. Legislators need to provide more funding to further explore and address the many facets of judicial stress. More generally, a shift in the legal system—from an adversarial approach to a more collaborative approach—would help to alleviate judge stress by creating a more therapeutic environment.

Conclusions

In this chapter we have attempted to summarize and critique available literature on judicial stress, its causes, and its prevention. Our examination revealed some relevant research but noted that much of the available work has significant limitations in terms of measurement, instrumentation used, sample size, and narrowness. Following a review of current interventions for judge stress, we also have offered detailed recommendations for possible future research that would relate judicial stress research to a broader concern about stress in other areas of life. We offer specific proposals for research that would be valuable, as well as how to accomplish that research, citing a number of instruments that seem worth reviewing for possible usefulness. Our recommendations are built upon a specific comprehensive model of judge stress offered by Miller and Richardson (2006), but which has not been tested to date in the research literature on judicial stress.

We closed our chapter with a substantial listing of proposed recommendations for policy changes and practices that seem worthy of consideration, even given the paucity of directly relevant research on judicial stress. These recommendations are derived from a review of the limited research that has been done (much of it by our team of researchers), as well as our examination of related research in other occupations and areas of life. We hope that our recommendations for future research and for changes in policy and practice are of use to those concerned about the negative effects of judicial stress on our nation's judges and on the efficient and fair operation of our justice system.

References

Adams, R. E., Boscarino, J. A., & Figley, C. R. (2006). Compassion fatigue and psychological distress among social workers: A validation study. *American Journal of Orthopsychiatry, 76,* 103–108.

Anti-Defamation League. (2005, March 9). *Investigation into murder of judge's family.* Retrieved from http://www.adl.org/learn/extremism_in_the_news/White_Supremacy/Lefkow_Update_3_9_05.htm?LEARN_Cat=Extremism&LEARN_SubCat=Extremism_in_the_News

Associated Press. (2006, June 13). Judge shot, wounded at Nevada courthouse. *USAToday.com*. Retrieved from http://www.usatoday.com/news/nation/2006-06-12-judge_x.htm

Beck, A. T., Steer, R. A., & Brown, G. (1996). *Beck Depression Inventory* (2nd ed.). San Antonio, TX: Harcourt.

Bornstein, B. H., Miller, M. K., Nemeth, R. J., Page, G. L., & Musil, S. M. (2005). Juror reactions to jury duty: Perceptions of the system and potential stressors. *Behavioral Sciences and the Law, 23*, 321–346.

Bremer, C. F. (2004). Reducing judicial stress through mentoring. *Judicature, 87*, 244–251.

Brusk, S., Sosa, N., & Kaye, R. (2005, March 11). Suspect's car found in downtown Atlanta. *CNN.com*. Retrieved from http://www.cnn.com/2005/LAW/03/11/atlanta.shooting

Butler, A. C., Chapman, J. E., Forman, E. M., & Beck, A. T. (2006). The empirical status of cognitive-behavioral therapy: A review of meta-analyses. *Clinical Psychology Review, 26*(1), 17–31.

Casey, P. (2006). *A national strategic plan for judicial branch security.* Retrieved from http://www.securitymanagement.com/archive/library/benchsecurity0706.pdf

Cerney, M. S. (1995). Treating the "heroic treaters." In C. R. Figley (Ed.), *Compassion fatigue* (pp. 131–148). New York, NY: Bunner/Mazel.

Chamberlain, J., & Miller, M. K. (2008). Stress in the courtroom: A call for research. *Psychiatry, Psychology and Law, 15*, 237–250.

Chamberlain, J., & Miller, M. K. (2009). Evidence of secondary traumatic stress, safety concerns, and burnout among a homogeneous group of judges in a single jurisdiction. *Journal of the American Academy of Psychiatry and the Law, 37*, 214–224.

CNN Wire Staff. (2011, September 14). Report: Police shoot Arkansas courthouse gunman dead. *CNN.com*. Retrieved from http://articles.cnn.com/2011-09-14/justice/arkansas.courthouse.shooting_1_fort-smith-police-metal-detectors-arkansas?_s=PM:CRIME

Court Security Improvement Act. (2007). P. L. 110–177, Chapter 7, 18 USC 119.

Daicoff, S. S. (2004). *Lawyer, know thyself: A psychological analysis of personality strengths and weaknesses.* Washington, DC: American Psychological Association.

Davis, M. H. (1983). Measuring individual differences in empathy: Evidence for a multidimensional approach. *Journal of Personality and Social Psychology, 44*, 113–126.

Dobbin, S. A., Gatowski, S. I., Ginsburg, G. P., Merlino, M. L., Dahir, V., & Richardson, J. T. (2001). Surveying difficult populations: Lessons learned from a national survey of state trial court judges. *Justice System Journal, 22*, 287–314.

Eells, T. D., & Showalter, C. R. (1994). Work-related stress in American trial judges. *Bulletin of American Academy of Psychiatry and Law, 22*, 70–83.

Everly, G. S., Boyle, S. H., & Lating, J. M. (1999). The effectiveness of psychological debriefing with vicarious trauma: A meta-analysis. *Stress Medicine, 15*, 229–233.

Farber, B. A. (1983). Dysfunctional aspects of the psychotherapeutic role. In B. A. Farber (Ed.), *Stress and burnout in the human service professions* (pp. 97–118). New York, NY: Pergamon Press.

Fautsko, T., Berson, S., & Swensen, S. (2012). Courthouse security incidents trending upward: The challenges facing state courts today. Retrieved from http://www.ncsc.org/sitecore/content/microsites/future-trends-2012/home/Better-Courts/1-1-Courthouse-Security-Incidents.aspx

Feldmann, T. B., & Bell, R. A. (1991). Crisis debriefing of a jury following a murder trial. *Hospital Community Psychiatry, 42*, 79–81.

Figley, C. R. (1995). Compassion fatigue as secondary traumatic stress disorder: An overview. In C. R. Figley (Ed.), *Compassion fatigue: Coping with secondary traumatic stress disorder* (pp. 1–20). New York, NY: Brunner/Mazel.

Figley, C. R., & Stamm, B. H. (1996). Psychometric review of compassion fatigue self-test. In B. H. Stamm (Ed.), *Measurement of stress, trauma, and adaptation* (pp. 129–130). Lutherville, MD: Sidran Press.

Flores, D. M., Miller, M. K., Chamberlain, J., Richardson, J. T., & Bornstein, B. H. (2008–2009). Judges' perspectives on stress and safety in the courtroom: An exploratory study. *Court Review, 45*, 75–89.

Gatowski, S. I., Dobbin, S. A., Richardson, J. T., Ginsburg, G. P., Merlino, M. L., & Dahir, V. (2001). Asking the gatekeepers: Results of a national survey of judges on judging expert evidence in a post-*Daubert* world. *Law and Human Behavior, 25*, 433–458.

Harris, D. J., Kirschner, C. L., Rozek, K. K., & Weiner, N. A. (2001). Violence in the judicial workplace: One state's experience. *ANNALS, AAPSS, 576*, 38–53.

Hightower, K. (2011, June 10). More gruesome testimony in Casey Anthony trial. *Associated Press*. Retrieved from http://abclocal.go.com/wpvi/story?section=news/national_world&id=8182356

Holmes, T., & Rahe, R. (1967). The social readjustment rating scale. *Journal of Psychosomatic Research, 11*, 213–218.

Ironson, G. H., Smith, P. C., Brannick, M. T., Gibson, W. M., & Paul, K. B. (1989). Constitution of a job in general scale: A comparison of global, composite, and specific measures. *Journal of Applied Psychology, 74*, 193–200.

Jaffe, P. G., Crooks, C. V., Dunford-Jackson, B. L., & Town, M. A. (2003). Vicarious trauma in judges: The personal challenge of dispensing justice. *Juvenile and Family Court Journal, 54*, 1–9.

Jenkins, D. M. (2001). The U.S. Marshals Service's threat analysis program for the protection of the federal judiciary. *Annals of the Academy of Political and Social Science, 576*, 69–77.

Joinson, C. (1992). Coping with compassion fatigue. *Nursing, 22*, 116–122.

Koerner, J. (1995). The essence of nursing—Creative compassion. *Journal of Professional Nursing, 11*, 317–366.

Lachman, M. E., & Weaver, S. L. (1997). *The Midlife Development Inventory (MIDI) personality scales: Scale construction and scoring* (Technical Report). Waltham, MA: Brandeis University.

Lustig, S., Karnik, N., Delucchi, K., Tennakoon, L., Kaul, B., Marks, D. L., & Slavin, D. (2008). Inside the judges' chamber: Narrative responses from the national association of immigration judges stress and burnout survey. *Georgetown Immigration Law Journal, 23*, 57–83.

Maslach, C., Jackson, S. E., & Leiter, M. P. (1997). Maslach Burnout Inventory. In C. P. Zalaquett & R. J. Wood (Eds.), *Evaluating stress* (pp. 191–218). Lanham, MD: Scarecrow.

McCann, I. L., & Pearlman, L. A. (1990a). Vicarious traumatization: A framework for understanding the psychological effects of working with victims. *Journal of Traumatic Stress, 3,* 131–149.
McCann, I. L., & Pearlman, L. A. (1990b). *Psychological trauma and the adult survivor.* New York, NY: Brunner/Mazel.
Miller, M. K., & Bornstein, B. H. (2004). Juror stress: Causes and interventions. *Thurgood Marshall Law Review, 30,* 237–269.
Miller, M. K., & Flores, D. (2007). Addressing the problem of courtroom stress. *Judicature, 91,* 60–69.
Miller, M. K., Flores, D. M., & Pitcher, B. J. (2010). Using constructivist self-development theory to understand judges' reactions to a courthouse shooting: An exploratory study. *Psychiatry, Psychology and Law, 17,* 121–138.
Miller, M. K., & Richardson, J. T. (2006). A model of causes and effects of judicial stress. *Judges Journal, 45,* 20–23.
National Center for the State Courts. (2002). *Through the eyes of the juror: A manual for addressing juror stress.* Retrieved from http://www.ncsconline.org/WC/Publications/Res_Juries_JurorStressPub.pdf
Osofsky, J., Putnam, F., & Lederman, C. (2008). How to maintain emotional health when working with trauma. *Juvenile and Family Court Journal, 59,* 91–102.
Ortlepp, K., & Friedman, M. (2002). Prevalence and correlates of secondary traumatic stress in workplace lay trauma counselors. *Journal of Traumatic Stress, 15,* 213–222.
Pearlman, L. A., & Mac Ian, P. S. (1995). Vicarious traumatization: An empirical study of the effects of trauma work on trauma therapists. *Professional Psychology: Research and Practice, 25,* 558–563.
Pines, A., & Aronson, E. (1988). *Career burnout: Causes and cures.* New York, NY: Free Press.
Rasmussen, B. (2005). An intersubjective perspective on vicarious trauma and its impact on the clinical process. *Journal of Social Work Practice, 19,* 19–30.
Resnick, A., Myatt, K. A., & Marotta, P. V. (2011). Surviving bench stress. *Family Court Review, 49,* 610–617.
Rotter, J. B. (1966). Generalized expectancies for internal versus external control of reinforcement. *Psychological Monographs: General and Applied, 80,* 1–28.
Salston, M., & Figley, C. R. (2003). Secondary traumatic stress effects of working with survivors of criminal victimization. *Journal of Traumatic Stress, 16,* 167–174.
Spielberger, C., Gorsuch, R., & Lusherier, R. (1970). *STAI manual for the state trait anxiety inventory.* Mountain View, CA: Consulting Psychologists Press.
Spoth, R. L., & Dush, D. M. (1994). Adult Health Concerns Questionnaire. In J. Fischer & K. Corcoran (Eds.), *Measures for clinical practice: A sourcebook* (pp. 200–202). New York, NY: Free Press.
Stamm, B. H. (2002). Measuring compassion satisfaction as well as fatigue. In C. R. Figley (Ed.), *Treating compassion fatigue* (pp. 7–119). New York, NY: Brunner-Routledge.
Stamm, B. H. (2009). *Professional quality of life: Compassion satisfaction and compassion fatigue (ProQOL) subscales, R-V.* Retrieved from http://www.proqol.org/uploads/ProQOL_5_English.pdf
State Court Administrators, Conference of Chief Justices and State Court Administrators. (2005). *Security and Emergency Preparedness Committee at*

the 57th Annual Meeting. Resolution 17. Retrieved from http://cosca.ncsc.dni.us/Resolutions/CourtAdmin/resolutionImportanceofCourtSecurity.html

Tan, A. L., Kendis, R. J., Fine, J., & Porac, J. (1994). Ego identity scale. In J. Fischer & K. Corcoran (Eds.), *Measures for clinical practice: A sourcebook* (pp. 200–202). New York, NY: Free Press.

Trippany, R. L., White Kress, V. E., & Wilcoxon, S. A. (2004). Preventing vicarious trauma: What counselors should know when working with trauma survivors. *Journal of Counseling and Development, 82*, 31–37.

Tversky, A., & Kahneman, D. (1973). Availability: A heuristic for judging frequency and probability. *Cognitive Psychology, 5*, 207–302.

U.S. Department of Justice, Office of the Inspector General, Evaluation and Inspections Division. (2007). *The United States Marshals service judicial security process* (Report No: I-2007–010). Retrieved from http://www.justice.gov/oig/reports/USMS/e0710/final.pdf

Weiner, N. A., & Hardenbergh, D. (2001). Understanding and controlling violence against the judiciary and judicial officials. *Annals of the Academy of Political and Social Science, 576*, 23–37.

Wexler, D. (1990). *Therapeutic jurisprudence: The law as a therapeutic agent.* Durham, NC: Carolina Academic Press.

Wexler, D., & Winick, B. (1991). *Essays in therapeutic jurisprudence.* Durham, NC: Carolina Academic Press.

Wexler, D., & Winick, B. (1996) *Law in a therapeutic key: Developments in therapeutic jurisprudence.* Durham, NC: Carolina Academic Press.

Zimet, G. D., Dahlem, N. W., Zimet, S. G., & Farley, G. K. (1988). The multidimensional scale of perceived social support. *Journal of Personality Assessment, 52*, 30–41

Zimmerman, I. M. (2000). Isolation in the judicial career. *Court Review, 36,* 1–6.

Zimmerman, I. M. (2006). Helping judges in distress. *Judicature, 10,* 10–15.

Part V

CONCLUSIONS AND FUTURE DIRECTIONS

13

Stress, Trauma, and Wellbeing in the Legal System: Where Do We Go from Here?

Brian H. Bornstein, Gwen Hullman, and Monica K. Miller

The preceding chapters summarize research on stress, trauma, and wellbeing in the legal system using a wide variety of methodologies, conceptual foundations, and populations. Because of this diversity of approaches, the recommendations for specific interventions and future research are somewhat idiosyncratic to each topic. We will therefore not attempt to summarize those recommendations here. Rather, this concluding chapter will briefly sketch the scope of the problem; offer some guiding principles for reducing stress; discuss two different populations that likely experience stress from their involvement with the legal system (namely, mediators and eyewitnesses) but have not yet been studied in this regard; and consider a few of the most fruitful ways that the legal system can address problems related to stress.

How Much Stress Is Too Much Stress?

To a significant degree, stress and trauma are unavoidable components of the legal system. For example, victimization is invariably stressful, often traumatic, and in many cases completely devastating. And the individuals who seek to prevent victimization and protect (potential and actual) victims, such as the police, necessarily expose themselves to stressful, and possibly life-threatening, situations. Efforts to reduce these kinds of stress would involve a much larger societal attempt to reduce crime and go well beyond the sorts of proposals contained in the present volume. Nonetheless, even accepting that victims, police, and others necessarily experience stress, the justice system can take steps to make their involvement as positive (or as little negative) as possible and improve their wellbeing.

As we argued in chapter 1, and as some of the other chapter authors have emphasized, some degree of stress can be a good thing. Police should be alert and sensitive to the threats involved in their work. Attorneys should feel pressure to advocate zealously for their clients. Judges and jurors should be aware of the enormous consequences that hinge on their decisions. And victims and witnesses should think carefully before making accusations and testifying. Indeed, as Rush and colleagues point out in chapter 5, a concern about what might happen if the courts make testifying *too* comfortable is one of the main reasons why interventions to aid children in court are so problematic.

One of the oldest principles in psychology is the Yerkes-Dodson Law, which holds that there is a nonlinear relationship between stress/arousal and performance, such that optimal performance results from an intermediate level of arousal. Too much is clearly disruptive—and, as the chapters in this volume illustrate, can have significant health consequences as well—but too little can also lead to suboptimal performance. Thus, although there is certainly room to reduce stress in legal contexts, it is probably undesirable—not to mention unrealistic—to attempt to eliminate it altogether. Even so, there are some general approaches and principles that could substantially reduce stress within the legal system, as discussed next.

Guiding Principles: Changing the People and the Environment

Stress is often seen as an appraisal of one's ability to manage the environment or situation one is in at the moment or for the long term (for review, see Taylor, 1999). As such, what is stressful to one person is not stressful to another. A professor might speak in front of a large group without any nervousness, but a student asked to speak in front of the same class may sweat, stutter, or have a panic attack. Because stress results from an inadequate "fit" between the person's resources and the environment, it is possible to manage stress by changing either the people or the environment (Taylor, 1999). The following sections offer some guiding principles for policymakers to consider in those endeavors.

Changing the People

It might be possible to help individuals gain the resources to respond effectively to the demands of the environment. Most individuals who experience stress related to their involvement with the legal system—either short or long term—could benefit from learning coping skills, using relaxation techniques, and seeking social support. Further, because low-level stressors can lead to habituation, some individuals (e.g., judges, police officers, community supervision officers) may not realize they are in danger of experiencing the physiological effects of long-term stress, such as immune system deficiencies, heart disease, and depression, until damage has already occurred. Knowledge of stress and how it can be managed is an important step in assisting individuals in managing a stressful environment, and the legal system can take many steps to address these needs, ranging from pamphlets to seminars.

In addition to *preparing* people to deal with stress, it might be possible to *select* the people who are best suited and thus the best fit for the environment. Judges, attorneys, caseworkers, and police, parole, and probation officers could be trained—starting in their schooling—to deal with stressors they will face on the job. Some students may be unaware of the demands of their future career. Proper career advising, guest speakers in classes, internships, and other hands-on training could help students realize the stressors they will experience if they pursue a particular career. Making students aware of the demands of their future careers can help ensure that only those with the proper personality and skills to handle a great deal of work-related stress (e.g., optimism, positivity, and ability to handle confrontations) will choose careers in the legal field. Some job testing and training (e.g., police academies) can address these issues very early on in the process, in order to select the individuals who are best suited for such careers.

Changing the Environment

While an in-depth overview of industrial/organizational psychology is beyond the scope of this book, it is important to note that any work environment can contribute to stress or promote wellbeing in a great number and variety of ways (Taylor, 1999). Some of these factors include one's workload, social relationships at work, career advancement, role conflict, and level of perceived control in the workplace. Often, these things can be managed by making changes to procedures and policies. For instance, role conflict can result from having conflicting demands from multiple sources in the workplace (e.g., supervisors and peers)—this stress can be addressed by implementing a clear chain of command, priority lists, and clear and frequent feedback. Employers can help reduce stress in the workplace by implementing changes that allow workers some free time to socialize and develop camaraderie, by restructuring workloads to prevent employees from becoming overwhelmed, and by allowing employees to be involved in their promotion and evaluation decisions.

The environment is also important to consider for those who have little say in the conditions of their employment. Stress is greatest when the environment is uncontrollable, unpredictable, ambiguous, and/or overwhelming. As such, any change in procedure that improves the environment can help reduce stress. For instance, allowing jurors to leave the courthouse during short breaks in a trial; fully informing witnesses of what will occur before, during, and after the trial; and explaining procedures in a simple and direct way (e.g., so that children, mentally ill litigants, or elders with diminished capacity can understand) are all ways of potentially reducing stress by changing the environment.

In sum, the legal system can address stress by helping to achieve a better fit between the person's abilities and the environment; the more a person feels capable of handling the environment, the less stress he or she will experience. These general principles can act as a guide for changes the legal system can make to protect all those involved, from witnesses to attorneys and from police officers to community supervision officers. It is important to note, however, that there is much that we still do not know about stress and its consequences, prevention, and reduction. Importantly, there are groups of individuals that have yet to be adequately studied, and thus much future research is needed. The next section details two such examples.

New Directions: Alternative Dispute Resolution and Eyewitnesses

As the breadth of topics covered in the preceding chapters illustrates, there are numerous populations of legal actors who experience significant stress. However, we make no claim to having exhausted the realm of possibilities, and in calling attention to the topic, we hope that future research will identify additional categories of individuals whose wellbeing is at risk from involvement in the legal system, so that interventions can be designed to assist them. Two such categories are mediators and eyewitnesses. Much research exists on both of these populations, but the research focuses mainly on procedural matters and the decision-making process, with virtually no attention paid to the question of wellbeing. In this section, we discuss the role of stress in these populations and sketch out possible research agendas.

Alternative Dispute Resolution

Alternative dispute resolution (ADR) includes a number of forms: adjudicative ADR (e.g., arbitration), evaluative ADR (e.g., settlements), and facilitative ADR (e.g., mediation or conciliation; McManus & Silverstein, 2011). Adjudicative ADR is characterized by the third party's ability to make a binding or advisory decision. Evaluative ADR usually involves attorneys working on a settlement, a judicial evaluation of a case (typically by a retired judge), or use of an expert to make recommendations on highly technical cases. Facilitative ADR differs from adjudicative and evaluative ADR because the neutral third party neither renders a decision nor evaluates the merits of the case.

Although both arbitration and mediation can be court ordered or voluntary, arbitration as currently practiced is usually binding, whereas mediation is nonbinding. "Nonbinding" means the outcome is dependent on the "willingness of the parties to voluntarily reach an agreement" (U.S. Agency for International Development, 1998, p. 5). Binding arbitration, on the contrary, results in a final decision made by the neutral third-party arbitrator. So, in mediation, mediators have less control over the outcome than arbitrators have in arbitration (Shapiro & Brett, 1993). Other differences between mediation and arbitration exist, but the nature of the experiences for practitioners of both processes is arguably similar; hence, they are often concurrently discussed under the umbrella of ADR.

Mediation, one type of facilitative ADR, is growing in popularity as an integrated part of the justice system in the United States (Emery, Sbarra, & Grover, 2005). Community mediation centers, family court mediation programs, small claims mediation programs, and, more recently, foreclosure mediation programs are now widespread. However, little research focuses on the wellbeing of the mediators.

Many models of mediation exist (reviewed by Beck & Sales, 2001), but most describe the mediator as a neutral third party assisting disputants with their own negotiation of a problem (Bingham & Pitts, 2002; McCorkle & Reese, 2005). Most mediators do not give advice, but instead guide a conversation that results in disputants' expressions of their own concerns, understanding of each other's perspectives, and sometimes development of potential solutions and/or agreements about a future state of affairs (Charkoudian, De Ritis, Buck, & Wilson, 2009; Kolb, 1983; Kressel, 2007; McDermott & Obar, 2004; Riskin, 1994; Wood, 2004). Handling the process of mediation can be a difficult task. Mediators have to attend to a multitude of factors during mediation sessions, which can be daunting. "They are concerned about staying within time limits, monitoring emotions, identifying issues, and developing a resolution, all while maintaining their acceptability to the parties" (Forlenza, 1991, p. 233). In most models of mediation, mediators balance these tasks, thus empowering the participants to solve their own issues, both relational and practical.

Mediators handle many types of cases, some of which embody deeply troubling issues such as bullying, foreclosure, divorce, and domestic abuse. Even less intense issues can bring about strong emotions, which can elicit protective reactions from mediators. Noah (2007) contended that mediators experience "compassion fatigue" or "secondary trauma" but that mediator burnout is absent from conversations in the profession (for more on secondary traumatic stress, see chapters 11 and 12). Sources of stress include contradictory demands of the mediation process (Kressel, 1985), challenging and difficult disputants, a lack of preparation on the mediator's part, and organizational demands of the mediation process (Roberts, 2007). Zetzel (1985) claimed that family mediators were especially prone to stress. As a result of the stress, some family mediators become emotionally involved and risk losing sight of fundamental mediation techniques, such as maintaining objectivity and refraining from advice giving.

In addition, mediators often are caught in a quagmire by working within a system demanding quantitative evidence of success in the form of agreements, a phenomenon labeled as "settlement mania" (Kressel, Butler-De Freitas, Forlenza, & Wilcox, 1989). At the same time, mediators are using a process that prohibits them from suggesting or enforcing an agreement. Many researchers have proposed additional or alternative outcome variables that measure success in ways different from reaching an agreement (Conlon, 2005; Duffy, 1991; Hollett, Herrman, Eaker, & Gale, 2002; Kressel & Pruitt, 1985; Poitras & La Tareau, 2009; Pruitt, Peirce, McGillicuddy, Welton, & Castrianno, 1993; Wall, Stark, & Standifer, 2001), although these benchmarks often are neglected in measures of success. The system, in this case, promotes goals that may run contrary to the process of mediation itself. Thus, it is no surprise that balancing system needs and the mediation process can become stressful.

A dearth of information exists about mediators' experiences with stress and stress management. Marketing and informational materials related to mediation tout stress relief for the disputing parties, and mediation training materials typically include guidance on handling disputing parties' emotions and stress (e.g., Ladd, 2005), but they lack guidance on handling the *mediator's* emotions and stress. For example, although Doherty and Guyler (2008) suggested that mediators and conflict managers be poised to avoid the negativity associated with conflict, they failed explicitly to address the stress that mediators encounter as part of the conflict resolution process. Doherty and Guyler recommended that mediators adopt an adult "life-position" (first suggested by Harris, 1969) to maintain a view that everyone involved in the conflict (including the mediator) is "OK," as opposed to a position in which judgments are made about the individuals involved in the conflict. Adopting the "I'm OK, you're OK" attitude can prevent some of the self-imposed criticism mediators sometimes experience during a mediation. This viewpoint, however, was argued in the context of helping the participants in the mediation, not helping mediators as individuals.

Although mediator stress rarely is the focal point of research, a few recommendations for managing it have emerged. Stress associated with the mediation profession could be mitigated by formal and informal support. Zetzel (1985) advocated for more formal support during the mediation process by using a comediation model involving mediator pairs. Comediation offers opportunities to "lean" on one's partner during mediation, thus relieving some of the stress associated with the process. Forlenza (1991) recommended that mediators attend conventions and join professional organizations to develop an informal support network of peers. Forlenza argued that mediators often work in isolation from other mediators, so developing a network of support, although challenging, is crucial, since peer support from professional groups helps mediators cope with stress (Blumstein & Wisch, 1992; Roberts, 2007).

Despite the suggestions from the mediation literature on formal and informal support, the literature has really not even begun to address concerns of mediator stress. Assessing the magnitude of stress, the frequency of stress, and the source of stress (e.g., mediator style, issue disputed, emotional intensity of parties) are good places to begin investigations of this topic. A mediator who mediates conflicts each working day, for example, is much more likely to burn out than a mediator who mediates a few conflicts per month. In the same way, a mediator who helps small claims court parties come to a payment plan agreement for an uncontested loan balance most likely would not encounter the same level of emotional stress as one who mediates a custody agreement including an interpersonally dysfunctional parent (Kressel et al., 1989).

The field of mediation has much to lose by not addressing the issue of mediator stress, as does the judicial system that depends on it. Unaddressed mediator burnout will result in mediators leaving the profession, and losing good mediators will hurt the judicial system (see chapters 10 [attorneys] and 12 [judges] for more discussion of burnout). "Mediation has emerged as the primary ADR process in the federal district courts" (McManus & Silverstein, 2011, p. 1), and it contributes to positive outcomes for society, such as reduced recidivism rates (Burrell, Gill, Timmerman, & Allen, 2009; Nugent, Umbreit, Wiinamaki, & Paddock, 2001), adherence to custody and divorce agreements (Bahr, 1981; Pearson & Thoennes, 1986), and reduced cost (Charkoudian, 2005; Riskin, 1994; Sander & Bordone, 2005). Even if they do not end up leaving the field of mediation, mediators who encounter long-term stress most likely will find themselves unable to perform to their fullest potential. This situation could result in a compromised mediation process and fewer benefits to the mediators, disputants, and legal system.

Eyewitnesses

The legal system includes not only those who have chosen a law-related profession, such as ADR professionals, but also laypeople who are unaffiliated with the legal system in a formal way. As discussed throughout the book, laypeople sometimes become part of the legal system on a temporary basis and, depending on the nature of their experience, may encounter stress. One such category of one-time or sporadic legal actors is eyewitnesses, who may be interviewed by legal authorities, shown a lineup for purposes of making an identification, or asked to testify in court.

Witnessing a crime is stressful and in many cases traumatic. This is true for bystanders and, even more so, for victims. Research shows that stress or arousal experienced by a witness at the time of the event generally has a negative effect on the reliability of eyewitness memory (Deffenbacher, Bornstein, Penrod, & McGorty, 2004), though there are certain respects in which stress can benefit memory, such as memory for central (vs. peripheral) details of an event (Reisberg & Heuer, 2006). Although considerable research has investigated eyewitness memory for stressful and/or violent events (Deffenbacher et al., 2004), little attention has been paid to stress that eyewitnesses might experience at later stages of their involvement with the criminal justice system.

Testifying can be stressful for eyewitnesses as well, especially when, as is usually the case, the person the witness believes committed the crime is seated a few feet away in open court (see chapter 5 by Rush et al.). Yet these two events—witnessing a crime and testifying about it in court—constitute the two endpoints on the timeline of eyewitnesses' involvement with the legal system; there is much in between, in the form of interviews with investigators and identification attempts. These experiences can be stressful also, and there are things that legal authorities can do to promote eyewitnesses' wellbeing. In the remainder of this section we discuss possible stress effects on eyewitnesses after the event has occurred, and we also explore several possible mechanisms that could explain those effects.

Interviews. Chapter 5 by Rush and colleagues describes the variety of procedural innovations that have been developed to reduce children's distress while testifying. These accommodations are important tools for reducing child witnesses' subjective distress, but they carry a potential cost as well. Prospective jurors often evaluate children's alternative testimony negatively, based in part on their expectancies for how children will behave under "normal" and alternative testimony conditions (McAuliff & Kovera, 2012).

Other child-focused procedures emphasize not their testimony at trial, but special interviewing techniques used during criminal investigations (e.g., using props, avoiding leading or misleading questions). The motivation for these methods is typically twofold: to minimize the child's distress and to maximize the amount of accurate information obtained, with particular concern about children's elevated suggestibility (e.g., Lamb, Hershkowitz, Orbach, & Esplin, 2008; Yuille, Hunter, Joffe, & Zaparniuk, 1993). In service of the former goal, significant time is spent building rapport with the child; and there is empirical evidence that children who are more comfortable and less anxious during the interview provide more complete and reliable information (Lamb et al., 2008; Yuille et al., 1993).

Significantly, rapport building is also an important component of the cognitive interview (CI), one of the best known, and most effective, interview protocols (Fisher & Schreiber, 2006). The CI is effective with nonstandard witnesses such as children and people with intellectual deficits, but it has been used primarily with traditional adult witnesses (Fisher & Schreiber, 2006). In their review of the CI, Fisher and Schreiber lament the paucity of research on different interviewing techniques, as well as the relatively small number of jurisdictions that have adopted the CI or a similar empirically validated technique. The same is true for interviewing techniques used with children; for example, there is no generally accepted protocol for interviewing child witnesses in the United States (Melinder et al., 2010). We agree with Fisher and Schreiber that more research needs to be done to develop and validate interviewing techniques that elicit reliable memory reports; we would add that these techniques should also bear in mind any detrimental effects that the interview procedure might have on witnesses' wellbeing and should take steps to minimize adverse outcomes.

Lineups. In contrast to interviewing methods, lineup identification procedures have received a great deal of empirical scrutiny (for review, see Lindsay, Ross, Read, & Toglia, 2007; Wells, Memon, & Penrod, 2006). Whether lineups are conducted live or, as is increasingly done, with photo arrays, a number of features of the identification task are potentially stressful. First, the task is an unfamiliar one, which could produce general anxiety. Second, witnesses are dealing with police officers. Although the officers are sure to be courteous and respectful toward witnesses in almost all cases, they are nevertheless strangers and authority figures. Many people are nervous about interacting with police officers, even when they have done nothing wrong. This anxiety is likely to be exacerbated if the identification takes place in the unfamiliar and often hectic setting of a police station.

Third, the actual process of making an identification decision can be stressful; these stressors likely vary depending on whether the eyewitness makes a positive identification. If the witness does recognize someone who the witness believes committed the crime, then seeing the perpetrator again is undoubtedly an emotional experience. The nature of those emotions would be highly variable depending on the characteristics of the crime and the witness, but would most commonly include fear and anger. Witnesses who make an identification—commonly referred to in the literature as "choosers"—would have the additional stress of knowing the consequences of their positive identification. These consequences pertain to the witnesses themselves—namely, their further involvement with the legal system as the case goes forward—and to the suspect, who could be detained, arrested, tried, and punished if ultimately convicted.

Nonchoosers—those who reject the lineup—face repercussions as well. They might feel like they let down the investigating officers, prosecutor, victims, and themselves. It would also be normal for them to experience anxiety from knowing that their decision could either lead to the release of the perpetrator—if the perpetrator is indeed in the lineup, but they failed to recognize him—or mean that the true perpetrator is still out there, as yet unapprehended by the authorities. All of the stressors associated with the identification task are likely to be greater for victim-witnesses than for bystander-witnesses.

Psychological and physiological mechanisms. Assuming that the task of recalling details of a witnessed event or identifying the perpetrator in a lineup is itself a negative emotional event, several psychological and physiological mechanisms might come into play. For example, stress leads to the increased release of glucocorticoids, the best known of which is cortisol (Het, Ramlow, & Wolf, 2005). Research has found that although cortisol at the time of encoding has mixed effects on memory, the administration of cortisol prior to memory retrieval has a significant negative effect on memory performance (Het et al., 2005; Wolf, 2009). Importantly, the effect is stronger for emotionally arousing material (Wolf, 2009), and crimes are frequently emotionally arousing events. Thus, when eyewitnesses retrieve information about a previously witnessed crime, as would occur during an interview or a lineup, witnesses who are more distressed at the time of retrieval should do worse. Little eyewitness research has addressed this possibility; because most studies have the retrieval phase follow the witnessed event closely in time and cortisol levels peak approximately 20 to 40 minutes after exposure to a particular stressor (Dickerson & Kemeny, 2004), it is often hard to tease apart witnesses' physiological reaction from stress due to the event and due to the retrieval attempt, respectively (Bornstein & Robicheaux, 2009).

The adverse effects of cortisol on memory retrieval suggest that police investigators should take steps to make procedures used with eyewitnesses less stressful. In addition to contributing generally to the witnesses' wellbeing, there could be benefits in terms of memory performance. Police might accomplish these ends by conducting interviews and (photo) lineups in the witness's home rather than at the police station, allowing a family member or support person to be present, or making special efforts to be a calming and reassuring presence.

In contrast to the research on cortisol, other research suggests that eyewitness memory might be superior for witnesses who are experiencing a negative emotion at retrieval. For example, according to mood congruency, a given mood tends to cue memories that are consistent with that mood (Neath & Surprenant, 2003). Mood congruency means that eyewitness memory for a negative event—namely, a crime—is likely to be better when the witness is in a negative mood (e.g., fearful or angry) at the time of retrieval than when the witness is in a positive or neutral mood. From the perspective of maximizing witnesses' memory performance, then, it might not make sense to do too much to put them at their ease; of course, any possible memory benefit has to be weighed against the cost in terms of the witnesses' wellbeing.

A final possible mechanism for the effect of one's emotional state at retrieval on eyewitness memory performance is the influence of emotion on information processing. Different negative emotions are associated with different appraisal tendencies (Smith & Ellsworth, 1985; Tiedens & Linton, 2001). Specifically, some negative emotions (e.g., anger) are associated with a greater sense of certainty than other negative emotions (e.g., fear). This distinction has potentially important consequences for eyewitnesses trying to remember an event. Consider, for example, a witness viewing a lineup who sees someone she believes to be the perpetrator. If seeing him again makes her angry, then she may be more confident in her positive identification than if seeing him again makes her fearful; and the eyewitness's greater confidence consequently makes the suspect's arrest, prosecution, and conviction more likely, even though eyewitness confidence and accuracy are not strongly correlated (Wells et al., 2006).

The higher degree of certainty associated with anger (compared to fear) also makes people engage in less systematic processing of information and rely more on heuristic cues. This could come into play in eyewitness retrieval situations in various ways; for example, one could predict that angry (as opposed to fearful) eyewitnesses would be influenced more by postidentification feedback, biased instructions, or nonverbal cues provided by the lineup administrator.

This brief discussion of psychological and physiological mechanisms associated with eyewitness memory retrieval suggests competing hypotheses for how stress might influence eyewitness performance. On the one hand, a cortisol-mediated stress response might impair performance; on the other hand, a negative emotional response such as stress might benefit memory via mood congruency; and a more nuanced view would predict different effects depending on the specific type of negative emotion. The eyewitness literature has heretofore largely ignored witnesses' emotional state at the time of retrieval. Future research should document the type and intensity of eyewitnesses' emotional experience when making, say, lineup identifications; consider eyewitnesses' wellbeing when devising procedures for examining them; and investigate the effect of eyewitnesses' emotional response on their memory performance.

Reducing Stress and Enhancing Wellbeing: Short-Term and Long-Term Recommendations

The chapters in this volume provide a veritable smorgasbord of techniques for reducing stress and enhancing wellbeing in the legal system. Some of these techniques have been implemented in a small number of jurisdictions, whereas others have been proposed but not yet implemented. Very few, if any, have been adopted on a large scale, and few have much in the way of empirical validation, though the vast majority of them make a great deal of intuitive sense. It is not our purpose to catalog all of those recommendations here; rather, we identify the most promising innovations, dividing them into short-term recommendations—that is, those the legal system should strongly consider adopting right now—and long-term recommendations, which seem promising but warrant further thought and study. In making these recommendations, we rely heavily on an analysis of the costs and benefits of the different techniques (see chapter 11 by Miller & Bornstein for a more detailed cost–benefit analysis of innovations for reducing juror stress). Indeed, one of the strongest arguments for implementing a procedure right away is that the costs are low, but the potential benefits in terms of wellbeing are substantial.

Short-Term Recommendations

Examples of inexpensive and relatively easy innovations include avoiding multiple interviews or lengthy trial delays for special populations, such as children and the elderly; providing jurors and witnesses with basic information before trial, via an orientation video or advance mailing; and providing legal professionals with referrals to mental health services. It should also be relatively easy to address some of police officers' health issues. For example, they might be allowed to bring their own food to work—rather than encouraged or required to eat in restaurants—and offered incentives for good fitness. The rationale for encouraging officers to eat in restaurants is to enhance their public visibility, which is a laudable goal; but there must be ways to achieve the same end without compromising the officers' cardiovascular health.

Elders and other vulnerable populations, who might be especially likely to experience stress from their involvement with the traditional adversarial court system, could benefit from less adversarial systems, like mediation. Thus, the existence of ADR options should be publicized for those who might not be aware that such programs exist.

Attorneys could make efforts to improve listening and communication skills with their clients. Efforts to understand the client's experiences, emotions, and desires (e.g., an apology from the wrongdoer) may help promote the wellbeing of the client, even if these efforts produce little tangible benefit in terms of case outcome. Of course, as the saying goes, "time is money," and attorneys may deem such things irrelevant to the legal case; but in the long run such efforts would allow clients to be more active in the case, have more positive wellbeing, and have an overall more positive perception of their legal experience.

For many individuals, informal support groups can provide some comfort that others have "been there before" and understand their situation. Caregivers in the foster care system would benefit from talking with other caregivers about the difficulties of raising children who have been removed from their home because of abuse and neglect. Similarly, legal professionals could create a network, perhaps in conjunction with already existing Lawyer Assistance Programs (see chapter 10), to support each other and provide a safe outlet for venting anger, fear, or frustration. Networks can be online or in person; regardless, they are not costly, as virtually all that is needed is the encouragement to form such connections.

Such efforts are all relatively inexpensive and hold promise for promoting wellbeing. While many are untested, they make intuitive sense and do not have obvious downsides. Thus, such short-term changes in policy, procedure, or behavior could have significantly greater benefits than costs.

Long-Term Recommendations

As researchers ourselves, we are accustomed to reading—and indeed, writing—that "more research is needed." The topic of stress, trauma, and wellbeing in the legal system is no exception to the rule. If the chapters in this book show anything, it is that there is a serious and dangerous lack of research in the area. The lack of research is serious because of the large potential consequences, for both individuals and society, of threats to wellbeing. And the lack of research is dangerous because in the absence of knowledge about the causes and consequences of stress, as well as the efficacy of various interventions, much time, effort, and expense could be wasted on ill-advised innovations. It is therefore essential to promote research on innovations, funded by the legal system and government agencies. It will be expensive—in both dollars and time—to conduct this research. But in the long run it is more expensive—in terms of operational inefficiencies, absenteeism, and burnout—not to. Of course, courts tend to operate on a tight budget, meaning that they might not be able to afford the up-front costs of conducting research on a particular innovation, such as debriefings for judges, even if they recognize that it would be desirable and ultimately cost-effective. It is therefore incumbent on researchers, and on legal professionals themselves, to place a priority on wellbeing and to devise cost-effective means for improving it.

A promising avenue for doing so is specialty courts, discussed in several chapters. We are loath to make a blanket recommendation for more specialty courts, as little research exists on their effectiveness (see chapter 2 by Sicafuse & Bornstein). We are, however, comfortable recommending that jurisdictions be creative in trying out specialty court pilot programs, and that courts and researchers do more to document whether or not they are effective. This effectiveness needs to be demonstrated in terms of costs and labor, as well as in the improved wellbeing of the participants.

Other long-term solutions involve changing the culture of legal work environments. Many of the stressors for police officers, community supervision officers, and even judges and jurors involve relatively mundane workplace hassles and inefficiencies. The research in chapter 9 revealed that some of the top stressors for probation officers were inconvenient scheduling of court appearances, being required to take work home, excessive paperwork, lack of recognition for good work, and inadequate support from the agency. Such internal stressors can often be addressed with policy and procedural changes in the agency; similar changes could promote wellbeing in any of the groups who work in the legal system. These organizational stressors are difficult to address and perhaps, to some extent, unavoidable. Nonetheless, recognizing the concerns and working in good faith to ameliorate them would be an important first step. Although it might seem glib to add that stress could be reduced by raising pay and lowering workloads, we will say it anyway. The majority of community supervision officers and judges cannot keep up with their caseloads, and it is a significant source of stress. Juror pay hardly offsets the costs of missing work for many jurors. The proper functioning of the justice system is an important enough goal that those who make it function should be compensated fairly and have the resources they need to do their jobs.

In these same work environments, an admission of stress is often seen as a sign of weakness. Employers should be more accepting of judges, attorneys, and officers who need to take a "mental health day" or a longer sabbatical. Changes can even start during the education of these professionals—for instance, by offering seminars on coping and wellbeing in law schools and police academies.

This brief summary makes it clear that there is much work still to be done. The legal system can be an exciting and rewarding place to work. Involvement in the legal system can also be a satisfying experience for "one-timers" such as litigants and victims, who get to see justice done up close and personal. Despite these positive aspects of working in or around legal contexts, the very nature of the issues that bring people into those contexts—as either lay participants or professionals—can be a significant source of stress and, in some cases, trauma. We hope that in calling attention to these matters, we have played some small part in improving the wellbeing of individuals who find themselves in these situations in the future.

References

Bahr, S. J. (1981). An evaluation of court mediation: A comparison in divorce cases with children. *Journal of Family Issues, 2,* 39–60.

Beck, C. J. A., & Sales, B. D. (2001). *Family mediation: Facts, Myths, and future prospects.* Washington, DC: APA Books.

Bingham, L. B., & Pitts, D. W. (2002). Highlights of mediation at work: Studies of the National REDRESS® evaluation project. *Negotiation Journal, 18,* 135–146.

Blumstein, E., & Wisch, P. B. (1992). Who nurtures the nurturer? A model of a peer support group. *Mediation Quarterly, 9,* 267–271.

Bornstein, B. H., & Robicheaux, T. R. (2009). Methodological issues in the study of eyewitness memory and arousal. *Creighton Law Review, 42,* 525–547.

Burrell, N., Gill, R., Timmerman, L., & Allen, M. (2009, November). *Victim-offender mediation: A meta-analysis.* Paper presented at the Annual Meeting of the National Communication Association, Chicago.

Charkoudian, L. (2005). A quantitative analysis of the effectiveness of community mediation in decreasing repeat calls for police service. *Conflict Resolution Quarterly, 20,* 87–98.

Charkoudian, L., De Ritis, C., Buck, R., & Wilson, C. L., (2009). Mediation by any other name would smell as sweet-or would it? *Conflict Resolution Quarterly, 26,* 293–316.

Conlon, D. E. (2005). Mediation and the fourfold model of justice. In M. S. Herrman, N. Hollett, & J. Gale (Eds.), *The Blackwell handbook of mediation: A guide to effective negotiation* (pp. 247–258). Malden, MA: Blackwell Publishing.

Deffenbacher, K. A., Bornstein, B. H., Penrod, S. D., & McGorty, E. K. (2004). A meta-analytic review of the effects of high stress on eyewitness memory. *Law and Human Behavior, 28,* 687–706.

Dickerson, S. S., & Kemeny, M. E. (2004). Acute stressors and cortisol responses: A theoretical integration and synthesis of laboratory research. *Psychological Bulletin, 130,* 355–391.

Doherty, N., & Guyler, M. (2008). *The essential guide to workplace mediation and conflict resolution: Rebuilding working relationships.* Philadelphia, PA: Kogan Page.

Duffy, K. G. (1991). Introduction to community mediation programs: Past, present and future. In K. G. Duffy, J. W. Grosh, & P. V. Olczak (Eds.), *Community mediation: A handbook for practitioners and researchers* (pp. 21–31). New York, NY: Guilford Press.

Emery, R. E., Sbarra, D., & Grover, T. (2005). Research & reflections. *Family Court Review, 43*, 22.
Fisher, R. P., & Schreiber, N. (2006). Interview protocols to improve eyewitness memory. In M. P. Toglia, J. D. Read, D. F. Ross, & R. C. L. Lindsay (Eds.), *Handbook of eyewitness psychology, Vol. 1: Memory for events* (pp. 53–80). Mahwah, NJ: Erlbaum.
Forlenza, S. G. (1991). Mediation and psychotherapy: Parallel processes. In K. G. Duffy, J. W. Grosch, & P. V. Olczak (Eds.), *Community mediation: A handbook for practitioners and researchers* (pp. 227–239). New York, NY: Guilford Press.
Harris, T. (1969). *I'm OK, you're OK*. New York, NY: Harper Collins.
Het, S., Ramlow, G., & Wolf, O. T. (2005). A meta-analytic review of the effects of acute cortisol administration on human memory. *Psychoneuroendocrinology, 30*, 771–784.
Hollett, N. J., Herrman, M. S., Eaker, D. G., & Gale, J. (2002). The assessment of mediation outcome: The development and validation of an evaluation technique. *Justice System Journal, 33*, 345–362.
Kolb, D. M. (1983). *The mediators*. Cambridge, MA: MIT Press.
Kressel, K. (1985). *The process of divorce*. New York, NY: Basic Books.
Kressel, K. (2007). The strategic style in mediation. *Conflict Resolution Quarterly, 24*, 251–283.
Kressel, K., Butler-DeFreitas, F., Forlenza, S. G., & Wilcox, C. (1989). Research in contested custody mediations: An illustration of the case study method. *Mediation Quarterly, 24*, 55–69.
Kressel, K., & Pruitt, D. G. (1985). Themes in the mediation of social conflict. *Journal of Social Issues, 41*, 179–198.
Ladd, P. D. (2005). *Mediation, conciliation, and emotions: A practitioner's guide for understanding emotions in dispute resolution*. Lanham, MD: University Press of America.
Lamb, M. E., Hershkowitz, I., Orbach, Y., & Esplin, P. W. (2008). *Tell me what happened: Structured investigative interviews of child victims and witnesses*. New York, NY: Wiley.
Lindsay, R. C. L., Ross, D. F., Read, J. D., & Toglia, M. P. (2007). *Handbook of eyewitness psychology, Vol. 2: Memory for people*. Mahwah, NJ: Erlbaum.
McAuliff, B. D., & Kovera, M. B. (2012). Do jurors get what they expect? Traditional versus alternative forms of children's testimony. *Psychology, Crime and Law, 18*, 27–47.
McCorkle, S., & Reese, M. J. (2005). *Personal conflict management*. Boston, MA: Allyn and Bacon.
McDermott, E. P., & Obar, R. (2004). "What's going on" in mediation: An empirical analysis of the influence of a mediator's style on party satisfaction and monetary benefit. *Harvard Negotiation Law Review, 9*, 75–113.
McManus, M., & Silverstein, B. (2011). Brief history of alternative dispute resolution in the United States. *Cadmus, 3*(1), 11. Retrieved from http://www.cadmusjournal.org/article/issue-3/brief-history-alternative-dispute-resolution-united-states
Melinder, A., Alexander, K., Cho, Y. I., Goodman, G. S., Thoresen, C., Lonnum, K., & Magnussen, S. (2010). Children's eyewitness memory: A comparison of

two interviewing strategies as realized by forensic professionals. *Journal of Experimental Child Psychology, 105*, 156–177.

Neath, I., & Surprenant, A. M. (2003). *Human memory* (2nd ed.). Belmont, CA: Wadsworth/Thomson.

Noah, L. L. (2007). *How do you know if you're conflict weary? If you have to ask…you are.* Pronoia Mediation. Retrieved from http://pronoiamediation.blogspot.com/2007/06/response-to-question-of-mediator-burn.html

Nugent, W. R., Umbreit, M. S., Wiinamaki, L., & Paddock, J. (2001). Participation in victim-offender mediation and reoffense: Successful replications? *Research on Social Work, 11*, 5–23.

Pearson, J., & Thoennes, N. (1986). Mediation in custody disputes. *Behavioral Sciences and the Law, 4*, 203–216.

Poitras, J., & Le Tareau, A. (2009). Quantifying the quality of mediation agreements. *Negotiation and Conflict Management Research, 2*, 363–380.

Pruitt, D. G., Peirce, R. S., McGillicuddy, N. B., Welton, G. L., & Castrianno, L. M. (1993). Long-term success in mediation. *Law and Human Behavior, 17*, 313–330.

Reisberg, D., & Heuer, F. (2006). The influence of emotion on memory in forensic settings. In M. P. Toglia, J. D. Read, D. F. Ross, & R. C. L. Lindsay (Eds.), *Handbook of eyewitness psychology, Vol. 1: Memory for events* (pp. 81–116). Mahwah, NJ: Erlbaum.

Riskin, L. L. (1994). Mediator orientations, strategies, and techniques. *Alternatives to the High Cost of Litigation, 12*, 111–114.

Roberts, M. (2007). *Developing the craft of mediation: Reflections on theory and practice.* Philadelphia, PA: Jessica Kinsley Publishers.

Sander, F. A., & Bordone, R. C. (2005). Early intervention: How to minimize the cost of conflict. *Negotiation, 8*, 1–5.

Shapiro, D. L., & Brett, J. M. (1993). Comparing three processes underlying judgments of procedural justice: A field study of mediation and arbitration. *Journal of Personality and Social Psychology, 65*, 1167–1177.

Smith, C., & Ellsworth, P. (1985). Patterns of cognitive appraisal in emotion. *Journal of Personality and Social Psychology, 48*, 813–838.

Taylor, S. E. (1999). *Health psychology* (4th ed.). Boston, MA: McGraw Hill.

Tiedens, L., & Linton, S. (2001). Judgment under emotional certainty and uncertainty: The effects of specific emotions on information processing. *Journal of Personality and Social Psychology, 81*, 973–988.

U.S. Agency for International Development, Office of Democracy and Governance, Bureau for Democracy, Conflict, and Humanitarian Assistance. (1998). *Alternative dispute resolution practitioners guide* (PN-ACP-335). Washington, DC: Government Printing Office.

Wall, J. A., Jr., Stark, J. B., & Standifer, R. L. (2001). Mediation: A current review and theory development. *Journal of Conflict Resolution, 45*, 370–391.

Wells, G. L., Memon, A., & Penrod, S. D. (2006). Eyewitness evidence: Improving its probative value. *Psychological Science in the Public Interest, 7*, 45–75.

Wolf, O. T. (2009). Stress and memory in humans: Twelve years of progress? *Brain Research, 1293*, 142–154.

Wood, J. (2004). Mediation styles: Subjective description of mediators. *Conflict Resolution Quarterly, 21*, 437–450.

Yuille, J. C., Hunter, R., Joffe, R., & Zaparniuk, J. (1993). Interviewing children in sexual abuse cases. In G. S. Goodman & B. L. Bottoms (Eds.), *Child victims, child witnesses: Understanding and improving testimony* (pp. 95–115). New York, NY: Guilford.

Zetzel, G. W. K. (1985). In and out of the family crucible: Reflections on parent-child mediation. *Mediation Quarterly, 7*, 47–67.

Index

W

Y

CPSIA information can be obtained at www.ICGtesting.com
Printed in the USA
BVOW010100131112

305362BV00002B/3/P

9 780199 829996